WE ARE LEFT
WITHOUT
A FATHER HERE

American Encounters/Global Interactions

A series edited by Gilbert M. Joseph and Emily S. Rosenberg

This series aims to stimulate critical perspectives and fresh interpretive frameworks for scholarship on the history of the imposing global presence of the United States. Its primary concerns include the deployment and contestation of power, the construction and deconstruction of cultural and political borders, the fluid meanings of intercultural encounters, and the complex interplay between the global and the local. American Encounters seeks to strengthen dialogue and collaboration between historians of U.S. international relations and area studies specialists.

The series encourages scholarship based on multiarchival historical research. At the same time, it supports a recognition of the representational character of all stories about the past and promotes critical inquiry into issues of subjectivity and narrative. In the process, American Encounters strives to understand the context in which meanings related to nations, cultures, and political economy are continually produced, challenged, and reshaped.

EILEEN J. SUÁREZ FINDLAY

WE ARE LEFT WITHOUT A FATHER HERE

Masculinity, Domesticity, and Migration in Postwar Puerto Rico

Duke University Press • Durham and London • 2014

Printed in the United States of America on acid-free paper ∞
Designed by Courtney Leigh Baker
Typeset in Quadraat by Westchester Publishing Services

Library of Congress Cataloging-in-Publication Data
Findlay, Eileen.
We are left without a father here : masculinity, domesticity,
and migration in postwar Puerto Rico / Eileen J. Suárez Findlay.
pages cm — (American encounters/global interactions)
Includes bibliographical references and index.
ISBN 978-0-8223-5766-7 (cloth : alk. paper)
ISBN 978-0-8223-5782-7 (pbk. : alk. paper)
1. Masculinity—Social aspects—Puerto Rico. 2. Migrant
labor—Government policy—Puerto Rico—History—20th
century. 3. Migrant agricultural laborers—Michigan—Social
conditions—History—20th century. 4. Puerto Rico—Politics
and government—1898–1952.
1. Title. 11. Series: American encounters/global interactions.
HQ1090.7.P9F56 2014
305.5′63—dc23
2014017561

ISBN 978-0-8223-7611-8 (e-book)

Cover art: Puerto Rico Division of Community Education Poster Collection, Archives
Center, National Museum of American History, Smithsonian Institution.

To

CONTENTS

ACKNOWLEDGMENTS

Many beloved people in Puerto Rico have sustained me over the years as I moved in, around, and through this project. Magaly Robles has given me undying friendship and creative inspiration across oceans and decades. I am grateful to José Flores Ramos for his wide-ranging scholarly work on gender in Puerto Rico, for his generosity in sharing ideas and sources, for his insatiable love of the intellectual life, and for his opening of home, family, and spiritual community. Rasiel Suárez and Annie Maldonado shared their lives, their home, and their spirits with me and my family during that first sabbatical leave so long ago when I first stumbled across the sugar beet migrant letters. Carlos Rodríguez, Laura Nater, Mabel Rodríguez, Jimmy Seale Collazo, and Marilyn Miller gave me loving support then, too. Thanks to Patricia Silver for all the many long conversations over the years, the collaborative searching for agricultural migrants, and our shared experience of gringas buena gente y solidaria en la diáspora.

I am grateful to Mark Overmyer-Velásquez and Blanca Silvestrini for inviting me many years ago to give the talk at the University of Connecticut that began this whole sojourn. My colleagues at American University Phil Stern, Andrew Lewis, Kathleen Franz, Katharine Norris, Amy Oliver, Shelley Harshe, Richard Breitman, and Allan Kraut read and commented on another early, unruly attempt to understand the sugar beet migration, as did Nancy Appelbaum. Ellen Feder was the first to see the book hidden in that crude chunk of writing. April Shelford agreed, encouraged me to "let it breathe" into its current form, and read several proposal drafts. Marisol de la Cadena, who always resides in my heart, encouraged me through the proposal writing process. Anne MacPherson commented thoughtfully on the archives portion of the introduction, and posed some provocative questions that I've never really been able to adequately answer. Karin Rosemblatt, Barbara Weinstein, and Mary Kay Vaughan kept me connected to the intellectual community of Latin Americanists at the University of Maryland. Francisco Scarano, Sue Ann Caulfield, Frank Guridy, Lorrin Thomas, Aldo Lauria-Santiago, Jorge Duany, Ismael García Colón, Emma Amador, Arlene Torres, Deborah Cohen, Lisa Leff, Dan Kerr, Mary Ellen Curtin, Kim Sims,

Margaret Power, Avi Chomsky, Cindy Forster, Ileana Rodríguez-Silva, and Ana Serra gave valued support as well.

As chair of my department, the late Bob Griffith ferreted out ways to fund my research trips to Michigan and Puerto Rico, nominated me for every feminist and teaching prize in the book, and invented the AU History Department's Clendenen fellowship, which gave me the space to actually finish a draft of the manuscript. Although he did not live to see it, this book is in large measure the fruit of his supportive labors. Thanks, also, to American University's College of Arts and Sciences for its funding and flexible course scheduling over the last few years.

I have had the exceedingly good fortune to have worked with fine archivists in the course of this project. José Flores, Milagros Pepín, and Hilda Chicón have been careful stewards of the collections of the Archivo General de Puerto Rico while showing me great friendship back to my first days in Puerto Rico, several decades ago. Julio Quirós generously opened the doors of the Fundación Luis Muñoz Marín to me. Susan Power at the Clarke Historical Library of Central Michigan University and Pedro Juan Hernández at CUNY Hunter's Center for Puerto Rican Studies were immensely helpful in locating and reproducing sources.

In Michigan, I was blessed with the time and energy of Sheriff Bob Banta, a lover of history who spent long hours photocopying the police records of Mount Pleasant for me. Donald Turner, who first responded to a simple announcement I placed in his local town newspaper, deeply shaped the Michigan portions of this book through his historical sleuthing, his sharing of both his own memories and his father's written memoir, and by organizing oral history interviews. He made this project his own and I am grateful to him for it. Thank you also to Anastacio Díaz, Elisa and Manuel Ochoa, and John Espinoza for the oral histories they granted for this book. Linda, Frank, and Walter Berry provided me with housing, sociohistorical insights, and oral history contacts in Michigan. Thanks to Emily Berry for facilitating so much of this and for her womanly solidarity in creativity.

Gratitude is also due to Jesse Hoffnung-Garskoff, for inviting me to the University of Michigan to present my early thoughts on this project, for his generous, unsolicited photocopying for me of crucial documents that he found in the course of his own research, and for his insightful conversations about and scholarship on twentieth-century Caribbean migratory experiences and race and gender politics in Puerto Rico. I am indebted also to a number of capable research assistants who have combed through newspapers and digitally photographed archival documents when I could not wrench time away from my family to do so: Adam Fenner, Carlos Martínez Ruíz, Alberto Ortiz, and Santiago Lebrón.

Valerie Millholland, senior Latin American editor at Duke University Press, has been waiting patiently for me to finish this book for many years. I have been extremely fortunate to have received her good judgment, caring editorial presence, and personal friendship for two books. The Latin American historical community will miss Valerie sorely as she moves into retirement. Thank you for holding out until I could finish this last labor of love!

The people who specialize in technical matters are the unsung heroes of book publishing. Thanks to Lorien Olive for tracking down and negotiating use of digital images; Sarah Adler for last-minute bibliographic, footnote, and formatting labor; and Gisela Fosado and Liz Smith for shepherding this book through the last parts of the production process. Julie Boser Rogers prepared the index with insight and great attention to detail.

A number of people read this manuscript from top to bottom. It is the better for all of their responses. Any remaining errors are, of course, my own. The two anonymous readers for Duke University Press improved the manuscript greatly with their comments. Thanks to Kate Haulman, who read a draft in a moment of great urgency and helped me rethink its structure. Andrea Friedman read the entire manuscript and gave me exceedingly insightful comments in the midst of her own parenting and publication whirlwinds. I am overjoyed that Patricia Alvarenga and I rediscovered our connection after so many long years away from each other's minds, just in time for her thought-provoking remarks on the book draft. My deep thanks also go to Dionisio Valdés for his incredibly detailed comments on this manuscript, his irreverent stance as a teacher, which I was fortunate enough to experience more than twenty years ago at the University of Wisconsin, his abiding respect for and solidarity with migrant agricultural workers, and his rigorous, far-seeing scholarship that follows their paths.

Ellen Feder has been living with this book nearly as long as I have. It would not exist without her. Her loving but firm exhortations to never give up, even in the face of great family demands, professional distractions, and just downright panic kept me going when I thought I never could. Her insightful comments on its concepts, structure, and intent have enlivened it far beyond what I have brought to it. Her own example as parent, community member, and scholar has served as a constant inspiration to me. Thank yous are completely insufficient, Ellen. You know how deep it all goes.

Nor can I thank Silvina Cerezo adequately for how she has contributed to this endeavor. Not only did she step in to free me from the weight of the family plumbing company and allow me to think concertedly again, she also combed through the petitions of thousands of anguished *boricuas* and allowed them to haunt her life, as they have mine for so long.

My family, while creating all the marvelously wild and love-filled distractions that have made the writing of this book such a long process, have also supported me through it. My in-laws, Marta and Reynol Suárez, provided child care, delicious food, unconditional love, and models for living a generous diaspora life. My sister-in-law, Tania González, offered laughter and wise counsel. My mother and father, Doris and James Findlay, have sustained me in body, soul, and intellect over the last thirteen years. They have listened to my excitement and fears, given me research and writing guidance, and taken charge of children and domestic duties more times than I can count. My mother spent countless days in Puerto Rico photocopying documents. My father traveled to Michigan to do archival and oral history research for me. Thank you for all that you do for me and for others every day, Mom and Dad, and for ensuring that this book could really exist someday. And finally, it goes without saying, an unending thank you to Amaya, Lucas, and Raciel, for everything that gives meaning to my life.

BREGANDO THE SUGAR BEET FIELDS

More than anything else . . . we need to keep telling stories about why the past
matters and why all of us should care about it. Nothing is more important, for only by
the neverending telling of such stories is the dead past reborn into memory to
become living history, over and over and over again. ▪ William Cronon, "Storytelling"

In June 1950, along with five thousand of his countrymen, Esteban Casas
Martínez boarded an airplane outside of San Juan, Puerto Rico, and headed
to the sugar beet fields of Michigan, where he expected to earn enough
money to make a down payment on a two-room house in his rural community. Thirteen months later, in July 1951, from the isolation of a tuberculosis
sanatorium in Puerto Rico, he penned a passionate letter to the head of the
island's Department of Labor. His wife and children were starving and facing eviction without his income. Casas Martínez had been unable to earn a
stable living since departing that June day. He had contracted tuberculosis
while working in the frigid Michigan fields. He would probably never be able

to do substantial work again if he were ever discharged from the asylum. Time and again, Puerto Rican government representatives had denied his claims for aid to his family and a pension. He felt a failure as a man and as a father. The state had failed him in turn. Casas Martínez cried out in a complex mixture of rage and supplication:

> This is YOUR fault, for having deceived me. . . . So you had better look at my case and resolve it this very week. Or else I WILL BE FORCED to resolve it myself. In my own way as a man. 'Cause you know I'm still strong, and I'll take up a collection to buy a ticket and then I'll go there personally [to San Juan]. If you really want to see me het-up. I'll get my rights like a man, because me, what I demand are my children's rice and beans and I'll get them, come what may.
>
> I'm asking you to resolve my case—I'm asking you, please. . . . Sir, I hope you forgive my attitude but it's that I'm so nervous witnessing this crime they're committing against me, please forgive the mistakes and bad handwriting.[1]

I came upon Casas Martínez's letter as I sifted through the mountainous files of the Archivo General de Puerto Rico (AGPR) in San Juan, looking for evidence of early Puerto Rican diasporic community building in the United States. Drawn in by Casas Martínez's vivid language and desperate circumstances, I photocopied the letter. However, I set it aside, since I knew that all the sizable Puerto Rican diaspora communities had formed in U.S. cities, most of them on the East Coast. Casa Martínez's letter decrying an ill-fated trip to rural Michigan seemed anomalous. As I continued to read through the AGPR documents, though, more angry, anguished letters from Michigan's countryside appeared. Before too long, I encountered even more documents: hundreds of letters and petitions for back pay alphabetized and ordered chronologically in binders as they arrived at the Puerto Rican governor's mansion, frequently adorned with the governor's handwritten comments in the margins; scores of newspaper clippings from Puerto Rico, the United States, Latin America, and Europe carefully mounted on yellowed backing by the governor's staff; multiple drafts of reports on the sugar beet fields and worried memos about something that government officials dubbed "the Michigan affair"—this was no normal, haphazard archival grouping.

Obviously, something of import had happened in this corner of the rural Upper Midwest. Clearly, too, the management of information about the migration and the study of these disillusioned men and their wives had been a top priority at all levels of the Puerto Rican government at the time the documents were generated. I doubled back on my archival tracks and began to trace the documentary trails I had initially dismissed. Why were so many Puerto Ricans in rural Michigan at a time when the scholarly consensus was that nearly all emigrants from the island were streaming to New York City?

As I began to piece together some of the answers to this simple query, however, even more questions emerged. What was it about this particular historical moment and context that created such an unprecedented flood of impassioned protests by emigrants and their island-based family members, when Puerto Ricans had been traveling to work in the far corners of U.S. territories for decades? Why did top-level Puerto Rican officials find the migrants' letters so threatening, at a time when the party in power and its leadership enjoyed more popular support than any other government in the history of the island? Why did the Puerto Ricans' protests garner so much attention when almost 100,000 other migrant workers had filled Michigan's fields every summer and fall for decades? These queries, in turn, led me into archival searches and scholarly literatures that stretched back decades into the broader Puerto Rican sociopolitical landscape and outward along the migratory paths of the Mexican American and Mexican agricultural workers who had long preceded the Puerto Ricans in Michigan. My quest to understand the context that had generated this unexpected Caribbean archival eruption, the motivations of the Puerto Rican migrants to Michigan, the meanings of their missives, the surprising solidarities they forged, and the possible legacies of their now-forgotten anger ultimately produced this book, which stretches from the mass political mobilizations and modernizing hopes of midcentury Puerto Rico, to the controversies caused by increasing Puerto Rican arrivals in New York City and Chicago, to the fields of Michigan, New Jersey, Texas, and beyond.

Casas Martínez, I found, was just one of more than five thousand Puerto Rican agricultural working men who had traveled to east-central Michigan in the summer of 1950 to cultivate and harvest sugar beets at the behest of Puerto Rico's populist government. The men expected the income earned in Michigan to lift them out of poverty and prove their capacity to be dignified breadwinners and fathers. In short, like many laboring Puerto Ricans during the island's populist era, these men and their wives were inspired by postwar promises of creating homes where women could expect financial support and protection and men could rule as financially successful patriarchs while domestically exerting their newfound political empowerment. Politicians in the United States and San Juan, for their part, intended for this migration to mark the beginning of a permanent, cyclical movement from the Caribbean to the Midwest for hundreds of thousands of under- and unemployed Puerto Rican men, "saving" both the Michigan sugar beet industry and impoverished Puerto Rican families. Puerto Rican politicians also hoped that a midwestern migratory circuit would intensify the massive flow of Puerto Rican emigration to the United States, deemed necessary for the island's economic development, but direct it away from New York City, where Puerto Ricans' arrival by the hundreds of thousands after World War II had met with a hostile backlash.

Touted as a grand experiment in migrant agricultural labor, sure to provide prosperity for workers and growers alike, Operation Farmlift soon exploded into disaster when a plane carrying laborers to Michigan crashed in the Atlantic Ocean, killing several men. Within weeks, the men working in the Michigan sugar beet fields and their wives in Puerto Rico began to protest vociferously the terrible conditions and pay they encountered, denouncing the betrayal of the men's aspirations to provide a decent livelihood for their families. Soon, they created a public uproar both on the island and in the U.S. Midwest that engulfed Puerto Rico's populist governor Luis Muñoz Marín and Michigan politicians alike. Giving it even greater weight, the Michigan controversy escalated in the midst of Muñoz Marín's party's campaign to ratify a new Puerto Rican constitution, which would reform, rather than sever, the colonial relationship between Puerto Rico and the United States. Puerto Rican officials scrambled frantically to contain the protests' potential political fallout.

Gender and Postwar Politics

The Puerto Ricans' denunciations of the sugar beet field exploitation lead us from the specificity of this particular agricultural labor migration experience into a fuller understanding of postwar Puerto Rican politics more generally. The protests from and about rural Michigan illuminate the conflictual historical production of manhood during post–World War II Puerto Rico, when populist invocations of national dignity ultimately confirmed, rather than challenged, U.S. colonialism. They tell a complex story about Puerto Rican working men's understandings of masculinity, dependency, and democracy in a time of great political hopes and subsequent disappointments. They show us how populist and colonial politics have built on preexisting definitions of manhood and family as they simultaneously helped create new ones. They also reveal the meanings rural Puerto Rican men and women gave to the exploitation of colonial agricultural labor migration—a crisis in the family economy, interpreted as a failure of fatherly responsibility, both by the individual men and by the paternalist Puerto Rican state and governor, which working people saw as their allies. "We are left without a father here" was a common refrain from the Michigan sugar beet fields.[2]

This book exposes the effervescent years of populist politics in Puerto Rico as a deeply masculinist project constructed by both working people and political elites—ironically, one through which many women, as well as men, hoped to carve out a space for themselves. It clarifies how the populist decades of the 1940s and '50s that so enduringly shaped Puerto Rican political life encouraged and incorporated gendered popular demands for homes, modernity, and dignity even as they excluded those voices deemed threatening to the core principles of productive modernity within a colonial framework. Finally, this book allows us to begin to analyze Puerto Rican male migrants as men, and most particularly as fathers—how their understandings of familially based masculinity shaped their experiences and choices.[3]

Indeed, this tale of populist mobilization, international rural migration, and their discontents allows us especially keen insights into the contested meanings of fatherhood for Puerto Ricans and how they could be mobilized for political purposes. Puerto Rican populist politics were deeply intimate.[4] The populist party that came to power on the island during the 1940s sought to empower and discipline Puerto Rican men into a set of fatherly rights and responsibilities, combining exhortations to free voting and active participation in unions and other civic associations with promises to fathers of economic dignity, social respect, and power over homes, wives, and children. Populists insisted, in addition, that fathers be present in domestic life and that they work hard to provide reliable financial support for their families. During this period, men made political and economic claims on the basis of being fathers. Political leaders staked their claims to legitimacy by asserting their fatherly capacity to protect and provide for their constituents. Women, in turn, made claims on men and the state by attempting to hold them accountable to their paternal responsibilities to individual families and to society as a whole. Assertions of fatherhood and its attendant rights and responsibilities, then, became an integral part of the practice and rhetoric of Puerto Rican politics at home and abroad during the mid-twentieth century, providing an important glue for new political alliances and understandings.[5]

Effective fathers needed homes and families over which to rule and for whom to provide. This anguished moment in the history of the island and its diaspora, when fathers of all kinds failed to comply with heightened expectations of them, appeared in the midst of the consolidation of a powerful set of discourses about domesticity during the postwar period in Puerto Rico. These discourses had their roots in populist colonial state policy, media representations, and popular yearnings. Throughout the 1940s and '50s, the imagining and building of stable, "respectable" homes became a central thread in popular mobilizations for justice while the Puerto Rican state physically destroyed homes deemed undesirable in its drive to transform the island into a properly productive, modern society. Government exhortations to create domesticity could ironically even include the promotion of men's complete absence from home as a precondition for familial prosperity, as the state encouraged male-only agricultural migration to the United States.

Despite differences in their definitions of desirable homes, Puerto Ricans did reach a deep consensus on the necessity of having them; the goal of domesticity, however variably defined, gained great power in the postwar years. It fueled popular interest in migrating to the rural Midwest, thus separating family members to stretch proletarian households internationally. Through the course of the 1950 Michigan crisis, Puerto Rican government officials, sympathetic U.S. journalists and organizers, the migrant farmworkers, and their family members all drew on the discourses of domesticity, family, and responsible fatherhood to legitimize their actions and protests. These domesticity discourses, not explicitly racialized distinctions, also quite effectively denigrated or erased fellow migrant workers of Mexican descent laboring in Michigan; they were deemed incapable of achieving the postwar goals of respectable patriarchal rule over a fixed home and the separation of men and women into public and private spheres.

Indeed, one fascinating element of these gendered rhetorics and ideals was their ability to absorb overtly racial talk in Puerto Rico, as well as in Michigan. Certainly, racial identities, racial relations, and racism did not cease to be issues on the island after World War II. Indeed, in arenas of Puerto Rican popular culture such as music and apolitical newspaper cartoons, references to racial identities and racial tensions took on considerable force during this period.[6] But in public political discussions, the intertwined discourses of modern family, domesticity, and fatherhood submerged racial concerns and differences even as they implicitly asserted the possibility and power of whiteness—or at least a distancing from blackness—as a dominant Puerto Rican identity. Powerfully gendered images and ideals helped to empty political discussions of racial references, while simultaneously drawing their power in part from the haunting historical memories of slavery, its physical insecurity, and its emasculation of enslaved men.[7] Political talk, then, whether oral or written, attempted to expand the meaning of slavery—and populism's economic development policies alleged liberation of the island from it—to include all Puerto Ricans, regardless of their racial identities or family histories. However, the visual images produced by both Puerto Rico's populist party and the island's privately owned mass media incessantly linked modernity, progress, and their attendant consumptive practices and productivity with whiteness. Whether carefully deracialized or explicitly associated with whiteness, the new domesticity and fatherhood discourses promised a social and economic security to women and a male authority over wives and children impossible during slavery in the nineteenth century and during the early twentieth-century "dead time" of sugarcane plantations' reign.

Both elite and popular actors mobilized the rhetorics of fatherhood and domesticity that undergirded the political debacle of Puerto Rican migration to the Michigan sugar beet fields. These discourses constituted contested social and political ideals and as such could become the language of political demands from below as well as the framework for communicating political expectations of the powerful. Proud fathers and peaceful, prosperous, benevolently patriarchal homes and families could represent a hopeful vision of Puerto Rican modernity and economic development for many. When these hopes were dashed, the same images could be invoked to express acute anguish and rage. The inability to fulfill deeply felt expectations could also provoke great shame and humiliation, rendering working men speechless and politically demobilized. Thus, the study of these discourses and the people who produced and used them is a history of emotion, as well as of political and cultural relations and meanings. Indeed, the power of emotions could fuel or defuse political action. It could also bury certain experiences, rendering them too difficult to recount and thus ensuring that they would not be shared with subsequent generations.[8]

Migration and Colonial Populism

Two historical processes converged in this moment of Puerto Rican masculine and family crisis. The first entailed frequent international migration in the face of chronic low wages and unemployment in Puerto Rico. Since the late nineteenth century, even before the United States invaded the island in 1898 and wrested colonial control of it from Spain, thousands of Puerto Ricans had been traveling to *buscar ambiente* in the United States and its imperial outposts—usually in large industrial centers such as New York City, but also to work in U.S.-owned agricultural enterprises in places as far-flung as Hawaii's pineapple plantations and Arizona cotton fields.[9] This long-standing survival strategy was facilitated by the winning of U.S. citizenship for all Puerto Ricans in 1917 and intensified exponentially in the post–World War II years, when approximately one-third of Puerto Rico's population emigrated to the United States.

In this latter period, Puerto Ricans began to arrive in the U.S. Midwest in substantial numbers, encountering many people of Mexican descent who had been working in the fields and settling in cities there for several generations. Thus, the postwar Midwest became the historic meeting ground of these two great migrations. Until now, work comparing the two groups or studying their encounters has solely examined large cities such as Chicago or New York.[10] This book examines the initial rural encounter between the two groups.[11] In the Michigan countryside, the political controversy that swirled around the Puerto Ricans' beet field experience was in large part structured around gendered constructions of alleged familial differences between the recently arrived Puerto Ricans and the better-established "Mexicans," most of whom were actually Mexican Americans who migrated to Michigan in family groups from Texas each year.[12] This historical moment at the first encounters of Puerto Rican men and Mexican-descent families with each other in a rural setting produced a very specific combination of fragile solidarity and discursively created differentiation and erasure.[13]

The second historical process that undergirded the beet field crisis was shorter but quite dramatic—a little over a decade of massive political effervescence, during which great numbers of urban and rural working people mobilized to elect and maintain in power a reformist political party, the Partido Popular Democrático (PPD), and its charismatic leader, Luis Muñoz Marín. In 1940, Muñoz Marín became leader of the island's Senate, and in 1948, Puerto Rico's first elected governor. The PPD's organizing activity channeled into electoral politics the widespread anger at colonial abuses and severe economic exploitation that had exploded in wildcat strikes, demonstrations against U.S. colonial rule, and other protests throughout the island during the 1930s.

This period saw an unprecedented expansion of Puerto Rican citizenship, in both legal status and democratic practice. Puerto Rican women won universal suffrage in 1936, earlier than many of their Caribbean and Latin American counterparts. A legislature dominated by the PPD equalized inheritance rights between legitimate and illegitimate children. Laboring Puerto Ricans, both men and women, threw themselves into political life on a larger scale than ever before, participating energetically in the PPD's organizing activities and joining labor unions, consumers' leagues, cooperatives, student groups, and veterans' organizations to invigorate associational life on the island. Most of the workers who flew to the Michigan sugar beet fields in 1950 were faithful PPD voters. Many had worked actively to bring the party and Muñoz Marín to power. Their expectations of both material prosperity in Michigan and of the political support due them by PPD leaders were grounded in the flowering of political mobilization, demands for social justice, electoral fervor, and new relationships forged with the state that marked the 1930s through the 1950s in Puerto Rico.[14]

Pushed by popular demands during these years, the PPD and Muñoz Marín sought to transform Puerto Rico, first basing their program on calls for social justice—higher wages, redistribution of land, legislation of social equality—and later turning to a grand drive for "productive modernity," based on the attraction of U.S. governmental and private capital for rapid industrialization, construction of infrastructure, and provision of social services. Part and parcel of the industrialization and modernization project, which became the centerpiece of the PPD's economic program, was the promotion—sometimes tacit, sometimes explicit—of migration from the island. The party's leaders judged migration necessary to decrease unemployment and battle an alleged problem of overpopulation in Puerto Rico. In addition to promoting properly domesticated families, these Puerto Rican elites' "aspirational modernity" also sought to cleanse the island of slavery's last vestiges, implicitly whitening both Puerto Rico's image and its populace's consumptive and cultural practices.[15] Although often overlooked in studies of Latin American populism, the PPD's socioeconomic project generated some of the most dramatic social and economic changes in all of the mid-twentieth-century reformist populist regimes of the region; in the space of two decades, the entire island effectively transformed from a largely rural, agricultural society to an overwhelmingly urban, industrial one.

Crucial, too, in Puerto Rico's populist years was the reformation of the United States' colonial rule in Puerto Rico, which had been enthusiastically received when the United States invaded the island and defeated Spain in 1898, but which by the 1930s had fallen into a deep crisis. By the mid-1940s, Luis Muñoz Marín and his faction of the PPD had decided to abandon any pretenses of interest in national independence, and instead attempted to expand elements of political home rule on the island while maintaining dependent economic ties between Puerto Rico and the United States.[16] However, in the post–World War II era of worldwide decolonization, overt colonialism had become equated with exploitation and national shame and humiliation. Ferociously debating, attempting to silence, and ultimately repressing Puerto Ricans advocating independence for the island, those who managed to ultimately consolidate power within the PPD sought to achieve national dignity and decolonization by claiming to make the U.S. empire more equitable, not by breaking from it. Colonialism could be remade into free association without changing its economic or broader political underpinnings, Muñoz Marín insisted, despite much dissent even among the PPD's ranks; allegedly, the island's drive to productive modernity depended upon it.[17]

The period covered by this book, then, provides us a unique opportunity to study the gendered workings of imperialism, populism, and migration simultaneously.[18] Seeing Puerto Rican populist attempts to redefine U.S. colonial rule as a dignified pact of mutual aid among an international chain of interdependent fathers, stretching from Roosevelt to Muñoz Marín to Puerto Rican working men, as a crucial underpinning of the Michigan migrants' dashed hopes for equal treatment as U.S. citizen-fathers allows us to examine afresh the power of the United States' colonial appeal as a potential source of equality, democracy, and economic development as well as the crushing pain of its limits.[19] Populism in Puerto Rico gained a good deal of its allure among the island's working classes from the gendered dynamics of its simultaneously inclusive and disciplinary politics. Luis Muñoz Marín in particular, and the Partido Popular Democrático more generally, provided a space where women's domestic labor won recognition as politically significant work, where women could organize their neighbors, exhort their husbands to action, and even run for political office themselves. But for all the openings it offered to women, the PPD also insisted that women remain within the roles of wife and mother, ultimately subordinate to both husband and party. In turn, the patriarchal empowerment that populist politics offered to men won endorsement from women through its insistence that men manage their families without violence and provide them with consistent financial support.[20] Early economic planners in the PPD also understood migration as a method to reduce the island's population and thus reduce unemployment by encouraging fertile women to work abroad as domestic servants. When this attempt failed, they recast migration as a way to make prosperous domesticity available to working families, even as it might demand their physical separation.

This book exposes the underside of this allegedly triumphalist populist period, recognized by all students and citizens of Puerto Rico as one of the island's great historical turning points. It attempts to unwrap the desires and hopes that modernity inspired in elites and plebeians alike. It calls us to reflect deeply on Puerto Rico's history, to examine the anxieties of apparently self-assured state officials planning broad socioeconomic transformations, to see how understandings of gender and implicit, yet powerful, racial codings shaped the changes that swept Puerto Rico during the postwar years, to feel the pain and social dismemberment experienced by those dislocated by these shifts, and, ultimately, to understand how even while losing many struggles, working-class Puerto Ricans still could thwart the plans of the powerful. For after the 1950 controversy and suffering in the sugar beet fields, Puerto Ricans refused to return to rural Michigan. They dashed politicians' and growers' dreams of massive, docile migratory labor flows into the fields of the Midwest.

Thus, this study also modifies the reigning leftist interpretation of the late 1940s through the 1950s as a period of the PPD's inexorable channeling and later repression of dissent. Certainly, Muñoz Marín and the PPD did eventually manage to construct a hegemonic cultural, political, and economic colonial order in Puerto Rico. However, Puerto Rican newspapers reflect this period's intense power negotiations. All over the island, physical conflict between men and women, strikes and work stoppages, struggles between labor union members and party leaders, and between local PPD activists and high-level party officials broke out persistently. Agricultural migrants and their families could shape the political terrain available to state builders, too.[21]

The Many Levels of *Bregar*

In *El arte de bregar*, Arcadio Díaz-Quiñones brilliantly captures such struggles in his analysis of the ubiquitous verb *bregar* in Puerto Rican speech. Díaz-Quiñones illustrates how *bregar*, much more than a simple phrase, constitutes a central political and cultural practice in Puerto Rican history.[22] For Díaz Quiñones, its most important meaning is that of negotiation, slipping from one position to another to "achieve a difficult balance between potentially conflictual elements." *Bregar* maintains dignity in the face of adversity. It entails struggle without a frontal clash, implying a pact or a dialogue between parties. "It . . . dodges the blows which daily life delivers, and, in some cases, astutely extracts favorable possibilities from the limited available spaces."[23] *Bregar*, needless to say, is often a weapon of the less powerful.

However, as Díaz-Quiñones points out, elites in Puerto Rico historically also *bregaban*—in relation to the United States and other foreign powers, but also with Puerto Rican working people. *Bregar*, then, is a hegemonic practice and set of meanings familiar to and used by all Puerto Ricans. Luis Muñoz Marín himself punctuated his speeches with the term *bregar*, sometimes passionately denouncing wrongs, at others avoiding such confrontations, attempting to forge a pact with the United States that gambled on its capacity to deliver enhanced benefits to Puerto Rico.[24]

Those who most poignantly lost this historic wager, Díaz Quiñones asserts, were the Puerto Ricans pushed and recruited into migration, ejected completely from the great colonial reformation effort on the island. He also reminds us that although Puerto Rico's modernizing populist *brega* has now definitively lost its glow, for several decades it constituted a grand, shining hope for millions of Puerto Ricans, who looked to a leader who truly seemed to speak their language and have the capacity to *bregar* on their behalf.[25] The demonstrations organized by working people on the island and the letters from the sugar beet fields voice the popular hopes of the period for authentic cross-class exchange and solidarity and also record the pain of their betrayal in the face of more powerful colonial pacts. In the end, the "violence of radical rupture" came wrapped in silence from those in state power, not from the angry protests of working men and women. Through it all, the sugar beet workers and their wives used their own skills of *bregar* to survive and even open new possibilities of camaraderie, both at home and abroad.

In my attention to how both the betrayal of imagined solidarities and the formation of new ones formed in transnational encounters, I hope to produce what Paul A. Kramer calls a "crossed imperial history," which develops a "localized turn toward global history," exploring "how imperial connections bridge and transform specific locations," analyzing historical actors and processes in different locations on an analytically equal footing, linking disparate national historiographies, and foregrounding agency of all kinds: resistance, collaboration, and "the sea of human agency not easily subsumed in either category."[26] Colonialism, populism, and migration—all broad, compelling themes—must be seen as historically specific products of particular social relationships and contexts. When we subject them to close analysis of this kind, we can discern how, even in the most exploitative of circumstances, empires, states, and local elites cannot contain the "sea of human agency." While institutional power can certainly be potent, historians should not solely emphasize the strategies of rule. In analyzing the workings of political and economic authority, we must also pay attention to its "vulnerabilities: to the places where the extension of control fell short of expectation, . . . where projects imploded."[27] By building unexpected alliances, challenging the wisdom and direction of social superiors, and refusing to participate in the plans of the state, even extremely marginalized groups such as agricultural migrants leave their mark on history. Such footprints in the past deserve acknowledgment and study, just as much as the more readily discernible historical imprints of the wealthy, powerful, or well-organized; they, too, have shaped the present.

Dancing in the Sepulchre: The Power of the Archival Trail

Sharing stories such as those of transnational agricultural migrants is not a transparent endeavor, however. The nation, desired or actual, wields great narrative-shaping power, as does the colonial/national archive, with its gendered assumptions of record keeping and classification. Indeed, the Michigan beet field controversy invites us to reflect on how the archive can be both a sepulchre—burying historical subjects in its drive for managing, controlling, and directing populations and in its classificatory logic—and a space for creative imagining.[28] Archives are always open to new possibilities, but also always limiting, simultaneously ensuring that we forget even as they allow us to reconstruct lost experiences.

Here, I hope to begin to answer Michel-Rolph Trouillot's and Antoinette Burton's calls to explore how archives "are constructed, policed, experienced, and manipulated."[29] Certainly, which documents are selected for archival preservation, the structure of the archive itself, whether users have access to the archives, and on what terms all shape the history that can be written. (Is the archive under construction or closed for lack of funds? Are the documents one seeks processed and cataloged? If not, can the user convince the archivist to allow him or her to view them?) I also query how historians' interactions with readily available archival sources are shaped by the questions we allow ourselves to ask—in this case, how the investment of Puerto Ricanist historians (including myself) in an island-based nationalism often has prevented us from seeing other histories and their importance to Puerto Rican experience.

First, however, a bit of personal history. My earlier archival research projects in Puerto Rico rested in large part on gaining access to previously unavailable or uncataloged documents. My ability to do this depended in turn on the relationships I built with archivists and fellow archive users, which, through the bonds of friendship and intellectual exchange we knit through the years I spent in Ponce and San Juan, opened up striking possibilities for source exploration and interpretation. Archivist friends allowed me to enter the entrails of the Archivo General to dust off uncataloged police records from the early twentieth century that had been languishing on the basement floor covered with pigeon dung and generously invited me to participate in the reorganization of the Ponce municipal archives for a full year, while the archive remained closed to the general public. Fellow researchers demanded that I continually rethink my assumptions about the meaning of the documents I encountered, as we recounted and debated our findings over long lunches and cups of coffee. I found that entering an archive also could mean stepping into a world of complex social relations, which literally created as well as framed my encounters with documents.[30]

The 1950 sugar beet field drama, in contrast, has remained "hidden in plain view" for sixty years. But the suffering, shouts, and political disappointment of the sugar beet workers and their wives, so compelling and troubling in their day, have been completely erased from Puerto Ricans' historical memory—this despite the fact that their documentary trail lies at the heart of the AGPR's collections, in the Fondo de la Oficina del Gobernador. The historical remains of the Michigan controversy are well organized, mentioned in the finding guides, and quite voluminous. A parallel evidence-generating process occurred in Michigan. Indeed, the volume of documents by and about the Puerto Rican migrants that the historian Dionicio Valdés found in Michigan archives and newspapers while researching the history of Mexican and Mexican American agricultural workers in the Midwest compelled him to dedicate an entire chapter of his book Al Norte to the Puerto Rican airlift, despite the Puerto Ricans' relatively small numbers in the region's overall labor force and brief stay there.[31] Why had the wrenching story of the migrants to Michigan (and probably many other equally compelling histories) been ignored for so long by me and other historians of Puerto Rican experiences? The answer, I believe, lies in a number of epistemological factors.

Official archives, historians have noted, are deeply imbricated with nation formation. An important foundational act of most modern states has been to establish archives as impressive physical spaces and fill them with the records produced and collected by the state. Official archives subsequently allow the state to keep track of and create various types of knowledge about its citizens while simultaneously asserting its own legitimacy. Such an archive is "a montage of fragments" that creates an "illusion of totality and continuity."[32] Imperial powers also use archives in hopes of documenting, controlling, and knowing their colonial subjects and territories.[33] National archives can build upon and become deeply intertwined with their colonial metropolis's interests, especially in a place such as Puerto Rico, which has remained a colony of the United States for over one hundred years and for four hundred more previously had been a colony of Spain.

However, historians in many parts of the postcolonial world, and certainly in Puerto Rico, are often struck more by national archives' fragility and incompleteness, and their underpaid staffs' heroic struggling against the difficult odds of lack of climate control, funding, and space than by their "panoptic" capacity for information gathering and distribution.[34] Such difficulties stand in stark contrast with the physical magnitude as well as the geographical, cataloging, and documentary reach of many imperial metropolitan archives, including the U.S. National Archives.

Particularly during and after World War II, when the populist politician Luis Muñoz Marín and his PPD gained and held state power for over twenty years, the Puerto Rican government began to fervently assert the island's national integrity in cultural matters—a matter made particularly urgent since the PPD leadership had become openly hostile to the idea of political or economic independence.[35] The PPD established the Archivo General de Puerto Rico along with the Instituto de Cultura Puertorriqueña as monuments to and essential building blocks in the process of defining and building Puerto Rico's "national culture."[36] The archive's holdings, though, particularly for the twentieth century, comprise only a fraction of the materials produced and received by state officials and agency offices—those documents considered important at the moment or of later "historic value."[37]

Consequently, the voluminous documentation of the Michigan workers, so carefully organized in a strikingly different way than the usual jumble of materials seemingly dumped into the AGPR straight from bureaucrats' file cabinets and closet boxes, marks the affair as undeniably significant—at least at the moment of the documents' production and collection. Clearly, Muñoz Marín and other party leaders considered these men's protests, the agitation by their wives, the media storm they stirred, the alliances they forged with union and church officials in both Puerto Rico and Michigan, and their increasingly angry threats to unseat Muñoz Marín in the next election of grave concern to PPD hegemony on the island, especially since the party had begun to build toward a referendum on a new constitution that, if approved, would enshrine the island's revamped colonial relationship with the United States. Reading the documents, one can feel the government officials' palpable worry about analyzing and controlling the eruption of discontent around the exploitation of migrants to rural Michigan—the careful alphabetization by last name of the letters from workers and wives, the painstaking follow-up to each letter with cautiously worded notes seeking to redirect the men and women's explosive rage and anguish, dutifully copied and clipped into place in the archival record, the conscientious filing of multiple copies of official and unofficial reports, the worried scribbles in red from Muñoz Marín and his advisors lodged in their margins, the newspaper articles meticulously glued to special backing paper, tucked away in chronological order.

This great archiving energy betrayed a deep worry about the sugar beet workers and their possible ripple effects. Their "unanticipated outbursts of distrust" demanded organization, classification, and tracking if they were to be understood, managed, and tamed. All this effort created a fastidiously organized archive of the sugar beet field crisis, which eventually passed to the larger national archive, apparently intact.[38] But the objects of this classificatory, managerial furor would not be contained. They continued to protest: the men "struck with their feet," leaving the rural Michigan labor camps to seek out urban allies in Detroit and Chicago; the women on the island carried their stories to union officials, radio announcers, and opposition newspapers in Puerto Rico, despite their poverty and frequent physical isolation. In the midst of this rising drumbeat of protest and popular anger of thousands of PPD faithful against their beloved governor, whom they had voted into office, for whose political projects they had mobilized in massive numbers, in whom they had placed their hopes for an improved future, and whom they now denounced as betraying his paternal commitments to them, the Nationalist Party uprisings of October 30, 1950, exploded in Puerto Rico and two members of the Party assaulted the residence of U.S. president Harry Truman in an attempt on his life.

The response was immediate—press coverage of the sugar beet worker crisis ground to a halt as all eyes turned to the nationalist threat (or "valiant stance," depending on one's political position). The Nationalist Party's protests against the PPD's complicity with U.S. colonialism met with a virulent crackdown of arrests, blacklisting, surveillance, political marginalization, and ideological diatribes linking proindependence organizations and individuals with communism, terrorism, sexual promiscuity, and insanity, among other things.[39] Public discussion of the sugar beet field challengers disappeared, despite the continuing arrival of their anguished missives at the governor's office. Thousands of men left Michigan, looking for work elsewhere in the United States, denied their promised airfare home. Many of the sugar beet workers do not seem to have made their way back to the island; instead, they went on to cities such as Milwaukee, Detroit, Chicago, and New York to seek industrial work, or accompanied Mexican Americans in their agricultural labor circuit to California and Texas, or moved into migrant labor camps in rural New York, New Jersey, Pennsylvania, and Florida, ultimately disappearing from Puerto Rico's archival record. Thus, the men's own physical diffusion and political demoralization, combined with the antinationalist consensual fervor in Puerto Rico that consolidated in late 1950 and endured for many more years, fueled by Cold War anticommunism and pro-U.S. zeal within the PPD, seem to have buried the Michigan tales of rage and suffering that had been so worriedly documented by Muñoz Marín's assistants.

But the Cold War, procolonial historical moment is only part of the history of silence that enveloped the sugar beet field crisis. Since well before the nationalist uprising of 1950, most historians of Puerto Rico have remained fixated, implicitly or explicitly, on the tension between Puerto Ricans' incipient attempts at nation formation and the enduring power of colonialism on the island. Whether demonized or held out as the redemption of an oppressed island people, nationalism has long resided at the core of most Puerto Rican historical projects, perhaps because the island's centuries-long colonial status imbues the issue with particular emotional power and political urgency. Historians of the island may have overlooked the impressive documentation of the beet field controversy partly because it does not fit into our previously conceived notions of what constitutes proper Puerto Rican history.[40]

Unlike the Nationalist Party and later movements for independence, the men and women who hoped for economic opportunity in the sugar beet fields of Michigan did not form an organized opposition movement battling to win political independence for an island nation. Rather, the migrants to Michigan and their female family members were by and large PPD faithfuls, who sought to hold Muñoz Marín accountable to his promises of dignified labor, political empowerment, and domestic prosperity. They did not challenge either the legitimacy of the PPD's proposed pseudo-nation or the colonial relationship between Puerto Rico and the United States. They did, however, insist on the right to respect as political equals, demanding that "imperial space be taken seriously."[41] The violence visited upon them by the Puerto Rican state was not the overt coercion it wielded against all those suspected of nationalist sympathies, but that of negation, rejection, erasure, the violence of forgetting. This silencing power is less easily identifiable now, much less easily denounced than the killing of peaceful Puerto Rican independence demonstrators by colonial police in the 1937 Ponce massacre, the antinationalist/communist hysteria of the 1950s, or the subsequent censorship and surveillance of those suspected of independence-related activism in Puerto Rico. Demoralized, challenging the Muñocista political project from within, and often unable to return to the island, the Michigan sugar beet workers could not win enduring recognition of their struggle for familial dignity and masculine redemption. Theirs was not a tale of stark opposition to Muñoz's paternalist pact with colonialism, nor did it nourish the teleological siren song of populist-led industrial development, which claimed to be ushering Puerto Rico into a beckoning modernity. Thus, the story of agricultural migrant workers isolated in the northern Midwest did not fit into the political and historical narratives being spun in the postwar years, which deepened in the ensuing decades. This book strives to open a space for uncovering not only this tale of the Michigan migration controversy, but many more forgotten, broken experiences that do not fit easily within the narratives of national struggle, whether heroic or threatening.

Second, and relatedly, historians of Puerto Rico have, until relatively recently, considered the island itself the sole spatial definition of the nation—a deeply ironic assumption, considering that massive migration out of the island began more than seventy-five years ago, and that more than 50 percent of all Puerto Ricans now reside in the United States. Since the sugar beet workers physically left the island, they literally disappeared from the geographic space that historians of Puerto Rico have considered their purview. Until recently, relatively few users consulted the section of the Oficina del Gobernador containing the Michigan sources; it is made up of documents about migrating Puerto Ricans—those no longer part of the legitimate nation.[42]

Concomitantly, research on the Puerto Rican diaspora, in full swing since the 1970s, developed autonomously from histories of Puerto Rico. In a mirror image of the island-based Puerto Rican blindness to migratory experiences, historians of the diaspora have sought to investigate urban migrant community formation in the United States, and thus have focused almost exclusively on New York City and, to a lesser extent, Chicago and Philadelphia. These historians have tended to draw primarily on oral histories, published government reports, and archives in the United States rather than in Puerto Rico.[43] Historians of both the island and its diaspora, then, have often spun "narratives of group identity [that] tend to aggrandize themselves by co-opting the materiality of spaces read back in time as the local bedrock of an inevitable history."[44]

Happily, historians of the island and of the diaspora are now dialoguing much more readily, but migrants to the rural Midwest continue to seem utterly marginal to the grand historical sweep of the recently redrawn Puerto

Rican map, which includes both island and urban diaspora communities.[45] The sugar beet workers, none of whom remained in rural Michigan and many of whom did not return to their homeland, do not fit such geographically rooted narratives. They remind us that the twinned, spatially bounded processes of community and nation formation, however important, do not encompass the totality of Puerto Rican historical experience. In writing the history of such eminently mobile people as Puerto Ricans, we need to try to trace the routes of physical movements themselves, as well as the relationships formed, the lessons learned, and the cultures forged in these processes, not restrict ourselves to the study of fixed settlements. The Puerto Rican workers' abandonment of the sugar beet fields and subsequent travels through the United States can help historians to "imagine . . . a somewhat more dynamic . . . model of historical analysis: one where the ground or space itself is ever moving, and those operating on it find themselves routinely adjusting themselves—whether by choice or otherwise—to its perpetual motion."[46]

The conceptual blinders of sharply delimited nations and communities are not the only challenge faced when trying to write such a history. The self-imposed silence of pain also plays a role in preventing personal or communal archival preservation of certain stories. For the men and women of the sugar beet field disaster, migration meant dislocation, anguish, and personal and political betrayal—not opportunity, as they had hoped (and as Muñoz Marín had promised). Histories of such experiences may well be "not contained in sensible narratives, but speak out as the remains of irreparable loss and violent discontinuity. They are objects stranded in the present as the debris of broken connections." Records of deep collective loss often "subvert the state-centered authority of the conventional archive."[47] Such stories of shame and perceived failure do not survive easily. They are painful to remember. Neither states, families, nor individuals yearn to recount such tales.

As a result, oral histories of the controversy and its aftermath have proved difficult—especially with Puerto Ricans. The sugar beet workers left the Michigan fields in many directions; their dispersion and the experience's disappointments meant that neither they nor their family members formed any sort of organization or network that would have allowed me to track them down sixty years later. Interestingly enough, my efforts to locate participants in or reminiscences about the sugar beet field debacle through appearances on radio talk shows as well as advertisements and letters to the editors in local midwestern and Puerto Rican newspapers netted me several responses from elderly rural Anglo-American Michiganians, but none at all from Puerto Ricans, either on the island or in the United States.[48] Certainly, my Anglo surname may well have discouraged Puerto Rican survivors of the Michigan migration from offering their memories, while it may have provided an incentive for nonmigrant Michiganians to contact me. Perhaps in the future, historians of Puerto Rican descent will have more luck than I in uncovering the personal memories and winding historical paths of the Michigan migrants.

Histories of unsuccessful projects also demand examination of what was imagined but did not come to pass—for both elites and working people. Such an analysis of the past is not highly valued in a discipline such as history, which is deeply invested in empirical evidence—if it cannot be proven to have been historically significant, of what use is it to historians? Thus, a further obstacle to reconstructing the Puerto Rican sugar beet field nightmare lies in its status as a failed project, for all involved. Despite its sensational importance in its own historical moment, the controversy did not create an enduring physical presence, political movement, or historical memory in either Michigan or Puerto Rico; it constitutes what Ann Laura Stoler has dubbed "historical negatives," efforts that "are absent from the historiography because they appear to be colonial debris, unfulfilled visions discarded in process." Although such plans of the powerful may have been scrapped eventually, they should not be ignored, Stoler insists. Rather, their analysis allows us to write the history of "what was deemed possible but remained unrealized"—an apt summation of the sugar beet fields' anguish.[49]

A final limit in writing a history of the sugar beet field struggles lies in the archive's gendered classification practices. Clearly, despite the workers' eventual erasure from historical memory in both Puerto Rico and Michigan, Muñoz Marín's archiving staff considered the migrating men potent—or at least problematic—historical agents at the time. The archival organization acknowledges this; the files of the sugar beet field controversy, whether letters of protest, press releases, commission reports, or petitions for back pay owed them by the Michigan growers, are organized around the male workers' voices and actions. Labels such as "Complaints from the Michigan Workers," "Michigan I, II, III, etc." adorn the scores of relevant boxes. Thus, a dense thicket of male voices, tracks, and fingerprints pointing to and from Michigan waits in the Archivo General de Puerto Rico, ready to be noticed by researchers.

Not so for the affected women, who were considered simply dependents of their husbands and partners, not historical actors in their own right. No files, boxes, or collections were organized around their letters, their demands for their husbands' return, their petitions for welfare benefits, or their investigations by social workers, despite the passage of a law in August 1950 that granted families of the sugar beet workers a special aid package—the only such concession ever made to families of postwar Puerto Rican migrants and an indication of the threatening potential power of the protests about conditions in Michigan. It is clear from the surviving letters from women scattered through the boxes of Michigan documents and from worried comments by their husbands that the sugar beet workers' wives exerted forceful, persistent pressure on both their husbands in Michigan and the government in Puerto Rico to provide income for their families' survival, turning the government's own triumphalist rhetoric of the family wage inside out. Sugar beet worker wives probably encouraged their husbands to file the thousands of petitions for back pay that fill an entire series of boxes in the AGPR's Fondo del Departamento del Trabajo; they may well have accompanied their husbands to the local union and government offices where the paperwork was done. After the passage of the August 1950 aid bill, women surely flooded into the offices of the PPD's burgeoning welfare state, demanding that they be given the food and cash "owed to the wives of the Michigan workers." Certainly, social workers subjected thousands of them to rigorous investigations, if Muñoz Marín's terse directive memos on the subject are to be taken seriously.

However, most of this activity remains unrecorded or unavailable to researchers. Sometimes women wrote their own letters; I incorporated these into my analysis. But more frequently, women's influence on their husbands' actions and concerns appear in occasional furtive, worried, backhanded comments from the men in their letters. The back pay *querellas* forms provided no space to record women's presence or interests in the petitions. The welfare cases were either not cataloged separately, as were the male sugar beet workers' documents, or not saved at all; the welfare benefit requests preserved in the AGPR are organized by municipality and by date of original contact with the local welfare offices—most beginning in the 1940s. The cases of sugar beet worker families, if collected, are impossible to distinguish from all the thousands of other rich files waiting for scholars to mine them. Thus, whether unnamed or not saved, women linked to the sugar beet worker controversy are largely untrackable in the archive, preventing me from dedicating the space due them in my own writings, unless I invent their actions—something prohibited by the disciplinary rules of historical writing. This problem is exacerbated by the frustration of my efforts to carry out oral histories. I have been denied access to the extraordinarily rich oral accounts of women's struggles and relationships with men and with other women that historians such as Heidi Tinsman, Ana Rosas, and Daniel James have mined so well in other Latin American contexts.[50] In the end, the archives have been my primary resource. They, and the androcentric assumptions of the people who created them, have pushed me to create an overwhelmingly male-dominant historical narrative as I try to challenge the many layers of silence surrounding the Michigan crisis of 1950.

Of course, my focus on the Michigan crisis and the agricultural front of migration also masculinizes this story. If this book were a history of the workers in the light industries opened during the PPD period, of the families who built homes on small *parcela* rural plots distributed by the PPD government during the 1940s and '50s, or of the proliferation of social services provided by the burgeoning Puerto Rican welfare state between 1930 and 1960, then women would necessarily loom much larger. Happily, some of these projects are already being researched by other scholars.[51] This book, however, remains grounded in the story of the migration to Michigan, which ultimately offers us primarily an examination of the intimate masculinist politics of populism and its workings in a colonial context, a topic worthy of its own investigation.

In the end, despite the disappointment of their aspirations for prosperous domesticity through agricultural labor migration, the sugar beet migrants and their wives did leave a powerful legacy of their own. By and large, Puerto Rican migrants rejected Muñoz Marín's pleas for them to continue to serve the Michigan growers throughout the long, cold fall of 1950. They also rebuffed the larger push for enduring, massive, cyclical Puerto Rican migration to the rural Midwest. (What role might women's pressure have played in this refusal of return? As of yet, we cannot definitively know.) No Puerto Ricans returned to the sugar beet fields in subsequent years, despite Michigan growers' persistent attempts to woo them. Ultimately, the workers' repudiation of the exploitative conditions of the rural Midwest set undeniable limits on the plans of the powerful. If the workers' dreams of migratory prosperity remained unrealized, so, too, did elite dreams of a steady stream of Puerto Ricans moving from the island to the midwestern countryside. The failure of this elite project—imposed by those it sought to recruit—remains what Ann Laura Stoler has dubbed an "arrested history," excluded from existent historiography.[52]

I have been constantly reminded, as I struggled with writing this "arrested history," that every process of remembering always entails forgetting. As Peter Fritzche comments, "we need to acknowledge the final impossibility of completely understanding or fully accounting for [historical] loss" and its effects.[53] We can know, however, that during the long months of 1950 and 1951, Puerto Rican state agents tried to wrestle into obedient compliance the shouts of indignation emanating from the sugar beet fields' exploitation, and to prevent them from dangerously ricocheting too far. State officials attempted to redirect the sugar beet workers' and family members' anger, to smother them in the governor's archive, confining them to bureaucrats' drawers, hiding them from view, denying their demands for respect and equitable treatment. But once placed in the national archive, open to the public, their traces remained for historians to notice, straining at the minutely detailed trusses of classification that contained them. Women left their marks as well as men, despite state agents' refusal to recognize their full historical weight, to acknowledge them as agents to be analyzed, neutralized, and known, like their male partners. Women's historical effects circulated below the surface of the readily available documentary record, calling out to be imagined, if not always proven.

Certainly, a state archive has its limits. These constraints can be crippling, completely excluding some experiences, consigning some stories to permanent debris status, burying others in the overwhelming weight of surrounding documents. But the archive can also "release meanings, tend mysteries, and disclose its own openness. . . . Dancing between remembering and forgetting, at once spanning them and within each, is imagining. . . . The archive, then, is a trilectic, an open-ended process of remembering, forgetting, imagining."[54] It is here, while critically conscious of our limits and responsibly imagining the untold aspects of the past, that creative history writing can thrive as we let the stories strain against the weight of the archive.

1

FAMILY AND FATHERHOOD IN
"A NEW ERA FOR ALL"
Populist Politics and Reformed Colonialism

Believe in yourselves! Don't think of yourselves as tiny or weak or inferior! The light of God is in the nature of all those men and women whom God has created in this world. Believe in yourselves! Have faith in your own strength and power to make justice and ensure your own futures. • Luis Muñoz Marín, "En la víspera de las elecciones," radio speech, 1940

[Muñoz Marín] put his ear to the ground, then dressed in shirt-sleeves without abandoning his lordly linen. . . . He transformed the ancient rhetoric . . . into phrases of frothy custard and succulent metaphors . . . into sparkling, economical verbs, inaugurating a new politics, disguising the society of old. . . . To what point did he console himself with the role of benevolent overseer? • Edgardo Rodríguez Juliá, *Las tribulaciones de Jonás*

The decade prior to the Michigan crisis of 1950 marked an era of mass organizing in Puerto Rico, of great popular hopes for change, and of the refashioning of politics. By 1940, vast numbers of urban and rural working- and middle-class people joined together to elect and maintain in power a new political party, the Partido Popular Democrático, which pledged to forge fresh political options on the island and to make "Bread, Land, and Freedom" available to all Puerto Ricans. Never before had a political party inspired such a massive mobilization of the Puerto Rican population. In its early years, the PPD was a sprawlingly inclusive organization, welcoming socialists and independence supporters of all kinds, working closely with the fledgling but bustling Communist Party of Puerto Rico, encouraging women to political action, and speaking passionately of the wounds of slavery that permeated many Puerto Ricans' hope for final deliverance into "freedom"—a broad term with many meanings. By the late 1940s, however, the PPD had begun to suppress autonomous political action within its ranks, its leaders simultaneously triumphant in their electoral success and anxious about the escalating demands made by laboring Puerto Ricans who organized as workers, veterans, consumers, housewives, and community residents. Beginning in 1950, PPD leaders worried particularly about winning popular endorsement of their plans to reform U.S. colonialism on the island, embodied in a referendum on a new political constitution. The protests from and about the Michigan sugar beet fields that exploded in mid-1950 surfaced out of and further fueled this complex political stew.

The PPD was led by the charismatic Luis Muñoz Marín, whose father had helped to found the Liberal Autonomist Party during the 1870s and had continued as a major player in Puerto Rican politics throughout the late nineteenth and early twentieth centuries. Many of the formally educated PPD founders had participated in the U.S. government's New Deal attempts to restructure the island's economy and provide a social service safety net to its poorest residents. In the process, they had accumulated experience in building relationships and hammering out policies with U.S. officials and politicians. Other party founders were seasoned union organizers, disillusioned with the island's stagnant politics and the intransigence of large, absentee-owned U.S. sugar corporations.

Puerto Rico's populist movement simultaneously legitimized "the people" as a historical force and exhorted them to focus their political energies on the compelling figure of Luis Muñoz Marín.[1] Muñoz Marín persistently presented himself as the great father of "the new Puerto Rico" and used a rhetoric that sidestepped racial differences while exalting national unity through gendered stability. He offered empathetic partnership with women, promised men paternal dignity and empowerment, and insisted that Puerto Rico's feminized colonial degradation could be transformed into a respectful international pact between modern, deracialized fathers. As he elaborated the PPD's vision of an all-inclusive Puerto Rico, Muñoz Marín forged a deeply personal, even passionate relationship with laboring Puerto Ricans. Among them were the men who headed north to Michigan in 1950, hoping to achieve the PPD ideal of prosperous domesticity through migration.

To understand the historical pressures out of which the PPD emerged, we must turn to the preceding decades. In 1898, the United States invaded

Puerto Rico and wrested control of it from Spain. The change of imperial ruler from Spain to the United States generated new colonial contradictions between intensified economic exploitation in the sugarcane fields and popular expectations of prosperity, democracy, and modernity. By the 1930s, political life on the island overflowed existing institutions as working families struggled with the gendered immiseration and disruptions of the Great Depression; women successfully agitated for universal suffrage; workers protested against complacent labor leaders and abusive employers; and criticisms of U.S. colonialism escalated. In its calls to social and political change, the PPD appropriated many of these demands, muting their radical edges and presenting them as inventions of the Partido Popular. Popular organizing shifted with the consolidation of PPD power. Plebeian demands for social justice continued, now both trusting in and pressuring the state to fulfill its promises. These autonomous political pressures simultaneously legitimized PPD power and unnerved the party's top leaders.

The Roots of Colonial Crisis

Throughout the nineteenth century, while a colony of Spain, Puerto Rican society was shaped by an economic counterpoint between the sugar-producing coastal regions and the coffee- and tobacco-producing mountainous center of the island. From 1820 to 1840, sugar plantations in Puerto Rico's coastal plains encroached on peasants who relied on informal, untitled land use to engage in subsistence agriculture. The sugar plantation owners imported tens of thousands of enslaved Africans to harvest and cut cane, unable to effectively coerce large numbers of the physically mobile, multiracial rural population into plantation labor.[2] By the mid-1870s, though, Puerto Rico's sugar industry had become rather moribund; slavery was abolished in 1873. Coffee and tobacco production, based in the hilly center of the island, took economic center stage. Impoverished rural Puerto Ricans moved between the coastal and mountainous regions, looking for work in burgeoning towns and in larger landed estates. By the turn of the twentieth century, they had begun to organize labor unions in cigar factories, urban artisan trades, and on the coastal sugarcane plantations.[3]

Working people's frequent physical movement and concomitant family and community building created an interracial society still marked by the island's persistently racialized geography—"blacker" coastal areas dominated by plantation production of sugar and "whiter" central mountainous regions where coffee and tobacco estates alternated with an impoverished peasantry dependent on estate wages as well as their own food crops. By the 1860s, plebeian Puerto Ricans, at least in the coastal areas, recognized that most people were of mixed racial heritage. Working people did not form racially segregated communities, even as the stigmatization of blackness persisted as a powerful current in Puerto Rico. Many laboring people did not identify as clearly black or white, although in their social networks, cultural attributes and styles, or regional identification, they may have tended more toward one end of the spectrum than the other. Racial identities among working people were often determined by one's social status or community reputation as much as by phenotype; they could also change over time or depend on the persons with whom one might relate socially. While maintaining more openness to popular culture than many elites in other colonies of the Spanish Empire, Puerto Rico's moneyed classes anxiously and vociferously asserted their own whiteness during the nineteenth century, distancing themselves from the possible racial impurities of laboring people and their own family histories. Race, then, became an ever-present yet subtle current in Puerto Rican politics, culture, and social relations during the nineteenth and early twentieth centuries. Sometimes, the racial intimacies, hierarchies, and identities rooted in slavery and complicated through long decades of internal migration, exploited and shared labor, and sexual relationships were discussed openly and overtly politicized. More frequently, they were addressed obliquely through the languages of sexual morality and respectability, wage slavery, merit, and communal belonging.[4]

In 1898, as part of its broader interventions into the Cuban and Philippine independence struggles, the United States invaded Puerto Rico and quickly defeated Spain's forces there. In this era of rising imperialist interests, the United States proclaimed itself Puerto Rico's new colonial ruler and great modernizing agent. Their colonialism, imperialist U.S. politicians and officials insisted, would be like no other—swathed in benevolence and inculcating modernity wherever it reached. The occupying power collaborated with liberal Puerto Rican elites to launch public health campaigns, build schools, and legalize divorce in Puerto Rico.[5] The United States also restructured the island's physical infrastructure and economy; U.S. capital streamed into Puerto Rico for the dredging of ports, the building of roads and bridges, the modernization of sugar mills, and the revitalization of the sugar industry. In addition, U.S. officials centralized political power and international economic dealings in the capital city of San Juan.[6]

In the process, the United States positioned itself as the primary example of modernity for Puerto Ricans. Whether imagined or directly experienced, the United States' economy, culture, and political practices came to represent the essence of modernity for most inhabitants of the new colony. For the rest of the twentieth century, Puerto Ricans' interpretations of modernity, whether utopian, dystopic, or disinterested, remained deeply historically intertwined with their experience of U.S. colonialism.

U.S. imperialists justified their invasion and continued colonial rule in Puerto Rico through gendered and racialized assertions about Puerto Ricans' alleged lack of modernity and consequent unfitness for self-governance. Although colonial officials conceded that there were a "few good men" among elite Puerto Ricans, they generally represented island elite men as either too ineffectual in their efforts to preserve social order on the island or too contaminated with the despotic political practices of their former Spanish colonial masters to govern properly. Thus, according to U.S. officials, male Puerto Rican elites might serve as allies in building the benevolent colonial project, but they clearly needed U.S. imperial tutelage; they were closer to obedient, docile, indecisive women than to the firm masculinity necessary for national sovereignty. Men of the laboring classes did not measure up either; they allegedly did not have the virile strength of character necessary for unrestricted political participation. "Manhood suffrage presupposes a basis of real, true manhood," thundered an early U.S. military governor. Not until 1904 did U.S. officials allow universal male suffrage, a right won by Puerto Ricans during the late 1890s under Spanish rule but revoked by the invading U.S. forces. U.S. colonial personnel also worried about laboring Puerto Ricans' "promiscuous" racial mixing. U.S. observers closely associated working-class Puerto Ricans' racial ambiguity with their propensity for living in consensual unions rather than entering into formal marriage. Colonial officials and observers puzzled over the suspect "reddishness" of white plebeians and the varied hues and phenotypes of children within a single family.[7]

For their part, Puerto Ricans of all social classes and racial identities initially enthusiastically endorsed the U.S. occupation of their island in 1898, although they did so for widely divergent reasons. Working men and women as well as feminists of various social classes saw a chance to build alliances with the United States' growing labor and women's movements. Puerto Ricans of African descent welcomed the connection with a nation that had fought a war to end slavery and where African Americans had organized to press for greater political, educational, and economic opportunities. All groups lauded the United States' democratic ideals, which they hoped to apply to themselves. Seeing that the U.S. political system afforded a good deal of autonomy to entering states, wealthy and professional Puerto

Ricans hoped to consolidate greater local political power than that accorded to them under Spain's restrictive colonial rule. They also expected to gain unrestricted access to massive U.S. markets for the island's sugar, tobacco, and coffee. Puerto Rican dreams of the modernity heralded by U.S. rule, then, could take many forms: social justice, economic prosperity, and political power all fit within its widening possibilities. Despite the ominous signs of Jim Crow consolidation in the U.S. South, the restriction of suffrage for working-class men, and the imposition of English as the language of instruction in public schools in Puerto Rico, Puerto Ricans across the social spectrum initially welcomed the North American intervention on their island, particularly because the United States was a decidedly more modern, liberal, and prosperous metropolitan power than Spain. Certainly, the United States' inspiring originating ideals, however imperfectly applied, offered a standard to which all civilized polities might aspire.[8]

U.S. imperialists, for their part, also enthusiastically welcomed Puerto Rico into their new 1898 stable of colonial possessions. U.S. capitalists and social reformers alike rapidly developed a great interest in Puerto Rico, which seemed a much less problematic colony to control than Cuba or the Philippines, which had developed broad-based armed struggles for independence from Spain. Sugar magnates bought up failing sugar plantations; the infusion of capital and technology fueled an implacable expansion of sugar production on the island that gobbled up land for decades. Excited by the evangelical possibilities, all the mainline U.S. Protestant churches established bases on the island and sent missionaries to lure Puerto Ricans away from Catholicism. The impressive success of organizing among tobacco workers, cane cutters, urban artisans, and sweatshop laborers in the first decades of the twentieth century caught the attention of the U.S. labor movement. By World War I, the American Federation of Labor (AFL) had established an enduring relationship with Puerto Rican labor organizers and institutions.[9]

Puerto Rican expectations of economic prosperity, democratic empowerment, and social justice had begun to wither by the end of the second decade of U.S. colonialism, however. U.S.-sponsored construction of roads and ports seemed designed to serve only the interests of U.S. sugar corporations. U.S. citizenship, granted in 1917 to all Puerto Ricans, did not guarantee equal political voice in Washington or on the island. Puerto Rico's laws still could be abrogated at will by the U.S. Congress or president. The island's governors remained federal appointees, all of them North American and for the most part incapable of or uninterested in speaking Spanish. To add insult to injury, Puerto Ricans were drafted into World War I by the United States. Sugar plantations reigned supreme in the island's economy, pumped up by U.S. capital and easy access to the United States' vast markets. The coffee industry, on the other hand, after its late nineteenth-century dynamism, lay moribund under U.S. rule. Small farmers and squatters rapidly lost access to land as the great sugar plantations consumed nearly all available flat land and brought new acreage under large-scale sugar production. The "dead time" of eviscerating unemployment for sugarcane workers between planting and harvest now stretched for more than six months of the year. Colonial officials sided consistently with U.S. corporations and Puerto Rican elites in labor conflicts. Likewise, they opposed broadening suffrage rights to Puerto Rican women.

Nevertheless, Puerto Rico's labor movement made steady membership gains during the first two decades of the twentieth century, launching a great island-wide organizing drive, leading a number of mass strikes in the cane fields, and actually garnering over 20 percent of the vote for the Socialist Party in the 1920 elections. During the 1920s, though, the leaders of the Puerto Rican labor movement turned away from their radical origins by privileging electoral politics over organizing for better work and living conditions, deepening their dependence on the funding and guidance of the increasingly conservative AFL, and eventually allying with the political heirs of the elite Liberal Autonomists of the nineteenth century. Encouraged by the AFL and its wealthy Puerto Rican political patrons, the Socialist Party even refused to endorse strikes by aggrieved workers during the 1920s.[10]

Both the alienation of the top echelons of traditional Puerto Rican labor leaders from the island's rank-and-file sugar workers and growing popular dissatisfaction with U.S. rule intensified during the Great Depression of the 1930s. Sugar prices dropped and male unemployment soared frighteningly high, even during the harvest months. Long-standing political allies such as the Socialist Party no longer consistently defended working-class interests. Many working-class families' only income came from the few cents that adult women and their daughters could earn sewing piecework for long hours each day or caring for wealthier women's homes and children. Don Rubén del Pilar, who grew up during the 1930s, remembered feeling as though "my stomach were one great, aching hole, never to be filled," as his father traveled from town to town looking unsuccessfully for work and as his mother's fingers bled from her never-ending sewing. He and his six siblings counted themselves lucky if they ate meagerly once a day. Crowds of men gathered desperately to seek work in the sugar fields. Even during the harvest, many were unsuccessful; during the seven months of dead time men were lucky to get a morning of work a week, to be paid with a few yuccas or sweet potatoes. Cash payments were unthinkable in many parts of rural Puerto Rico.[11]

Protests against such conditions escalated throughout the 1930s in Puerto Rico, often organized by the new Nationalist or Communist Parties; both political parties openly denounced the intertwined exploitation of poverty and colonialism. Some seamstresses also tried to organize unions; they demanded fair wages, the right to protest employer abuses, and government regulation and investigation of home-based needlework conditions, while insisting on the necessity of maintaining women's right to earn income from their homes. Working-class feminists continued to press hard for universal female suffrage as well, insisting that the voting rights conceded only to literate Puerto Rican women in 1928 constituted a democratic farce.[12] U.S. repression of the Nationalist Party, which openly advocated independence for Puerto Rico, increased exponentially; policemen fired into nationalist demonstrations on several occasions, killing peaceful protesters.[13] Through the course of the 1930s, then, spiraling poverty and political repression pushed many Puerto Ricans to resent U.S. rule and protest against their material and political conditions as never before. This generalized crisis had a gendered underpinning. More women than ever were forced to provide the sole income for their families; men's long-standing identity as familial financial providers was shaken to its core.

Coping with Crisis

Facing an undeniable crisis in their colonial regime, U.S. officials in Washington attempted to reestablish their legitimacy by instituting elements of New Deal reforms in Puerto Rico. Emphasizing economic development and state services more than the promise of democracy that had so permeated the United States' initial occupation of the island in 1898, assertions of the United States' role as the bearer of modernity again proliferated. However, U.S.-funded attempts at forming rural cooperatives and state-owned businesses, providing a bare modicum of basic welfare services to impoverished families, and constructing subsidized housing, schools, and health clinics fizzled by the end of the 1930s, leaving laboring Puerto Ricans still deeply impoverished and often critical of U.S. rule.[14]

A new cohort of liberal, socially reformist Puerto Rican intelligentsia emerged during the 1930s, though, forging a shared vision by participating in the colonial agencies charged with implementing the new modernization efforts. After the rapid disbanding of the U.S.-sponsored Puerto Rican Emergency Relief Administration, a group of these Puerto Rican reformers, including Luis Muñoz Marín, drafted the famous Chardón Plan in 1934, which called, among other things, for the construction of infrastructure to benefit the majority of Puerto Ricans, the enforcement of the long-standing Five Hundred Acre Law, which endorsed the redistribution of "unproductive" landholdings larger than five hundred acres, and the mass dissemination of birth control.[15] Even as dissatisfaction with U.S. rule escalated on the island through the 1930s, the new liberal Puerto Rican intelligentsia infused the United States' reforming efforts with the language of both nationalism and development. The island's prosperity depended on its close relationship with the United States, these middle-class reformers insisted. Colonial benevolence could be ensured by shaping the metropolis's programs to serve Puerto Rico's interests. Indeed, economic development through the savvy use of U.S. funds could eventually render Puerto Rico capable of national independence, some of them argued.

Many of this new generation of Puerto Rican liberal reformers and New Deal technocrats joined with veteran union activists to establish the PPD in 1938. This was a charged historical moment, preceded by working-class feminists' triumph in obtaining universal women's suffrage in 1936, large wildcat strikes by sugarcane workers, and by an ominous act of colonial repression dubbed the Ponce Massacre, when in 1937 police fired on a peaceful group of Nationalist Party demonstrators, killing eighteen and wounding more than two hundred. Thus, from its inception, the PPD faced a gendered crisis of deep impoverishment, combined with the imperatives of incorporating a new female electorate, which doubled the potential voting population, responding to a restive working class in the cities and sugar regions, and dealing with an active anti-imperialist movement that was gaining the sympathies of increasing numbers of Puerto Ricans, in both rural and urban areas.

The founding of the PPD also coincided with the birth of a revived Puerto Rican labor movement, embodied in the Confederación General de Trabajadores (CGT), whose leaders rejected the antistrike, collaborationist positions of the Socialist Party and its now AFL-affiliated union. Within a few years the newly formed CGT won elections to represent more than 140,000 workers across the island and claimed the loyalty of the vast majority of Puerto Rico's organized cane workers. Until its splintering in the mid-1940s, the CGT worked closely with the PPD while retaining its autonomy from the party, successfully pressing for the payment of hourly wages rather than piecework rates, the establishment of an island-wide minimum wage, workers' injury and unemployment insurance, and housing free from sugar company control.[16] Throughout its years of political power, the PPD drew on these demands and others made by both union organizers and feminists, periodically implementing them and enjoying the popularity these moves afforded the party. Rarely, however, did Luis Muñoz Marín or other top PPD officials acknowledge the origins of these political positions in the autonomous social movements that had preceded the PPD's rise to political dominance.[17]

Muñoz Marín, the PPD, and Populist Paternalism

In 1940, when his party won a plurality of the popular vote, Muñoz Marín became the leader of the island's Senate. In 1944, the PPD gained an impressive majority in island legislative elections, and in 1948 Muñoz won a smashing victory to serve as Puerto Rico's first elected governor, accompanied by a PPD legislative majority. At the helm of the PPD and alternately neutralizing or persecuting his political rivals, Muñoz Marín effectively dominated the island's politics for the next two decades. From the founding days of the party, Muñoz Marín asserted himself as the public face, even the personification, of the PPD and its vision of social change and progress. Traveling through the countryside during the late 1930s and early 1940s, conversing with rural and urban laboring Puerto Ricans in fields, kitchens, roadside taverns, union meetings, and town plazas, Muñoz Marín spoke in many tongues to many audiences. He authored and produced a free newspaper called El Batey that presented him as the embodiment of the party. Committed "Populares" carried copies of the newspaper throughout the countryside, into city neighborhoods, and to émigré communities in the United States. Muñoz Marín's voice emanated from radios in the most remote mountaintops of the island.

Explicating, exhorting, praising, denouncing, Muñoz Marín spoke directly to his listeners as would a parent, a friend, a teacher, or a pastor. He preached with religiously inflected zeal to impoverished rural people, weaving folksy metaphors and plebeian grammatical structures into his calls to everyday Puerto Ricans to believe in themselves as agents of history. For Puerto Rico's middle classes, elites, and U.S.-educated technocrats who hoped to modernize the island, Muñoz Marín and his party wielded the language of science, technology, and planning. And in polished English, crafted in his youth while living in the United States, Muñoz Marín spoke to U.S. economic and political power brokers of investment, democracy, and colonial reform, presenting Puerto Rico as an international model of capitalist development and "peaceful, not radical" decolonization—the poster child for Cold War modernity dreams.

The PPD era, Muñoz Marín promised, marked the dawning of a Puerto Rico that could satisfy everyone's needs, ensuring the dignity and well-being of all. Modernity, he insisted, could expand its parameters to include the promise of social justice and national dignity, as well as access to new material objects and ideas. Land distribution, decent wages, a home of one's own, gender complementarity, an end to racial degradation and the shame of a past steeped in slavery, a political voice for all Puerto Ricans, regardless of wealth or gender—all were deemed possible within the PPD's vision of a modern, transformed Puerto Rico, one founded on collaboration rather than overt dominance. The terms of these collaborations, however, whether within the family, community, political party, or international political economy, often remained obscured. Would they simply modify hierarchical power relations, or radically transform them? Would political power ultimately rest in the hands of the people, as promised, or in the hands of party elites and their colonial patrons?

For many Puerto Ricans, especially among the working classes, the PPD's early calls for Bread, Land, and Freedom—just wages, land reform, and independence of political expression and affiliation—and the party's recognition of the exploitation they endured in the terrible, grinding reality of the cane fields, tobacco factories, and coffee estates, did indeed constitute an age of the people, one that brought them hope of personal and collective dignity, material and familial stability. Muñoz Marín's denunciation of the dead time that they had long been living—the hunger and deprivation associated with the months of unrelenting unemployment between sugar planting and harvest that haunted Puerto Ricans each year—resonated deeply with laboring people.

> These past . . . years have been that tragic thing called "the dead time," the time when there is no work, nor planting, nor progress, nor creation; the time when life is put on hold and grasped onto in whatever way until a better time can arrive. Dead time for the Puerto Rican peasants, with neither furrow nor seed, neither planting nor harvest! Time of waiting, while the earth is still giving forth nothing, that dead time . . . that our peasants know with pain in their bones and with desperation in their spirits—that has been the last twenty-four years of our public life![18]

When Luis Muñoz Marín and other reformers founded the PPD in 1938, they drew on the popular language and demands that had resonated throughout the island for decades and escalated so intensively during the 1930s. They also powerfully stirred many who had not previously participated consistently in electoral politics. With women's universal suffrage finally approved, women of all social classes voted in large numbers for the PPD. Landless men and women alike, living and working on the Puerto Rican coffee estates in the mountainous interior of the island, long marginalized from the working-class political ferment of the coastal cities and sugar plantations, also responded to Muñoz Marín's call for political engagement and social reform.

Many people who became fervent Populares would forever remember the 1940s as the "beginning of representation," when they managed to attain a modicum of both personal and political dignity.[19] For those who had long fought for social justice, the early PPD platform and political practices signaled a sea change as well. Now the local state might serve as an ally, an advocate, a trusted mediator in their conflicts with employers or colonial officials. Soon after winning seats in the Puerto Rican legislature, the PPD pushed for passage of the Ley de Tierras, which prohibited corporations from owning estates larger than five hundred acres and facilitated the expropriated land's redistribution to individual families or to state-run cooperatives. The PPD encouraged working people to join labor unions—indeed, several high-profile PPD legislators were labor organizers themselves. In the early 1940s, the party often intervened on unions' behalf, passing labor-friendly legislation, participating in workers' mass demonstrations, and mediating strikes. As in Peronist Argentina, Cardenist Mexico, and Brazil under the early Vargas regime, participants in the PPD strove to articulate a new notion of politics. This certainly included a potent sense of the power of one's vote, but extended far beyond the simple act of exercising electoral choice. Activists in the PPD and newspapers in the late 1930s and early 1940s also called on poor women and men to participate in the social and economic life of the island, whether in producing more goods in the new factories, utilizing modern agricultural techniques, joining unions and consumer leagues, or organizing local volunteer labor brigades to build schools, cooperatives, and recreation centers.

Muñoz Marín, in particular, expressed himself in a vocabulary "both visionary and believable," addressing specific economic issues confronting the Puerto Rican poor. He "took working-class consciousness, habit, life-styles, and values as [he] found them and affirmed their sufficiency and value."[20]

FIGURE 1.1 • The *pava* (large hat worn by rural jíbaro men) symbol of the PPD, overshadowing the stage at a public political meeting. "Luis Muñoz Marín y otros líderes del Partido Popular Democrático durante uno de los mítines efectuados en la campaña eleccionaria de 1964," *El Mundo*, October 8, 1964, photographer unknown. Courtesy of Colección Periódico El Mundo, Universidad de Puerto Rico, Recinto de Río Piedras.

He "touched the skin of hope" for Puerto Ricans.[21] Concomitantly, the PPD transformed the term *jíbaro* (hillbilly) into a central icon of Puerto Rican identity.[22] Its campaign emblem became "the face under the big hat called the 'sombrero pava.' Remember it well: make a cross underneath the only insignia of the P.P.D., *which is the face of a human being just like you*" (fig. 1.1).[23]

In the early days, while building the PPD, Muñoz Marín "glorified the everyday and the ordinary as a sufficient basis for the rapid attainment of a more just society."[24] He was fond of stating, "The people know the statistics of their own stomach, of their own scarcity, of their own observation, of their own suffering, in every part of this island."[25] He acknowledged Puerto Rican working people as anguished yet worthy agents of history. The party's slogan of Bread, Land, and Freedom and its excoriation of the "vampire" absentee sugar corporations that "sucked the lifeblood from the island" called out to wage workers, small-holding peasants, descendants of slaves, small business owners, and all those yearning for relief from crushing debt and exploitation.

Poor rural people's metaphors and experiences, which had long been silenced or ridiculed by the powerful, now became central to the language of politics. Those who voted unthinkingly for the traditional parties were "livestock brought to the slaughter, who knew not why they are sold."[26] Creating state-run markets that would guarantee reasonable food prices and undercut price-gouging merchants would mean "not killing the hen who lays golden eggs; no, it means dividing up the hen's eggs better and making sure that everyone pays for her feed."[27]

Muñoz Marín also delivered his speeches in the impassioned tones and rhythms of a skilled preacher.[28] He created passages reverberating with religious overtones, calling Puerto Ricans to participate in their own collective social and political resurrection. "You can be your own salvation! Choose a new life now!" he often cried. "Be not unthinking children! Be men and women as God wanted you to be!"[29] Muñoz Marín similarly excoriated his opponents in biblically resonant terms, calling for the people of Puerto Rico to vote them out of office, as Jesus had overturned the tables of the money changers in the temple—"those who charge exaggerated prices for the sole cruel reason of enriching themselves, at the cost of others' needs. Cruel, anti-social, anti-Christian motivation, corrupter of consciences and of the goodness which God wished to place in the souls of his children."

Just as importantly, Muñoz Marín explicitly spoke to both women and men, frequently using a surprisingly gender-inclusive political rhetoric:

> You are not children who must always be spoken to sweetly. You are men and women with responsibilities of men and women who deserve to be told the truth. All of you are part of this democratic work which we are making all together.[30]

> Believe in yourselves! Don't think of yourselves as tiny or weak or inferior! The light of God is in the nature of all those men and women whom God has created in this world. Believe in yourselves! Have faith in your own strength and power to make justice and ensure your own futures.[31]

He acknowledged both women and men as workers, struggling with the desperation of unemployment and with the worry of providing for their families.[32]

At other points, Muñoz Marín addressed the particularities of working Puerto Ricans' gendered experiences. Impoverished men could not fulfill expectations to provide economically for their families. As a result, women suffered terribly. Thus, Muñoz Marín empathized with both men's failings and women's struggles in his speeches. He articulated new political possibilities rooted in decades-old gender norms and practices—fresh dressings for old wounds.

Indeed, Luis Muñoz Marín spoke to working women's travails more powerfully than any other male politician of his generation. He denounced the exploitation of women as wage workers, always in the context of familial labor. Muñoz Marín described time and again in his speeches how women knew suffering more intimately than anyone else, caring for children who died of malnutrition and lack of medical care, struggling to feed their offspring on miserable wages—or no wages at all. But Muñoz Marín also acknowledged women's unrelenting, unpaid domestic labor. "Pushing the iron, washing the modest clothes in the river, lugging water in a can on her head, . . . sustaining on her shoulders all the life within the walls of her shack. . . . The hands that push the iron and split open as she washes the clothes are part of the material body of that woman peasant!"[33] Muñoz Marín thus publicly validated women's heretofore invisible domestic work and gave it political value. Reproductive labor of the sort discussed by Muñoz Marín in his speeches to women had never before been politicized by male organizers. Anarchists and socialists in Puerto Rico, both male and female, had certainly denounced women's exploitation as wage workers and had even, in the early years of the twentieth century, powerfully broached the subject of sexual exploitation. But unpaid domestic labor remained outside of the realm of even these early radicals' political discussion.[34]

Women, Muñoz Marín insisted in these speeches directed at them, inspired him with their persistence, self-sacrifice, and courage. In their daily domestic struggles, women became the model for PPD activists. He also recognized women as political actors themselves, crucial in the votes they cast, in the influence they could wield over men's voting behavior, and in the public opinion they could mobilize. Indeed, Muñoz Marín asserted, women were often more steadfast in their political commitments than men.[35]

When their male partners failed them and women faced the deprivation and desperate worry of single motherhood, Muñoz Marín pledged that the PPD would step in to provide stability and safety. In classic Muñocista syle, he presented himself as the embodiment of the PPD, he and the party fused into one powerful, pulsating self: "I want to work my spiritual hands to the bone helping those women, just as they work their physical hands to the bone, wearing their lives out as they raise their children! I want to spend all my life's energy in taking those cans of water from their heads, in giving them a little more security in obtaining mouthfuls of food, in placing all the force of a modern and just government into alleviating their lives which are so noble and so serious and so wise and so filled with suffering."[36] Such words, vowing never-ending commitment in a quasi-marital pact, converted the PPD into much more than a political institution. Rather, Muñoz Marín positioned himself and the party as helpmeets, substitute husbands, offering "the strong arm of government, on which [women] could lean, and which would alleviate [their] children's suffering."[37] Such pledges must have resonated deeply for many women.

In the early years of the party, women seem to have responded enthusiastically to the PPD's call, rooted in familiar experiences and familial paradigms, positing an ideal masculinity both kind and powerful, promising to let women rest in the protecting arms of the party and its leader, and encouraging women's political activism. Through the early 1940s, women, some already active in unions, frequently served as local PPD *cuadro* organizers. Along with men, they jammed PPD mass rallies and island-wide assemblies, voted for PPD candidates, and exhorted their family members to do the same. They formed Mothers' Committees to ensure decent housing and public health services for their communities. They even ran for local political offices themselves, including mayoral positions in several towns.[38] The PPD's building years, then, offered a political opening to women, many of whom vigorously grasped the opportunity.

However, in the Muñocista and PPD lexicon, women could only be mothers or daughters, sisters or wives. The emphasis on the drudgery of domestic labor may have spoken powerfully to women's daily material conditions and struggles, but also reinforced a vision of their inexorable fusion with the heterosexual family. However necessary their presence might be to a successful political project, the PPD never represented women as independent, autonomous organizers, workers, or community members. Ultimately, women's value lay in their experiences as family caregivers and in their potential transformative powers over men, not in their worth in and of themselves, or as fully independent actors.[39]

Indeed, for all of his inclusion of women in his political manifestoes, Muñoz Marín did not speak solely, or even primarily, to women. The PPD also sent a powerful message of masculine redemption and male power—however tempered—to laboring men. Muñoz Marín never suggested that men take up domestic work, or that women should live or work independently from a patriarchal family setting. Women should be political agents, but they were expected to build the PPD and confirm its power—and ultimately, the PPD was decidedly male. This was evident both in the makeup of the party leadership at the island and local community levels, and in the party's visual iconography, which idealized either whitened peasant men or burly European-looking industrial proletariats.[40]

Muñoz Marín's fiery speeches often repeated themes such as his 1940 call to taxi drivers as "'the fathers of their children who need the bread provided by justice.'"[41] Muñoz Marín frequently invoked *bregar* as a manly, dignified practice, an empowered shaping of society—"'You must use your hands to *bregar*, as hands of men, with the present and with the future!'"[42] "Be free men," he called, and advocated using the vote as a weapon to prevent the rich and corrupt politicians from "putting their hands under the roof of your humble home and robbing there the last little bit of justice which remains to you."[43] The cry "'Believe in your manhood!'" punctuated early PPD discourse.[44] Muñoz Marín defended Puerto Ricans' masculine dignity in language that resonated on many possible levels: freedom from colonial indignities, freedom from the chattel slavery that lurked in many Puerto Ricans' past, freedom from the current misery of poverty, freedom to both protect and control one's family and dependents.

Carefully avoiding explicit racial references, Muñoz Marín presented this defense of masculine honor not only as a political project, but as his own intensely personal, individual mission to the many exploited men of the island. "I want to teach you to be free men for your whole lives. Men free in their hearts, men free in their consciences, men free in their understanding, men free in their dignity! Free men! This must be for your whole lives! Free men!" "While the old *mogollas* lie, deceive, confuse, distort, threaten, coerce, and praise each other for buying men like beasts, I am the only party leader in Puerto Rico who speaks a truly Christian language, who defends men as men instead of using them as things, who defends the forgotten man instead of deceiving him."[45] Speeches such as these, which called on men to refuse "being enslaved in the name of a single political party or leader," certainly must have resonated especially powerfully for those Puerto Ricans of African descent who still shared stories of the horrors of slavery. It also called out to impoverished rural men in general who had lived their entire lives in terrible deadening debt to local landowners and U.S. sugar corporations, directly dependent on these hated employers not only for store scrip to feed their families but for the very shacks in which they slept. In the 1930s, many Puerto Rican men lived decidedly unfree lives—deeply, painfully dependent on abusive landowners and employers. In the early PPD years, then, Muñoz Marín's passionate pledge to "free all men from slavery" echoed powerfully throughout the island, expansively inclusive in its call. Perhaps because of its careful avoidance of explicit racialization, it could effectively speak to many people, regardless of their racial identities. Simultaneously, however, its compelling power was rooted in the experience of chattel slavery that had marked Puerto Ricans' past.[46]

Historians of gender have shown us that populist leaders can gain legitimacy in part by their reputations as generous fathers or as virile womanizers.[47] Muñoz Marín constructed an image of himself as the perfect combination of both these manly elements, one that acknowledged colonial power while affirming the island's right to dignity. Muñoz Marín initially married a woman from the United States, with whom he had two children. But as his political career accelerated, Muñoz Marín left this North American first wife for a Puerto Rican woman whom he honored for many years as his common-law wife and the mother of his third child, until finally marrying her the year before his election as governor of Puerto Rico. Muñoz Marín's public sexual life, then, simultaneously confirmed men's right to extramarital affairs, the honor and value of Puerto Rico versus the United States, and the importance of recognizing and financially supporting all children one might father.

Indeed, Luis Muñoz Marín positioned himself as the great father of the modern Puerto Rican nation—seemingly visionary, empathetic, and generous.[48] Muñoz Marín promised to converse about rural issues in his free newspaper El Batey the same way "'the problems of a family are discussed in the batey (front yard) of their home.'"[49] The visual images of Muñoz Marín produced during the early 1940s in Puerto Rican newspapers, news clips, postcards, and posters continually asserted this parental, teaching role for the leader (fig. 1.2). Holding informal tertulias with a group of peasant men on a rural road, walking with his arm around the elderly, caring for bereft widows and wives, Muñoz Marín constantly appeared as an honorable, knowledgeable father, in intimate relation with the people, and on whom they could depend.[50]

Working people's letters to Muñoz Marín from the 1940s were filled with both respect and an intimate familiarity; they spoke to him not simply as a dispenser of resources and information, but also as a relative or as a trusted confidante. Men and women crowded into the mass meetings where Muñoz

FIGURE I.2 • Luis Muñoz Marín speaking to families gathered in the small mountain town of Utuado. "Luis Muñoz Marín dirigiéndose a gente aglomerada en Utuado," El Mundo, c. 1964, photographer unknown. Courtesy of Colección Periódico El Mundo, Universidad de Puerto Rico, Recinto de Río Piedras.

Marín spoke, waving and shouting to him in passionate physical and verbal dialogue (fig. 1.3). "Between us and Muñoz, that distance of state never existed," mused the author Edgardo Rodríguez Juliá upon Muñoz Marín's death in 1980.[51] At Muñoz Marín's funeral, working-class women hurled themselves upon his coffin, crying out "'Papá Muñoz! He is like my father! . . . I was with him in 1940. . . . I don't want to leave him, I want to go with him, wherever he may go. Look at his product, look at what he did! . . . He put an end to latrines, an end to misery!'"[52]

While calling on working Puerto Ricans to believe in themselves as agents of history, and encouraging them to identify personally and collectively with him and the PPD, Muñoz Marín also left no doubt regarding who was to lead and who was to follow. He structured many of the articles in the PPD newspaper El Batey as didactic catechisms that posed questions and then provided clear, memorizable answers. Thus, the newspaper established an omnipotent voice of knowledge, authored primarily by Muñoz Marín himself (figs. 1.4 and 1.5).[53] "God has seen fit to give me intelligence. . . . The intelligence which God has given me, I transfer to you! Through my words, all of you

FIGURE 1.3 • Women calling out to Luis Muñoz Marín, awaiting his arrival at a speech. "Damas con pancartas y banderas del PPD saludando con alegría durante recibimiento al gobernador Muñoz Marín en 1949," *El Mundo*, August 2, 1949, photographer unknown. Courtesy of Colección Periódico El Mundo, Universidad de Puerto Rico, Recinto de Río Piedras.

FIGURE 1.4 • RIGHT, TOP. Luis Muñoz Marín imparting his wisdom to the masses, 1948. "Luis Muñoz Marín pronunciando discurso en la convención del Partido Popular," *El Mundo*, August 1948, photograph by Samuel A. Santiago. Courtesy of Colección Periódico El Mundo, Universidad de Puerto Rico, Recinto de Río Piedras.

FIGURE 1.5 • RIGHT, BOTTOM. The PPD's newspaper claimed that the people who crowded into the Sixto Escobar Park to hear Luis Muñoz Marín speak at the PPD convention in 1948 constituted "the largest crowd ever gathered in Puerto Rico" (*El Batey*, September 1, 1948). "Multidud presente en el Parque Sixto Escobar durante la Convención del Partido Popular Democrático," *El Mundo*, August 1948, photograph by Samuel A. Santiago. Courtesy of Colección Periódico El Mundo, Universidad de Puerto Rico, Recinto de Río Piedras.

FIGURE 1.6 • *Promesa Cumplida* (Fulfilled Promise), 1944. The caption below the two joined images states: "The votes which you give to the Popular Democratic Party will NOT count as votes for independence nor for statehood, nor for any other form of future political 'status.' They will count, now as always, only as votes in favor of implementing the Popular Party's social justice and economic program. THIS IS LUIS MUÑOZ MARIN'S WORD WHICH HE GIVES TO ALL OF YOU."

s votos que ustedes den a favor del Partido Popular Democrático NO s
contarán como votos en favor de la independencia o de la estadidad
o de cualquier otra forma de "status" político futuro

-contarán, ahora como antes, exclusivamente como votos a favor de que sig-
plantándose el programa de justicia social y económica del Partido Popula

TA ES LA PALABRA QUE LES DA A TODOS USTEDES LUIS MUÑOZ MARI

can see as clearly as do I! God gave me intelligence so that the humble ones of my people could see, not to blind them or confuse them! God did not give me land, but he gave me intelligence. And the intelligence that he gave me, I turn it over to you, all of a piece. Use it! Use it! Good God, use it!"[54] Apparently, within the dominant PPD framework, working-class Puerto Ricans themselves did not possess insight. The power of intellect necessarily traveled in only one direction—from Muñoz Marín to "the humble folks" whom he called to him as his followers.

The powerful visual image *Promesa Cumplida* (Fulfilled Promise; fig. 1.6) perhaps best exemplifies the compelling, complex mixture of paternalism and identification Muñoz Marín sought to promote between himself, the people of Puerto Rico, and the PPD. Produced by the PPD during the 1944 electoral campaign, which brought it a smashing island-wide majority, this image was made into posters and postcards to be distributed to the Puerto Rican populace at large. In the upper left-hand corner floats the small image of a thin white man, dressed in rough peasant garb and the classic pava hat. He drapes his arm gently over his horse and looks ahead and down. The rest of the visual space is occupied by a photo of Muñoz Marín leaning against the palm-thatched wall of a country bohío in a pose parallel to that of the diminutive jíbaro. Muñoz Marín, however, looks out to the horizon, surveying the countryside that stretches out around him, envisioning the future of "his" island. Brow furrowed, lost in thought, dressed in shirtsleeves, Muñoz Marín appears as an approachable yet visionary leader, identified with the people, connected to the land, imagining beyond current limits. Leader, father, teacher, preacher, in this image Muñoz Marín both embodies and leads the people. "The people," in turn are decidedly male (and white), but are not marked by an overwhelmingly masculinist power. The relationship between "the people," represented poignantly by an individual jíbaro, and Muñoz Marín remained deeply intimate, albeit undeniably hierarchical.[55]

Colonialism as Familial Pact

Like all good fathers, Muñoz Marín promised to restore his national family's dignity and honor by bringing it prosperity and protecting it from abuses by more powerful parties—such as the infamous sugar corporations or the U.S. government. Instead of exploitation, he promised partnership and mutual respect between men of different classes and between the United States and Puerto Rico, mediated through his person and his political party. Muñoz Marín's status as beloved political father was cemented in partnership with the people; consequently, he pledged to intervene on their behalf. Muñoz Marín recognized Puerto Ricans as people worthy of dignified lives; he, in turn, could claim the power of having been recognized as a competent leader by the United States. Thus, the PPD's discourse proclaimed a new day of honorable brega between potential adversaries, transformed into a great international chain of interdependent fathers and sons.

In the early 1940s, Muñoz Marín sometimes defiantly denounced attempts by U.S. politicians to limit or reduce Puerto Rican electoral and legislative autonomy. At these points, he defended his people with righteous anger.[56] More frequently, however, as the decade wore on, Muñoz

Marín spoke in terms of solidarity and alliances, of restoring Puerto Rico's national honor by transforming the bitter, exploitative colonial relations of the 1930s into a relationship of trust and mutual benefit between Puerto Rico and the United States. In these later speeches and writings, Muñoz Marín's language shifted from the relatively gender-inclusive rhetoric of internal political empowerment and mobilization to a powerfully masculinist discourse of fatherhood and fraternity. From Franklin D. Roosevelt to himself to the PPD to the everyday male citizens and soldiers of Puerto Rico, Muñoz Marín traced a palpable thread of loyalty and mutual support.[57] True to form, he posited himself as the perfect bridge between the two nations. Born as the Americans invaded Puerto Rico ("The American regime and I arrived together to Puerto Rico") and raised in both places, perfectly bilingual and bicultural, the two societies "came to understand each other as brothers" in his person.[58]

Guided by Muñoz Marín, Puerto Ricans would escape the "economic and political dependency" of the past, under which they resembled "children under tutelage and protection," and where men worked under coercive conditions, implicitly as slaves or dependent landless laborers. Puerto Rico's relationship with the United States needed to become one of "a deep and honorable recognition of men's rights and the value of their dignity," Muñoz Marín proclaimed. Puerto Rico as a nation was growing up into manhood, and deserved to be treated as such. The PPD would supplant colonial exploitation with proud equal citizenship in the United States, the democratic exercise of island self-government, and fraternal economic cooperation between the two nations.[59]

This new collaboration within colonial parameters excluded the possibility of separation from the United States. By 1946, Muñoz Marín and other top PPD officials brooked no discussion of independence within the PPD ranks, proclaiming that members of the PPD could not also belong to proindependence organizations. Moving from an earlier position that proposed leveraging U.S. resources to develop enough of an economic base to make a gradual transition to independence, Muñoz Marín and most other party top-brass in the later 1940s embraced a permanent, if modified, dependency on the United States. High-ranking PPD officials insisted that the party's goals of Puerto Ricans electing their own governor, reinstituting school instruction in Spanish, and amplifying industrial employment on the island signaled the turn from exploitative colonialism to a familial pact (*convenio*), despite their refusal to consider altering the underlying economic and political relationship between Puerto Rico and the United States. Economic development for the island, they decided, was only possible through direct access to federal government funds and U.S. private capital; political independence would destroy this potential.[60]

One working-class PPD member put it this way in the 1940s: "'Look, here is father. He is the United States. We are his colonies. You could make yourself independent, and he would grant your wish. But later, when you close the door, you will want to return to the table once more."[61] A PPD campaign song from 1944 also reasserted the message, in simple language that linked economic security, local domesticity, and ongoing ties to the United States:

> The Popular party does not stand for independence
> He who tells you that
> Wants to deceive you.
> Only social justice
> So that you may live quietly
> And together with your family
> Create a decent home.[62]

Muñoz Marín and PPD officials continually sought throughout the latter half of the 1940s to recast the U.S.–Puerto Rican relationship as familial rather than colonial. The more powerful of the two partners would serve as a father, generously dispensing resources to his loving son, now a fully grown man with goals and plans of his own. The son's plans, however, were always formed in consultation with his father. Each man would recognize both the enduring ties between them and the right of the other to masculine honor and respect. Thus, the familial language used by PPD officials and propaganda helped render reformed colonialism more palatable to Puerto Ricans. Familial metaphors provided Puerto Ricans with a familiar, nonthreatening, but dignified language with which to reconceptualize their understandings of self and community in relation to the United States. In short, Muñoz Marín insisted that a new international *brega* had begun.[63]

These assertions crystallized in discussions of legislation introduced into the U.S. Congress in March 1950 and signed into law by President Truman six months later, in July 1950. Muñoz Marín and his close associates in the PPD insisted that Public Law 600, which ensured Puerto Ricans' right to choose their own political representatives and the form of local government, but which kept other political and economic aspects of the relationship between the two polities intact, constituted a compact between two mutually consenting parties, enshrining the principle of government by consent. Puerto Rico would now be a "free associated state," not a colonial possession of the United States. The

PPD leadership immediately launched a campaign for a popular referendum on a new constitution for Puerto Rico, which would make permanent this recasting of the political relationship between the two nations.

In the summer of 1950, then, the Michigan crisis potentially jeopardized a decade of hard work convincing Puerto Ricans of the reality of a reformed relationship with a paternal metropolis. The sugar beet workers' angry missives denouncing the exploitation they encountered in Michigan threatened the constantly repeated PPD claim to be moving toward fraternity, dignity, and equality with the United States. As a result, they provoked close surveillance by government officials and immense concern about the possible derailment of the ratification of the new constitution. Both the protests' sharp edges and the broad reverberations they evoked on the island lay in the Michigan experience's betrayal of many Puerto Ricans' newly heightened hopes for a more familial, mutually respectful collaboration with the United States.

Popular Organizing, *Bregas* from Below, and Anxious Responses from Above

The migrant workers' protests were not a historical anomaly, however. They were part and parcel of the broader post–World War II historical moment in Puerto Rico—a time when diverse groups of islanders mobilized in massive numbers to demand concessions from their government, creating a political culture of social protest, undergirded by a complex paternalist *brega*. Historians have generally interpreted the late 1940s as a time of increasingly consolidated PPD hegemony, with Muñoz Marín and a tightened inner circle of advisors successfully neutralizing proindependence activists, members of the Puerto Rican Communist Party, and other dissidents. While the long-term narrowing of the PPD's initial political pluralism is undeniable, a close examination of the historical record also reveals a striking amount of political effervescence during these years, often unnerving to those in power. Between 1947 and 1950, a plethora of groups mobilized to claim the attention and allegiance of the state. The constriction of the PPD was perhaps not teleologically ordained, as some historians seem to assume. Rather, the very strength of the demonstrators' public presence may well have helped intensify the PPD leadership's conviction that it needed to purge dissenters, even as it conceded to some of the growing popular demands.

Sugarcane and factory workers, consumers, students, and World War II veterans, among others, all established organizations to defend their interests and engaged in mass public protests to express their demands. Often these claims were couched in the language of family and home. Throughout these local conflicts, laboring Puerto Ricans frequently expressed a deep faith in their organic connection to top-level state officials, especially Luis Muñoz Marín, although they refused to accept a passive role in the great changes sweeping their island. The people had been called upon to make history, and they insisted on doing so, even as they clamored for paternalist intervention by the trusted powerful.

The 1940s witnessed intense workplace-based mobilizations for social justice. Historians such as Gabriel Villaronga place the high point of such organizing at the island-wide sugar strike of 1942, which brought together a wide range of unions and political leaders, including Muñoz Marín and the U.S.-appointed governor, Rexford R. Tugwell.[64] Massive strikes continued to rock the island's cities, ports, and sugar fields well into the 1950s, however.[65] Stevedores, railroad workers, ironworkers, laborers at the island's newly established cement plants—so crucial for the booming construction projects on the island—as well as sugarcane cutters, grinders, and even white-collar employees all organized industry-wide work stoppages during the closing years of the decade. Teachers struck in 1946, setting off a wave of union activity among other Puerto Rican professionals. A sugar strike in 1949 brought 76,000 workers onto the picket lines in the space of two days. Workers in newer, state-facilitated industries such as leather, shoe, cardboard, glass, and clothing production also shut down their factories, demanding better wages, working conditions, and the recognition of their unions. Taxi drivers protested their low pay and organized an island-wide union; part-time cafeteria workers and security guards insisted on gaining full-time status. In small towns and large cities all over the island—from Guánica, Fajardo, and Yabucoa to Lajas, Aguadilla, and Mayagüez—labor protests exploded in these years of PPD power.[66]

Combative unions, then, were a ubiquitous presence in Puerto Rico in the 1940s, especially in the coastal, sugar-producing areas. Their struggles filled the newspapers; their members occupied public plazas, marched through cane fields, and surrounded factories. Their lively meetings took place in private homes, taverns, and church halls. Unorganized workers clearly were aware of these developments. They sought out union representatives to help them improve work conditions or prod unresponsive governmental agencies into action. Puerto Ricans of African descent sometimes turned to unions when suspecting racial discrimination in job recruitment. Indeed, the strike became a common method of protest among both nonunionized workers and other groups such as the Consumers' Congress, which pressed for price reductions in basic foodstuffs.[67]

Government officials often mediated labor conflicts, not infrequently meeting many, if not all, the workers' demands. Sometimes even Muñoz Marín himself stepped in to broker agreements in particularly contentious strikes. Other labor conflicts were resolved in the Puerto Rican courts; some judges evinced clear union sympathies, as did various island labor regulatory agencies such as the Committee for Minimum Wage Regulations.[68]

Over the course of the 1940s, these organizing efforts did indeed win important gains for wage laborers, although most of them went to unionized workers, especially in the sugar industry. Unions in a wide range of trades, sometimes supported by U.S. labor organizations, successfully pressed for local contracts for death and injury benefits, paid vacations, and automatic union membership, as well as higher wages. By mid-1948, in response to pressure by organized labor, the PPD passed national legislation regulating the sugar industry, which established minimum hourly wage rates, a maximum forty-eight-hour work week, and an eight-hour work day, as well as double pay for overtime. Cane cutters also won caps on the amount of sugar they could be required to haul at a time. Payment by the numbers of agricultural tasks performed or the quantity of cane cut or ground (*por tarea* or *por ajuste*) was expressly prohibited; workers were protected from discrimination by employers if they refused such payment. Through court decision, preventing employees from forming unions became punishable by law and nonviolent strikes were confirmed as legal. Workers' compensation for workplace injuries increased. Sugar workers even won a modicum of unemployment insurance—a tiny bit of dependable male income for the dead time.[69]

True to form, Muñoz Marín positioned himself as the great father of labor unions, lovingly dispensing resources and wisely guiding warring parties out of seemingly impossible impasses between capital and labor. In April 1944, Muñoz Marín announced the rare state appropriation of a sugar mill in a radio speech—"a gift from me to you, the people." A few years later, just days after taking office as governor, Muñoz Marín signed the law establishing unemployment insurance for sugar workers as their "Three Kings Day present." He promised to resolve labor disputes if unions came to him personally; negotiating with large employers behind closed doors, he often convinced capitalists to cede some ground in bargaining. At his bidding, the government bank Fomento guaranteed back pay for wronged workers at Operation Bootstrap–funded factories. Muñoz Marín pledged that the people could count on the laws passed by his party and signed by him personally to protect them; his law would be a source of justice.[70]

Unions, not surprisingly, by and large saw the Puerto Rican state as an ally during the 1940s. They often called upon national officials, including Muñoz Marín, to force municipal officials as well as private employers to bargain with them. They insisted that the Department of Labor investigate shady labor recruitment agencies and applauded the PPD's new labor laws and attempts to institute workplace safety regulations. Unions were joined by investigators from the PPD's Department of Health in decrying the horrible housing and sanitary conditions faced by sugarcane cutters.[71]

Unions were not the only groups organizing during the late 1940s, however. Puerto Ricans of African descent sometimes asserted solidarity with U.S. blacks "who [fought] for their rights and continue[d] to improve their nation." Other Afro–Puerto Ricans insisted that possible racial discrimination in hiring practices by U.S.-based private labor recruitment agencies be investigated. During these years, also, housewives and wage workers (many of whom were probably women as well) joined together to form an island-wide Congress of Consumers, which insisted upon price controls for food and other basic household items such as soap and cooking oil. Students at various branches of the University of Puerto Rico protested against heavy-handed administrators who sought to restrict freedom of expression and political activity on campus. Groups of single working mothers resisted eviction from their homes, insisting that they were honorable women who deserved state protection.[72]

Male veterans of World War II also formed their own organizations and lobbied, demonstrated, and wrote letters to the press "defending their legitimate interests." Thousands of them gathered at the capitol building in San Juan to support a measure for special pension payments to veterans. They demanded preference in job hiring and the acquisition of homes; they pressed for access both to the new public housing apartments and to low-interest mortgages for home purchase in new suburban developments. They joined with unions (many of them were members of both types of organizations) to insist on the necessity of unemployment insurance, a minimum wage, and social security benefits. Calling on their history of military service to the United States, presenting themselves as the essence of virility, and thus claiming a privileged citizenship status, these men became a force to be reckoned with, persistently demanding that they be honored materially and socially for their sacrifices "on the altar of democracy and freedom" during World War II.[73]

The language of family and fatherhood ran throughout the demands articulated in the vibrant popular mobilizations of the 1940s.[74] Consistently, the arguments made by labor unions of all kinds were couched in the language of providing for families. Higher wages and more humane working conditions for union members did not just benefit individuals, the unions insisted; entire families enjoyed the increased buying power, more settled homes, and social security afforded by labor's gains. They empowered men and guaranteed stability to their wives. (Unions during the 1940s and '50s consistently represented wage workers as male, despite the high number of women earning wages.) Consumer advocates pointed out that price controls would ensure better nutrition, healthier families, and thus happier homes. Mothers could manage household budgets with less worry; men could more reliably aspire to successful fatherhood. Finally, many of the rallying cries at popular demonstrations explicitly centered on access to homes—veterans, single mothers fighting eviction orders, and unions all made a safe, secure home of one's own choosing into a central demand of the PPD era.

Through all of these protests ran intertwined currents of simultaneous political critique and faith in benevolent paternalist intervention. These groups squarely denounced abuses by the powerful, who could be local government officials as well as greedy merchants, sweatshop owners, university administrators, or huge sugar corporations. They organized impressive demonstrations and publicized their demands in the press. Not infrequently, they bravely faced down police forces called out to quell their protests. Like the unions, simultaneously combative and collaborative, other groups showed a marked tendency to call on national government leaders—Muñoz Marín primary among them—to intervene on their behalf. Thus, even while local conflicts continued to explode and laboring people refused to accept the economic and social status quo, Muñoz Marín's personal charisma as well as popular belief in the PPD's ultimate trustworthiness seems to have persisted among many of those making demands for change. These two currents that constituted the Puerto Rican political practices of *bregar*—challenge to power and collaboration or negotiation with trusted, paternalist power wielders—wove in and out of most of the period's massive mobilizations, sometimes in deep tension with each other. They would deeply mark the beet workers' response to their own crisis in the faraway fields of the northern U.S. Midwest.

This *brega* pattern is also evident in the internal conflicts that rent the PPD during the late 1940s, particularly those surrounding the process for choosing the party's candidates for office. By 1948, controversies exploded in municipalities all over the island as local party activists rebelled against new rules stating that candidates for office would no longer be chosen at local party assemblies, but by juntas and subjuntas appointed by Muñoz Marín and a small group of top party officials. In Cayey, for example, several thousand Populares protested at the city's popular assembly and insisted that a primary election be held to decide who would be the PPD legislative candidate from the area. They agreed to take their case to Muñoz Marín, so that he could "intervene to save the party," but insisted that if he did not agree to a primary election, they would picket the island-wide assembly, to be held a week later.[75]

In several of these cases, the popularly selected candidates were women. The supporters of the popularly chosen female candidate for mayor of Río Piedras, María Luisa Guerra, appealed to Muñoz Marín to intervene on her behalf. They assured their community that they "trusted in Muñoz Marín's promise" to remove the corrupt current mayor. They swore to vote for whoever Muñoz Marín designated as the PPD candidate, but hoped that it would be Guerra. Guerra herself, however, did not leave matters solely to her party's supreme leader. She took her candidacy battle into the poorest neighborhoods of the city, speaking on radio shows and meeting with constituents in marketplaces and in their homes.[76]

Needing to maintain their popular political base, but also anxious to placate U.S. investors and politicians who sought a quiescent citizenry and labor force, Muñoz Marín and his top advisors were often unnerved by this animated organizing that threatened to bubble out of control. As Danny James has pointed out for Peronists in Argentina, "For those who controlled . . . the apparatus of power . . . [populist] oppositional culture was a burden."[77] These men reigned over an anxious state. They were bent on gaining and maintaining political power, which they understood as rooted in popular legitimacy, but worried about managing the tumultuous transition. More and more quickly, they moved to silence dissent, to narrow democratic practices, and to neutralize autonomous political actors, even as they continued to pass and enforce legislation supporting popular demands. By 1948, with mass demonstrations continuing and demands for social justice escalating, the PPD began to move in earnest against those who "threatened the social peace."

Proindependence activists already had been banned from the party in 1946. Now, charismatic local party activists, autonomously minded unions and their organizers, and energetic women Populares all found themselves marginalized from decision making, undercut in local elections, and subjected to public smear campaigns. Muñoz Marín moved to purchase controlling interests in several significant island-wide newspapers.[78] Even high-ranking members of the PPD such as Vicente Geigel Polanco, a former head of the Labor Department, member of the Puerto Rican Senate, and ultimately Muñoz Marín's right-hand man, was fired when he refused to endorse the new Puerto Rican constitution of 1952, insisting that it simply "put a pretty mask on enduring colonialism."[79] Muñoz Marín's earlier exhortations to "freely believe in yourselves" ended; by 1948, his speeches singularly emphasized following the party's lead. Social action, Muñoz Marín now insisted, consisted solely of voting for the PPD, which would provide for the people. For the PPD top leadership, the party's commitment to popular empowerment had ended; the great pluralistic democratic opening was closing. The time of protection, direction, and regulation was now at hand.[80]

By the end of the decade, images joining Muñoz and "the people" continued to proliferate, but they had begun to emphasize hierarchy much more than the personalized, intimate relationship between the Puerto Rican populace and their charismatic leader that lay at the core of early PPD visual images. A prime example is the huge centerfold spread produced in January 1949 by El Mundo, an important island-wide daily newspaper, celebrating Muñoz Marín's election as governor of Puerto Rico (fig. 1.7). Here, the page is dominated by two gigantic photos of Muñoz Marín looking off into the future. Underneath these portraits of Muñoz Marín unfold multiple replications of an image of racially ambiguous men bending down to hoe young cane plants. This line of agricultural workers appears to be hoeing inexorably from the past into the future. However, the laborers, who form a marching, faceless mass of interchangeable men, completely stripped of individual character, only look down, into the earth. It is the dapper Muñoz Marín who looks up and far into the distance. Still clearly a visionary paternal figure, Muñoz is now portrayed as undeniably omnipotent, leading the masses of hardworking, unimaginative, unquestioning people toward their inexorable progress.[81]

But the people were neither unimaginative nor unquestioning. The seeds of political heresy, sown throughout the 1930s and into the 1940s, were not easily strangled. Activists who supported independence began to defect from the PPD's ranks and join the newly formed Partido Independentista de Puerto Rico. The Nationalist Party continued to pen critiques and organize protests against the PPD's economic and political program. Opposition newspapers like El Imparcial vociferously criticized Muñoz Marín's antidemocratic actions. Autonomous union leaders denounced the draconian steps taken by Muñoz Marín and his allies.[82]

FIGURE 1.7 • "Don Luis Siéntese!," El Mundo, January 2, 1949, 37–38.

Other ripple effects continued as well, less easily traced than these explicitly politicized rebuttals, but ultimately no less meaningful. By 1950, when the five thousand men left Puerto Rico for the Michigan sugar beet fields, working people in general had developed intensely heightened expectations of the state, based on their more than ten-year experience of mass democratic participation, and the new government's promises of equity, social justice, and economic development. Rural Puerto Rican men, in particular, anticipated that their hard labor on behalf of the populist project finally would bear fruit in the fulfillment of long-held masculine yearnings. After years of fighting for the cause, as many sugar beet workers termed it, they had won the right to previously unavailable resources, alliances with those in power, and a sense of manly dignity. Populism in Puerto Rico had promised the economic, social, and political empowerment of men *as men*.

The sugar beet migrants also felt a deep personal connection to Luis Muñoz Marín. He was a father, like the men who had placed him in office— their political comrade, dependent on their good will and energetic labor to remain in office. But he was also *their* father—and they, his sons—not a distant, omnipotent politician. Thus, when facing the intense exploitation of the Michigan sugar beet industry, Puerto Rican working men would appeal to their government, and to Muñoz Marín in particular, as both fathers and sons, virile partners and dependent children, articulating a complex mixture of manly defiance and deference. In this political *brega* saturated with familial overtones, so much a part of the political culture of postwar Puerto Rico, they demanded and begged the paternal state to fulfill its responsibility to them so that they, in turn, could provide for their own families.

This, they understood, was their right, and they insisted upon it. In the eyes of the state, however, hierarchy trumped the workers' claims of familial solidarity. The migrant workers in Michigan felt this betrayal as a simultaneously personal and political affront. Their shock and outrage, products of this particular historical moment and its impassioned political expectations and commitments, fueled the intensity of their protests as well as politicians' nervous reactions to them.

2

BUILDING HOMES, DOMESTICITY DREAMS, AND THE DRIVE TO MODERNITY

Comfort . . . the dream of every family man, just as much as of all housewives. The homes in Bay View are spacious and comfortable. Your husband will feel so happy in Bay View that he will never want to leave, never succumb to outside distractions. • "Aquí sí hay," *El Mundo*, May 12, 1947

Puerto Rico is carrying out a gigantic, dramatic effort to endow the nation with a modern industrial plant that will permit our people to incorporate themselves into a brighter destiny. • Manos a la Obra, *El Imparcial*, 1948

Fatherhood was not the only familial current fueling the Michigan controversy in 1950. Aspirations to domesticity, embodied in a stable, individually owned home and a successful male breadwinner who exercised legitimate authority over his dependents, also helped mobilize thousands of men for the airlift to Michigan and echoed through the bitter protests against the conditions the men encountered there. Dreams of domesticity had become particularly potent in Puerto Rico by 1950. Throughout the 1940s, the PPD made the massive construction of homes in both rural and urban areas a central element in the party's political program, as it responded to and fueled popular demands such as those we saw in chapter 1. The heightened availability of homes for working people in Puerto Rico converged with the intensification of public discourses that exhorted Puerto Ricans to embrace modernity and industrialization as their primary socioeconomic goals and asserted the centrality of domesticity to the construction of a modern society.[1]

The PPD and the Puerto Rican press linked the possibility of owning a home of one's own with the creation of benevolently patriarchal, stable families and with an insistence on industrialization as the sole option for the island's economic development. Agriculture belonged to the exploitative past; rapid industrialization and urbanization held the key to a truly modern Puerto Rico, intoned PPD leaders. Indeed, the original 1938 PPD slogan of "Bread, Land, and Freedom" could have been refashioned by 1948 into "Bread, Home, and Security," based in the political imperative for a stable, "hygenic" home. In the eyes of the state and citizens alike, democratizing home ownership emerged as an important goal of this new era that was to sweep away the "dead time" of the past.

Inciting Puerto Ricans to embrace modernity, to aspire to "developed" status, the PPD-era policy and culture makers also hoped to restructure the family and the internal workings of the home. By gaining industrial employment and winning expanded workplace rights, state officials and working Puerto Ricans alike dreamed of islanders having more material goods, more economic stability, and access to a home and private space as never before. In exchange, PPD functionaries and politicians insisted, like many of their Latin American counterparts, that "even very poor men should settle down, marry, and commit to becoming producers for the nation and providers for families. This [was] a productive, domesticated, hetero-normative, and nationalist masculinity . . . the hegemonic masculinity of the family man."[2] According to PPD doctrine, the family man, in turn, should be able to rule authoritatively, albeit benevolently, over his home and dependent wife and children.

Overall, the state proclaimed, modernity could have only one face in Puerto Rico. Industrial productivity was the only possible path to economic prosperity. Abandon the land, PPD leaders cried; agriculture was incompatible with modernity. Only certain kinds of homes, also, were acceptable. As the PPD marginalized dissenters and purged independence supporters from its ranks, it also razed squatter communities—the spatial counterpart to its political deradicalization delineated in chapter 1. And while the PPD continued its practice of avoiding explicitly racialized language, the visual images circulating through the Puerto Rican press during this period implicitly yet powerfully asserted that the consumption of new domestic goods and heightened industrial production would whiten the island, effectively distancing Puerto Ricans and their cultural practices from the exploitation and degradation of slavery and blackness.

These incitements to transform Puerto Rican society were simultaneously a lived reality for some and uneasy discursive assertions of the teleological power of processes whose outcomes were not at all assured during the 1940s. Indeed, despite PPD officials' insistence on the industrial drive to modern domesticity's inevitable power and prosperity, this project remained plagued with uncertainties and tensions, as did PPD political hegemony.[3] Eliminating "diseased, decadent" squatter communities provoked fervent protests from enraged residents. The mushrooming factories so triumphantly heralded by the press and the government never managed to provide adequate employment for islanders. Male economic power and stable social status remained unattainable for most. The process of industrialization produced a seemingly never-ending stream of Puerto Ricans encouraged to migrate to the United States in search of work, among them the Michigan sugar beet workers. Murderous violence lurked at the heart of family. Increasingly frequent divorces undid the ties of patriarchal marriage. The constant talk about domesticity, then, constituted a worried defense of an uncertain economy and worldview, as well as an expression of elite and popular desires.

Las Parcelas: Land Reform and Rural Homes

It is . . . an integral part of the moral purpose and the aims of dignity and economic freedom embodied in the public policy of the Legislature, to furnish the means whereby the social class of *agregados*, or, that is, of agricultural laborers *enslaved through the fact that they are not the owners of even the lot where they have their homes,* will disappear from Puerto Rico; and to that end the Legislature states the fundamental right of all human beings who live exclusively by the tilling of the soil, *to be the owners of at least a piece of that land which they may use to erect thereon,* in the full enjoyment of the inviolability guaranteed by law for the homestead of the citizen, *their own homes, thereby delivering them from coercion and leaving them free to sell their labor through fair and equitable bargaining.* [emphasis added] • "Statement of Motives," Ley de Tierras de Puerto Rico, Ley 26, 19

One of the PPD's earliest legislative acts was to distribute small plots of land (*parcelas*) to sharecropping families. The famous Five Hundred Acre Law, which decreed the expropriation of all corporately owned properties of more than five hundred square acres, was finally deemed enforceable by decision of the U.S. Supreme Court in 1940. The law provided for a variety of land reform strategies, including the establishment of state-owned agricultural cooperatives that shared profits with their workers, and the creation of smallholder farming plots. However, most of the PPD's land-reforming energies poured into establishing the tiny *parcelas*, which were to be distributed at no cost to the new owners and owned only in usufruct; the right to occupy the land could be passed down to one's heirs, but the land itself could never be sold. *Parcelistas* were required to erect a home on the *parcelas* within 120 days of their land grant.[4]

As is evident from the Land Law quote above, these plots were considered to herald the final extinction of slavery and its experience of deep material deprivation in Puerto Rico. Now "the people of Puerto Rico would have the opportunity to create thousands of proprietors who presently are dispossessed men."[5] No longer would rural working people's access to housing depend on the whims of a quixotic or abusive employer (fig. 2.1).[6] This was a significant transformation in the lives of the rural poor, who no longer lived in constant fear of eviction; gone were the days when rural laborers could be coerced into working solely for inadequate shelter. For impoverished Puerto Ricans in the countryside, gaining access to a stable home meant the ability to assert a modicum of autonomy and dignity vis-à-vis their employers (fig. 2.2). The distribution of upward of 45,000 *parcelas* during the 1940s won the PPD an extremely loyal base in the Puerto Rican countryside.[7]

The original definition of an *agregado*, the class of Puerto Ricans eligible to receive a *parcela*, although not explicitly gendered, did ensure that most recipients would be men. An *agregado* had to be a head of household (*jefe de familia*), live in the countryside in a house or on land belonging to someone else, own no land, and, most importantly, survive solely on wages earned in agriculture. Since the majority of rural women earned income from sewing and other domestic labor such as laundry as well as from occasional agricultural wages, even single mothers were generally excluded from *parcela* ownership.

The PPD's distribution of *parcelas* consolidated its political base in rural areas. However, *parcela* grants were expressly intended not to create an independent peasantry. Rather, the land was destined solely to provide permanent homes for the rural poor.[8] The size of the plots—not more than three *cuerdas* (a unit of land measurement equaling 0.97 acres), no less than one-quarter cuerda—might leave room for a family garden or a small livestock pen, but it certainly did not offer the possibility of escaping wage labor altogether. *Parcelistas* remained rural proletarians, albeit ones with increased bargaining power. Over time, the size of the plots was limited more consistently

FIGURE 2.1 • Barracks-like *agregado* housing on a coffee plantation near Lares, 1956. Such structures were similar to the *barracones* where enslaved people were forced to live during the nineteenth century. Elsie Hoffman Barrett, *Houses Near Lares*, March 1956. From the Lehman Puerto Rico 1940s–1950s Collection. Courtesy of Fundación Luis Muñoz Marín.

FIGURE 2.2 • *Parcela* home, 1944–1947. Unlike families in *agregado* plantation housing, this *parcelista* family has its own, physically separate home, with a trench dug around its perimeter to keep the house free from rainwater seepage. A plantation stretches in the background, but around the house on their *parcela* plot the family has planted *plátano* (plantain), *yautía*, *batata* (sweet potato), *calabaza* (squash), and *gandul* trees. A mango tree is on the left. All these crops helped sustain *parcelista* families through the "dead time." H. Clair Amstutz, *Family Home*, c. 1944. From the Lehman Puerto Rico 1940s–1950s Collection. Courtesy of Fundación Luis Muñoz Marín.

to one-quarter cuerda. Thus, as PPD land reform efforts unfolded through the 1940s, access to land translated into the ownership of a secure, however humble, home—not into economic independence from exploitative large landowners nor into the creation of a class of small farmers.[9]

By the mid-1940s, PPD officials were carefully planning the creation of small rural communities through the targeted distribution of *parcelas*. The state began to build roads and, later, provide sewer and electrical services to the *parcela* communities. By the late 1940s, *parcela* villages were planned in conjunction with the construction of light-industry factories; basic infrastructure and employment were to be part of the creation of stable homes and a geographically fixed rural labor force, hopefully uninterested in swelling urban squatter communities. Ironically, however, as Ismael García Colón notes, many *parcelistas* used their new homes as a launching pad for international migration. Assured of an uncontested residence for their wives and children, male *parcelistas* more readily made the decision to migrate to the United States to look for work. Party officials do not seem to have foreseen that the gendered migration practices developed by rural Puerto Ricans might effectively reposition women as heads of household, at least temporarily, even as men gained the formal legal status of jefe de familia and *parcela* owners. The women in *parcela* families seem to have been more likely than the men to gain employment in the light industries built near the new communities. This may have played an important role in men's decision to migrate off the island.[10] Thus, *parcela* distribution supported the process of industrialization that PPD officials soon began to see as the only hope for Puerto Rico's economic future, even as it may have created quite unexpected gender dynamics within *parcelista* households.[11]

Las Urbanizaciones: Industrial Development, the Remaking of Cities, and Urban Home Construction

The PPD emphasis on industrialization was part of the belief in developmentalist economic policies that swept the Western world in the post–World War II era. Despite its condescension toward "backward" peoples and nations, its general contempt for local cultures and socioeconomic practices, and its lauding of Western European / North American industrial capitalism as a universal model for attempts to end poverty, the discourse of development through large-scale capitalist industrialization promised economic growth and reduced inequality to all. Its insistence that "no society would be permanently relegated to a lesser standard of living" was a welcome message for many in regions struggling with the legacy of colonialism. Indeed, developmentalism asserted "that all human beings could hope to share in the magic of modernity, and that the lessons of history could provide the signposts for a better future."[12] As such, it found an eager audience among the new leaders of Puerto Rico, who emphasized the possibility of economic resources and markets made available by the United States, while they sidestepped the negative aspects of the history of U.S. colonialism on the island.[13]

During the late 1940s and throughout the 1950s, Puerto Rico did, in fact, undergo a sweeping process of industrialization and of construction of physical infrastructures that transformed both people's lives and the island's geography. Fueled with private U.S. capital and federal funds, factories seemed to spring up daily, shoes, glass, paper, and cement tumbling from their doors. But industrialization and urban development more broadly were also created discursively; they were celebrated as proof positive of a new era and promoted incessantly as the only appropriate route for the island's prosperity, security, and dignity. State development advocates curtly dismissed alternate economic visions, such as large-scale redistribution of land, or attempts to create collectively or individually owned small farming communities, as "romantic" or "ridiculously utopian." The land in Puerto Rico, PPD publications insisted by the late 1940s, was hopelessly unproductive for anything other than growing sugar, good only for constructing homes, not for producing food or other agricultural items. "Land was not to plant, but to build."[14] Only factories on a large scale and ever-closer ties with the United States could provide an adequate economic future for the island. "Our people did not resign themselves to the languid existence which accompanied an almost exclusively agricultural economy. They intuitively understood that in a world tied to the development of the machine, denying the machine meant missing the path of progress. And lingering in History is deterioration, is backwardness, is decadence, and is a sin paid in hunger and pain."[15]

Such a vision had to be sold to the Puerto Rican people, who had little experience with factory labor. By the late 1940s, PPD publications, advertisements, and newspaper columns promoting industrialization had become ubiquitous on the island, appearing in every major media outlet, both print and radio. Even the staunchly oppositional newspaper El Imparcial ran the weekly PPD economic promotional column Manos a la Obra and reproduced the party's advertisements for industrial development, which allegedly would bring "more work, more income, more profit, and more happiness" to the island.[16]

FIGURE 2.3 •

Advertisement of the
Compañía de Fomento
Industrial de Puerto
Rico. Such ads promoted
industrialization as an
integral part of the PPD's
"war against sickness,
hunger, and misery."
They appeared frequently
in all the Puerto Rican
newspapers of the era
and generally occupied
a full page. El Imparcial,
September 3, 1950.

During World War II, this developmentalist discourse fused with a bellicose language that endorsed the struggle against fascism. Invoking the "battle for production" became quite common by 1945; this was the only way to end hunger on the island, the PPD proclaimed.[17] Party propaganda repeatedly portrayed the production battle as a large, clean-cut, European-looking man moving cogs in giant wheels as his muscular torso bulged (fig. 2.3). Virile men working in concert with machinery embodied development. This, in turn, promised productive whiteness—the future of an island striving to escape the exploitation of the sugar plantation and its roots in chattel slavery on the one hand, and, on the other, the malnourished disempowerment of the isolated rural jíbaro.[18]

Evangelizing as it educated its citizenry about industrialization and triumphantly announced the weekly opening of new factories, the PPD insisted that rapid, untrammeled industrial development was not only desirable, but possible. Its propaganda invoked a quasi-religious faith in the power of science and technology to bring an abundant modernity to Puerto Rico.[19]

Puerto Rico is carrying out a gigantic, dramatic effort to endow the nation with a modern industrial plant that will permit our people to incorporate themselves into a brighter destiny. . . . We would do many other things if we believed them possible! And nothing should be impossible for us. Faith can move mountains. Above all, if we have, along with faith, technology, machinery, and perseverance. Faith can move mountains, but not so quickly as boxes of dynamite and a parade of bulldozers. There are still some among us who disdain technology. However, technology is only the extension of a hand. And it is the hand which can open the doors of tomorrow to us.[20]

Despite the official PPD enthusiasm for technology, urban development, and factories, apparently not all Puerto Ricans were so easily convinced. All the state's exhortations to believe blindly in the power of the machine betrayed a deep anxiety; the industrialization project had to be sold aggressively to the Puerto Rican public. The authors of the newspaper column even openly admitted their worry, as they mentioned those who continued to "disdain technology." Indeed, a variety of union organizers and intellectuals on the island openly contested this vision of industrial development as a panacea for Puerto Rico's impoverishment.[21] The cartoonist Filardi, whose work ran regularly in the daily newspaper El Mundo, was one of the sharpest public critics of the Muñoz administration's development proposals. In the cartoon shown in figure 2.4, he pictured a working-class man's house condemned by a sign (probably referring to the U.S. funds and ideologies fueling the state's projects) that reads "Avenue of the North will pass through here." Dwarfed by the airplane-like scrolls embodying state plans for highway development, the man wonders "And ME? What plans will I make?" as he peers trepidatiously at the zooming plans.

Indeed, as Filardi noted, the PPD push for economic development did not stop with the creation of factories. Funded by federal monies in the United States' booming postwar economy, the Puerto Rican government also launched a massive effort to build all manner of physical infrastructure in practically every corner of the island. Sewer and plumbing systems brought potable water to more than 300,000 families in just a few years, often to entire towns at a time. Electricity grids and dams introduced lights and other electrical services to rural and urban working-class communities alike; often the arrival of sewer systems and electricity was celebrated with public ceremonies, replete with musical bands and speeches from local PPD and union leaders. The San Juan airport and coastal wharfs were rebuilt to handle increased international traffic. New paved roads, some of them multilane, wended their way through the island. Medical clinics and rural schools, parks and bridges appeared for the first time in many areas.[22]

FIGURE 2.4 • Filardi, "Mientras tanto . . . ," *El Mundo*, January 20, 1948, 6.

An entirely new urban landscape emerged during the 1940s and '50s as well. Large, multifloor buildings rose from the ground seemingly overnight. Banks, hospitals, apartment buildings, and department stores sprang up, primed to serve the new consumption needs of urban residents.[23] Perhaps the most striking change in Puerto Rico's urban landscapes, however, was the explosion of huge suburban housing tracts, which consumed mangrove swamps and defunct sugar plantations alike. Carefully designated for either the discerning, individualized housing tastes of well-heeled urban professionals (figs. 2.5 and 2.6) or the mass production of small, prefabricated homes for working- and lower-middle-class families (fig. 2.7), these sprawling "urbanizaciones" transformed and vastly extended the face of urban Puerto Rico.[24]

Democratizing proper home ownership became a central element of PPD allure. In 1956, Muñoz Marín promised that "almost all families should manage to have their own home, which, although modest, can be decent, comfortable, and a shelter for the material and spiritual health of the family."[25] Almost a decade earlier, the Puerto Rican Land Authority had developed plans for small prefabricated cement homes to be sold cheaply to *parcela* residents. Architects also worked in teams to design small urban homes with sturdy, readily available materials, within the price range of working-class families (fig. 2.8). The PPD mobilized Federal Housing Administration home loan funds, administered through the newly established private bank, Banco Popular, and the government's Banco Fomento. Federal Housing Administration mortgage application offices opened in every sizeable town on the island. Thousands of low-cost houses in suburban tracts such as the massive 5,000-home Puerto Nuevo development near San Juan were built in the space of just a few years in the late 1940s.[26] Many could be purchased for a down payment of only $100. "Take advantage of this opportunity to become a homeowner. You can modify it, increase its size, build balconies for it. Your relatives and friends can move to this neighborhood now also and become property owners immediately. It's wonderful to be able to say, THIS IS MY HOUSE!"[27]

Los Arrabales: Razing "Unworthy" Homes and Residents' Resistance

As the urbanizaciones and other urban construction swallowed up land surrounding the island's major towns and cities, government bulldozers also began to systematically destroy the shacks built by impoverished rural families who had migrated in large numbers to urban areas from the countryside, looking for work. These multiracial squatter areas or *arrabales* often included hundreds of families apiece. After years of existence, many had become tight-knit communities where residents formed extended family networks and helped each other through the vagaries of life on the economic margins. Composed of tiny houses made of discarded wood, plastic, and other scavenged materials, the *arrabales* were frequently built in swamps and other "unusable" geographical areas, linked together by simple board walkways and muddy footpaths. Many *arrabal* residents owned their homes, although not the land on which they were constructed, and frequently bought, sold, and paid rent on houses within the communities.[28]

FIGURE 2.5 • A home in one of the more luxurious urbanizaciones of the San Juan area. The very composition of the photo, marked by a spacious sky, large automobile, and shining street, signals comfort, roominess, and prosperity. Luke Birky, *House on Teniente Ramirez Street in Hato Rey*, c. 1950. From the Lehman Puerto Rico 1940s– 1950s Collection. Courtesy of Fundación Luis Muñoz Marín.

FIGURE 2.6 • Bay View— "Seen from the sky, it's like Paradise!" *El Mundo*, May 26, 1947. Suburban sprawl consumes an entire peninsula of the island.

Vista desde el Cielo
es como un paraíso...

BORINQUEN HOME CORP.

FIGURE 2.7 • One of the scores of suburban communities built for working-class families in Puerto Rico. "Vista aérea de la Urbanización Bayamón Gardens mostrando sus calles curvas y su falta de vegetación," El Mundo, June 13, 1964, photographer unknown. Courtesy of Colección Periódico El Mundo, Universidad de Puerto Rico, Recinto de Río Piedras.

To outsiders, however, *arrabal* buildings seemed haphazardly thrown together and their impoverished residents dangerous. In the newspapers and government publications of the 1940s, *arrabales* became the physical and discursive foil to the hopeful, concrete-filled modernity of the urbanizaciones. The PPD and its supporters in the press portrayed *arrabales* as uninhabitable places, breeding grounds for disease, prostitution, and crime. They were allegedly the essence of decadence—the opposite of the "hygienic," sturdy homes being built with the state's support. They represented the utter absence of domesticity and modern whiteness. *Arrabales* existed in all the major urban areas of Puerto Rico, but the most (in)famous of them were El Fanguito, located along the mangrove swamps of Hato Rey, just outside of the capital city, and La Perla, located on the rocky shores of the sea at the outskirts of the colonial center of Old San Juan. During the 1940s, both of these communities appeared frequently in the U.S. press as well as in Puerto Rican

FIGURE 2.8 • Ideal working-class family, rendered speechless upon entering their model new home. "Primera familia en ocupar su casa en Puerto Nuevo mirando la urbanización desde su balcón," El Mundo, July 31, 1948, photograph by Hamilton Wright. Courtesy of Colección Periódico El Mundo, Universidad de Puerto Rico, Recinto de Río Piedras.

newspapers as the embodiment of evil, decadent, uninhabitable slums. Images like figure 2.9, from Life magazine, proclaimed that these squatter-created spaces were closer to pigsties than communities, drowning their inhabitants in a sea of mud and reducing them to animals. The photo's original caption reads: "Sanitary facilities are completely lacking in El Fanguito. . . . Junk, garbage, animals, children, laundry and human excrement all fight for the same little space in the sun."[29]

Eliminating arrabales became an important goal of the PPD's modernization project by the late 1940s. Providing homes to working people might be

FIGURE 2.9 • The public face of the *arrabal*. Images like this filled the Puerto Rican and U.S. press alike in the mid-1940s. "Puerto Rico: Senate Investigating Committee Finds It an Unsolvable Problem," *Life*, March 8, 1943.

important to the PPD political project, but development-minded officials deemed only certain kinds of homes acceptable. In order to become a "clean and organized" nation, the *arrabales* had to be razed, and their residents forcibly relocated, generally to the new public housing projects being built in the larger cities and towns of the island.[30] Impoverished squatters had neither the financial resources, the political clout, nor the cultural capital to merit residence in the ultramodern urbanizaciones. Thus, the construction of the modern Puerto Rican urban landscape was predicated upon the destruction of the *arrabal*. Luxurious urban areas such as the "Mile of Gold," the capital's new financial district in Hato Rey, filled with high-rise banks and office buildings, were erected on land previously occupied by *arrabales*.[31]

State officials planned to forcibly relocate *arrabal* residents to the public housing apartment buildings that emerged in tandem with the suburban neighborhoods during the postwar period. The state poured great effort into justifying its destruction of the *arrabales*, producing many advertisements for their new public housing projects. One such article featured two arresting images, the upper one a drawing of the planned cement buildings, and the lower one a photo of three men happily beginning the demolition of a ramshackle, zinc-roofed building made of rough boards and labeled "Condemned," linked by a lengthy text that began: "Advancing one step more in our goal of eliminating *arrabales* from this community." The advertisement boasted of plans for thirty-four buildings, including 280 apartments, a community center, and streets and avenues—allegedly a veritable urbanización for the poor.[32]

Many *arrabal* residents fought back against the PPD bulldozers and their forced dislocation, sometimes physically confronting the police. They wrote to powerful politicians in both the United States and Puerto Rico, insisting that they had been conceded the right to build homes on government-owned land for more than a decade. They met with opposition newspapers to denounce the destruction of their homes, often winning editorial support for their cause. For example, the caption to a photo of hollow-eyed, angry *arrabal* families titled *Without Shelter*, which dominated the front page of *El Imparcial* (fig. 2.10), read: "These citizens of Barrio Amelia, of the town of Cataño, are today without shelter, because they built their houses on land owned by the Insular Government, which had not been zoned for this use. Their homes, some built and some in the process of being built, were destroyed [the] day before yesterday by a brigade of the Housing Authority. The neighbors say that the official action constitutes 'an abuse.'"[33]

Shantytown community members organized mass marches, insisting on the right to retain their current home locations and, unlike the organized war

FIGURE 2.10 • "Sin Albergue," El *Imparcial*, May 20, 1949, 1.

veterans, refusing to move into public housing projects. One speaker declared, "'I can't read or write, but I know that the Housing Authority has to publish a plan or regulation or something official before destroying people's homes. None of us has seen anything like this before. . . . Today, in this gigantic demonstration, we will decide whether Puerto Rico wants freedom or slavery. . . . Now [by forcing us into the housing projects] the Government wants to make us slaves for our whole lives!'"[34] Evidently, the PPD was not the only organization that could mobilize the language of slavery for its political purposes. All over the island, *arrabal* neighbors rejected the PPD plans for development and vociferously faced down the government bulldozers; their protests joined the other mass demonstrations of the postwar era to make for a worrisome political atmosphere.

The paternalist populist *brega* noted in chapter 1 emerged, however, even in these *arrabal* demonstrations, undeniably the most sharply antigovernment of all the protests of the late 1940s. For example, an attorney for the organization Workers United in Favor of Free Homes, which helped organize the marches, suggested that the *arrabal* residents abandon all attempts to challenge the relocation through the court system. A much more effective strategy, he insisted, would be to meet with Muñoz Marín directly to negotiate a resolution. (Whether or not the rest of the demonstrators agreed with this proposition was not reported in the press.)[35] Ironically, by 1959, one of the most powerful organizational presences in the few San Juan–area *arrabales* that managed to survive the razings of the previous decade was the local PPD committee, which was peopled by community leaders aspiring to respectability and which served as a medium for expressing protests as well as distributing material resources. Party control was never permanently ensured, however; several years later, a majority of the remaining *arrabal* residents in the San Juan metropolitan area rejected the PPD in the polls.[36]

Constructing a Modern, Whitened Domesticity

As government bulldozers razed squatter communities and battled their residents throughout the island, state agencies embarked on a project not only to encourage the building of "decent, hygenic" homes, but to shape what occurred within their walls. In the countryside, *parcela* homes and the new status and stability they provided their male owners would form the basis of a recognizable, patriarchal domesticity, PPD officials hoped. Government publications spent long passages instructing rural families how to create an orderly domestic space, with animals penned outside and tools and kitchen utensils tucked away in distinct places. The family should eat together at regular mealtimes around a single table, using a special set of dinner dishes (the "legitimate pride of all housewives"). Rural PPD agents, sent to provide *parcelistas* with "technical assistance," also sought to discourage the long-standing practices of people and animals freely moving in and out of rural homes; women sewing, repairing farm implements, and doing laundry while cooking outside under a makeshift roof; and family members serving themselves whenever hungry out of a common pot of food, warmed over an open flame. The new respectable rural domesticity, the state anticipated, would more closely approximate a bourgeois household, clearly delineating between public and private, income-earning and domestic tasks, sleeping and eating spaces, family and individual time.[37]

This newly constituted domestic sphere, while peopled primarily by women and children, was to be happily presided over by men, who would inspire enthusiastic collaboration from their wives. Rewarded for their "decent, hard work," successful rural patriarchs allegedly led their harmonious families in loan applications to state banks that would "depend on a man's character rather than on the quantities in his pocket," in cooperative agricultural labor, in repairing and beautifying the home and its surrounding yard, and in sharing bountiful meals (fig. 2.11).[38] Rural couples in such a domestic sphere would be properly demure, focused on income-earning production, not on creating unmanageably huge families (fig. 2.12).[39]

Consistently, the visual images of this idealized rural domesticity depicted racially white, tidy, and neatly dressed families. The new rural family and domesticity made possible by *parcela* distribution, the official PPD images announced, marked an end to chaotic poverty, rooted in the exploitation of slavery. All rural families, no matter how poor, might now aspire to an orderly, honorable life, free of racial stigmatization, filled with simple material comforts. Becoming a model PPD jíbaro, in effect, whitened as it brought prosperous order to the nation.[40] For some plebeian Puerto Ricans, visual messages like this and the whitened burly male industrial proletariat may have comprised a compelling call to liberation; ideally, all Puerto Ricans could escape slavery's historic degradations through the PPD's program. Those who unswervingly identified as Afro–Puerto Rican, however, may well have recognized the consistent whiteness of visual representations of respectability as deeply racist. In these sorts of venues, the articulation of the PPD project provided no space for those who might assert a proud, distinctively black identity; decency and progress could only be coded as white.[41] Such visual images of modernity, unequivocally rooted in whiteness, lay in tension with the expansive PPD language of slavery and freedom that strove to include all exploited Puerto Ricans, regardless of their racial identifications.

In the island's cities and towns, the new sprawling suburban homes were not only a badge of familial economic stability but also an undeniable sign of the Puerto Rican populace's move into whitened modernity. Made of cement, ensuring solidity, permanence, and resistance to the hurricanes, fire, and vermin that plagued the ramshackle wooden residences of the countryside and the *arrabales*, the urbanización homes were to be filled with the new appliances marketed at every turn in urban shops, newspapers, and street corners: electric fans, refrigerators, lightbulbs, washing machines, toasters, and irons—cooling, cooking, and cleaning implements that required the presence of electricity and heralded the transformation of domestic labor and space. A whole new aesthetic of domestic urban modernity emerged in the advertisements for these items. With their sleek, shining metal sides, gently whirring motors, and efficient functionality, the appliances were caressed by carefully coiffed, white housewives exclaiming at the comfort, abundance, and pleasure of their new lives: "Philco fans—Sensational, Sumptuous!" "A whole world fits in your Kelvinator refrigerator!" "Caloric,

agricultor de recursos limitados que quiera progresar se acerca
una oficina local de la Administración de Hogares de Agricultura para llenar y presentar su solicitud para un préstamo. Estos se
en para que el prestatario pueda adquirir una finca, para que
ade o mejore la que posee o para que se refaccione. El pro-
ma de la AHA descansa sobre el carácter de los hombres más
que sobre la cuantía de su bolsa.

El prestatario y su familia revisan sus cuentas y repasan el plan
la finca y del hogar concertado con la AHA. Esta le ha facilitado fo
dos a unos 700 agricultores pobres para comprar fincas. El promed
de estos préstamos es de $4,651. El total prestado se acerca a un
tres millones de dólares.

t prestatario cultiva el "pan de cada día." La AHA hace también
estamos de refacción. Su cooperación en este sentido alcanza a unas
50 familias rurales. El monto de ellas se acerca a los siete mi-
mes de dólares. Unos cuatro mil prestatarios han saldado sus cuen-
s. AHA tiene hoy 10,555 clientes activos. El promedio de clientes
morosos no llega al veinticinco por ciento.

Mejorar la dieta de sus parroquianos, haciéndola apetitosa, vari
y nutritiva, es uno de los objetivos de la Administración. Milla
de prestatarios cultivan huertos y consumen sus hortalizas. El
grama de préstamos de la AHA tiende a provocar un desarrollo
mónico entre la finca y el hogar rural, con el propósito de que
traduzca en el mejoramiento de la vida campesina.

FIGURE 2.11 • The proper sort of rural family would be created through a
state-sponsored loan and land ownership program, which would reconstitute
the family, with the father established as a loving, successful patriarch. Here
we see him applying for a government improvement loan, aided by a friendly
bureaucrat and his affectionate, modestly sized family, and producing crops, all
culminating in a happy domestic scene at the bountiful dinner table, centered
on a well-scrubbed, carefully dressed couple. The wife demurely looks down,
while her husband beams across the table. (In the originals, all the jíbaros are
light skinned.) "La AHA y su obra en Puerto Rico," El Mundo, April 20, 1947, 9.

FIGURE 2.12 • Another example of the PPD's vision of a model rural family: erect, well-fed, healthy, calm, ready to work but serene in their labor, small in number, united behind the father, unmistakably white, and looking steadily to the future. Notice that the little boy's clothes are not designed for work, unlike his parents'. He has a potential future in the middle class. This particular image appeared frequently in El Mundo and El Imparcial in 1949 as part of the PPD's campaign to encourage sugar companies to participate in the state's fledgling unemployment insurance program. It generally occupied nearly a full page.

the most modern gas stove! Made of porcelain outside and in! Caloric is elegant; it's economic; it's precise!" (figs. 2.13 and 2.14).[42]

These dreams of modern domesticity promised to banish to a nightmarish past the smoke-filled, wood-burning *fogón* kitchen tacked onto the back of ramshackle shacks, the hours of trudging to the river to carry water, the heat and hunger of the sugar fields' dead time, and the malnutrition of children. Puerto Rico, the ads proclaimed, had entered the future. Happiness through domestically oriented consumption of U.S.-produced goods was within the people's grasp. Women's household labor would be reduced and transformed, brought within a comfortable, clearly defined domestic space (fig. 2.15). Children would be well fed and perpetually happy. Men's experience of domestic space would be pleasurably expanded, obviating the need for the traditional male diversions of taverns, cockfights, *bolita* gambling, and domino playing on street corners (fig. 2.16). All could relax and enjoy together the tranquility of a new domesticity, inexorably tied to Puerto Rico's relationship with the indisputably modern and prosperous United States.[43]

Laid out in geometrical grids, planned and constructed on a massive scale, the urbanizaciones were heralded as "paradise on earth, with all the advantages and comforts of a truly modern city." Their sturdy homes

FIGURE 2.13 • Housewife exclaiming at her efficiently designed, full-to-the-brim refrigerator. Advertisement for Muebleria La Luz, *El Imparcial*, June 29, 1949, 11.

FIGURE 2.14 • "The Modern Kitchen Is a Pleasant Place," *El Imparcial*, October 10, 1948.

FIGURE 2.15 • Washing clothes in the river: every plebeian woman's lot. This was the sort of physically grueling, publicly performed reproductive labor that the new domesticity promised to obviate. Clayton Gingrich, *Washing Clothes*, c. 1946. From the Lehman Puerto Rico 1940s–1950s Collection. Courtesy of Fundación Luis Muñoz Marín.

FIGURE 2.16 • The homosocial space of a rural tavern. Photograph by Louise Rosskam for the Office of Information for Puerto Rico, 1945. From Laura Katzman and Beverly W. Brannan, *Re-viewing Documentary: The Photographic Life of Louise Rosskam* (Washington, DC: American University Museum, 2011).

La Casa de sus Sueños
AL ALCANCE DE SU MANO
EN LA MEJOR URBANIZACION DE PUERTO RICO.

Ahora y en el Reparto Baldrich —"la mejor urbanización de Puerto Rico"— usted puede poseer la casa de sus sueños. Estamos construyendo en esta moderna, céntrica y saludable urbanización un número limitado de residencias de elegante diseño y con todas las comodidades. Estas casas estarán a la venta dentro de poco. Con gusto daremos más informes a quien los solicite.

FIGURE 2.17 • "Nuestras Felicitaciones al Reparto Baldrich," El Mundo, May 6, 1947, 20.

allegedly provided a domestic space powerful enough to obviate the extra-marital liaisons that Puerto Rican men had long considered their right.[44] "Comfort . . . the *dream of every family man, just as much as of all housewives.* The homes in Bay View are spacious and comfortable. Your husband will feel so happy in Bay View that he will never want to leave, never succumb to outside distractions." Here, heterosexual parents could harmoniously bond together and raise "strong and healthy children."[45] Advertisements for houses in the upscale Baldrich urbanización in Hato Rey emphasized their spacious size and individual tailoring to their well-heeled owners' specifications, often imitating the design of North American ranch-style homes. In such images, both husband and wife exclaim in pleasure at the sight of their new house; a home such as this was not only a woman's desire (fig. 2.17).[46]

In a lengthy feature in the newspaper El Mundo, working-class families who have moved into the barely finished, modest homes in the massive sprawl of Puerto Nuevo exclaim, "'This is mine!' 'It's so quiet here!'" A long section of the article describes how new homeowners, especially the women, are inventing individualized domesticity out of the basic conformity of the houses' design. The caption to these photos reads: "The first family to in-

FIGURE 2.18 • "Señora Prado guardando platos en gabinete de cocina de su nueva casa en Puerto Nuevo," *El Mundo*, February 27, 1949, photograph by Hamilton Wright. Courtesy of Colección Periódico El Mundo, Universidad de Puerto Rico, Recinto de Río Piedras.

stall themselves in Puerto Nuevo was that of veteran José Prado. His little son seems to have immediately felt 'at home.' To the right, Mrs. Prado dedicates herself to arranging the small but comfortable kitchen" (fig. 2.18).[47]

Such discourses of domesticity fed the PPD understanding of a model working-class family of "high moral fiber." Party officials envisioned a Puerto Rico where laboring men and women together could comfortably fulfill clearly demarcated patriarchal gender roles—where abundance put an end to both material misery and unnervingly blurred gender lines. Ideally, men were to be the sole breadwinners; women, freed from the stress of wage earning, were to dedicate themselves to the care of husbands and children.

This PPD vision of domesticity and the family enshrined long-standing ideals of Puerto Rican laboring men. Even radical male union organizers in the early twentieth century who rejected institutionalized marriage as "women's slavery to the church and society" and who supported women's emancipation through wage work and the right to vote had dreamed of creating a peaceful, gently patriarchal working-class domesticity. Once capitalism's exploitation had ended, they insisted, "their" women would be ensconced within the home, economically dependent on their partners, and happily meeting the domestic desires of male workers.[48] Highland landowning peasant men probably also responded positively to the PPD policies promoting domesticity. They equated independence from both parental and estate owner authority with establishing a long-term marital relationship and setting up their own household on a tiny plot of land. Eric Wolf notes that "this partnership require[d] the subordination of the woman to her husband." Ideal rural patriarchal power in this "independent jíbaro" vision rested unequivocally in the hands of fathers; women owed their husbands sex on demand, the production and care of many children, meal preparation and service, and intimate physical care, as well as all wages they might earn.[49]

The PPD domesticity discourses may well have appealed to working Puerto Rican men precisely because they resonated with ideals that they embraced but could rarely, if ever, achieve. Agregado men in the coffee-producing areas of the island's interior neither had access to land of their own nor earned sufficient income to effectively enforce dependable female submission.[50] Puerto Rican proletarian families, both rural and urban, lived a reality far from the PPD ideal as well. Historically, most had depended on multiple wage earners—mothers, other adults in the household, and younger family members. In towns and in the coastal sugar-producing regions with deeply entrenched wage economies, plebeian Puerto Rican women earned and controlled their own wages and exercised a "strong voice in household affairs," while men strove, often unsuccessfully, to be "a dominant and deciding figure at all times." In these parts of the island, women frequently headed household units or changed male partners several times during their lives, challenging the domesticity ideal even more dramatically. Even in the mountainous centrally located rural areas, where generally two parents raised children jointly, the majority of couples were not legally married, living in long-term consensual union instead.[51]

By 1949, more men did serve as the sole household source of income in Puerto Rico, but even then, only 55 percent of all rural men and 41 percent of all urban men could claim this position. It is probably safe to assume that among the rural proletariat, from whose ranks most of the sugar beet migrants were drawn, the percentage of sole male breadwinners was even lower. Conflicts over the production and distribution of economic resources within plebeian households were commonplace. Men also asserted the right to have multiple sexual partners and to control women's sexual activity. Women actively contested these principles, particularly when men were unable—or refused—to provide sufficient financial support for them and their children. Thus, familial conflicts between men and women—not infrequently spiraling into violence—were an ever-present part of laboring Puerto Ricans' daily existence.[52]

The PPD implicitly admitted this in its discourse on domesticity. Men needed to be reformed in order to "create a decent home." The state joined women in publicly condemning domestic violence, excessive male possessiveness, and men's financial and sexual philandering. The PPD did confirm that both women and men could work to ensure the viability of their local communities, as long as women did not assert too marked an autonomy from the men in their lives. Government officials, posters, publications, workshops, and films urged working men to take charge by dependably caring for women and children, as well as ensuring their containment within a benevolently patriarchal family and community.[53] Thus, the PPD's definition of domesticity empowered women to a certain extent, legitimizing their interest in responsible, caring male partners who would help raise children and dependably support their families financially.

In some senses, the PPD's gendered project for modernity promoted important elements of late nineteenth- and early twentieth-century Puerto Rican feminists' demands—an end to male extramarital wanderings and violence against their families, men's responsibility to provide consistent financial support for women and children, and women's right to earn their own wages—but only after erasing their feminist origins and analysis of social conflict.[54] The PPD version of domesticity still required a strong male head of household, to whom women were always to be lovingly subordinate. Fathers were now officially expected to be benevolent; marriage was to be a mutual partnership. But husbands and fathers remained patriarchs.[55] They were to rule over harmonious, safely hierarchical families, stripped of the gender conflict that haunted the economically insecure households of traditional Puerto Rico.

Muñoz Marín's popularity grew in part from his promises that his government would create the conditions to make such a benevolently patriarchal family possible. Financial provision for partners and offspring long had been a cornerstone of masculine expectations, although it was an ideal rarely attained (and sometimes actively shirked). Impoverished laboring men lived with their own gendered suffering, like the man living in Hato Rey who lit himself on fire after months of looking for work. Better to kill oneself than see one's family starve, his neighbors reported.[56] In exchange for working men and women's votes and organizing energy, Muñoz Marín promised to

FIGURES 2.19 and 2.20 • Women workers in new Puerto Rican factories, manufacturing hats and dolls. These PPD-approved photos communicated that even while women worked outside the home, they could help produce domesticity. In these photos, attractive, well-dressed women demurely focus on their clearly indisputably feminized sewing tasks, in spotlessly clean workplaces. These pictures betray no hint of the low wages they were paid or the conflicts over familial authority and financial priorities in which the women may have been embroiled at home. Louise Rosskam, *Straw Hats Being Manufactured in the Cabrer Hat Factory, Ponce Puerto Rico,* February 1947, and *Making Dolls in the Manual Industries Division of the Puerto Rico Industrial Company. Near Isla Verde, Puerto Rico,* May 1947. Reproduced in Laura Katzman and Beverly W. Brannan, *Re-viewing Documentary: The Photographic Life of Louise Rosskam* (Washington, DC: American University Museum, 2011).

end the exploitation in Puerto Rico that produced such acts of desperation. This, he pledged, would translate into consistent, decently paid employment for men, who would thus win their long-denied masculine dignity. Women, in turn, would finally be able to concentrate their energies on the domestic sphere, raising children, feeding and caring for their families and communities without fear of eviction, hunger, spousal abandonment, or violence.[57]

The democratization of political power, home ownership, and economic opportunity under Muñoz Marín, then, was a gendered class project; Muñocista and PPD rule allegedly would finally usher the entire nation into respectable, secure, male-headed domesticity. For the first time in Puerto Rican history, all men could be "real fathers," with a home and family to rule over and the means to provide for them. Women, in turn, could hold men to this standard. Thus, the new state project sought to establish an effective, reformed patriarchy.[58]

However, despite the state's insistence on the goal of domesticity and its probable attractiveness to many laboring Puerto Ricans, it remained an official ideal rarely reached. During the 1940s, stable employment remained a chimera for most of the Puerto Rican poor; the jobs created could not keep pace with the number of people seeking work. Working-class men generally did not earn sufficient wages to support a family without women and children's income. Women challenged men's claim to exclusive decision-making rights within the household. Indeed, the very industrialization program set in motion by the PPD threatened to undermine the possibility of women's enclosure in the home by pulling working-class women even further into wage work; the majority of the workers employed in the new factories opened during the 1940s and '50s were women, not men, as the PPD had projected. For most Puerto Ricans, the figure of the sole male breadwinner remained, as Helen Safa points out for a later period, a myth, not a lived reality.[59] In the constant talk of domesticity and men's "wages to support a family," PPD propaganda attempted to confirm the powerful certainty of these as-yet-unrealized ideals, just as it sought to assert the teleological power of industrial modernity.

Scholars have not yet carefully studied the effects of the PPD's early industrialization program on gender relations within the working-class family. However, Sidney Mintz tantalizingly reports that the factories established by the PPD government during the 1940s and '50s near the *parcela* communities provided many rural women with their first chance to work away from the home and earn their own income free from male surveillance (figs. 2.19 and 2.20). This wage labor and increased physical mobility may have changed rural women's life options, but Mintz notes that it did not alter rural men's desire to control women's physical movement and sexuality. Helen Icken Safa also comments on the tensions generated by the long-standing patterns of plebeian Puerto Rican women's active economic role in the family, whether through wages or transfer payments from the state, and working men's inability to consistently exercise dominant familial authority due to low wages or unemployment.[60] Thus, the Puerto Rican laboring family was hardly conflict free, as the PPD asserted it could become once the island had truly modernized.

Echoes of the gender conflict and sexualized violence that many women experienced surfaced in daily lurid reports of spousal and lover murders splashed across the pages of island newspapers. Often, they focused on women killed for threatening to leave their partners. Clearly, patriarchal authority was not as loving as the PPD asserted. Nor was it as hegemonic as men might wish, since it often had to be imposed by force.[61] Passionate debates also raged about the rapid increase in Puerto Rican divorce rates during the 1940s. By 1950, one of every six marriages ended in divorce; close to 60 percent of these couples had been married for less than five years.[62] Women struggled to enforce child support payments from separated male partners.[63]

The lived reality of many people's lives belied official rhetoric, but the daily gender struggles between Puerto Rican working men and women could have made the dream of harmonious gender relations wrapped in modern, comfort-filled domesticity even more powerful for some. For others, the constant reporting of marital violence and disintegration may have functioned as an effective policing mechanism, threatening the possibility of familial chaos. At the very least, by 1950, the discourse of domesticity and the myth of the sole male breadwinner had become powerful resources on which both the Puerto Rican state and its citizens could draw. They became an integral element of the massive social movement mobilizations of the late 1940s. They fueled the sugar beet workers' desires to migrate to Michigan in 1950 and their anger upon encountering terrible exploitation there. They would also become a potent political weapon in the hands of the Michigan migrants' wives, who insisted upon their right to receive sustenance for themselves and their children from their husbands' grueling labor abroad. A home and a male income that could reliably provide healthy familial shelter and food, the Michigan workers and their families insisted, as did many other Puerto Ricans during these years, was not only a seductive call of modernity promoters. It was a right owed them by the state, one that could become threatening to government officials.

3

REMOVING "EXCESS POPULATION"

Redirecting the Great Migration

Emigration on a grand scale has been recognized by the Government of
Puerto Rico as one of the most important elements of our plans to combat the
island's economic dilemma. . . . Our plan does not consist exactly of expelling our excess
population; we want to find them a place to live outside of Puerto Rico, where they
can be happy, self-sufficient, and provide a positive contribution to their
new surroundings. • Jesús Piñero, governor of Puerto Rico, October 1947

Populist compassion morphed into "expertise"; the ruler gradually distanced
himself from the transcendental experiences of his people. In this politics of migration, the
Puerto Rican had become a "problem"; ultimately, inefficient compassion was exiled,
banished from the nation. • Edgardo Rodríguez Juliá, *Las tribulaciones de Jonás*

In 1940, on the eve of the election that would bring his party to a position of power in island politics, Luis Muñoz Marín invoked the "150,000 Puerto Ricans, pushed into the sea," forced to emigrate to New York City "just to avoid dying of hunger."[1] Within a few short years, his empathetic recognition of migrants as part of the Puerto Rican nation would shift into a consistent representation of them as "excess population," a "problem" to be "disposed of" by relocation to the U.S. mainland, where "after two generations, the problem of Puerto Ricans . . . will no longer exist, simply because by that time [because of assimilation] there won't be any more Puerto Ricans there."[2]

As we have seen, by the mid-1940s, Muñoz Marín and many other high-level PPD leaders turned away from their earlier social justice program of "bread, land, and liberty." Instead, they aggressively promoted "productive modernity," which privileged industrialization over substantive land reform and began to purge independence advocates and other dissenters from the party's ranks. These changes accompanied a shift from critiquing colonial and elite exploitation of Puerto Ricans and the island's resources to blaming Puerto Rico's poverty on overpopulation. Concomitantly, the PPD government began to encourage migration from Puerto Rico as an indispensable element of its development strategy. Hundreds of thousands of Puerto Ricans left the island during the PPD years, seeking *mejor ambiente* (a better life). They may well have been spurred on by the promotion of new homes and consumption of innovative domestic items so ubiquitous in government and mass media discourse. Migration, then, fused with both state and popular desires for modernity and prosperity.[3] Faced with a hostile backlash against the huge increase in Puerto Rican emigration to New York City, by 1947, the PPD attempted to channel migrants to other locations in the United States. The Puerto Rican state simultaneously moved to systematize, regulate, and ultimately wrest control over recruitment for the U.S. labor market from private, U.S.-based agencies.

The Puerto Rican government's strategies for migration promotion outside of New York City were deeply gendered. Defending Puerto Rican migrants against charges of failed masculinity, wanton womanhood, and a lax work ethic, PPD officials launched a public relations campaign proclaiming Puerto Ricans' traditional family values as they asserted Puerto Ricans' right as citizens to move freely from the island to the United States. In 1947, officials sought to train women on a large scale for domestic service in U.S. households. When this project fizzled, the Puerto Rican Department of Labor turned again to the popular issues of strengthening home and family. Puerto Rican men migrating to work in U.S. agriculture, the new official discourse proclaimed, would both consolidate the new fraternal relationship between the two nations and create a new transnational domesticity, one that ironically required men's long-term absence from the home, but that would allegedly ensure modern abundance for the impoverished wives and children who remained in Puerto Rico. Agricultural labor, then, should be the focus of future migration to the United States, which had to be continued at all costs. "Excess" Puerto Rican men should not aspire to the industrial, urban employment so energetically promoted on the island.

Certainly, concern about Puerto Rico's alleged overpopulation did not begin with the PPD. Discussion of the issue began at least in the early 1930s, when New Deal reformers, Nationalist Party members, socialists, feminists, and Catholic clerics debated the use of birth control in Puerto Rico. By the late 1940s, however, the invocation of overpopulation reached a fever pitch. Over and over again in the postwar years, PPD officials, journalists, and intellectuals asserted that Puerto Rico's primary problem was its overpopulation: it was an island with "lots of people and very little land." References to an incessantly increasing population made the "battle for [industrial] production" absolutely urgent—a matter of life or death.[4] U.S. liberal policymakers and social scientists also leaped into the fray, echoing the assertion that Puerto Rico's "primary trouble is not American imperialism. . . . Overpopulation is the most ominous threat to the island's future."[5] The newspaper El Mundo echoed top PPD officials' use of the term "Super Populated," a "chronic condition" of the island that created a burning need for birth control (including sterilization of women) and mass emigration.[6] By 1948, much of the rural populace that had mobilized to put the PPD in power was deemed by the top party brass to be surplus population, fit only for migration. Quotes like the following filled the pages of Puerto Rican newspapers and politicians' speeches in the postwar years:

> The population increase in Puerto Rico has reached uncommon proportions. . . . We are the most rapidly reproducing people in the world. We add about 20,000 to our working population every year, but the scarcity of land means that these workers cannot be absorbed by agriculture here. . . . Currently, the increase in migratory movement is decreasing the pressure on our resources from excess labor force. But this is not enough. It is imperative to open new channels to emigration. . . . To the men and women who raise families in Puerto Rico, we should tell them without subterfuge or equivocation what a danger Puerto Rico with 5 million inhabitants would pose to the future of their children.[7]

Leaders of the unions most closely affiliated with the PPD agreed that emigration to the United States was the only hope for the effective reduction of unemployment on the island.[8]

International labor migration was nothing new to Puerto Ricans. Since 1898, thousands of Puerto Ricans had traveled to buscar ambiente in the United States' industrial urban centers such as New York City and in its imperial outposts in places as far-flung as Hawaii's pineapple plantations and Arizona cotton fields. This long-standing survival strategy transformed into an outpouring of people in the post–World War II years, however, when approximately one-third of Puerto Rico's entire population emigrated to the United

States. Fueled by ongoing economic hardship on the island, the proliferation of options for low-cost air travel, government promotion of migration, and dreams of gaining permanent access to prosperous modernity, Puerto Rican migration during the 1940s focused almost entirely on New York City.

Marta Suárez, who grew up in a working-class neighborhood of the Puerto Rican city of Mayagüez during World War II, remembered, "The people who had left for New York seemed so much more sophisticated than us when they came back to visit. They brought money we didn't have; they knew about all sorts of things like elevators and subways and 'building supers'; they even looked whiter because they never went out in the sun! Oh, how I wanted to go there, too!"[9] More than 300,000 Puerto Ricans would arrive in New York between 1940 and 1950, most of them in the second half of the decade.

The "Invasion" of New York City

As the Puerto Ricans' great postwar migration dramatically swelled their numbers in New York City, the New York English-language press began to hysterically denounce the new arrivals. Despite New York's long history as a point of entry for immigrants and as a focus of emigration for Puerto Ricans themselves, the postwar Puerto Rican arrivals were deemed "unique"—threatening like no other.[10] "600,000 PUERTORICANS COME TO DINNER—THEY FLEE DARK FUTURE IN THE SUN TO BECOME CITY'S PROBLEM BROOD" a New York Daily News headline screamed.[11] Puerto Rican migrants to New York were consistently portrayed as an invasion of subhuman creatures or sinister natural forces. "Creeping," "crawling," "seeping," "flooding," "swarming," "teeming"—their arrival constituted "a bloodletting" of the island and its pestilence. They "clotted" Spanish Harlem. "An immutable flow of lava from an erupting volcano, . . . they disrupt the economy and customs of their newly adopted city."[12]

Puerto Ricans allegedly brought their island "problems" to New York. First and foremost, unsurprisingly, was overpopulation and its correlation, overcrowding, which commentators seemed to blame on the people living in such terrible conditions.[13] "At night the walls of the tenements in Spanish Harlem bulge with the hideous overcrowding which grows worse with every passing week. Everything that New York City stands for in the way of progress, culture, and communal leadership is forgotten in the areas where the Puerto Ricans have moved in."[14] Rarely did the New York press acknowledge overcrowding as a problem rooted in the lack of affordable housing in the city. Rather, New York journalists frequently expressed disgust at the Puerto

FIGURE 3.1 • "Puerto Rican Migrants Jam New York," *Life*, April 25, 1947, 27.

Ricans themselves living in the tenements.[15] The Puerto Ricans' high rates of tuberculosis also posed a threat to public safety, journalists insisted.[16] Newspaper reporters identified young Puerto Rican men as criminals, participants in gangs alongside newly arriving African Americans, which were supposedly pushing Italians, Irish, and eastern Europeans out of their long-established neighborhoods.[17] Puerto Ricans also allegedly suffered from an "education famine," having little interest and certainly no discipline in sending their children to school or enforcing teachers' rules.[18]

Most powerfully, however, the New York press linked Puerto Ricans with poverty, crippled families, and an alleged dependence on state welfare payments. The *New York World-Telegram* created a media blitz disparaging Puerto Ricans' "relief culture," featuring daily articles on the theme through much of 1947. The *New York Times*, the *New York Daily News*, and *Life* magazine also propagated the stereotype on numerous occasions, claiming that Puerto Ricans took taxis directly to relief offices from the filthy planes that transported them to New York. *Life* featured photos such as figure 3.1, which claimed to capture "Puerto Ricans and others jamming" New York City welfare offices. Which of the people in this picture were actually Puerto Rican is impossible to know, although the caption leaves the impression that it is the vast majority.

Puerto Ricans' demands for welfare benefits supposedly strained public budgets, creating an economic crisis for the city and state of New York. In this sense, Puerto Ricans were like their homeland, which depended heavily on infusions of federal aid from the United States to survive.[19] The hysteria about Puerto Ricans and their alleged "relief abuse" pushed the New York legislature to propose a bill requiring a two-year residency for access to benefits and spurred years of welfare fraud investigations in New York City.[20]

Oversexed, unproductive Puerto Rican men allegedly did not work, as they produced an overabundance of babies. Puerto Rican women, for their part, the New York newspapers trumpeted, were largely unwed mothers, having children with different men, and refusing to follow respectable family practices in the process.[21] For all the sexual energy they invested in physical reproduction, the New York press claimed, Puerto Rican men (and women) were decidedly not entrepreneurial in economic matters. Men supposedly were unable to find work, while the allegedly few Puerto Rican women who did not seek welfare worked for miserable wages in sweatshops, purportedly earning more than the tragic men in their families and upsetting respectable gender norms in the process. When journalists recognized that Puerto Rican men did earn income, they dramatically feminized their labor. "When [these men] manage to find jobs, they work in small factories, soldering lipstick cases, making zippers. . . . They are the big city's men behind the scenes. They wash the dishes, make the beds, clean the offices, launder the clothes, change the tablecloths."[22] Thus, according to postwar U.S. journalists, Puerto Rican men were decidedly masculine failures, and Puerto Rican women, when not overproducing babies, were decidedly nondomestic, swelling sweatshops to earn low wages. The full-page photo from *Life* magazine in figure 3.2, for example, visually presents the Puerto Rican father as the antithesis of a virile wage earner. Rather, the father here is swallowed up by the family and its domestic space, markedly diminished in power and physical size, apparently skilled only at producing children. The looming, gaunt faces of the elderly woman and the girl in the photo's foreground threaten the possibility of becoming public wards. Such a family, with no male wage earner striding at its head, could not contribute to New York's economy; it could only drain the city's budget.

Puerto Ricans' miserable conditions combined with their allegedly inherent passivity, which, ironically, was said to easily lead them into becoming leftists—another persistent theme in the increasingly anticommunist New York newspapers. The mainstream New York press repeatedly noted that large numbers of Puerto Ricans voted and campaigned for Vito Marcantonio of the American Labor Party, who "duped" them into believing that his socialist-inflected populism and proindependence positions could help them. Marcantonio was known throughout New York as a fervent advocate

FIGURE 3.2 • "Puerto Rican Migrants Jam New York," *Life*, August 25, 1947, 29.

of workers' rights, quality public education, and direct political action. He spoke out passionately in defense of Puerto Ricans' cultural integrity and sharply denounced U.S. political and economic exploitation of the island, calling frequently for Puerto Rico to become independent.[23]

At the center of this hysteria lurked the terrifying fact that Puerto Ricans were citizens of the United States. Unlike other immigrants, they could not be prevented from coming to New York. They also had the right to vote in the United States—and exercised this right enthusiastically. And they had the right to receive public welfare benefits. According to the editorial board and several reporters at the *New York World-Telegram*, Puerto Rican relief seekers formed an unholy communist alliance with radical social workers, collaborating to "bring down the American system." All in all, Puerto Ricans' "abuse of citizenship" posed a powerful threat to the "sanity and sanitation" of New York City.[24]

Puerto Ricans mounted their own responses to these virulent attacks. They organized public demonstrations against the *New York World-Telegram* offices, accompanied by Vito Marcantonio and other allies. They wrote letters to the editors of the *New York Times* and the *New York World-Telegram*, as did a few North American educators and settlement house workers who insisted that Puerto Ricans had a rich culture and were very committed to paid work and education for their children. Puerto Ricans also flooded the head of their island's legislature, Luis Muñoz Marín, with demands that he defend Puerto Ricans' dignity by refuting the slander against them in New York.[25]

Re-presenting and Redirecting the Multitudes

Beginning in 1947 and intensifying its efforts after Muñoz Marín's election as governor in 1948, the Puerto Rican government mounted a counterpublicity campaign. The 1947 speech of then governor Jesús Piñero, distributed to news outlets all over Puerto Rico and the United States, launched these efforts to remake (not end) the huge Puerto Rican exodus from the island. Piñero declared war on "disorganized" emigration from his "superpopulated" homeland, even as he asserted the unequivocal right of Puerto Ricans as U.S. citizens to freely move to their colonial metropole. Puerto Rican migration to the United States, Piñero proclaimed, should be focused outside New York City. In the future, it should flow particularly to agricultural areas of the United States. Piñero also presented the Puerto Rican government as a rational, stable institution with whom capitalists could do business, and in whom U.S. politicians could trust. PPD officials were not moved by political passions or corrupt desires for power, Piñero reassured his readers. Rather, they were judicious planners, men of reason, bent on introducing a panoply of scientific methods for social and economic reconstruction of the island. In subsequent years, the PPD continued this message, as its officials sought to counteract negative publicity about Puerto Ricans in New York City, direct Puerto Rican emigration away from the city, and take control of labor contracting outside New York away from private recruitment agencies.[26]

Officials in the PPD cultivated relationships with journalists at the *New York Times*, *Life*, *Esquire*, and *Time*. They commissioned and publicized a high-profile social science study of Puerto Rican immigrants with Columbia University, ultimately published in 1950 as a book titled *The Puerto Rican Journey*. They produced documentary films and educational materials on the island's "great Operation Bootstrap experiment" that were distributed to TV and radio stations, movie houses, church groups, and Boy and Girl Scout troops along the East Coast of the United States. Puerto Ricans, they insisted, were similar to previous immigrants from Europe. Given the chance, they would assimilate into mainstream U.S. society even more easily than their predecessors; they were already U.S. citizens and passionate participants in U.S. cultural activities like baseball.

Creating an image of ordered domesticity in migrant families, invariably led by a responsible male breadwinner, was crucial to these efforts. Puerto Rican government-sponsored materials and press releases also featured white Puerto Ricans in visual representations and downplayed the island's racial diversity. PPD officials hoped that such presentations would resonate positively with the broader post–World War II enshrinement of white middle-class domesticity in the United States (fig. 3.3).[27]

Once firmly ensconced in power on the island, the PPD also successfully promoted its new modern, industrialized vision of Puerto Rico in New York. The *New York Times*'s shift in reporting on Puerto Rico was so rapid that it verged on the surreal. In the space of a few months, it changed from a steady drumbeat of denouncing the alleged threat that Puerto Rican migrants posed to New York to enthusiastic praise of Puerto Rican persistence in the face of adversity and to excitement over the changes introduced on the island by the PPD and its Operation Bootstrap industrialization project.[28] Every month during 1948 and 1949, the *New York Times* reported on new factories, hotels, and suburban housing projects being built in Puerto Rico, paired with glowing proclamations about the "visionary new leaders" who were now guiding the island, particularly Luis Muñoz Marín. These articles often featured photos of industrial spaces and sprawling housing developments, all on a grand scale, overwhelming in their modern, technological

FIGURE 3.3 • "A Puerto Rican family at home watching television (circa 1950s)." Original photo published by Office of Government of Puerto Rico in the U.S. collection, c. 1950. Reproduced in Edgardo Meléndez Vélez, "The Puerto Rican Journey Revisited: Politics and the Study of Puerto Rican Migration," CENTRO 17:2 (2005): 192.

grandeur. Working-class Puerto Ricans themselves rarely appeared in these photos.[29] The irony of heralding massive housing construction on the island while tens of thousands of Puerto Ricans emigrated to the United States each year seemed lost on both U.S. journalists and Puerto Rican officials.

Life magazine also succumbed to the PPD's charms, with its January 1949 article "A New Puerto Rico Shows Off" featuring photos of open-shirted, large-gutted politicians and nattily dressed capitalists negotiating business deals on Puerto Rican beaches. The arrabal El Fanguito made its obligatory appearance, but now the new steel-and-glass skyscraper offices of the Banco Popular rose gracefully in the distance behind the shantytown's muck, a harbinger of the economic prosperity sure to come (figs. 3.4–3.6).[30]

Other national U.S. publications followed suit: Time, Newsweek, and Reader's Digest all began to run articles on the "new Puerto Rico." Puerto Rican male workers, when discussed, were now referred to as "clever, adaptable, and industrious, reacting marvelously to responsibility," engaged in "feverish activity." According to New York Times reporter Charles Grutzner, who ran a revisionist series on Puerto Ricans in late 1948, Puerto Rican women in New York City now ensured that "Homes are Kept Clean"—"Despite Ugly

FIGURES 3.4, 3.5, and 3.6 • Three images from "A New Puerto Rico Shows Off," *Life*, January 29, 1949, 20, 22, 24. The headline for the second photo read: "The Island Begins to Find Answers for Its Old 'Unsolvable Problem.'"

Surroundings, Social Worker Says Women Instinctively Tidy."[31] PPD officials promoted Puerto Rican men as productive, skilled agricultural workers, glad to be "aiding U.S. farmers." The *New York Times* began to run articles featuring large photos of happy Puerto Rican field laborers picking strawberries in New Jersey and mushrooms in Pennsylvania. "A tired and perspiring worker comes in with a good haul," the caption for the photo of one hardworking Puerto Rican laborer proclaimed; while another informed the public that the dapperly dressed, good-looking men joking with each other in a bunkroom reminiscent of summer camp "pick on an average of 100 quarts of berries a day" (figs. 3.7 and 3.8). In this rural context, it seemed, Puerto Rican men could regain their productive potential and serve as a counterbalance to the images of diseased, dispossessed Puerto Rican hordes flooding the streets and tenements of New York City.[32]

Thus, the Puerto Rican government launched a sophisticated propaganda campaign in the U.S. national press, lauding the island's capacity for industrial development within the context of untrammeled U.S. investment, its men's potential for labor productivity, and its women's desires for respectable domesticity. Such gendered assertions underlay Muñoz Marín's aggressive promotion of himself and Puerto Rico as effective Cold War deterrence figures, allowing the PPD to capitalize well on U.S. policymakers' Cold War

FIGURES 3.7 and 3.8 • Agricultural migrants proudly displaying their productive masculinity. Warren Weaver, "Puerto Ricans Aid Up-State Farmers," *New York Times,* June 16, 1949.

worries. In the post–World War II period, fears of communist influence were escalating, populist nationalist political regimes were emerging throughout Latin America that often came into direct conflict with U.S. interests, and leftist-inspired decolonization movements were forming around the world that criticized the United States as a hypocritical colonial power. The promotion of Puerto Rico's "peaceful, democratic revolution" that did not reject U.S. political or economic tutelage gained Muñoz Marín greater international visibility. It also encouraged U.S. funding for the PPD modernization project. The U.S. government began to sponsor tours of Puerto Rico by political and intellectual leaders from the Global South and the United States. By mid-1950, the *New York Times* could paternalistically proclaim without a trace of irony, "Puerto Rico is providing a notable example of enlightened control from a governing power and energetic, intelligent progress on the part of the governed. The whole of Latin America has been watching the Puerto Rico experiment with interest and often with admiration. As evidence of 'American imperialism,' Puerto Rico will stand examination by our harshest critics."[33] As in 1898, when Puerto Rico served as the enthusiastic and allegedly docile colonial subject in the eyes of U.S. power brokers, providing a crucial counterpoint to troublesome nationalist revolutions in Cuba and the Philippines, Puerto Rico could once again stand as proof positive to the world of the United States' benevolent influence. In the Cold War world, Puerto Rico under Muñoz Marín's guidance could help advance the Truman project of what Greg Grandin has dubbed "liberalism at home and internationalism abroad."[34]

However, the previous noxious discourses about Puerto Ricans did not die so easily. Certainly, by 1949 and 1950, the text of many U.S. newspaper and magazine articles provided a sociological explanation of the difficulties Puerto Ricans faced in New York. They tended to analyze the broader social conditions confronted by Puerto Ricans and often dismissed assertions of "natural" Puerto Rican tendencies toward crime, poverty, or disease. These later articles frequently explicitly rejected the blame heaped upon Puerto Ricans in previous years. However, their sensationalistic headlines still blared messages of alarm about Puerto Ricans: "City Problems Created," "Health and Housing Strained as Mass Movement Adds to the Big Colonies Here." Also, the sociological approach to understanding Puerto Rican migrants, crystallized in the Columbia University study *The Puerto Rican Journey*, still assumed that the Puerto Ricans living in New York City constituted a problem that desperately needed to be resolved—not a resource to be cherished, as many Puerto Rican activists and their allies insisted. *Time* magazine's article "The World They Never Made" echoed many others both by insisting that the previous assumptions about Puerto Rican relief mongering were incorrect and by uncritically recycling some of the most damaging images of oversexed, unproductive criminality.[35] In short, the discourses of the Puerto Rican menace remained alive and well, even at the heart of attempts to change them.

Officials in the PPD were not deterred, however. While musing about the possibilities of sending Puerto Ricans to other Latin American countries such as Venezuela and the Dominican Republic, most of the party's top leadership's efforts to redirect workers away from New York City continued to focus on the United States.[36] If officials hoped to reduce the out-migration's "chaotic" nature while increasing its flow and directing migrants away from the city, they would first have to wrest control of geographically dispersed labor recruitment from the private companies who had established themselves as migrant labor brokers in Puerto Rico.

Before 1947, the Puerto Rican Department of Labor had limited its role in migrant labor contracting to sporadic review and approval of privately sponsored labor agreements.[37] Private companies, such as Rolly and Miranda, Samuel Friedman, and Castle, Barton, and Associates made contacts with potential employers and signed contracts with Puerto Ricans on the island, promising workers housing, long-term employment, and higher wages in the United States than those prevalent on the island. Advertisements by these agencies for employment outside New York filled the Puerto Rican newspapers. Many such businesses opened semipermanent offices on the island in the early 1940s. The conditions women and men workers encountered upon their arrival in the United States rarely matched what the recruitment companies had promised, however. Working conditions themselves were often difficult at best. Housing was frequently inadequate or nonexistent. Employers tried to control workers' lives when off duty, and often did not provide enough working hours to earn the promised income. Frequently, the contracts were simply oral agreements and completely unenforceable (fig. 3.9).[38]

Throughout the mid-1940s, stories circulated in Puerto Rico about the abuses of these recruitment agencies, which lured unsuspecting workers into exploitative situations and then tried to force them to remain. Perhaps the most celebrated of these cases was the 1946 emigration of 362 young Puerto Rican women to Chicago, recruited by Castle, Barton, and Associates to work as domestic servants. Many of the women were horrified at the treatment they received from the employing families and incensed at their employers' frequent refusal to pay the promised wages. Unlike many of the earlier recruited groups, who were less numerous and without local allies,

FIGURE 3.9 • The innocent Puerto Rican worker is lured to emigrate by "promises of work which are never fulfilled," dangled before him by illegal airfare agencies, based in the United States. Filardi, "La carnada," El Mundo, March 10, 1948, 6.

the Puerto Rican women stayed in touch with each other through afternoon teas organized by the Chicago YWCA. They also managed to make contact with two politically active Puerto Rican graduate students at the University of Chicago: Elena Padilla, a budding anthropologist, and Munita Muñoz Lee, the daughter of Luis Muñoz Marín himself, at that point president of the Puerto Rican Senate.

Elena Padilla, a brilliant undergraduate at the University of Puerto Rico, was one of a handful of students picked by the university's rector, Jaime Benítez, to study at the University of Chicago, his alma mater. Padilla's early experiences in Chicago organizing on behalf of the Puerto Rican contract workers profoundly shaped her subsequent career and intellectual trajectory; she was continually marginalized within academic institutions, despite her pivotal role in the creation of studies that have formed some of the core documents of the field of Puerto Rican Studies. Padilla ultimately completed her PhD at Columbia University and contributed to the groundbreaking *People of Puerto Rico* volume, along with anthropologists Sidney Mintz and Eric Wolf. She also served as a key researcher for Columbia University's Puerto Rican Journey study, commissioned by the PPD government to defuse public anti–Puerto Rican hysteria in New York City. Unlike Mintz and Wolf, who went on to become academic luminaries, Padilla refused to accept a full-time permanent university post, choosing instead to fuse her scholarship with community-based activism and carving out a career as an important public intellectual who remained largely unacknowledged in academic circles. Padilla's field notes from the *People of Puerto Rico* project were not archived by Columbia University, as were those of her (later famous) male collaborators. In addition, Puerto Rican male academics, deeply invested in an anti-imperialist nationalism, also accused Padilla of being apolitical because of her insistence on the importance of Puerto Ricans' "private" cultural beliefs, racial attitudes, and social practices, as well as relationships between Puerto Rican migrants and different ethnic and national groups that did not fit within the nationalist paradigm; these Puerto Rican male intellectuals neglected her work as well.[39]

Munita Muñoz Lee was the daughter of Muñoz Marín and his first wife, Muna Lee, a North American lyrical poet, skilled literary translator, and feminist born in Mississippi and raised in Oklahoma. The two were married in 1919. Muna Lee's fascinating transnational life, artistic production, and enduring political commitments are for the most part shrouded in silence among Puerto Ricans. Lee raised her two children, Munita and Luisito, primarily with Muñoz Marín's mother, the two women living together in New

Jersey, Puerto Rico, and New York City while Muñoz Marín traveled about occupying himself with politics. Lee was a passionate feminist activist herself, joining a group of Latin American feminists who forced their way into the 1928 Pan-American Congress in Havana, Cuba, to demand that its all-male participants take up women and children's rights as central concerns of the organization. A committed suffragist on behalf of all Latin American women, Lee also worked for the National Women's Party to advance labor protections for working-class women in the United States during the 1930s. Puerto Rico remained Muna Lee's permanent place of residence and her primary place of identification long after her relationship with Muñoz Marín effectively ended; she died there in 1965. As mentioned in chapter 1, Marín's second wife, Inés Mendoza, who was Puerto Rican, and with whom he maintained an openly acknowledged live-in sexual relationship from about 1935 (complete with two children), is generally recognized as his life partner and legitimate wife by most Puerto Ricans to this day. Inés Mendoza and Muñoz Marín married the day after his formal divorce from Muna Lee in November 1946, just as his daughter Munita and Elena Padilla were organizing Puerto Rican public opinion in defense of the women contract workers in Chicago.[40]

Sharing in the social justice fervor sweeping Puerto Rico even as they were recruited into the ranks of the new U.S.-trained intelligentsia, Padilla and Muñoz Lee threw themselves into an impassioned defense of the Puerto Rican women workers, writing letters of protest to Muñoz Marín, making contacts with journalists and Department of Labor officials in Chicago and Puerto Rico whom they convinced to investigate the women's conditions, and networking with both seasoned leftists in the New York City diaspora community and labor advocates on the island. They also helped the women locate local factory employment, housing (sometimes letting them sleep in their own University of Chicago dormitory room), and travel funds to New York City.[41]

The result, despite Luis Muñoz Marín's long-distance attempts to dampen the women's international cross-class organizing efforts, was a public relations eruption, precursor in miniature to the scandal caused by the Michigan beet field fiasco. Puerto Ricans on the island, angered by the mistreatment of *jóvenes engañadas* (deceived young women—a term often used for innocent virgins seduced by predatory men), eventually prompted investigations by the Illinois and Puerto Rican Departments of Labor, the YWCA, and the Women's Bureau of the federal Department of Labor. Attempting to minimize opposition criticisms and the women's complaints, the PPD government blamed the "minor problems" in Chicago on the "privately-engineered" nature of the women's emigration. Ultimately, the Puerto Rican legislature managed to pacify its critics by passing a bill that established standards for closer regulation of collective emigration contracts.[42]

The Chicago controversy brought to a head concerns about the shadowy network of private employment agencies that had been recruiting Puerto Ricans for years to work in the United States. By late 1947, when Governor Piñero released his statement about Puerto Rican development and migration, PPD leaders were determined to crack down on the informal labor contractors. They began to more aggressively follow up on worker complaints and pursue sanctions against labor recruitment companies that did not ensure satisfactory working conditions.[43] While trying to edge out the private labor agencies, the Puerto Rican Department of Labor also began to develop employment contracts itself, meeting with fruit and vegetable growers' organizations and politicians in California, Washington state, Delaware, Pennsylvania, New Jersey, Connecticut, and rural New York.[44] The Puerto Rican government found itself not only in the midst of potential conflicts of interest—it had pledged to protect workers but also needed to accept wages low enough to be attractive to agricultural employers—but also in competition with the furtive private recruitment agencies.[45]

Several times in the late 1940s, government officials decided not to finalize contracts with growers who insisted on lower than subsistence wages, only to discover that informal labor contractors had continued with the deal and were attempting to send Puerto Ricans to do the rejected agricultural work. Once, the illegal dealings were stopped by the island's Department of Labor officials just as the labor recruiters were ushering Puerto Rican workers onto unlicensed airplanes at the San Juan airport. One of the best known of the labor recruiters, Samuel Friedman, based in Philadelphia, even debated the head of the Puerto Rican Department of Labor in the Puerto Rican press, insisting that the government's attempt to regulate Puerto Ricans' labor conditions in the United States would damage employment opportunities abroad.[46]

In an attempt to develop its own managed labor flow out of the island, the PPD government set up a training program for women domestic workers, intended as an alternative to the Chicago fiasco. Actively promoted by the newspaper El Mundo, whose editorial positions recently had become enthusiastically progovernment, the program was planned to quickly expand to eight training centers, all offering three-month courses in conversational English, kitchen utensil washing, cleaning and arranging furniture, polishing silver, proper methods of answering doors and telephones, food service, and modern laundering techniques. Hundreds of thousands of women might be trained annually in these centers, once they were up and running, El Mundo trumpeted.

Not only could this effort solve the island's overpopulation issue by relo-cating women of prime reproductive age, the local press coverage also as-serted that the young students would not be destined for life as degraded *criadas* (servants). Rather, they would graduate from their training courses as "respectable women," well versed in both English and the creation and main-tenance of modern domesticity. Their migration would also be undeniably respectable, carefully supervised by state officials and employing families alike, contained within homes. These women would not be moving freely about on the streets, working in factories or creating excess babies, either in Puerto Rico or in the United States. Caring for the homes and children of U.S. middle-class and wealthy families, these reconstructed working-class Puerto Rican women ideally would confirm the benevolently dependent relationship between the United States and Puerto Rico. Allegedly provid-ing gentle tutelage for the colonized as well as grateful modern caretaking by them, the large-scale employment of Puerto Rican women within the U.S. do-mestic sphere would safeguard and facilitate the process of migration, teach-ing assimilation through respectable household work as it counteracted the "problem of overpopulation."[47]

The opposition El *Imparcial*'s reporting on these governmental migra-tory plans for women implicitly revealed their ephemeral nature, however. Large numbers of domestic service jobs never materialized in the United States, and few women seem to have even applied to enter the program in Puerto Rico. The well-publicized negative experience of domestic workers in Chicago may have deterred young Puerto Rican women from entering the training programs. Also, the seductive images of modernity propagated by both commercial advertisements and the Puerto Rican government dur-ing the postwar years may have undercut working-class women's willing-ness to work as servants; all the messages incited them to be proud mis-tresses of their own homes—not to care for someone else's. Overall, Puerto Rican women migrants appear to have preferred independently seeking U.S. factory employment to accepting the government's circumscribed migrant job offerings. Finally, U.S. families seem not to have treated their female employees as kindly as the Puerto Rican government had hoped; a Spanish-language newspaper in New York City reported that the wages paid to the handful of state-imported Puerto Rican domestic workers undercut state minimum wage laws governing this type of labor.[48] Ultimately, the grand dreams of the Puerto Rican government to export fertile Puerto Rican women to work in "properly supervised" U.S. homes fizzled, destroyed by the reluctance of working women to follow a script of internationalized domestic subordination and of U.S. employers to provide decent wages and working conditions.

Puerto Rican men, however, were another matter, the Puerto Rican government hoped. The majority of them already worked in agriculture on the island, planting and cutting cane, picking coffee, and harvesting tobacco. Why could they not find employment in U.S. agriculture as well? This seemed to be the perfect answer to Puerto Ricans' swelling numbers in New York City—send them to the U.S. countryside and keep them there; prevent "urban problems" and backlash from hostile U.S. citizens. Indeed, Fernando Sierra Berdecía, the director of the Puerto Rican Department of Labor, stated this baldly to his New York–based colleagues at the Puerto Rican Migration Division: "We want to place workers. There can be no argument on that score. But we do not want to place them where we think they will create a problem."[49] Working-class Puerto Ricans, then, were the potential problems—not the local hostility or exploitation that they might encounter in the United States. The only exception to this general rule was the U.S. South, where Jim Crow racial segregation reigned supreme. PPD officials, particularly Sierra Berdecía, remained staunchly opposed to sending Puerto Ricans there.[50]

The PPD launched a campaign to convince northern and western U.S. growers to hire Puerto Ricans instead of other "foreign nationals"—Mexicans in California and Washington, and on the East Coast, West Indians, especially Barbadians and Jamaicans. PPD officials also argued vociferously to the U.S. Department of Employment Services that because of their U.S. citizenship, Puerto Ricans should be considered domestic laborers and thus given priority over other international migrants in agricultural hiring. Here again, maintaining Puerto Rico's "benevolent" colonial relationship with the United States was crucial for the government's arguments. For years PPD officials negotiated with politicians, government bureaucrats, and growers alike, trying to gain an agreement that would consolidate a privileged hiring status for Puerto Rican agricultural workers. In his frustration, the PPD attorney for labor matters in the United States opined that the Puerto Rican government should wage a "second American Revolutionary War" to keep all non-U.S. citizens out of the migrant labor market.[51]

Through the late 1940s, PPD officials and their attorney in the United States were able to sign several contracts for hundreds of workers at a time, but their hopes for opening up tens of thousands of agricultural jobs remained stymied. Growers on the East Coast continued to hire many more workers from other countries; not only did their governments frequently accept lower wages than those demanded by the PPD Department of Labor, but their lack of citizenship rendered them relatively easy to deport. Puerto Ricans, on the other hand, as citizens could remain "freely wandering through American cities," leaving difficult rural conditions or simply moving on to urban employment once their farm contracts ended.[52] This tendency of Puerto Ricans to leave the fields for industrial or urban employment plagued both growers and PPD officials—contracts and newspaper articles reiterated that government protections could only be assured for those workers who remained at their original contract site. Those who deserted their posts to look for higher wages, better conditions, or an urban community could not count on any support from the Puerto Rican government. Such workers not only exposed themselves to the danger of unmediated exploitation, they also created a terrible situation for their countrymen, stirring up resentments against Puerto Ricans that would limit the possibility of future employment for others. The frequency of such published concerns hints that Puerto Ricans often used farm labor on the U.S. Eastern Seaboard as a stepping stone to urban life in New York City, but also in cities like Hartford, Albany, and Philadelphia.[53] Likewise, Puerto Rican state officials insisted that those Puerto Ricans who migrated on their own, or under promises of employment from any party other than the Puerto Rican government itself, had no one but themselves to blame if they encountered oppressive conditions.[54]

Hollow Promises

And encounter such conditions they did. Puerto Rican male migrants periodically denounced their experiences on U.S. East Coast farms in the island press—usually in the opposition newspaper El Imparcial—and organized some collective protests during the postwar 1940s. Without consistent political allies, however, their objections did not create the media storm produced in the Michigan beet fields; without gendered sympathy for "wronged womanhood," they could not even cause as much of a stir as the women in Chicago. Clearly, though, Puerto Rican men migrating to work in U.S. agriculture in the years prior to 1950 expected respectful treatment, knew the terms of their contracts, and called on both the Puerto Rican government and Puerto Rican unions to enforce them.

Island-based unions did not ignore migrating agricultural laborers. In 1947, the autonomous Confederación General de Trabajadores union demanded that unions exercise oversight of the contracts for migrant work signed with private recruiters and called on U.S. unions to independently investigate the conditions of Puerto Rican workers on the mainland. In subsequent years, the Unidad General de Trabajadores union, led by communist organizer Juan Saez Corales, sent investigators to labor camps in New Jersey. The UGT condemned the conditions suffered by Puerto Rican workers on U.S. farms, even under government contracts, and held the Puerto Rican government responsible for them.[55] However, embattled by the postwar PPD purges of independence sympathizers and probably focusing their energies on the large island-based labor actions, these independent unions did not maintain consistent support for migrant farm workers.

Through 1947, letters from agricultural migrants reporting abusive conditions on East Coast farms appeared from time to time in the Puerto Rican press; most of them had migrated under the auspices of private employment agencies. The PPD government and island newspapers found it easy to lay the blame for these situations at the feet of the "ruthless recruiters."[56] In the spring of 1948, however, Fernando Sierra Berdecía boasted that the Puerto Rican Department of Labor had confirmed an employment contract for two thousand workers in the fruit and vegetable farms of New Jersey. El Mundo and El Imparcial both lauded the contract's terms: free medical care, free good-quality housing, an hourly wage of 55 cents per hour, and a guarantee of a minimum of forty hours per week from April 1 to November 1.[57] More would be hired in Delaware soon. Several hundred might be heading to Washington State as well.

Workers in the mid-Atlantic states soon put the lie to the government's promises of dignified labor and work conditions. By May, complaints had begun to arrive in the New York office of the Puerto Rican government's Migration Division. Several workers wrote to the opposition island press reporting death threats from growers when workers insisted on the payment of back wages. They pointed out that despite their U.S. citizenship, they were paid 20 cents an hour less than American field-workers, lost substantial amounts of money to extra pay deductions ("taxes" not levied on "Americans"), and were forced to live in shacks that looked like rabbit warrens. "Here, the dogs live and sleep in more decent conditions than the Puerto Ricans." Following the traditions established over the preceding years in Puerto Rico, these workers announced that they were organizing "for their mutual defense" and demanded wages, tax payments, and housing equal to those of U.S. workers. Workers in Delaware also furiously countered New York and San Juan government officials' findings that their contract, after a few "minor problems," was now being honored in full. They replied that the growers were insisting on paying por ajuste (by the quantity picked), rather than by the hour, as the contract stipulated. Others wrote in anger "to make all Puerto Ricans aware what it means to leave on the expeditions organized by the Department of Labor. Every day, groups of Puerto Ricans arrive here, deceived by these accursed expeditions. . . . Two years of negotiation with these people and the Puerto Rican government doesn't know that this is a joke? We're sending a warning to all our countrymen so that they won't continue to be deceived."[58]

Clearly, the Puerto Rican Department of Labor's promises of agricultural worker protection under their contracts rang hollow. Leading PPD officials in New York City feared sending monitors out to rural labor camps on a regular basis; they did not want to irritate the growers or county agricultural boards who controlled the approval of future contracts.[59] Consistently through the late 1940s, Sierra Berdecía and other local Puerto Rican government representatives dismissed those Puerto Ricans who protested the conditions they encountered while working under government contracts on the farms of the U.S. Eastern Seaboard as "malcontents" who lacked experience in agricultural labor and who suffered from an "incapacity to adjust to new cultural situations." "A barber or a mechanic or a business clerk will have great difficulty adapting to rural life if he hasn't experienced it before. This problem of adjustment is the most serious issue that people emigrating to the farms of New Jersey face."[60] According to the Puerto Rican government officials, problems in U.S. agricultural employment lay with the Puerto Rican workers, not with the conditions and pay imposed upon them. In their urgent desire to encourage emigration from the island, PPD officials refused to honor the underlying principles of the worker protections recently passed in Puerto Rico.

In the summer of 1949, the New Jersey fields erupted again, when 250 Puerto Rican men who had begun the growing season working in Washington State were transferred by the Puerto Rican government to New Jersey after complaining of not being paid in full by Washington growers. Upon arrival in New Jersey, the transferred workers refused to begin work there, insisting that beginning a new contract could invalidate their claims against employers in Washington. They elected two spokespeople who promptly filed a formal complaint with the PPD's Migration Division office in New York City and demanded an immediate meeting with a top official of the Puerto Rican Department of Labor. Manuel Cabranes, the director of the New York City Migration Division office, traveled to address a mass meeting of the 250 angry men. After several hours of negotiations, during which Cabranes promised to throw the full force of the PPD legal team into the enforcement of the men's claims against Washington growers and brought the labor camp supervisor in to promise plenty of lucrative work in the New Jersey fields, the men finally voted to begin work in their new location.[61]

Once again, the PPD seemed to have defused an unnervingly restive labor situation, this time in the heart of the colonial metropolis. Shipped en masse from one end of the United States to another, the men drew on their island experiences of union democracy, negotiation, and strikes to force their government to the bargaining table. Although combative in their demands for respect, they continued in recent Puerto Rican political tradition, trusting in the goodwill and effective advocacy of the PPD. Challenges to power and trust in its potential benevolence intertwined again; as in Chicago, la brega's ambiguous politics had become transnational.

But true to form, Puerto Rican workers continued to press their demands when they found that justice had not been adequately served. A few weeks later, the *Philadelphia Daily News* reported that the federal secretary of labor had ordered an investigation into the contracts, hours, and salaries paid to Puerto Rican workers in New Jersey fields—probably as a result of the three-day work stoppage organized earlier by the transferred workers from Washington. Apparently, New Jersey employment services officials had approved contracts treating Puerto Ricans as foreign workers who could be paid less than the minimum state wage, despite the fact that they were U.S. citizens. In early September, 322 men representing workers housed in five different large New Jersey labor camps met in Philadelphia to announce that they were founding the Puerto Rican-American Agricultural Union. Welcoming the presence of a Puerto Rican who was president of the Camden, New Jersey, chapter of the Congress of Industrial Organizations (CIO), a representative of the Puerto Rican Labor Department from New York City, and a Puerto Rican lawyer resident in Philadelphia for more than twenty-five years, the men demanded pay equal to that of U.S. citizens and set up a steering committee composed of delegates from each labor camp. In a strange turn of events, they also elected Samuel Friedman, the notorious private labor recruiter from Philadelphia, to be the president of their fledgling organization. Notes on planned activities of the new union mentioned that it would generate lists of names and locations of employers and Puerto Rican workers in rural New Jersey—information that Friedman could have used lucratively in developing his own labor contracts.[62]

It is unclear what this move to elect Friedman as a leader signified. He may have engineered the entire incident himself in order to continue his public pressure on the Puerto Rican government to stay away from developing contracts with agricultural employers. Certainly, Friedman had plenty of

contacts among Puerto Ricans in the Philadelphia area and had been building relationships with island Puerto Ricans as well for years. The presence of
the CIO representative and hundreds of workers from the New Jersey labor
camps undercuts this interpretation, however. Puerto Ricans may have
been engaged in their own recruitment strategies, trying to access Friedman's possible clout with local employers. In classic *brega* politics, Puerto
Rican laborers may have been attempting to attract to their cause as many
powerful agents as possible—both U.S. and island based (note the presence
also of a representative of the PPD's Migration Division in New York). Certainly, Friedman had his own reasons to try to insert himself into this new
Puerto Rican labor organization, but we should not assume that the workers were his simple dupes. Newspaper reports do not record the discussions
undertaken by the labor camp delegates prior to their votes; we cannot tell at
present whether Friedman's election was contentious or imposed upon the
whole convention by a small group.

Worried about maintaining popular support on the island in the midst of
a massive cement industry strike there, Luis Muñoz Marín himself jumped
briefly into the fray, stating that he supported the New Jersey government's
investigation and was appalled that this sort of a "slipup" could have occurred. Fernando Sierra Berdecía granted a special interview to El *Mundo* in
which he asserted that agricultural work had no set minimum wage in the
United States. Puerto Rican workers, he insisted, were earning more than
the usual agricultural wages in New Jersey and rural New York. A few weeks
later, however, the New Jersey investigator contradicted Sierra Berdecía by
finding that Puerto Rican agricultural laborers had, indeed, been underpaid. They had the right to back pay; the Puerto Rican government could
help them file claims. El *Mundo*'s headlines proclaimed "Muñoz Intervened,"
despite providing no evidence of further efforts on his part on behalf of
Puerto Ricans in the New Jersey fields.[63]

Salvation in the Sugar Beet Fields?

After these collective Puerto Rican worker demands for justice, growers in
the mid-Atlantic states pulled back from large-scale agreements with the
PPD Department of Labor. By early 1950, Sierra Berdecía and Alan Perl, the
attorney for the Puerto Rican Department of Labor, were desperate. They
had made no headway in their attempts to win formal legal priority for
Puerto Ricans in northern agricultural interests' labor recruitment efforts.
No large-scale employment contracts had been signed for the coming spring

and summer. The flow of emigration off the island had to be increased, but New York City was bursting at the seams; the hard work of the PPD publicity teams to calm press coverage there was in jeopardy.

Alan Perl urged Sierra Berdecía to consider meeting with Louisiana sugar growers, despite the repugnance of their racial segregation policies; Sierra Berdecía refused. If the U.S. South remained off limits, Perl concluded, the Puerto Rican government had only one viable option left; he had been meeting with a man named Max Henderson, who represented sugar beet growers in Michigan. His organization, Michigan Field Crops, had made a verbal offer to employ five to eight thousand Puerto Ricans in the summer and fall of 1950. If this deal were sealed, it could be the key to creating a massive migration to the vast fields of the U.S. Midwest, far enough from New York City to prevent workers from "defecting" there, as they did from Eastern Seaboard farms.[64]

Eventually, tens, perhaps even hundreds of thousands of workers could be employed in the Upper Midwest, PPD officials soon began to assert. The *bracero* program, which for years had brought hundreds of thousands of Mexican workers to the United States, had run into legislative problems. If Puerto Ricans could supplant Mexicans in the international agricultural migrant labor flow, the island's "population problem" would certainly be solved. At the very minimum, the northern growing and harvest seasons of June through November meshed perfectly with the rhythms of sugar production; these were the months of Tiempo Muerto, when the Caribbean sugar fields offered no employment to the masses of Puerto Rican working people.

As talks with Max Henderson continued and his offer to employ five thousand Puerto Ricans in the Michigan beet fields during the summer and fall of 1950 solidified, along with promises for many more thousands of jobs in the future, PPD officials began to excitedly ruminate that such a migratory pattern could serve the Puerto Rican government well and also help meet working people's demands for stable, secure homes on the island. By migrating several months each year to earn a respectable income during the Puerto Rican sugar industry's "dead time" of June to November, male agricultural workers would not be consistently physically present to preside over their households. Their regular remittances, though, would enable their wives to create properly domestic homes, ready for their return. Cane cutters' wives, remaining in Puerto Rico, would now be able to enjoy stable homes and raise healthy, productive children.[65] Thus, fathers' emigration would help create Caribbean domesticity for women and children. The rural Puerto Rican family had to be stretched thousands of miles in order to be reconstituted in an acceptable form.

Concomitant with the sugar beet field deal, then, a domesticity ironically premised upon the absence of male heads of households became crucial to the Puerto Rican government's promotion of migration both in Puerto Rico and in the United States. Officials of the PPD painted the Michigan endeavor in particular as a permanent, cyclical movement, grounded in creating a sharply gendered but stable home in Puerto Rico, with women and children firmly anchored on the island, while the men ranged about earning a respectable income in the vast agricultural lands of the United States. Large Puerto Rican families would not "invade" rural mainland communities, as they had allegedly done in New York City. On the contrary, "the Islander is a responsible family man and cannot bear the thought of his family suffering hunger and hardships for lack of money which he can send them if he works hard. He is anxious to return home at the end of the season to his family and to his job during the sugar season. . . . We have reason to believe that about 98% of the workers return to Puerto Rico at the end of the agricultural season in the mainland."[66] Such an arrangement would confirm the new, allegedly collaborative relationship between the United States and Puerto Rico. Cooperation, not colonial exploitation, would mark interactions between the two peoples. "This way the continental farmers get the benefit of Puerto Rican workers and Puerto Rican workers expand their period of employment to eight or nine months a year. An American solution to an American problem."[67]

Thus, the sugar beet fields' promise of domestic harmony was a transnational proletarian one, not the classic bourgeois model so idealized by the ruling party in Puerto Rico. It depended on stretching the rural laboring family far beyond the limits of the island and on the prolonged absence of male heads of households from the very homes they hoped to rule. It claimed to serve the interests of both U.S. growers and working-class Puerto Ricans. It proclaimed a new, nonexploitative day for the previously contentious colonial relations between the United States and Puerto Rico. Ultimately, it would fail quite bitterly on all fronts, but no one knew this in the heady days preceding Operation Airlift to Michigan in the spring of 1950.

4

ARRIVING IN MICHIGAN
The Collapse of the Dream

I am now a Puerto Rican orphan, fatherless, and you were my father because I insisted upon it, lending you a hand so that you could be such. I helped you to become the father of all Puerto Ricans, but now I can help to find another father who will fight for his children when it is necessary. It's never too late and I am still young. • Antonio López Santiago

In March 1950, Puerto Rican Department of Labor officials, committed to stimulating migration, but eager to divert the massive flow of Puerto Ricans away from New York City, signed a contract with Michigan Field Crops to airlift five thousand men to the sugar beet fields of Michigan. Politicians in both the United States and Puerto Rico heralded the contract as the "biggest mass migration in commercial aviation history."[1] Officials at every level of the Puerto Rican government understood its importance. The newspaper El Mundo proclaimed momentously, "It is crucial that this excursion of workers to Michigan not fail. It has opened an opportunity for work, for this year and subsequent ones, to thousands of Puerto Rican workers. It also establishes

Salen 186 Obreros a "Buscar Ambiente" en Michigan

Recibiendo las últimas instrucciones, advertencias y consejos antes de abandonar por algunos meses la Isla para ir a ayudar a la agricultura continental a mantener su producción alta, un grupo de obreros agrícolas boricuas aparecen en la foto reconcentrados en una de las oficinas del Negociado de Empleos y Migración. En sus manos está el contrato de trabajo que han de firmar antes de sa-lir hacia Michigan, a trabajar en las plantaciones de remolacha, pepinillos, habichuelas tiernas y otros vegetales. Cerca de cada uno, a la mano, las maletas conteniendo ropa y enseres personales. La señora Petra América Pagán de Colón, directora del Negociado y el señor Rafael Arzuaga, funcionario del mismo, dan las instrucciones a los emigrantes. (Foto EL MUNDO.)

FIGURE 4.1 • Michigan airlift workers "seeking a better environment" in the sugar beet fields. El Mundo, June 2, 1950, 1.

a relational bridge for future emigrations to different points in the United States, which still is the land of opportunity."[2]

Puerto Rican state publicity for applications to the Michigan field operation enveloped the entire endeavor in an aura of scientific, regulated planning. The pro-PPD newspaper El Mundo displayed photos of top officials of the Division of Employment and Migration ceremoniously meeting the men departing for Michigan to review their belongings, explain their contracts, and "orient them for successful integration upon arrival" (fig. 4.1). This was a weighty state ritual, pointing toward a future filled with many more like it. The well-dressed, orderly men photographed seated in airplanes headed to Michigan, armed with their work contracts, constituted the chosen troops for the agricultural arm of Puerto Rico's drive toward productive modernity.[3]

The migration clearly held great appeal to laboring Puerto Ricans as well. Puerto Rican men flocked to the Michigan Program's recruiting stations, hoping to become successful breadwinning patriarchs—an as-yet only dreamed-of status for these men struggling with unrelenting unemployment or terribly low pay on the island.[4] Prosperous domesticity, they hoped, would now be within their families' grasp, even as they left their homes behind; the government had promised steady work, decent wages, and collaboration with American farmers. Modernity awaited them in this escape from the colonial oppression of Puerto Rico's cane fields and coffee farms.[5]

The migrants and their families could not know, however, that the sugar beet fields of Michigan were no less exploitative than the Caribbean sugarcane plantations from which they hoped to liberate themselves. Rural Michigan had undergone its own transformations since the introduction of sugar beet production; by 1950, the state's agricultural economy depended heavily upon tens of thousands of temporary migrant laborers who suffered terrible work and living conditions. In 1950, the majority of the sugar beet workers, who had for decades formed the backbone of Michigan's seasonal agricultural workforce, were actually U.S. citizens—Mexican Americans who traveled north from Texas each spring. However, rural Michiganians of European descent excluded from local citizenship rights these Tejanos who arrived every year to tend and harvest crops.

When the Puerto Rican men landed in the sugar beet fields, they were hailed by Michiganians as impressively modern migrants—responsible, hardworking fathers who stepped from airplanes, leaving their families behind at home, marking their adherence to proper domestic arrangements. But all expectations of modernity ended in disaster; the Puerto Ricans' anticipation of collaborative hard work, helping to sustain the U.S. sugar beet industry while sending ample paychecks back to create domesticity and prosperity in the island, quickly shattered. Colonial-like abuses, they found, were alive and well in the fields of Michigan. Equal, dignified U.S. citizenship was a chimera. Luis Muñoz Marín, their trusted political father, had failed them. They, in turn, were reduced to failed fathers themselves. Their enraged responses, rooted in their elevated expectations, past experiences of political mobilization, and the paternalist language of the Puerto Rican *brega*, would soon create a crisis for their beloved governor and his North American allies.

The Puerto Rican government's insistence that this latest migratory wave marked an important battle in the island's "war for modernity and progress" reverberated ironically through the history of midwestern sugar beet production. Sixty years earlier, many rural Michiganians themselves had responded enthusiastically to the promise of prosperous modernity through growing sugar beets. In the 1890s, nascent sugar beet companies in the United States seeking to fuse the crop's large-scale agricultural production with the factories needed to process it into granulated sugar fervently promoted a turn to near monocrop sugar beet planting in the Upper Midwest. This move to a globally marketable agricultural product, the sugar beet executives trumpeted, would modernize rural Michigan, Minnesota, and North Dakota, simultaneously bringing industrial jobs to small midwestern towns and nurturing the fortunes of local family farmers.[6]

Sugar beet companies invested primarily in building beet-processing factories in the northern midwestern countryside, rather than in owning land. The corporations' representatives did exert tremendous pressure on local farmers, however, to concentrate on sugar beets as a profitable cash crop with a national and even global market reach, unlike the regionally marketed food crops generally produced in Michigan. Once farmers in Michigan and elsewhere in the northern Midwest began to plant sugar beets on a large scale, the companies tried to assert control over crucial aspects of the crop's agricultural production as well, setting prices to be paid farmers, requiring large amounts of acreage to be dedicated to sugar beets (thus reducing farms' crop diversity), and establishing rigid schedules for the delivery of the sugar beets to the processing factories.

After the Spanish-American War of 1898, sugar beet capitalists also developed a sophisticated lobbying arm aimed at price supports for U.S.-produced beet sugar and at limitation of the cane sugar now flooding into the United States from its new tropical acquisitions of Cuba, the Philippines, and Puerto Rico. The sugar beet corporations pressed hard for stiff tariffs to be imposed on Cuban sugar and argued strenuously for Philippine independence in order to exclude its sugar from the United States. Puerto Rican sugar, produced in a colony with no strong independence movement in the early twentieth century and less threatening in its production levels, received less attention from the anti–tropical sugar lobbyists. Beet sugar, the lobbyists argued, should be prioritized over cane sugar not only because of its U.S.-based production; it was also inherently much more civilized, cultivated and harvested by native, white citizens. Cane sugar, on the other hand, was planted, cut, and ground by dark-skinned foreign workers, sweating away on backward tropical plantations, evoking haunting images of slavery and brutal colonial relations. In sugar beet corporate rhetoric, cane sugar production rested on exploitation; beet sugar supposedly embodied the free labor and democratic practices of yeoman U.S. farmers of western European descent.

But as sugar beet capitalists continued to try to limit the importation of cane sugar from abroad, by the 1910s they eagerly sought immigrant seasonal labor to cultivate and harvest the thousands of tons of sugar beets produced on upper midwestern farms, which had quickly outstripped local farmers' capacity to produce with their own families' labor. The sugar beet corporations generally provided the funds, transportation, and propaganda apparatuses necessary to recruit field-workers on a large scale. First, the sugar beet fields received eastern European families, often brought on trains from large urban centers such as Buffalo, Cleveland, and Chicago in the years surrounding World War I. Later, sugar beet corporations recruited thousands of Mexicans seeking work after the upheavals of the Mexican Revolution and the rural displacement that accompanied the postrevolutionary explosion of large-scale commercial cotton cultivation in northern Mexico; by 1927, 75 percent of the sixteen thousand migrant sugar beet workers in Michigan were Mexican. The massive deportations of Mexican workers during the anti-immigrant hysteria of the 1930s pushed sugar beet companies to train their sights on Mexican American families living in South Texas. These Spanish-speaking U.S. citizens were later rejoined during World War II by relatively small numbers of single Mexican men arriving through the auspices of the *bracero* program. Throughout the 1940s, however, and certainly by 1950, when the Puerto Ricans arrived, the sugar beets were tended and harvested primarily by Tejanos.[7]

Thus, in sugar beet-producing areas of the U.S. Midwest, geographically mobile, meagerly remunerated migrant labor quickly became crucial to the survival of the new, modern system of family farming, now driven by the mass production and industrial processing of a single crop for global markets. Despite sugar beet growers' and company representatives' constant invocation of the traditional family farm in Michigan, local sugar beet farmers' labor relations, crop production strategies, and markets had radically changed within a few decades.

In the process, labor practices themselves shifted dramatically. Like the tropically produced cane sugar with which it competed internationally, sugar beet cultivation required a terribly grueling labor regime. The backbreaking stoop work required in the manual weeding, thinning, and harvesting of the giant sugar beets was widely recognized as the most demanding of all Michigan crops. It remains etched in the memories of Michigan farm owners and ex-migrant workers alike, even more than forty years after its disappearance due to mechanization. Anastacio Díaz, a Puerto Rican who had spent several years cutting cane on the island and who had "enjoyed" agricultural migrant work in New Jersey, subsequently tried his hand at working in Michigan sugar beets for a single growing season in 1949. This gentleman, brought to Michigan by a small independent labor recruiter a year before the great Puerto Rican airlift there, lasted only a few weeks in the sugar beet fields. He remembered: "That was the worst thing that I had ever done in my life! That work—it was AWFUL! Working bent over for twelve hours a day, hauling those great beets out of the ground—they weighed like balls of iron, it seemed! And how our backs hurt so terribly! Even the cane fields didn't hold a candle to how horrible that sugar beet labor was! Picking asparagus and strawberries in New Jersey was easy work—but those sugar beets—I'll never forget them."[8]

Bitter conflicts between local growers and the sugar beet companies over prices, land use, and subordination to factory schedules often exploded around the turn of the century. They continued to simmer through the 1930s, but by the early 1940s, the overwhelming need for large amounts of cheap, temporary labor seems to have brought farmers and sugar beet corporations to a relatively stable truce. Growers' associations, many of them originally founded to defend farmers' interests against the looming authority of the beet sugar companies, had by the end of World War II dedicated themselves to collaborating with the sugar beet corporations in the recruitment of migrant labor during the height of cultivation and harvesting seasons.[9]

Thus, the prosperity of modern Michigan sugar beet farmers and corporations alike quickly came to depend on the exploitation of peoples considered racially distinct and inferior by members of the permanent communities of the midwestern countryside. Massive numbers of migrant workers, paid excruciatingly low wages and afforded only marginal living conditions in the interest of higher profits for both growers and companies, had become the silent underpinning of modern family farm prosperity. Perhaps northern sugar beet harvests and tropical cane cutting were not such different endeavors after all.

The ubiquitous presence of outsider workers throughout the summer and fall became the unremarked centerpiece of rural Michigan's economy.

Sweating in the fields from sunrise to sundown, living in tents, refurbished chicken coops, and dusty shacks isolated far away from the growers' homes, seasonal migrant laborers remained invisible in the public chatter about native Michiganians' community events, even as their unrelenting, grinding work grew into an indispensable element of farmers' success. Maintaining the image of the independent Michigan family farm required that the plight of the state's migrant agricultural workers be "buried deep, as far as it could be buried."[10] The public documentary silence surrounding the tens of thousands of these ubiquitous workers is truly stunning. Post–World War II censuses, news stories, town directories, and newspaper columns about local residents' lives and community events made no mention whatsoever of agricultural migrants.[11] The local media explosion around the 1950 Puerto Rican migration to Michigan is even more striking when viewed in the context of the otherwise pervasive silence on migrant workers. Agricultural migrant laborers did surface periodically in police records; for example, 2.5 percent of the arrests between 1948 and 1951 in Mount Pleasant, Michigan ($N = 2,318$) were of Spanish-surnamed men, listed as originating in either South Texas or Mexico (overwhelmingly the former). None of these arrests received any comment in the local press, however, except, tellingly, those of the two altercations among Puerto Rican sugar beet workers in the summer of 1950.[12]

Michigan postwar novels and personal memoirs, however, tell a different tale. Here, migrant workers of Mexican descent constituted a powerful symbolic and thematic presence. In the 1950 novel *Cloud of Arrows*, for example, the poverty and degradation of Mexican American migrant laborers continually surfaced to contradict both Michigan's natural beauty and the luxurious lifestyle lived by its small-town elites.[13] Long-term elderly residents of sugar beet areas also remembered the migrants from South Texas vividly, even as they spoke of the migrants' poverty-stricken circumstances as natural and their cultural differences as frightening: "They used to come in trucks, lots of 'em, their children and all, jammed in. They stayed in these little places, only the size of a bed. You couldn't call them houses, even. They were a little scary, you know—they didn't know any English."[14]

Certainly, the fates of different migrant groups in the Michigan sugar beet fields varied over the decades. Many of the ethnic Germans who migrated from Russia to become synonymous with migrant sugar beet labor at the turn of the twentieth century were able to assimilate into the ranks of the prosperous farmers of German descent in Michigan. Land ownership and permanent settlement in Michigan were much more difficult for the Hungarians, Bohemians, Poles, and Romanians who followed them. By the late 1920s, however, when Mexicans dominated the migrant population, 88 percent of eastern European women migrants to Michigan sugar beet areas planted their own vegetable gardens; 60 percent owned chickens and 41 percent kept their own cows from which they could get milk, butter, and cheese.[15]

Mexican and, later, Tejano migrants never enjoyed such women-organized autonomous food production while working in the Michigan sugar beet fields; they were generally not granted gardening privileges, much less the possibility of permanent housing. Indeed, sugar beet company spokespeople claimed in the 1920s, as they were first recruiting Mexicans north, that Mexicans had no desire to become landowners, despite their country's recent revolution, fought in large part by peasants struggling to gain access to land. Sugar beet corporation representatives portrayed Mexicans as hardworking, docile people who would not stay in Michigan. Unlike the eastern Europeans, who had sought to remain and become citizens, Mexicans allegedly had an "innate homing instinct," which would draw them inexorably back to their native land.[16] This rhetoric reverberated uncannily, despite its alternative logic, with the assurances offered decades later by Puerto Rican officials in the small-town Michigan press of 1950 that Puerto Rican men would return home to their families at the end of the sugar beet harvest.

The early assumption of Mexicans' perennial return to their homelands, facilitated by the relatively fluid movement of people back and forth across the U.S.-Mexico border prior to 1920, soon took on the power of state coercion when during the late 1920s and '30s hundreds of thousands of people of Mexican descent suffered deportation from the United States, regardless of their citizenship or legal immigrant status. By the end of the 1930s, "Mexicans" of all kinds, whether born in the United States or not, were assumed in many parts of the country to be illegal, invading foreigners. "Mexican migrant labor was . . . constructed as an imported workforce. . . . Casting Mexicans as foreign distanced them both from Euro-Americans culturally and from the Southwest as a spatial referent: it stripped Mexicans of the claim of belonging that they had had as natives, even as conquered natives."[17] Permanent Michigan residents of European ancestry, who by the 1940s considered themselves white, continued to consider even the Tejanos, whose birthplace in Texas they readily acknowledged, as suspicious foreigners; their physical mobility, Spanish language, degraded living conditions, and invisible, sweated labor marked them as indelibly other. Citizens of Michigan they decidedly were not, regardless of whether they had been born in the United States.[18]

By 1950, when the five thousand Puerto Rican men eagerly signed up to "fly to prosperity" in the Michigan sugar beet fields, the structure of Michigan family farms had shifted even further. By the mid-twentieth century, most middling to prosperous farmers, regardless of the crop, employed seasonal migrant laborers during growing and harvest periods. The sugar beet areas depended primarily on Mexican American labor from South Texas; Michigan Field Crops, the largest Michigan sugar beet grower cooperative, contracted sixteen thousand Tejanos in 1949. Bay County alone received six thousand migrants from twenty-three counties in South Texas. Several thousand impoverished white and African American migrants arrived as well each year in Michigan's cherry, apple, and other fruit-producing regions from southern states, including Arkansas, the Missouri Ozarks, Kentucky, Louisiana, Georgia, and Tennessee. Michigan vegetable and fruit growers also experimented during the postwar years with recruiting Jamaicans and Bahamians. Throughout the late 1940s and early '50s, however, Tejanos dominated the massive migrant labor force in Michigan, second only to California's in its numbers.[19]

While growing dramatically in size, by the postwar period, Michigan family farms had been drawn into a matrix of regional industrial agribusiness that attempted to manage nearly 100,000 migrant workers each year. Behemoth corporations like Green Giant gobbled up the hundreds of small local companies dedicated to canning fruits and vegetables. Michigan acreage planted in sugar beets increased by 30 percent in just five years; in Bay County alone, the sugar beet acres leaped from 9,500 to 12,600 in a single year.[20] The individualized paternalism that had shaped the earlier relationship between hired hands and most Michigan farmers producing food for regional markets had nearly disappeared. In its place had emerged a giant industrial system, with growers quite distanced from the people who harvested their crops. As a local Michigan man mused in 1950,

> I don't believe the implications of the revolution in agriculture which has taken place in the last forty years are fully recognized. I grew up on a farm and worked on the farms until I was through college every summer. While I was a hired man I ate with the family, I talked over wages with the boss, it was a face-to-face relationship, but that is not true . . . in the employment of this migratory labor. . . . It is a fiction that John Smith, a farmer, employs a family of Spanish-speaking workers, . . . or whatever they may be who operate his field. I say "fiction," because when the representative of an industry recruits 10,000

or 13,000 American citizens in Texas, or 5,300 in Puerto Rico, or 13,000 in Mexico . . . it is as much of an industry problem as an industrial responsibility, as when the auto industry of Detroit, where I work, sends out orders or requests for more workers there.[21]

Indeed, any remaining hired hands who shared ethnic, cultural, and community identities with farmers and their families resisted association with sugar beet cultivation. This was left to "lowly migrants."[22]

Growers' associations reached across crop specializations to try to coordinate the passing of workers from one crop to the next, as farmers' labor demands shifted geographically through the summer and fall. These cooperatives also attempted to reduce the wage competition among farmers, which experienced migrant workers were sometimes able to manipulate to their advantage; grower organizations like Michigan Field Crops set across-the-board pay rates and labor terms for their member farmers, usually based on the acreage or pound picked, rather than on hourly wages. They also negotiated relations between the farmers and large agricultural corporations, such as Monitor Sugar, Michigan Sugar, or Green Giant.[23]

These developments in Michigan paralleled the rise of large-scale corporate agribusiness in the rest of the United States, a process that began in many parts of the country during the 1920s and '30s but accelerated dramatically during World War II. Agricultural corporations across the nation sought out a different sort of labor force. They needed massive numbers of workers in order to produce a constant surplus of laborers to whom extremely low wages could be paid. Such workers had to be migratory as well, moving in when needed and away once superfluous in the production process. After agricultural laborers' attempts at organizing unions on the West Coast across national and linguistic lines during the 1930s, corporate growers turned to the practice of contracts between national or local colonial government officials to bring foreign temporary laborers to their fields in a hopefully more controlled way. This "imported colonialism," deemed necessary during World War II's labor emergency, revived a practice common throughout much of the nineteenth century, but which had been outlawed in 1885, because of its resonances with slavery's denial of workers' rights to choose employers, quit, or move about physically. The bracero program, initiated between the U.S. and Mexican governments in 1942, was the most massive of these endeavors, ultimately bringing hundreds of thousands of Mexican men to work in U.S. agriculture over the course of more than twenty years.[24] In Michigan, however, in 1950, the huge migrant population remained a patchwork of domestic and foreign contract workers, which growers attempted to keep segregated by race and nationality. Tejanos constituted the vast majority of the migrant workers, particularly in the sugar beet fields.[25]

Despite the growers' attempts to recruit and manage smooth labor flows from outside the state, migrant labor in Michigan continued to be a messy, uncontrollable phenomenon in 1950. Growers had to contend with the ever-present allure of Michigan's urban centers, to which migrants on the farms "absconded" whenever possible. Entry-level work in auto plants could garner $1.50 per hour—more than quadruple the wages of a rural migrant laborer. But a complete transition to city life was difficult to accomplish. Growers held migrants' pay until the end of the season in order to keep them tied to the fields, and full-time, permanent work in the cities was not always readily available.[26]

The Mexican Americans from South Texas, who made up the great majority of the state's migrant laborers, presented the most complex challenge to Michigan growers. By the end of the 1930s, almost all the *betabeleros* from the U.S. Southwest drove in private trucks to Michigan in groups from their home communities. This, in addition to their intimate knowledge of both the sugar beet crop and the surrounding areas, gave them a distinct advantage over new workers dependent on the sugar beet growers for their transportation.[27]

Tejanos generally arrived in rural Michigan in late May, before the weeds grew too high. By exploiting all available family members' labor, they could accomplish several complete rounds of weeding, blocking, and thinning the sugar beet plants by late summer. They sought out better fields and less oppressive employers, and negotiated higher pay rates for fields with particularly advanced weeds. The women also trekked to nearby towns to purchase food in bulk and thus stretched their weekly family allowance further than if buying in high-priced grower-owned rural stores. In the long idle weeks between the sugar beet cultivation and harvest, the mobile Tejanos traveled to other parts of the region to crate apples and cherries, and pick cucumbers and corn, earning additional income. Some went to area cities such as Saginaw, Bay City, Detroit, and even Duluth and St. Paul, Minnesota, to work as temporary day laborers, and if they were very lucky, to work in factories. By 1950, Mexican Americans had established settled communities in all these cities, from which they continued to migrate annually to rural Michigan to work in the sugar beet and fruit harvests.[28]

Despite their relative autonomy of movement, Tejanos suffered terrible exploitation at both ends of the rural migratory cycle. In South Texas, rural and small-town Mexican Americans experienced intermittent, badly paid employment at best—even those with skills such as bricklaying or oil pipeline repair. They generally had no choice but to live in racially segregated areas with little to no access to plumbing, consistent schooling, or the right to vote. In Michigan, migrant field-workers frequently had to walk a mile or more to reach water wells from the ramshackle housing provided to them. The food rations, when offered, were meager and often rotten. Monetary advances for food were usually only a few dollars in cash or in company store credit each week for the sustenance of entire families. Pay was calculated based on acreage cleared or amount picked, not on an hourly wage; this system pushed parents to send their children into the fields to work grueling long days in all kinds of weather in order to increase the family's income.

Despite being U.S. citizens, Tejano migrant workers also generally lacked access to services such as health care and education in Michigan. Their constant physical movement and concomitant lack of a permanent, fixed place of residence condemned them to an effective state of noncitizenship. Michigan and federal labor regulations expressly excluded farm laborers, including children, from their protections. Michigan public health clinics commonly denied care to agricultural workers if migrant laborers could not provide proof of local residence for an entire year. Babies born to migrant working women in Michigan were three times more likely to die than those born to permanent residents. Many local school officials either ignored migrant children or resisted their entrance into Michigan classrooms. Only one out of every twenty-one migrant children eligible for school was enrolled in September 1950, although they were not explicitly barred from attending. Many migrant children in Michigan as old as thirteen or fourteen had never been in a school at all.[29]

Some level of public interest in the plight of migrant laborers had been building nationwide since the 1939 publication of John Steinbeck's epic novel *The Grapes of Wrath* and a series of federal hearings on migrant farm labor organized during the 1940s. By the late 1940s, some of Michigan's Consumers' League chapters, public health professionals, and education advocates had begun to press periodically for improved housing, wages, and social services for migrant agricultural laborers, the most sophisticated among them arguing that support for such workers and their families should be organized along their migratory paths, rather than through the piecemeal state-by-state methods that generally ended up failing them.[30]

In Michigan, however, most of these early petitions fell on deaf ears, whether in the state's governmental agencies or in its rural communities.

Indeed, Dionicio Valdés concludes that the 1940s marked increasingly intense discrimination against Tejanos in the Upper Midwest. Violent backlash was not uncommon by the end of the decade. While some local newspapers reported approvingly about Ku Klux Klan gatherings across the nation, many permanent Michigan residents were convinced, one person testified, "that every Texan family has syphilis. That is the common assumption. They are afraid to have these youngsters on the property. It is appalling ignorance." The minister of a Presbyterian church in Bay City had to hastily leave the state in 1947 "because, in his attempt to have something done [to change migrants' conditions], the people got aroused and hounded him out."[31]

Such responses to persistent social justice activism on behalf of migrants ensured that the fledgling outreach programs for migrant workers in Michigan organized by mainline Protestant denominations during the 1940s remained relatively toothless. Most of this work was dedicated to organizing family recreational evenings, hymn sings, and providing Bible classes and day care for migrant children. Very few of the volunteers denounced the terrible living and working conditions of the migrant families, reproducing the public silence on such matters among Michiganians. Instead, the church volunteers often collaborated closely with the growers, discouraging "discontented murmurings" among adult field-workers and urging the laborers to work through the end of their contracts. The outreach workers' main interest seemed to be in the migrant children, who they saw as more open to the Protestant religious message. Evangelizing volunteers strove to teach the children "more hygienic ways of living," assimilate them into Anglo-American culture, and convert them from Catholicism to Protestantism. Periodic comments in the outreach reports about migrant children's ravenous hunger or terrible housing were always cheerily swept aside in the glowing accounts of the "love and deep affection" that blossomed between church volunteers and migrant youngsters.[32]

The Catholic Church in Michigan also established some social services in the 1940s for rural migrant workers, such as a health clinic in the city of Saginaw. More radical individual Catholics in Detroit periodically called for unionization of migrant workers and decried their exploitation. Father Clement Kern of Detroit was one of the most consistent of these Catholic voices in Michigan from the mid-1940s until his death in the 1980s. He fought tirelessly for better material conditions for Michigan's migrant laborers.[33]

Institutionally, however, the Catholic Church accomplished little in the way of consistent advocacy on behalf of seasonal agricultural laborers prior to 1950. William Murphy, the Catholic Bishop of Saginaw Diocese, stopped short of pressing for workers' collective organization and instead emphasized "ministry to the migrant soul" and access to basic social services such as health care. Similar efforts to provide Spanish-language mass, religious instruction, and "wholesome recreation activities" were launched by priests "imported" from Latin America by the Saginaw Diocese during the late 1940s and 1950s who were assigned to ten different parishes around the state during the summer months. These clerics seem to have avoided openly denouncing migrants' working and living conditions.[34]

The Tejanos persevered as best they could, though, placing a premium on physical mobility rather than fighting for political recognition in Michigan or membership in Michigan unions. Before 1950, the vast majority of the Tejanos in Michigan traveled and labored in extended family groups. Tejana women procured and prepared food, cleaned the meager home quarters, mended clothing, and cared for children in addition to working ten- to twelve-hour days in the fields, generally not sleeping more than three or four hours per night. When possible, they cooked food and washed clothes for single male migrants in order to earn extra income. Such efforts allowed Elisa Ochoa and her husband Manuel to put a down payment on land in Croswell, Michigan, where they eventually settled after years of migrating back and forth from South Texas. Children as young as six also periodically worked in the fields; by the age of fourteen almost all labored full time beside adults. An older man generally served as the head of each household; he received all pay for the entire group at the end of the harvesting season, which was calculated based on amount of acreage cleared and picked rather than hours worked. The older men also maintained work discipline over women and junior members of the group. Through immense collective effort and sacrifice, Tejano families often managed to bring savings with them back to Texas.[35]

The Turn to Puerto Rican Migrants

By importing Puerto Rican workers, the Michigan sugar beet industry representatives hoped to eventually ease their dependence on the relatively autonomous Tejanos, who comprised the majority of the sugar beet labor force in Michigan. The sugar beet industry also feared that recent pressure from the U.S. labor movement, most notably the National Farm Labor Union, spelled the end of the federal government's bracero program, which had begun to bring temporary agricultural workers from Mexico.[36] The new Puerto Rican workers, unfamiliar with the Michigan context, unable to move about independently, and tied to their families who still resided in their homeland, appealed greatly to sugar beet growers and corporations. To both Puerto Rican government officials and Michigan agriculturalists, this seemed a match made in heaven.

Eulalio Torres, the PPD's point man for public opinion management and worker oversight in Michigan, met with local reporters and community leaders to quell their worries that Puerto Ricans would remain in the area after the harvest. He assured them that these were a "higher type of worker"; all the Puerto Ricans had been submitted to police background checks, medical examinations, and employer references. They were "steady, married men" whose wives and children would remain on the island. Despite their status as U.S. citizens, the men would certainly return to their families once the harvest was over in December. This was also the beginning of sugarcane season; since the majority of the men had been employed regularly in the cane fields, Torres claimed, they could return to their jobs there.[37]

On the island, the Puerto Rican government painted the Michigan migration as part of a grand cause, emblematic of the new reciprocal relationship between the two nations, in which Puerto Rico would aid the United States. Island newspapers quoted Michigan growers in claiming that one-third of the sugar beet yields would be lost without the Puerto Ricans. "'These men are good workers and literally have saved our harvest.'" Other articles announced that from Florida to Hawaii to New Jersey, Puerto Rican agricultural laborers had demonstrated their "work ethic, good faith, and spirit of service" by uplifting U.S. agriculture. The New York Times as well as Michigan newspapers echoed this redemptive rhetoric.[38]

While allegedly bolstering the fortunes of both U.S. agriculturalists and Puerto Rican workers, the Michigan migration also served a powerful individual political need. Fred Crawford, the Republican representative to Congress from Michigan's sugar beet–growing Eighth District, was a longtime Washington ally of Puerto Rican governor Luis Muñoz Marín. Crawford had worked as a sugar beet company executive from 1917 until he won his Michigan congressional seat in 1934. Since then, Crawford had continued to influence inter-American sugar politics, sitting on the Congress's Committee on Territories and Insular Affairs and the Public Lands Committee, vantage points from which he could survey and build relationships with elites from the U.S.-controlled sugar-producing islands of Puerto Rico, Hawaii, and Saint Croix, among others. As a senior member of these committees, Crawford had supported the passage of Puerto Rico's 1941 Land Law (a product of the first PPD-dominated island legislature, which had the potential to break up large sugar estates and thus reduce sugarcane production in Puerto Rico), advocated for U.S. aid to Puerto Rico, coauthored the legislation that authorized direct elections for the island's governor in 1948, defended Puerto Ricans when they were not accepted into the U.S. Marines after World War II, and forcefully promoted the new PPD constitution, which proposed reform rather than rupturing of colonial relations with the United States. A fervent anticommunist, Crawford touted Muñoz Marín's political and economic project of modernizing colonial reform as a powerful antidote to potentially more radical rumblings elsewhere in Latin America and the Caribbean. By 1950, then, Luis Muñoz Marín had accumulated a decade of weighty political debts to the Michigan politician.[39] Now Crawford faced a tough battle with a labor union–backed candidate to maintain his seat in Congress, accused by many in his district of spending too much time on foreign policy issues and neglecting his own constituents' concerns. If Puerto Ricans filled an important gap in Michigan's sugar beet labor needs, Crawford might quiet such criticisms.[40]

The Puerto Rican sugar beet field migration, then, lay at the nexus of a complex network of colonial alliances and dependencies, all portrayed by the PPD press in Puerto Rico, Crawford, and head executives of Michigan sugar beet companies and grower associations as part of a new relationship of reciprocity between Puerto Rico and the United States. Puerto Rican workers would alleviate an alleged labor shortage for sugar beet growers; the sugar beet harvest, in turn, would ease Puerto Rico's crippling unemployment. One sugar beet representative waxed eloquent in his recapitulation of the PPD's developmentalist discourse: "Many persons do not realize that Puerto Ricans are American citizens the same as Hawaiians or Alaskans. They are entitled to the same rights and conditions granted any citizen. . . . Puerto Rico has an advanced educational system and the country is trying desperately to establish a sound economy."[41]

Fred Crawford also drew on PPD rhetoric when he proclaimed, "They have a pressure of population in Puerto Rico which is no less than fantastic." Consequently, Michigan needed to "absorb" 25,000 to 50,000 Puerto Ricans per year and "work them into our society, into our institution in agriculture and industry, and thus provide some place in the sun for them. . . . It is the duty of the people of the United States to fix it so they can have work." Otherwise, the island would become a resource-sucking tax burden, Crawford warned.[42] Michigan agriculturalists' benevolence could provide a dignified, migratory way of life for working Puerto Ricans. Colonialism could be transformed into collaboration, with politicians on each end claiming that their constituents would uplift the others.

A Masculine, Modern Migration

Working-class Puerto Ricans responded enthusiastically to the calls for travel to Michigan. From all over the island, men lined up by the thousands for the opportunity to participate in this great modern international physical movement of men. The applicants for the Michigan Program came from every single municipality on the island. Based on a random sample of the applications saved by the Puerto Rican Department of Labor, 7 percent lived in major urban areas, 28 percent in the mountainous municipalities in the center of the island, and 65 percent in rural coastal areas where sugar production reigned supreme. They ranged in age from twenty-one to fifty-two; 55 percent were in their twenties, 35 percent in their thirties, and 10 percent were mature fathers (and perhaps grandfathers) in their forties and fifties. Some 94 percent of the men had been agricultural laborers their entire lives, and 23 percent of these tended food crops, often in conjunction with coffee or tobacco. Also, 67 percent of the agricultural laborers worked in sugarcane fields, either as their sole source of income or moving back and forth from cane cutting to coffee, tobacco, or food crop cultivation. Only 1 percent of the applicants owned more than a small *parcela*-sized plot of land, and 6 percent of the applicants were artisans such as carpenters, painters, and masons, or exercised other nonagricultural professions such as clerk, messenger, or restaurant waiter. Half of these men, however, even those living in bustling urban centers such as Santurce or San Juan, split their time between agricultural wage earning and their artisanal occupations—an indication of how linked rural and urban life continued to be in Puerto Rico. Unsurprisingly, given its general avoidance of explicit discussions of race, the PPD government did not record information on the applicants' racial identities. However, we can gather from newspaper photos that the migrants to Michigan were quite a multiracial group; they encompassed a wide range of skin colors and phenotypes. Eighty percent of them had dependents for whom they were economically responsible—sometimes as many as eight or ten—although only half of them were formally married. This also is no surprise, given the propensity of Puerto Rico's laboring population for living in consensual union. Prosperous modernity, enabling respectable proletarian domesticity, seemed within these men's grasp as they waited in long lines to relate their personal information to the interviewers.[43]

Disaster awaited the hopeful men, however. An airplane carrying sixty-two workers to Michigan crashed on June 5, 1950, a few days after the airlift began, killing twenty-seven of the men. While the Puerto Rican legislature briefly halted all flights to the sugar beet fields until safer (and more expensive) airlines could be contracted, Luis Muñoz Marín quickly moved to assure the sugar beet industry representatives that they would not have to bear any of the increased costs, even if this meant charging the men for transportation.[44] No notice of these new arrangements, needless to say, was passed on to the workers filling the planes to Michigan.

The crash drew international attention to the airlift. The men were transformed overnight into martyrs and celebrities in Puerto Rico.[45] In Michigan, "an aroused public" worried about another potential "invasion of foreigners." More liberal voices in the Michigan press continued to insist that Puerto Ricans were destined to be allies in sugar beet production.[46]

The Puerto Rican government now had to explain and defend the airlift even more carefully. The opposition newspaper El Imparcial pounded out criticisms of the Puerto Rican government for not inspecting the planes properly and not insisting from the outset on the use of a regulated international airline.[47] In response, the pro-PPD newspaper El Mundo trumpeted the news repeatedly in the days following the tragic crash that thousands of men continued to board the planes in a valiant act of fatherhood, even risking death in their resolve to provide for their families. Photos of grieving, hungry wives and children of the men killed in the crash reminded the Puerto Rican public of the domestic needs that fueled the brave "agricultural troops'" departure for "the cause of Michigan." One widow cried "'I didn't want him to go. He did it because he wanted to save some money to buy us a little house.'"[48] Images of the men waiting in orderly, even cheerful fashion at the airport appeared continually. Such representations likened the Michigan migrants to the Puerto Rican soldiers departing for Korea to "save democracy."[49]

In an act that brought accolades in the Michigan and New York City press, Luis Muñoz Marín quickly made arrangements with Pan American and Eastern airlines to carry out a massive transportation operation, sending nine nonstop two-thousand-mile flights a day between Puerto Rico and the Bay City, Michigan, airport. Journalists and politicians alike touted the "largest emergency airlift in commercial aviation history" as a sign of the cooperation between Michigan and Puerto Rico.[50] Even small-town Michigan newspapers broke their stoic silence about migrant farm labor to publish lengthy articles about the airlift.[51] The hair-raising story of the plane crash and the sensational airborne efforts to save both workers and the sugar beet harvest transformed the arrival of the Puerto Ricans in Michigan into a thrilling tale of the potential dangers and redemptive possibilities of modern technology.

"A critical shortage of migrant field hands that threatened what is expected to be a $14 million sugar beet harvest next fall will now have been averted, and the miracle of modern air transportation will have again broken through the obstacles of time and space."[52] Photos of the huge airplanes and their dashing flight crews filled the pages of local newspapers, with headlines like "Operation Farmlift Bigtime Aviation Job."[53]

Hundreds of people from all over the sugar beet region of central Michigan crowded into the Tri-City airport outside Bay City to see the Puerto Ricans land. County sheriffs had to be called in to contain the excited Michiganians from pressing too close.[54] Sixty years later, rural Michigan residents still vividly remembered the Puerto Ricans' arrival, as they disembarked from roaring airplanes, dapperly dressed in shiny dress shoes, jaunty hats, suit jackets, and ties. Contemporary Michigan press photos of the men portrayed them as happy vacationers, with their crisp hats, formal suits, and carefully packed luggage in hand. This seemed a different sort of agricultural migration indeed, its modern, adventurous aura a far cry from the dusty, unkempt vehicles filled with Mexican Americans that lumbered into Michigan from Texas each spring.[55] Excitement filled the air as the Puerto Ricans boarded the trucks that would transport them to the sugar beet fields.[56]

A Crisis of Fatherhood: Protests from Michigan

Buoyed by the cheering crowds who greeted them, their PPD-sponsored contracts that guaranteed them several months of solidly remunerated work, and their own government's drumbeat of valiant manhood and familial sacrifice for the cause of prosperous, modern domesticity and collaboration between the United States and Puerto Rico, the Puerto Ricans could hardly have known that they would encounter the terrible wages, repulsive housing, and degrading conditions with which Texans of Mexican descent had long contended. Within weeks of their arrival in Michigan, Puerto Rican workers began to protest their living conditions and contract violations in letters to family members and island newspapers, particularly the opposition daily El Imparcial. This rapid explosion of worker outrage was particularly striking, given the Puerto Ricans' inability to communicate effectively with each other in Michigan. Unlike the impressive but short-lived New Jersey demonstration of 1949, where the aggrieved Puerto Rican men had already shared a journey to work on farms in Washington State before being transported en masse to a New Jersey migrant camp that housed hundreds of them together, the men in the sugar beet fields were isolated from each other on individual farms. Initially, they could not have known whether fellow Puerto Ricans beyond the small groups of six to ten men housed on each farm might be protesting their situation.

But protest they did, and quite vociferously. They might have been considered excess citizens by politicians, but these agricultural workers expected to be treated with dignity, live in sanitary housing, and earn an hourly wage from which they could send frequent payments home. The years of political and labor mobilization in Puerto Rico had taught them this much. The men were also keenly aware of the power of the press; not infrequently, they sent separate notes to family members instructing them to share their letters with newspapers in Puerto Rico before sending them along to Luis Muñoz Marín's offices. They also wrote to the Red Cross and to the Puerto Rican government's offices in New York City. They exhorted their wives to travel to San Juan to personally exert pressure on the central government there. They even wrote to popular musicians like the famous *décima* composer Tonín Romero, asking them to write songs about the horrors of Michigan sugar beet exploitation and sing them in concerts and on radio programs.[57]

Often, individual men composed protest letters on behalf of themselves and the rest of their work crew. Generally, these "field scribes" wrote in flowing penmanship, fluid language, and impeccable grammar; they seem to have served as informal worker lawyers, reading contracts carefully and insisting on their enforcement. Other Puerto Rican migrants penned their protests in cramped, shaky handwriting, scratching out misspelled words with great difficulty. Whether highly articulate or barely literate, these migrants drew on the popular political mobilizations of the preceding decades in Puerto Rico. "Workers have rights that cannot be ignored!" they shouted. "Contracts must be honored! We must have hygienic housing!"[58] Throughout the months of July, August, and September 1950, El Imparcial provided almost daily reports of problems in Michigan, summarizing the bundles of worker letters that arrived at their offices and printing some letters in their entirety. The newspaper soon sent a reporter to Michigan to cover the story (fig. 4.2).

Despite the almost immediate flood of letters to Puerto Rican newspapers protesting Michigan conditions, PPD officials minimized the problems, while the pro-PPD newspaper El Mundo maintained a studied silence about the protests. Instead, El Mundo obsessively discussed the Puerto Rican government's success in ensuring airline regulation to avoid future plane crashes and printed several letters from readers praising the government's speedy, effective intervention in regulatory matters. The newspaper printed only two letters of protest from Michigan-based workers after the pressure to investigate the sugar beet field exploitation had become unbearable.[59]

FIGURE 4.2 • A group of workers in Michigan who wrote protest letters to the Puerto Rican press. The photo's headline reads: "They Describe Horrors in the Michigan Countryside." "Protestan de maltrato," El Imparcial, July 9, 1950.

Manuel Cabranes, head of the New York City Migration Bureau office of the Puerto Rican government, visited the sugar beet fields in late June, only three weeks after the men had arrived. Although he heard many bitter complaints, he reassured the Puerto Rican reading public that the workers' pay would be adequate. Eulalio Torres, sent from the Chicago office of the PPD Migration Bureau in June, insisted that the main problem was "a lack of orientation among our men" and assured his superiors on the island that "with rare exceptions, [he] found that the directors of the company and their employees were humanitarian people, very interested in the well-being of the recently arrived workers."[60] El Mundo even published a propaganda piece from the Michigan growers' representative, Max Henderson, claiming that all the workers "are very enthusiastic about their life and work conditions."[61] The Puerto Ricans working in the sugar beet fields could not have disagreed more.

The men warned that they were scattered on farms throughout a 1,200-square-mile radius, with no mobility or means of communication other than occasional company trucks. They lived jammed eight to ten men in one-room cabins or tents with little to no plumbing or cooking facilities, sleeping on the ground, or on beds of bug-infested straw, frozen and soaked to the bone in rainy weather from the uncontrollable leaks in walls and roofs. They were unable to communicate with the farmers, if they ever actually saw them. The only source of provisions was high-priced rural stores where the company truck drivers took them to spend their weekly food allowance of $5. This meager amount, which frequently ran out before the end of the week, leaving them without food for days at a stretch, was their only regular access to cash. Michigan Field Crops insisted on holding all pay until the end of the harvest season in December, despite the Puerto Rican contract's clear statement that the men were to be paid biweekly. In addition, the sugar beet industry supervisors calculated eventual pay based on their own measurement of acreage cleared, planted, and tended, rather than the Puerto Ricans' expected hourly rate. When Puerto Ricans protested this method of payment, they were told "only Americans were paid by the hour." Citizens of the United States they might be, but the Puerto Ricans discovered that, like the Mexican Americans from Texas, Michigan growers and work supervisors considered them exploitable foreigners, not equal collaborators in "the cause of the harvest."

Growers also charged workers inflated rates for work-related medical costs. Finally, despite promises to the contrary, Michigan Field Crops deducted alleged costs of the Puerto Ricans' transportation—not only from the island but also to and from the fields each day—from pay balances. These deductions left pay "advances," when they were delivered, of $1 to $7 for many weeks'—sometimes months'—worth of grueling twelve-hour-per-day work. Not infrequently, men even received statements that they owed the growers money. "If we refuse to go where they take us, they order us to be thrown into the street with nothing to eat. . . . They wake us up at 4:00 AM and they bring us back at 7:00 PM. . . . The coffee arrives as cold as the tongue of a dead man. I tell you, we are worse off than prisoners in a concentration camp."[62]

The Puerto Rican workers agreed that piecework pay, even if delivered, would be untenable. Unionized cane cutters had fought hard to eliminate piecework (al ajuste) in Puerto Rico's sugarcane fields during the 1930s and early 1940s. The PPD legislature's implementation of a minimum hourly wage, which attempted to claim these struggles as the party's provenance, marked an important advance for island workers. For some men, the resentment engendered by the *ajuste* payment may have stemmed from a clash of expectations rather than actual experience with hourly wages alone. Piecework payment was still practiced in Puerto Rico for a few job categories in both sugar and coffee production. Payment *al ajuste* in Puerto Rico, however, was made weekly, not at the end of the season, as in rural Michigan. Certainly, the workers traveling to harvest beets hoped to escape the exploitation implicit in piecework wages. In addition, home needlework, performed by more than fifty thousand rural women, probably including many mothers, wives, and daughters of the sugar beet migrants, remained one of the few industries in Puerto Rico still paid solely "by the bundle" in 1950. Thus, the sugar beet industry's insistence on paying the men *al ajuste* rather than by the hour was doubly demeaning. It evoked both the exploitation that Puerto Rican men struggled to surmount, and women's work—by 1950, piecework was a degrading, even feminized payment method.[63]

Complaints of substandard housing and insufficient food also voiced humiliations far deeper than simple material deprivation. As we have seen, for the landless *agregados,* building one's own home on a separate *parcela* plot of land constituted an essential assertion of dignity and autonomy from large landowners, escaping the most degrading aspect of rural impoverishment. Likewise, buying food in a company-controlled store on credit to the landowner had been a bitter daily enactment of rural wage laborers' near bondage. Responding to worker demands, the PPD had instituted a number of important changes during the 1940s that challenged such relations of power in the countryside, including the *parcela* program, the abolition of payment in store tokens, and the severing of direct relations between local stores and large landowners. In 1948, Eric Wolf reported that "the free wage worker is no longer interested in obtaining [company-provided housing and credit], which are part of a lower standard of living. He recalls how personal relationships with a landowner also made him dependent on a single individual."[64] Single-sex collective housing in agricultural labor evoked echoes of the *barracones* in which enslaved workers had been forced to live. Thus, the sugar beet fields' lack of independent housing and purchasing power meant both the erasure of the last decade's gains and the betrayal of PPD promises of a prosperous, modern future. They constituted, in essence, the denial of domesticity—even the return to slavery.

Puerto Ricans were no strangers to hard agricultural labor—cutting cane and picking coffee was grueling, badly paid work. But this situation, they chorused, was worse than any exploitation they had experienced in Puerto

Rico—or even in other migrations to the United States.[65] Not only were they not paid, but they suffered terrible personal treatment—kicked awake in the morning and forced to work when seriously ill. Pablo Tirado, for example, faced down an abusive supervisor who tried to force his hunger-weakened coworkers into the fields. "During those days when our food ran out, I went to work, but the others, who were terribly weak, couldn't get up. Then the boss wanted to make me go make the other two work. Only God and my own discipline saved he and I from going to the point of no return. But my attitude and my eyes told him everything, and he never tried to approach me again."[66] Others exclaimed, "These Americans are savages. . . . From what I have seen, these people are not human."[67] Indeed, these northern fields evoked the most oppressive part of Puerto Rico's past; repeatedly the workers cried out that they had been sent to plantations, to be treated as slaves.[68] And under these conditions—twelve-hour days for nothing but inadequate food—the Puerto Ricans were not far from the truth. Such condemnations exposed the bitter reality behind the PPD's claims to be building a fraternal, familial relationship with the United States.

The men felt this lack of independence in the sugar beet fields particularly acutely in women's absence. Working-class men throughout Puerto Rico refused to mend clothes, clean homes, cook, wash dishes and clothes, or empty chamber pots. These domestic tasks were unequivocally women's responsibility; no self-respecting man would perform them under normal conditions. Women's physical care, serving of food, and sexual availability were some of the few daily pleasures and experiences of power for working-class men. Isolated and without transportation in Michigan, the sugar beet workers could not even visit local towns to find prostitutes or other female domestic care. Such enforced heterosexual abstinence must have been even more acutely painful since they were unable to keep their own partners on the island under proper sexual surveillance. For Puerto Rican men, "it [was] an indescribably humiliating experience for a man to be made a cuckold." In Puerto Rican towns, cities, and the sugarcane regions, this must have been a substantial worry, since women commonly left partners who proved unable to provide financially.[69] Thus, men's concerns about sexual control of women on the island, as well as wage and reproductive labor, underlay the Michigan migrants' protests.

The contradictions between Luis Muñoz Marín's promised international *brega* and the men's lived reality screamed from El Imparcial's headlines about the Michigan debacle: "'Slavery in the middle of the twentieth century and under the North American flag, symbol of liberty.'"[70] The pact with the

United States that guaranteed honorable collaboration in place of the infantilizing colonialism that had long humiliated Puerto Rico seemed a pathetic chimera. "The United States, which we thought was our country, and our President Truman have betrayed and forgotten us," wrote Tito Oriol Colón to Luis Muñoz Marín. He apologized for his sharp words, which he hoped would not "damage the friendship between Puerto Rico and the United States. . . . Señor Luis, I am sure that you know President Truman well, the workings of his heart also. Please don't let these people in Michigan punish Truman's brothers and the other migrants here. We Puerto Ricans are ready to leave our island to give our lives for democracy and fight against Communism [in Korea]. We shouldn't be abandoned to evil like this."[71]

When workers threatened to call on Puerto Rican government officials to investigate conditions, they faced jeers from North American employees of Michigan Field Crops: "You people don't even have a government."[72] Exploitation, threats to masculine pride, and colonial disempowerment resonated together and put the lie to hopes of *bregando* a mutually respectful international relationship between dignified fathers.

The sugar beet fields of Michigan, then, constituted the worst imaginable conditions—denying the men the right to the small pleasures of female physical care and sexual services, erasing the possibility of developing a paternalist relationship with the landowner, refusing them the dignity of a calculable, reliable weekly wage, and reducing them to utter physical dependency, sometimes wrapped in openly colonial garb. The combination of structural exploitation and capricious abuses the Puerto Ricans encountered in the sugar beet fields threatened to strip them of their hard-won manhood in many ways. Over and over again, workers protested at how they had been "deceived like children" (*engañados como nenes*). They had been dehumanized, practically reduced to animals; migrants to Michigan frequently wrote of being "treated like pigs," "sold like cattle to a slaughterhouse," "killing ourselves working like oxen."[73]

But through it all, the Puerto Rican workers asserted their status as honorable men. They and their wives spoke proudly of them being "good husbands, good fathers, and above all, hard-working, despite being of humble background." They reminded the government of their military service in World War II, fighting to defend the United States where they now, ironically, suffered such cruel conditions. "I have continued to fulfill my obligations, like a gentleman. . . . I have been one of the best, doing my duty by the farmer, helping him resolve his problems."[74] They knew how to stand up to adversity. They wanted very much to work, but not for "this irresponsible company."[75]

An urgent fatherly responsibility also permeated every single one of the letters. Even before mentioning their own hunger and suffering in the beet fields, these men cried out in a chorus of desperation—"Our children will starve in Puerto Rico if we do not send them money!" Wives' daily requests for money and vivid descriptions of the suffering of families on the island intensified the men's heartfelt concern for their families. "What is it worth, Mr. Governor, for us to eat, if our children and wives cannot?"[76] "Our wives are asking us to send them money, even if it's just to buy a pound of rice. Even though we are working we can't send them anything—we're going crazy!" The men invoked the suffering and undeniable human value of their families to counteract the grinding, dehumanizing exploitation they faced each day.[77]

A Defiant Edge: From Petition to Protest

Repeatedly, the Puerto Rican agricultural migrants called on Luis Muñoz Marín to help them provide for their families—as the father of the nation, he had the responsibility to support them in fulfilling their paternal responsibilities.[78] Numerous letters employed the classic paternalist language of political supplication—"I come before you, as if you were my father, to request that you do right by this humble Puerto Rican."[79] A few even linked Muñoz Marín with God and divine intervention, as was common in letters to the governor throughout the 1940s.[80]

But now, in this moment of disillusionment and crisis in a foreign land following years of populist mobilization on the island, most letters from Michigan contained an egalitarian edge absent from other migrants' expressions of need. Of the sugar beet field letters kept in PPD archives, 65 percent articulated either a direct defiance of Muñoz Marín's authority or a mix of political egalitarianism, warning, and petition for paternalist intervention. Only one-third of the sugar beet workers wrote to the governor solely as humble supplicants. This stands in stark contrast to those sent to Muñoz Marín from earlier émigrés; between 1945 and 1949 more than three-fifths of the letters that Puerto Rican migrants penned to their governor from the United States deferentially requested that he provide them with aid, employment, or other resources. Even when recounting PPD activism in order to legitimize their pleas, petitioning letters to Luis Muñoz Marín from the 1940s did not have the egalitarian, often even demanding or warning tone that permeated so many of the sugar beet migrants' missives from Michigan.[81]

Miguel Casul, for example, assured Muñoz Marín that he had fought in World War II "for the Americans' cause"; he had fought for the cause of justice in Puerto Rico by organizing for the PPD; he was willing to continue struggling for the "cause of Michigan with [his] labor"; but he needed to know that those in power would fulfill their responsibilities to support him in his struggles. "As a poor man I have many who follow me and we all helped to raise up [subir] our glorious Popular Party." He closed his letter by placing himself on an equal footing with Muñoz Marín: "I bid you farewell as a man who has fought and who will continue to fight together with you as a compatriot."[82] The majority of these workers were not simply humble supplicants, beseeching a superior for his charity. Rather, they presented themselves as political equals, honorable men, on whose shoulders rode the leader of their nation.

Even many of those who used the language of paternal hierarchy slipped subtle criticism into their letters. Marcial Montalvo wrote: "Since today you are the father of Puerto Rico, we have no one to whom to deliver our complaints, go and see what you can do, since you are near to my father and kids. Even if it was only a peso which I earned with my sweat, I always helped them, but then I took off to this place to see if I could earn more money to keep helping them and now all I can do is die of the cold." Montalvo created a subtle, yet stinging contrast between his own ability to care for his family, even when penniless, and Muñoz Marín's failure to deliver on his promises of support. Montalvo had proven his own fatherly capacity time and time again. What of Muñoz Marín?[83]

Workers and their wives frequently referred to their political activity on behalf of Muñoz Marín and his party. They thus asserted their right to official attention and implicitly demanded that the state—and Muñoz Marín personally—comply with a basic political quid pro quo: We put you into office. Now you owe us. Brega con nosostros. Deal with us. "I ask you as the faithful Popular that I have been, that you change your mind and if you put this project together to help us, the neediest of Puerto Rico, and if you keep on helping us, we will keep helping you, if only with our vote—we have nothing else to give." "We want to remind Mr. Muñoz Marín of when he was poor and he would travel through the backroads with us 'guayucos'; we ask him to help us now, before our children and wives die of hunger." Others gave their anger full rein: "Ask Rodolfo Rodríguez how we did political work in our community, spending long days without eating, just working on your behalf. And look at how you do nothing for us now."[84] These working men had offered their vote and labor as political activists, expecting the state's protection, advocacy, and access to a decent wage and stable home in exchange. They mixed requests for paternal protection with assertions of political partnership. Within their invocations of faithful party work lurked an implicit threat: We created your power. We can take it away as well.

Indeed, as conditions in the sugar beet fields failed to improve, the growers continued to withhold pay, and Puerto Rican state representatives refused to intervene systematically on behalf of the workers, many men and their wives unveiled these threats. Their letters burned with anger. Gloria López of Caguas, a worker's wife, raged: "Do you think that we can last three months without eating? You certainly wouldn't be happy if the government stopped paying you for that long." Others asked, "How would you like to be one of us?" or commented sarcastically, "It seems that this contract was not made by a worker, but one who wants to live off the workers."[85]

Some of the sugar beet workers began to openly and angrily challenge PPD hegemony—22 percent of the letters written directly to the government, and at least 45 percent of those published in El Imparcial between July and December 1950, were unequivocally defiant. "Mi estimado Luisito," Teófilo Caro commenced, with crackling sarcasm, not only denying Muñoz Marín his customary title of "don" or "Señor," but reducing him to the dimunitive, childlike form of address, "Luisito, you know that the elections are two years away and I think that the Popular Party has lost more than 5,000 votes." Everyone in his family was a fervent Popular, Caro recounted. All of them had worked hard on behalf of the party. "But if you don't cooperate with my family at home and here," they were all poised to vote against Muñoz Marín.[86] The poor, once politically empowered, could be dangerous if betrayed, Rafael Arroyo warned. "They said that we would have good housing and beds. Where is that? They said that in Michigan the pay was good and there was abundant work. Where is that? . . . You had better fight for us because 5,000 men can easily defeat your party."[87] The poor had built this government. They considered it theirs. Rural working men and women could bring it down, some insisted, if it no longer served them.

Fully one-half of those who did retain some elements of supplication in their letters now mixed their pleas with enraged defiance or political warnings, speaking as both vulnerable sons and wronged fathers. Inocencio Ortiz swore that his paternal dignity had been destroyed. He would not succumb again to such treatment. He also desperately needed Muñoz Marín's help in the moment, however.[88] Speaking warmly, intimately, as if a trusted advisor to the governor, Rejustino de Jesús warned Muñoz Marín of a potential storm of opposition, even as he asserted his political loyalty and asked for protection:

I want you, Honorable Don Luis, as our leader in Puerto Rico, to tell me if you have authority to protect us or not.

You know very well that your offerings to the people of Puerto Rico are great and among them is the cooperation of the workers. We need your aid now if you are going to need us in the future. Mr. Marín, I don't want you to take this as a criticism of the United States, but since you are the only one who can resolve this case with your power, you must protect us. I have heard many criticisms of you here, some founded and some unfounded.

I will not stop being a Popular because of the false agreements, but as a good citizen I want our suffering workers to be watched over. We cannot let this go any further. Now is the time to correct them. And as I told you before, "You are the only one who can save" our situation.[89]

The sons of Puerto Rico had been empowered by their sustained political activism and Muñoz Marín's promises of solidarity and prosperity. They could now demand, threaten, and advise even as they sought fatherly intervention from their leader. Their *brega* had developed a new edge, threatening to break the restraints of Puerto Rico's paternalism.

The Puerto Rican migrants to Michigan seem to have been deeply moved by the PPD's rhetoric, which had called upon them to leave their homes in order to sustain them. Expectations of increased material comforts, private space, and sturdy homes with which to envelop their wives and children fueled the men's decision to join Operation Farmlift. But now, abused, hungry, and without pay for weeks, the men raged at their inability to perform fatherhood effectively. Now they had neither women's presence and succor nor a claim to patriarchal legitimacy. Their absence meant economic desperation, not abundance. Domesticity had been denied, fatherly responsibilities thwarted.

Fatherhood operated on many levels in this postwar political moment, however. Not only the migrants were failing in their paternal duties. Muñoz Marín had led his sons into a situation that sent them sliding back into exploitation reminiscent of slavery and the most naked of colonial brutalities, not into a prosperous modernity created by collaboration between equal partners, as he had promised. This was a shocking betrayal of fathers, by their own political father.

The Puerto Ricans' response came swiftly and sharply, honed by their recent experiences in political organizing on the island. Calling out to family members, the press, unions, local government officials, and the governor himself in Puerto Rico, they vividly and persistently denounced the abuses they encountered in Michigan. Elevated in island public opinion for their braving of dangerous air travel to advance the cause of both Puerto Rican and Michigan prosperity, these men's protests resonated deeply with their homeland's public. They particularly worried PPD officials in this historical moment, when Puerto Ricans were debating the merits of a new constitution and its framing of U.S. colonial rule. In Michigan, too, in the backyard of Muñoz Marín's colonial benefactor Fred Crawford, where they were supposed to be opening the way for tens of thousands more future emigrants, migrant workers' discontent posed potentially acute problems. Puerto Rican politicians feared that the migrants' protests might scuttle the PPD's well-laid plans for colonial reform, payment of international political debts, and redirection of the island's excess population. Their political ramifications grew even further in the eyes of anxious officials as the migrant men built connections with liberals in Michigan's urban areas and with Tejano migrants, and as their women family members launched their own multifaceted *bregas* back on the island.

5

THE *BREGA* EXPANDS

Puerto Rico has contributed its sons in two wars to defend democracy. We four are all veterans of these wars. The American People can rest assured of our co-operation in this new conflict as we did in the other two wars—fighting under the same flag and the same God. We want to complete this harvest. We want to support our families. • Saturno Quiñones and the Committee of Publicity, Unionville, Michigan

I could not be a priest for five minutes if I did not stand up and protest against the horrible concept that men with families can get along without money to send to those families! • Father Clement Kern, September 1950

Puerto Rican beet workers' multiple *brega* strategies were not limited to their relationship with Luis Muñoz Marín and their government. Tejanos whom they met in the sugar beet fields offered them aid, information, and acts of solidarity. The Puerto Ricans launched collective protests, built relationships with church outreach volunteers, and wrote to Michigan newspapers to publicize their exploitation. Many Puerto Ricans also defiantly left the sugar beet fields entirely, often in groups. Some made their way to Detroit, following the advice of friendly Tejanos. They found encouragement in that city's Holy Trinity Catholic parish, where they organized jointly with Mexican Americans to denounce the treatment they had endured. The priests at

Holy Trinity also connected the Puerto Ricans with Detroit labor activists and other liberal sympathizers. Moved by the Puerto Ricans' stories and their presentation as faithful fathers struggling to create domesticity in their homeland, urban social reform advocates in Michigan in turn helped create a public outcry in the local press about the conditions these migrants faced.

Thus, the Puerto Ricans managed to recruit allies in far wider circles than their physical isolation in the fields might suggest was possible. Back on the island, female relatives of the sugar beet workers continued to pressure both the migrant men and the Puerto Rican government to provide an acceptable resolution of their families' economic crises. These combined efforts forced the Puerto Rican press and state to acknowledge the severity of the situation, when in August 1950, the island legislature passed a historic bill allotting funds for aid to the Michigan migrants and their families.

Both Michigan and island strategies for denouncing the sugar beet exploitation drew heavily on the expectations of domesticity with which the Puerto Rican government's propaganda had saturated the Michigan migration, asserting the Puerto Ricans' worthy citizenship in respectable gendered terms that distanced them from the implicitly racialized language of disrepute and disease that plagued their fellow islanders in New York City. Tragically, these domesticity discourses also helped erase or even denigrate the Tejanos' presence in Michigan, despite the Mexican Americans' own long history of labor in the sugar beet fields and their support of the Puerto Rican migrants. Such political language, then, created false distinctions between migrant groups in the spotlight of public concern, even as the migrant laborers reached out to each other in solidarity.

By late summer, thousands of the Puerto Rican workers had left the beet fields, determined to assert their dignity and find less exploitative work. They and their women relatives' refusal to accept the terms imposed upon them in Michigan forced the growers and the Puerto Rican government to make concessions. In an effort to stem the mass rejection of sugar beet labor, the growers offered a new contract to the workers and the PPD government passed a law—the first of its kind—offering financial aid to the Michigan workers' families. The attempts by the powerful to appease popular concerns had little effect, however; by midfall, fewer than 25 percent of the original migrants remained to finish their contracts with Michigan Field Crops. For a moment, Muñoz Marín's fatherly glow seemed to have lost its power, at least for these survivors of its betrayal.

In the midst of this political crisis, though, exploded another more dramatic one, which would eclipse its predecessor. The PPD state's fusion of repression and anticommunist hysteria in response to the Nationalist Party's rebellion of November 1, 1950, distracted the Puerto Rican public from the earlier crisis of the sugar beet fields, and facilitated the migrants' permanent political marginalization or physical dislocation.

Michigan Solidarities

Despite their relative isolation from each other, many of the Puerto Rican migrants crossed paths rather quickly with Tejano families. The Puerto Ricans' letters hinted at a diversity of experience with the Mexican Americans they met in the sugar beet region. Consistently, they acknowledged the Tejanos' greater resources and longer experience in the area. Puerto Ricans also wrote that when employed as supervisors and truck drivers Mexican Americans could be just as abusive as the growers, deducting unauthorized amounts from their pay and giving preferential treatment to other Mexican Americans.[1] Most often, however, Puerto Ricans acknowledged the solidarity they experienced with Tejano field workers. Mexican Americans shared food and shelter, offered insights, and eventually provided transportation into the migrant job network that stretched throughout the Midwest and West Coast. Tejanos also shared information about potential allies in the region, pointing the way to Father Clement Kern's parish in Detroit.

Mexican Americans themselves could be advocates for Puerto Ricans. The twenty-three men led by Álvaro González Reyes, who had served as a member of the PPD organizing committee back home in Camuy, for example, told of a "Mexican friend," Joe Chávez, living on a neighboring farm, who had written petitions for them, "a man who has been the only one who has done anything he could for us. . . . He has been almost a father to us." Chávez's caring paternal interventions starkly contrasted with the lack of protection offered them by the Puerto Rican state. This kind advocate was probably the Tejano Joseph Chávez who testified in the hearings held in Michigan during September by the President's Commission on Migratory Labor. This man enjoyed a relatively privileged position among Michigan migrant laborers, having returned to the same farm near Bay City for five years, where he and his family lived in a concrete house with electricity.[2]

Building on the knowledge gained from Tejano allies and on their island's political culture of party propaganda and union organizing, Puerto Rican beet workers reached beyond their isolation on the remote farms to communicate with Michigan permanent residents. On June 23, only two weeks after their arrival in Michigan, a group of fifteen Puerto Rican workers left the farms to which they had been assigned in Saginaw County to gather at a countryside road crossing in protest. By the time the local sheriff arrived to examine the situation, the group had grown to forty men, who demanded a meeting with a Puerto Rican government official. Echoing the events a year earlier in New Jersey, the men finally agreed to return to work after speaking with a Puerto Rican official and a representative of Michigan Field Crops.[3]

Sixty Puerto Rican workers who had the relative good fortune to be housed together in a migrant camp near Eaton Rapids made a deep impression on a small group of Protestant church women accustomed to providing summer recreational activities for Tejano children. Shocked to find this group of single men in a camp occupied in past years by Mexican American families, the church ladies were even more surprised when the Puerto Ricans "immediately" protested their conditions, showing the church workers contracts that guaranteed three meals per day and hourly wages paid biweekly. After several weeks of no pay other than their minimal food allotment, the men were enraged. "And they struck. They would not even take the $5 [for food]." While persistently expressing outrage at their working and living conditions and their inability to send funds to their families on the island, the Puerto Ricans "came to be great friends" with the women, visiting them in their homes and requesting English lessons, "to better communicate with Americans."[4]

The political utility of such communication became apparent before long. In late July, just as top Puerto Rican state officials were visiting the beet fields in response to political pressure on the island, a group of Puerto Rican workers on a farm near Unionville, calling themselves "the committee of publicity," sent a letter to the *Detroit Free Press*. Their leader, Saturno Quiñones, thanked the people of Michigan for being "very friendly and without discriminating due to race, language, or position" in their treatment of Puerto Ricans. He wrote of "fraternity between the United States and Puerto Rico," invoked his and his coworkers' status as World War II veterans, and expressed their willingness to "cooperate in this new conflict [the Korean War] as [they] did in the other two wars—fighting under the same flag and the same God."[5]

A month earlier, Saturno Quiñones and eleven other men had been some of the first to pen an indignant letter to Luis Muñoz Marín, describing their terrible living and working conditions in great detail and insisting that he intervene to end the exploitation of all Puerto Ricans in Michigan. They closed their communication to Muñoz Marín quite formally: "We Puerto Ricans and American citizens hold the Puerto Rican government responsible for this situation. We respectfully request that your honor take the appropriate actions to resolve this problem." Muñoz Marín's top aide, Gustavo Agraít, marked this letter in red as urgently requiring a thank you from the director of the Department of Labor. However, this response clearly was not satisfactory; when their own government failed them, the men, at least those who remained on the farm a month later, seem to have attempted to seek out new allies, using different tactics.[6]

Clearly, Quiñones and his coworkers were not blindly celebrating U.S. benevolence in their letter to the Detroit newspaper; they were acutely aware of the migration's exploitative conditions as well as the potential weight of their U.S. citizenship. Rather, they were engaging in a sophisticated brega, utilizing different tactics to speak to a variety of audiences, attempting to build alliances with a broader Michigan public beyond the hostile treatment they faced in the fields. If they employed the discourse of militarized, masculine reciprocity, of cooperation in the struggle against a common enemy, the committee of publicity seems to have hoped, they might indeed spark such collaboration with urban Michigan residents—this time, against an opponent much closer to home. Such political moves insisted on Puerto Ricans' right to full citizenship in the United States' emerging liberal postwar polity.[7]

Over one hundred Puerto Rican beet workers—among them Pablo Tirado, who had faced down the abusive farmer—managed to walk several days through the countryside or catch rides in the dead of night to arrive in Detroit where they found their way to the Holy Trinity Catholic parish of Father Clement Kern, the priest renowned in the area as an advocate of labor rights and migrant agricultural laborers.[8] These Puerto Ricans probably discovered Holy Trinity Parish through the help of Tejanos. At Holy Trinity, Father Kern and his assistant from Mexico, Father Talavera, urged the men to record descriptions of their recruitment, exploitation, and subsequent departure from the fields: "They put us on trucks and sent us out to work without eating. And how could we work for $19 an acre when we were 8 men and *we were all fathers of families* and the farmer said that if we didn't like it we could walk to New York along the highway and we left, walking, walking 200 miles."[9] In mid-July, a group of these Puerto Ricans and several Mexican Americans held a public meeting supported by Talavera and Kern where they announced the formation of the Beet Workers' Defense Committee, an organization that would publicize the plight of all those suffering in the Michigan fields. Taking advantage of contacts offered by Father Kern, the Puerto Ricans began meeting with AFL and CIO representatives, social workers, teachers, members of the Detroit Consumers' League, and local journalists.

Within a few weeks, they had forced a discussion of their situation within the Michigan Department of Labor and had pushed Michigan Field Crops to the bargaining table with Puerto Rican government officials.[10]

The Puerto Rican migrants' organizing efforts had other ripple effects. Interested labor organizers, for example, brought liberal activist Presbyterian minister R. Norman Hughes of Bay City to investigate Puerto Ricans' working conditions.[11] After a group of Puerto Rican workers showed him through the camp where they were "imprisoned," an appalled Hughes returned with Leonard Jackson, a *Bay City Times* reporter, and Democratic State Representative Robert Chase, a sympathetic prolabor politician, in tow. Jackson, in turn, produced a national award-winning series of newspaper articles in the *Bay City Times* denouncing the Puerto Ricans' suffering. Representative Chase used the Puerto Ricans' plight to condemn treatment of migrant workers in Michigan as "'man's inhumanity to man.'" The Puerto Ricans' accusations of mistreatment, unfair pay, and contract violations rapidly became a contentious issue in Fred Crawford's reelection battle. The debates they engendered also undergirded much of the testimony in the Saginaw hearings of the President's Commission on Migratory Labor and its final report.[12] The sugar beet field workers, then, developed multifaceted, strategic *bregas* with European Americans: collective protests; building relationships with individuals; use of the press to celebrate a fictitious but potential solidarity between equals; and, whenever possible, pushing their North American allies to publicize their denunciations of agricultural exploitation in Michigan.

Women *Bregando*

Back on the island, the migrants' women relatives also spoke as political actors, using a variety of tactics. Some, like Carmen González Crespo, mobilized the paternalist familial discourse of the PPD in their appeals for government intervention: "I simply ask that you place your noble heart into the most perfect union with this mother of a family to . . . return to our side the man who is father of his children and who only with his presence can alleviate the arduous task of creating happiness in our family."[13] Virginia Nieves took a different tack. She simultaneously proclaimed her loyalty to the PPD and threatened Muñoz Marín: "Remember that we are yours, and will always be. I don't want this letter to get into the newspapers or the radio because I find those sorts of things embarrassing. But if nothing changes, I have the right to complain, and I can make public the letters my husband sends me."[14] Felícita López de Vásquez fairly shouted in her letter to Muñoz Marín:

And the worst of all is that after we, the poor, built up a government as worthy as ours, now we have been forgotten and our situation worsens every day, to the point that our husbands have been deceived and sent to serve foreign countries and then they don't pay them. And we wives don't receive any aid from the government; they just talk at us all day in the newspapers and over the radio. Mr. Governor, if you don't change your tactics and protect us some other way, this brilliant handiwork that we made can come tumbling down.[15]

Female anger and disillusionment spelled great potential political trouble—as much as, or perhaps even more than, the male migrants'. The women were still resident on the island. Not only could they vote, they were also adept at mobilizing community opinion through informal social networks. Several of the female relatives of Michigan migrants whose letters appeared in the Archivo General de Puerto Rico's archival collections on the crisis had also served as organizers or officers of local neighborhood PPD committees or were members of unions; they wielded particular institutional clout.

Throughout the island, women relatives of Michigan migrants wrote hundreds of letters and made innumerable personal pilgrimages to government offices in San Juan and local towns asking for aid, investigation of conditions in Michigan, and airfare to bring the men back home. They forwarded their husbands' letters to Muñoz Marín and to a plethora of government agencies and press offices to illustrate the gravity of the situation. They visited the offices of newspapers to publicize their and their husbands' suffering. They spoke on the radio. Thus, while Puerto Rican men struggled to earn income and sway public opinion in Michigan, their partners, wives, and mothers helped create acute public awareness in Puerto Rico of the migration's human costs.[16]

The women also wrote frequently to their husbands asking them to send money, sometimes accusing them of squandering the imagined riches earned p'allá afuera.[17] The men in Michigan read these letters aloud to each other as they arrived in the daily mail deliveries, creating an inescapable collective awareness of their families' needs on the island.[18] Women's pressures on both the Puerto Rican state and the workers in the beet fields ensured that men's responsibilities to support their families financially remained a primary focus of this crisis's public face. By sending private letters to the press and to the government, the sugar beet workers' partners and mothers elevated family news into a transnational political crisis. They had used "one of the most powerful of female weapons: the weapon of scandal, the loud venting of information and accusation in a manner that forced public resolution of a matter heretofore private or discreet."[19] The PPD's promises of husbandly support clearly had failed. Neither their own partners nor the Puerto Rican state had complied with their pledges of benevolent patriarchal protection. The women's actions reminded all parties involved that leaving families behind did not mean the end of men's financial responsibility to them.

Women's individual pressures on their partners and sons expressed privately the tensions flowing through working-class gender relations over the earning and dispensing of income within families. Men also worried about the frightening prospect of their partners leaving them for more reliable family providers. As noted in chapter 4, this possibility loomed large for the male migrants; Puerto Rican women had a long history of seeking out more dependable sources of male income if prevented access to a partner's wage.[20] Thus, the letters from the Michigan migrants' wives that constantly pressured the men to send money home carried weighty veiled threats for their husbands.

However, these potentially bitter gender conflicts remained concealed in the public controversy over the exploitation of male workers on Michigan farms. Women's letters to newspapers and politicians breathed not one word about their worries of men squandering the income earned abroad. The possibility of men's sexual alliances with women other than their wives, a prominent theme in many male-dominant historical processes or social movements throughout Latin America, was also absent from the public discourse about the Puerto Rican sugar beet field crisis.[21] Rather, when speaking or writing in public, working men and women collaborated in creating a political discourse that located all sources of discord outside of the family. Their protests defended exploited yet honorable fathers and denounced the failure of politicians' paternalism. This is not surprising, considering that women family members, male sugar beet workers, and Puerto Rican state officials all were deeply invested in presenting the workers as responsible family men, unswervingly faithful to the wives and children who remained on the island, and posing no threat—sexual or otherwise—to the U.S. communities to which they had traveled.

Working women and men sustained another discourse rooted in the PPD ideals of modern domesticity. For years, Puerto Rican government officials had exalted the role of housewife and had insisted that in the new, modern Puerto Rico, women should be contained within the home. They had continued these assertions in their propaganda efforts in New York City and in Michigan. Now working women turned these domestically focused representations to their own uses. Women relatives of the Michigan migrants presented themselves, and were also generally portrayed by the press and the male migrants, as being utterly homebound, completely dependent on their husbands' wages, passive victims of U.S. farmers' rapacious profit mongering and of the Puerto Rican government's neglect.

Certainly, Puerto Rican working-class women could not easily thrive without a male income, but probably relatively few were housewives with no income. Most women of the rural laboring classes earned income of their own; this money often constituted a substantial part of their household budget. Raising and marketing livestock, eggs, and produce from small family plots, taking in washing and piecework sewing, manufacturing and selling home-brewed liquor, cooking and vending prepared foods, and selling tickets for *bolita*, the ubiquitous illegal lottery—Puerto Rican women had long engaged in a constant *brega* of their own to ensure their families' survival.[22]

The Michigan migrants' wives and partners also did everything in their power to keep themselves and their families alive. They demanded the attention of officials at the government's housing agency, insisting (often in vain) that they be given privileged access to apartments in the new public housing projects. They attempted to negotiate medical services for ill parents and children. They applied for additional jobs everywhere they could think, took up peddling, and played creditors against each other, taking new loans to pay off old debts. They leaned on extended families for food, clothing, shelter, and money to pay bills. They gleaned help from neighbors and fellow community members as well, like José Cáceres Vélez, a small-town store owner who fed his emigrant friend's wife and children for almost three months as they waited for their husband's Michigan earnings to arrive.

But all their resourcefulness was not enough. Women's anguish intensified as money from abroad failed to materialize. By late August 1950, many had sick children and elderly parents whose medical conditions had become quite grave from lack of treatment. Scores of families suffered evictions from inability to pay rent. All were deeply in debt and faced the end of their credit extensions from local stores—"Now," they chorused, "we will surely starve!" The women's and their husbands' deepening indebtedness constituted a spiraling internationalized family economic crisis.[23]

The helpless wife, like the faithful, hardworking father, became a primary icon of the Michigan scandal, one that could goad as well as beseech. Denunciations like this one peppered public discussions of the beet field disaster: "It was clear that married men with families were unable to wait until 'the work was completed' to send money to their families or to live themselves. . . . Certainly, their families could not perform the biological miracle of living without eating until some remote future date."[24] Women relatives of the Michigan migrants simultaneously exposed the cruel reality of the PPD's rhetoric of genteel domesticity and used this discourse's power to lend legitimacy to their demands for state intervention.

Indeed, women became crucial mediators of information. Their persistent demands on the state, funneling of anecdotes to the island press and radio stations, pressure on their husbands in Michigan, and constant conversations in the houses, streets, marketplaces, and agency waiting rooms of Puerto Rico fed the political crisis that so unnerved Muñoz Marín and his inner circle of advisors. The women's grievances recognized no geographical boundaries.

The Crisis Widens: From Puerto Rico to Michigan and Back Again

Events unfolding in Washington, DC, intensified the effects of the beet field–related denunciations. In July 1950, after several years of negotiation with the PPD government, the United States agreed to allow a voter referendum in Puerto Rico on a new constitution for the governance of the island. The United States hoped that this move would alleviate the international pressure for decolonization that had built after World War II. Puerto Ricans would now be able to constitute their own local government; the U.S. Congress would no longer be able to alter the structure of the insular government unilaterally. Puerto Ricans would not, however, be offered the options of becoming a U.S. state or of choosing national independence. Thus, the paths opened to Hawaii and the Philippines, respectively, were denied to Puerto Rico. In addition, Puerto Rico would still remain subject to federal laws and regulations. Despite the fact that the new document did not substantively change the terms of the political or economic relationship between Puerto Rico and the United States, top PPD officials touted it as a profound transformation of the colonialism under which their island had chafed for so long. They based their claims on a clause which stated that the relationship between the two polities would now be considered a compact, a freely chosen affiliation. If confirmed by popular vote, PPD leaders insisted, the Estado Libre Asociado would embody the fruition of the long-discussed dignified collaboration between the two peoples. Economic and political dependency on the United States could not be colonial if the Puerto Rican people voted to endorse them.

The debates over Puerto Rico's political status, quite heated since the purges of independence supporters from the ranks of the PPD in the latter half of the 1940s, intensified even further. Independence advocates denigrated the new constitution and its referendum as a continuation of colonialism in new garb, while PPD leaders faithful to Muñoz Marín's vision passionately defended it as the necessary next step toward the island's economic and political well-being.[25] Thus, in 1950, the PPD top brass were deeply embroiled in a tug-of-war with their own citizens over what Paul Kramer calls "the politics of recognition"—"a calibrated mixture of empowerment and disenfranchisement" that would eventually stabilize colonialism.[26]

Puerto Rican state officials strove mightily to promote their own vision of the terms by which Puerto Rican sovereignty would be determined. Ultimately, the Puerto Rican electorate's approval of the Estado Libre Asociado's constitution in June 1951 and its eventual ratification by the U.S. Congress and the United Nations would consolidate this type of flexible hegemonic colonialism in Puerto Rico.[27] In the summer of 1950, however, the outcome of these political struggles was quite unclear.

To the anxious leaders of the PPD, the sugar beet field crisis seemed capable of derailing their whole drive toward confirming a new colonial political order. It exponentially multiplied the intensity of the plethora of demands advanced by the variety of groups discussed in chapter 2, telescoping these persistent calls for decent wages and working conditions, social respect, and a stable home of their choice into a single, bitter outcry. The migrants to the Michigan beet fields seemed impossible to demonize. They had been heralded by the government itself as the harbingers of Puerto Rico's emigratory future. They had valiantly continued to "struggle for the cause" of good relations between the United States and Puerto Rico by risking death by airplane crash. For the most part, they positioned themselves as faithful PPD members, not advocates of independence. These men were neither political mavericks nor contenders for state power. They had the attention of the liberal and opposition press, both in Michigan and in Puerto Rico. Vito Marcantonio, the leftist, proindependence congressman from New York City, who had developed a large base of support among Puerto Ricans there, also took up the sugar beet migrants' cause.[28]

The potential for political fallout from the Michigan scandal, then, PPD leaders feared, loomed much larger than the possible loss of several thousand votes from men already physically removed from the island. The alternately anguished and angry protests by beet workers and their wives exposed the continuing exploitation experienced by Puerto Rican migrants to the United States. In challenging the sugar beet field debacle, Puerto Ricans invoked their U.S. citizenship, their honorable man- and womanhood, and their right to respectable domesticity as powerful discursive weapons. In so doing, they implicitly raised profound questions about the workings of power in the postwar drive for modernity. Indeed, as Paul Kramer points out, despite its hegemonic masking power, "the politics of recognition also left colonial subjects with discursive resources."[29] The protests surrounding the Michigan migration could be interpreted to signify that colonial oppression had smashed hopes for honorable collaboration. The public scrutiny that the denunciations provoked potentially struck at the heart of the PPD's long-term political and economic project. It should not surprise us, then, that Muñoz Marín ordered his staff to carefully monitor all beet field–related events and communications, thus creating the impressive collections of documents held in the Archivo General de Puerto Rico.

Indeed, within a few weeks of the first disillusioned letters' publication on the island, Tomás Méndez Mejía, the national director of the General Confederation of Workers, Puerto Rico's combative opposition sugar industry union, had toured the beet fields. He returned to the island appalled at what he had seen and heard from his compatriots there. Fighting against PPD attempts to break up his union and in the midst of negotiating a relationship with the CIO in the United States, Méndez Mejía called a press conference on the island. There he denounced the beet workers' suffering and announced that the Michigan branch of the CIO had also found the treatment of farm workers deplorable.[30]

The PPD, as the alleged defender of the island's working classes, could no longer maintain its public silence on the Michigan debacle. Muñoz Marín did not visit the beet fields, but he had already sent many other top officials there to carry out investigations and mediate for the workers—the directors and their staffs of the New York and Chicago offices of Migration Services, and the lead representative of the Puerto Rican government on labor affairs to the U.S. federal government, to name just a few. On July 24, the head of Puerto Rico's Department of Labor, Fernando Sierra Berdecía, flew to Michigan to "discover the truth of the situation." Several weeks later, he confirmed many of the workers' allegations. Migrants and their families on the island had forged a new set of alliances on both the mainland and the island and had pressured their newly elected government back into the *brega*.[31]

The PPD's attempts to calm the worker outrage emanating from Michigan were much less successful than in the earlier New Jersey and Chicago migration controversies. Many more migrants had traveled to Michigan, and negotiation with them en masse was not possible. Sierra Berdecía and the other PPD officials assigned to managing the Michigan situation were unable to visit all, or even most, of the widely dispersed Puerto Rican workers in Michigan. Those migrants who did obtain meetings with government officials often remained dissatisfied, since their material circumstances did not change substantively. Their women partners on the island, left without dependable male income, continued to press for state intervention.

The widespread chorus of protest from Michigan, coupled with its complex international political context, created ever-larger political ripples in the U.S. Midwest and on the island. Puerto Ricans throughout the region—professionals in Detroit, industrial workers in Lorain and Youngstown, Ohio, recent emigrants to Chicago, all took up the cause of the sugar beet workers. They joined with local labor and church reform groups in Detroit, Bay City, and Saginaw to pressure the growers to improve the Puerto Ricans' conditions and pay.[32] Newspapers all over Michigan reported on the men's protests. The *New York Times* covered the crisis throughout the summer and fall of 1950. The *Bay City Times* ran a series of articles in August 1950 exposing the exploitative conditions (for which the reporter won the American Newspaper Guild's national prize for outstanding journalism). Newspapers in Italy, France, and Spain reported on the story as well.[33]

Picking up on the Puerto Rican workers' and government's drumbeat of respectable internationalized families, those who denounced the conditions of the beet fields and expressed sympathy for the Puerto Ricans' suffering consistently presented the workers as honest, honorable, hardworking family men, who had arrived to pull the beet industry out of a difficult situation. Over and over again, journalists, reformers, and U.S. labor and Puerto Rican state officials invoked the hunger and dependency of wives and children waiting desperately for wages to arrive in Puerto Rico. The linked images of honorable, wronged male wage earners in the U.S. beet fields and women's passive, homebound suffering (with the domestic sphere now extended to include the entire island) provided the conceptual underpinning for public outrage at the Puerto Ricans' treatment. A telling excerpt from Father Clement Kern's fiery speech at the federal hearings in Saginaw was reprinted in several newspapers: "'I could not be a priest for five minutes if I did not stand up and protest against the horrible concept that men with families can get along without money to send to those families.'" A Detroit labor newspaper confirmed this rhetoric in its article titled "Time Study Needed: Beet Workers Sleep on Ground in Michigan as Families Sell Furniture to Eat in Puerto Rico."[34]

Mexican Americans Denied

The public portrayal of Puerto Ricans contrasted markedly with that of Mexican American Tejanos who had labored in Michigan under terrible material conditions for decades. Except for Father Clement Kern, who persistently called for a union of all migrant laborers—but who was quoted consistently in 1950 Michigan newspapers referring solely to Puerto Ricans—urban journalists and others sympathetic to the Puerto Ricans remained silent about the plight of Mexican Americans and other sugar beet field laborers, erasing the other groups' long history of suffering and struggle in the region. Local Catholic newspapers decried Puerto Ricans' exploitation and scolded other media outlets for simply glorifying the technological success of the airlift, but said nothing about the tens of thousands of other migrant farm laborers in Michigan. National and local press coverage of the September 1950 federal hearings in Saginaw covered Puerto Ricans' testimony with great drama, but usually did not even mention the Tejano witnesses who also spoke. The Committee for the Defense of Beetworkers, although founded by a combination of Tejanos and Puerto Ricans with the Mexican priest Father Talavera, was generally referred to by the media as an organization established by Father Kern solely in conjunction with Puerto Ricans who had left the sugar beet fields.[35]

Mexican Americans appeared most frequently as the assumed but unstated contrast to the Puerto Ricans' manly, honorable, and disciplined work: "The fields have never looked so clean." "The farmers say: 'The best men we ever had,'" Puerto Rican officials and Michigan journalists alike trumpeted. Such comments attempted discursively to heal the wounds of emasculation reported by the Puerto Rican workers. Others criticized the system of family field labor used by the growers and most Mexican Americans as "artificial," the nefarious opposite of the dignified separation of Puerto Rican women from sugar beet production, which seemed a more natural family form.[36]

The director of the Puerto Rican Department of Labor, Fernando Sierra Berdecía, visited the sugar beet fields in July 1950 and commented on the earning and survival strategies Tejanos had developed.[37] Sierra Berdecía seemed not to consider the Tejanos' circumstances so miserable; exploitation, in his rendering of the situation, seemed reserved only for Puerto Ricans, who in their ignorance suffered unconscionable abuse at the hands of the rapacious sugar beet industry. Perhaps most obviously, Sierra Berdecía noted, women did not accompany the Puerto Rican men to tend to their needs or to labor alongside them in the fields. The family-based migrant housing, provision, and labor system in Michigan was at complete odds with the Puerto Rican ideal of autonomous individual male wage earners supporting a dependent family located in a separate, private sphere. Sierra Berdecía insisted that the Puerto Rican migrants' familial dispersion, with single men working for wages in Michigan and women and children assigned to the "home space" of the island, was much more respectable than that of the Tejanos who allegedly threw women and children into the field and carted full families around the country in a roving, unhygienic mass.[38]

Other brief direct mentions of Mexican American beet workers in public, written contexts often openly denigrated them. A *Detroit Free Press* article lauding the labor of the Puerto Ricans inserted a quick reference to police arrests of drunken Mexicans. The *Detroit Times* presented the Puerto Ricans as dapper, orderly, civilized men, U.S. citizens honoring and sheltered by U.S. democracy, a clear counterpoint to the diseased "Mexicans and Negroes" who comprised 50 percent of the patients in the local tuberculosis sanatorium:

> The Puerto Ricans are called "stoop workers" because of the back-bending work required of them. But few of them appear to deserve the name. Most of them are wearing sports jackets, slacks carefully pressed and sports shirts open at the neck. They step carefully around the mudholes at the airport so that their clean summer shoes will not be soiled. They are fancy dressers, most of them, despite their poverty. They are also hard workers, once their overalls are unpacked. . . . Most of the 5,000 workers will live in portable shacks resembling Detroit's voting booths.[39]

Thus, Puerto Ricans' defenders deemed them more respectable, more deserving, even more American, than Mexican Americans. They were presented as upstanding citizens, who had been shockingly denied their basic rights to life, liberty, and the pursuit of happiness. Ignoring the existence of the over 100,000 other migrant workers in the region (most of whom were American citizens as well), the journalist Gordon Blake wrote of the Puerto Ricans' experience: "This incident will ever remain a blot on the escutcheon of American justice and fair play. While we are fighting to make the world safe for democracy, America, it seems, is becoming less and less safe for Americans."[40] Despite their legal status as citizens, their consistent residence in the mainland United States, and their military service in U.S. wars, Mexican Americans apparently were not considered as fully American as Puerto Ricans. They had long been considered invisible or invading foreigners, discursively fused with allegedly illegal Mexicans; the liberal sympathy for Puerto Ricans only continued this pattern.[41]

This resulted in part from Puerto Ricans' supposedly more respectable gendered labor patterns, emphasized continually by the Puerto Rican government. Eulalio Torres, for example, in his meetings with Michigan journalists, helped produce passages like this one: "The greatest percentage of the men being brought to Michigan are married men with families. In previous years, men, women and children all made the trip to Michigan. But now only the male laborers are being brought from Puerto Rico. Families must remain at home. . . . All are clean and well-dressed. They have good luggage and are young and healthy. They are a far cry from the motley crowds that used to roll into Michigan each spring."[42]

Other factors certainly influenced the different portrayals of the two groups. The long-standing relationship of Puerto Rican cane cutters, tobacco rollers, and stevedores with U.S.-based unions that had been organizing on the island for decades stood them in good stead; the CIO had begun a new organizing drive in Puerto Rico just as the Michigan scandal exploded. The industrial labor movement in Michigan's cities increased dramatically during the postwar years, expanding membership rapidly and electing candidates sympathetic to labor's concerns at the state level. Consequently, the protesting Puerto Ricans found an interested public among Michigan's politicians, organizers, and journalists linked to the labor movement as well as among the women leaders of Michigan's Consumers' League chapters in Flint, Detroit, Bay City, and Lansing.[43] Mainline Protestant denominations also harbored preexisting interests in Puerto Rico, having established missions and active congregations there after the U.S. invasion of the island in 1898. Liberal church members and pastors who were already involved in organizing for international peace and racial justice in Michigan cities also took up the Puerto Ricans' cause.[44]

In addition, the Puerto Ricans were clearly temporary workers. Small in number when compared to the other migrant groups laboring in the midwestern fields, and yearning to return to their families in the Caribbean, they posed no permanent settlement risk. Their children did not swell school populations, introducing threatening "foreign" influences to rural communities, as did the Tejanos' children. Isolated on farms without transportation, Puerto Rican sugar beet workers were unable to visit local towns and disturb the peace with fiestas and communal public presences.[45]

Finally, and perhaps most importantly, the Puerto Ricans arrived in the beet fields relatively politically empowered. They had brought the PPD and

Luis Muñoz Marín to power on the island. They had helped build a fresh political culture of protest and electoral organizing in Puerto Rico. They were flush with expectations about encountering material prosperity and equal treatment as citizens of the United States, expectations nurtured continually by PPD propaganda in Puerto Rico. Indeed, PPD rhetoric often equated the reformed relationship between Puerto Rico and the United States with the new relationships being promoted between men and women on the island. Both would be emptied of their previously oppressive, conflictual elements, to be replaced with harmonious mutual respect.[46] Thus, the migrants' rapid and persistent denunciations of the conditions they encountered in Michigan were in large measure the result of a potent combination of empowerment, organizing skills, and the deep disillusionment that their exploitation engendered. The workers' protests, in turn, fueled both liberal outrage in the United States and attention from the Puerto Rican press and political leadership.

Dionicio Valdés argues that Mexican Americans, on the other hand, after long generations of direct experience of U.S. racism and suffering even worse economic and social conditions in the Southwest, neither brought with them to Michigan a sense of political empowerment nor experienced shocking disillusionment there. Rather, for them, Michigan represented less virulent institutionalized racism and slightly better pay than they experienced in Texas. Consequently, despite their readiness to organize for better conditions in other contexts, Tejanos do not seem to have produced significant individual or collective protests in Michigan during the immediate postwar period. Valdés dryly comments on the difference in both protest strategies and reformist responses to Puerto Ricans and other farm laborers in the region: "Operation Farmlift [the 1950 Michigan experiment with Puerto Rican workers] was not unusual for the lack of justice that accompanied it, but rather for the publicity that attended that injustice."[47]

Lauded prior to their arrival, linked to the modern lure of the airplane, less socially problematic, and actively protesting exploitative conditions in gendered terms acceptable to Michigan residents, Puerto Rican agricultural workers temporarily became more deserving of liberal sympathy than Mexican Americans. Interestingly, this public, primarily urban response in Michigan differed profoundly from the racist diatribes Puerto Ricans often confronted in New York City, where they were settling by the hundreds of thousands during the same period.

Refusing to Work: The Migrants Strike with Their Feet

The Puerto Rican workers left the sugar beet fields in droves. Most, however, could not make it back to the island. The Puerto Rican Department of Labor managed to transfer hundreds to vegetable fields in New Jersey, New York, and Washington State, but many sought work elsewhere on their own. By August 1950, two months after the sugar beet field debacle began, only two thousand of the original five thousand men remained, and they continued to leave at a rate of more than seventy-five per day. At least 450 ultimately made it to Detroit, where Fathers Clement Kern and Carlos Talavera offered them hospitality, helped them look for work, and urged them to make their exploitation public.[48]

Panicked now at the prospect of facing a fall harvest with a drastically reduced labor force, Michigan Field Crops offered to renegotiate the contract with Fernando Sierra Berdecía, the director of Puerto Rico's Department of Labor. Under fire from Puerto Rican unions and island opposition groups, Sierra Berdecía refused to meet with the Michigan Field Crops representative. He lambasted the organization in the Puerto Rican press as a front for Michigan Sugar Company, the northern equivalent of the exploitative sugar corporations that had so mistreated Puerto Rico for generations. However, trying to juggle the need to placate both Puerto Rican popular opinion and Michigan grower interests, Sierra Berdecía insisted that Michigan farmers and citizens at large were not at fault in the public relations debacle. Rather, "in everything possible, the individual farmers helped our workers. . . . The entire community of Michigan has understood the problems of our workers with profound sympathy. . . . The farmers' judgment of our workers as industrious and efficient law-abiding people has been shared by the whole community. Our obligation now is to cooperate with the workers and the broader Michigan community. We will cooperate however humanly possible to ensure the completion of the harvest under just and reasonable conditions."[49]

Michigan Field Crops representatives finally sat down directly with Muñoz Marín to discuss a way to save the sugar beet harvest. They offered a new contract that promised to pay an hourly wage on a biweekly schedule, improve housing standards, and provide centrally cooked, nutritious food.[50] In addition, bending to the pressure exerted by women relatives of the Michigan migrants, the Puerto Rican legislature passed Law No. 1 on August 23, 1950. The legislation allotted funds for (1) aid to families of the Michigan beet workers, (2) return to Puerto Rico of Michigan workers medically certified as ill and unable to work, and (3) payment to beet workers of transportation costs to other jobs in the United States. For the first time in its history, the Puerto Rican state had taken action to directly, materially alleviate the plight of emigrants and their families. It had been pushed into this position by protests from Michigan migrants and their wives and mothers.[51]

The Puerto Rican government made much of this legislation, but those hoping for relief found little to celebrate. Women and their families wrote bitterly to the government denouncing the meager amount of charity available—one basket of food, a pair of shoes, a single rent payment. "Is this what our husbands went to Michigan for? A single bag of food!" "I am a respectable housewife," a woman living in the countryside outside the small town of Gurabo announced. "I refuse to submit to a government investigation in order to receive this measly aid! If you insist on entering my home, I have the right to complain and show the letters which my husband sends me. Here is one, just so that you know that I am not lying." If the state invaded her privacy, then she would shove her private worries into the public sphere. Carmen Seda Miranda, on the other hand, a politically savvy resident of the infamous *arrabal* La Perla located just outside of the capital, demanded that the government grant her an investigation; what she really needed was an apartment in one of the new public housing projects—not the paltry state offerings that sought to placate Michigan workers and their wives.[52]

For the men in the sugar beet fields, too, the new contract terms offered by Michigan Field Crops were too little, much too late—with good reason. I could find no evidence that these changes were ever actually implemented. Indeed, the Puerto Ricans may have won the discursive battle for respect and respectability, but their protests against the exploitative conditions they encountered in Michigan did not yield concrete changes in their living and working conditions. The CIO never made good on its alleged interest in organizing rural Michigan workers. The federal hearing commissioners moved on to other venues.

Michigan Congressman Fred Crawford, enraged at the Puerto Rican government's confirmation of the workers' allegations, under pressure in his district to respond to criticisms of his role in brokering the migration deal that was now hemorrhaging its supposedly docile family men, and worried about expanding investigations into his own electoral affairs, accused Sierra Berdecía of "playing politics at home" and insisted that if this harvest were saved, the combination of beet and cane sugar interests could guarantee employment for twenty thousand men the following year. Behind the scenes, he fired off letters scolding Muñoz Marín for letting the situation get out of hand.[53]

After assuring Crawford that he would "smooth things over with the men," Luis Muñoz Marín wrote to all the Michigan beet workers on August 25, 1950.[54] In his letter to the workers, and in subsequent radio addresses in Puerto Rico, Muñoz Marín acknowledged the company's contract violations, and assured the workers that the catastrophe was not their fault, but stopped short of accepting responsibility himself. He explained the August 23 legislation, reassuring the migrants that their families would receive some relief, and summarized the new agreement with the growers. Finally, after noting that no one was required to remain, he urged the men to stay through the harvest, as long as Michigan Field Crops upheld the new agreement. The letter, meant to "mobilize the workers for the cause of Michigan" by reaffirming the paternal pact of protection and solidarity between Muñoz Marín and his "political sons," seems largely to have backfired.[55]

The Puerto Rican migrants astutely read Muñoz Marín's letter as an insistence that they remain in the sugar beet fields, fulfilling a long-violated contract, in order to prove their and Puerto Rico's honor. Most interpreted the document as Muñoz Marín's siding with the sugar beet growers, "leading them again to the slaughter"—at best a frightening mistake by their leader, at worst a profound betrayal. Their leader's assurances of fatherly protection rang hollow. One man wrote, "They are abusing the Puerto Rican worker. His dignity and decorum has been trampled by the Michigan exploiters, exploiters like those who you have so often condemned." Only 927 men of the original five thousand signed the new contract. Barely eight hundred remained in the Michigan countryside for the fall sugar beet harvest. Emilio González wrote mournfully to Muñoz Marín, "I have stayed on and am loyal to your project. But everyone else has gone."[56] The few remaining Muñocista devotees were left literally standing alone in the frozen fields, a tragic embodiment of the destruction of the PPD dream of prosperous internationalized domesticity.

Maximino Cordero was one of these faithful few. Cordero was one of the many literate artisans living in the island's urban areas who frequently ended up as spokesmen and scribes for their field mates in Michigan. He had built houses and done smaller-scale carpentry work in Puerto Rico and four years earlier had migrated to Utah, where he spent seven months as a mechanic's assistant in the copper mines. Before moving to the San Juan area, he had planted and tended food crops for many years in rural Puerto Rico.[57] A member of the PPD organizing committee in his neighborhood, Cordero wrote, "[We] fought ever since the Partido Popular began to establish itself until we managed to make you governor of Puerto Rico. . . . I received a letter from you just before the elections; my wife and I and seven other family members proudly gave our vote to you."[58] On September 4, 1950, Cordero wrote of his joy at hearing from his wife about the aid package passed in Puerto Rico and of his deep despair upon receiving the letter from Muñoz Marín urging him to continue serving such an exploitative employer. "This was for me, as for many others, a great sadness." All of the other six men in his work crew subsequently left Michigan, hoping to find work somewhere else.[59]

As the author of the first letter to arrive at Muñoz Marín's office in response to the governor's circular to the beet workers, Maximino Cordero and his wife would be the recipients of Muñoz Marín's greatest populist performance of the sugar beet crisis. Not only did the governor personally respond to Cordero's letter, as his aide Gustavo Agrait urged him to do, he and his Puerto Rican wife, the beloved Doña Inés Mendoza, paid a visit to Cordero's wife and children in their tiny two-room house in a shantytown that hugged the edges of the new middle-class suburban tracts of Hato Rey. Here, in a domestic space where the rejected Puerto Rican past of the poverty-stricken *arrabal* met the heralded modern future of the island, Luis Muñoz Marín and Doña Inés made a last-ditch effort to save the midwestern migration project. They listened to Maximino Cordero's wife Regalada's tale of suffering, accompanied by a media entourage snapping photos and hanging on the governor's every word (fig. 5.1). Doña Inés left a gift of $5 to buy the children shoes and urged Regalada to keep her little ones in school. Muñoz Marín pronounced from this most humble of domestic spaces that Cordero and the other remaining sugar beet workers had been terribly wronged, acknowledging the power of their protests. Despite their bitter experiences, however, Muñoz Marín insisted, the migrants to Michigan were still masters of their fates; they could freely choose their futures. They could stay in Michigan, where they could now work under dignified conditions, ensured by his newly negotiated pact with the sugar beet growers. They could thus prove their own and their country's honor beyond a shadow of a doubt, or they could return home. Work was also plentiful in Detroit and in Minnesota, Muñoz Marín assured the workers and their supporters. A manly modernity still could await them in the United States if they followed the PPD's lead to urban jobs in the Upper Midwest.[60]

Later that day, after the public political theater had ended, Muñoz Marín slipped a one-hundred-dollar money order into an envelope, which he sent to Maximino Cordero in Michigan. "I beg you not to tell anyone that I am sending you this money, because it would be impossible to send it to every-

FIGURE 5.1 • "Gobernador visita esposa obrero en Michigan," *El Imparcial*, September 9, 1950, 4. Even this fiercely oppositional newspaper printed Muñoz Marín's speech at Cordero's home in full. As in his letter, Muñoz Marín urged the men to remain in Michigan "out of their own free will." The man in the bottom righthand snapshot is Maximino Cordero; the woman to the right in the main photo is his wife, Regalada. Doña Inés is sitting on the left. Muñoz Marín occupies his classic position, front and center, leaning toward his constituent as he listens to her woes and instructs her on how to escape them.

one," Muñoz Marín wrote. "I have done this in your case because I have been able to sense how in your home they want you to return and worry about your health. Your wife and daughters are good people; it gives me great satisfaction to help in some way." Muñoz Marín seems to have believed deeply in his persona of the Great Father, carrying out such a hidden ritual act of charity, which could have had little public political purpose. If his charisma had been shredded, he could at least try to win the heart of this individual worker and thus bind him into political reciprocity.[61]

In the fall of 1950, however, neither public performances nor private acts of atonement could save the rural midwestern migration experiment.[62] Viviano Rodríguez sadly commented from a Michigan Field Crops placement in Minnesota, "My dear sir, I read a pamphlet signed by you and dated August 25 where it says that you feel a deep concern for us; well I don't believe it because you insist that we return to Michigan, knowing that the company did not come through for us [*no cumplió con nosotros*]."[63] The men had honorably fulfilled their promises to work well and hard, but had received nothing in exchange. Their strenuous labor in the fields and in Puerto Rico on behalf of the PPD had all come to naught. "We want to reflect well on our country, but we have been sold out. How wonderful to have such a good Government which does nothing for us after we helped to build it."[64] Perhaps Antonio López Santiago said it most passionately, but his words resonated through scores of letters that arrived in San Juan in subsequent weeks: "I am now a Puerto Rican orphan, fatherless, and you were my father because I insisted upon it, lending you a hand so that you could be such. I helped you to become the father of all Puerto Ricans, but now I can help to find another father who will fight for his children when it is necessary. It's never too late and I am still young."[65]

Some men stayed in Michigan, stranded through lack of cash or debilitated physical condition, or trying to be dignified *cumplidores*. "Even though almost everyone has left, we do not want to trample your word in the dust and we will fulfill the promise that you gave these people here."[66] Most, however, departed as soon as possible, looking for work anywhere they could find it, or seeking sustenance in the established diaspora communities of Chicago and New York City.[67] The men frequently left in groups, like the sixteen from Guayama and Salinas who "put their suitcases on their heads" and caught a ride to Ohio.[68] Others left individually, hoboing on trains and trucks, traveling with Mexican American migrant families, or using their few precious dollars to catch buses. Many Puerto Rican sojourners in Michigan ended up criss-crossing the United States seeking a livelihood; they reported having traveled to Mississippi, Arkansas, Pennsylvania, Florida, Texas, Colorado, Missouri, Washington, and Indiana, among other places—often in concert with Tejano families. Others sought work in the industrial centers of Milwaukee, Detroit, Chicago, Gary, Indiana, and Cleveland.[69]

They also crowded into the Migration Bureau offices of the Puerto Rican government in New York City, demanding to be given passage back to the island. The office's director, Manuel Cabranes, sent a panicked cable a few weeks after Muñoz Marín's August letter: "Situation regarding return Michigan workers becoming more critical STOP Have now 36 men in office refusing work and aid except passage home STOP more reportedly on way New York STOP public opinion being organized against us on this issue by government enemies STOP will arrange transportation some paying."[70] Those who did not make it to New York and Chicago also sent floods of letters back to the Puerto Rican government in San Juan, recounting their plight and asking for airfare to return home.[71]

To a man, these workers clamored for the returnee fund of Law No. 1 to be expanded. They insisted that all of the Michigan workers were victims of an unjust labor arrangement, not just physically disabled ones. They were honorable working men. They had labored long and hard and had received literally nothing as recompense. They had complied with their word and their contracts and had represented their nation well; the U.S. growers, however, had violated their rights and their dignity, and endangered their families' survival. Now, since the experiment in rural midwestern migration had failed, they deserved the right to return, to reunite with their families to piece together the shreds of domesticity remaining for them. Once more, they requested some sort of compassionate *brega* from their state.

The Puerto Rican government's response, however, was unyielding. There would be no aid for the men to return to the island. There was no room for them there. They were now part of the surplus population. At a press conference in October, Manuel Cabranes insisted that the beet workers could find work in urban areas of the United States and that his office would help them to relocate. He continually deflected questions about workers' desires to return to their homeland. The aid funds allocated for workers, he said, were "to avoid them becoming public wards in the continent"—not for their repatriation. Even Fernando Sierra Berdecía, the head of the Puerto Rican Department of Labor, the government's single apparent advocate for the sugar beet workers, who after finally visiting the men in their miserable surroundings had denounced the exploitative industry with passion and disdain, strongly urged Muñoz Marín not to allow the men to return. Ending colonial displacement clearly was not in the cards for these migrants.[72]

Their ignominious expulsion from the nation in such a penniless state provoked great shame in the men unable to find work in the United States. Reduced to begging their wives for transportation money home (usually in vain, since the women had no extra funds either) rather than returning triumphantly with abundant resources to share, the workers struggled mightily with this further challenge to their fatherly honor and authority. Their defiant refusal to work under extremely exploitative conditions—an act insisting on their own inherent worth and dignity—had not freed them. They had become degraded dependents themselves: "I don't know what I'm going to do, I'm half crazy because you know that without money, a man is nothing."[73] "I blush at having left my home in search of daily bread, and after having worked like a slave arriving back home with my hands in my pockets."[74] Another man's petition to his wife not to share his letter recounting his miserable state ended in threats, a desperate demand that his manly authority not be further undone: "I had better not find out that anyone else has seen this letter."[75]

Once again, the men faced the agonizing reality of betrayal by their alleged political allies. Contrary to promises made to many of them before boarding the planes for Michigan, the Puerto Rican state had never made any provisions for their return. Now, disillusioned, angry, and potential mobilizers of opposition at a delicate political moment on the island, when the PPD was mounting a campaign for a referendum on the new colonial constitution, these men were even more undesirable than before. The public rhetoric of internationally reconstituted domesticity had been a farce. The men were separated from their families, with no ability to provide for them. Migrant families would not be reunited, at least not on the island. Eventually, state officials hoped, workers' wives, partners, and children would join the men in the United States.[76] For many, this migration had become, in effect, a permanent economic exile.

Even those sugar beet workers who eventually managed to return home faced a desperate situation. Unemployment still haunted the island, and their families were mired even deeper in debt than before. Creditors hounded them, demanding payment for having sustained their families during their absence. The state provided little to no assistance in finding jobs or intervening with creditors. Which was worse, to be wandering, cold, and afraid p'allá afuera in the United States, or to be at home, a constant drain on the family and ashamed of one's failure as manly provider?[77]

To make matters worse for the migrants to Michigan, the Nationalist Party's armed rebellion on the island and attempted assassination of U.S. president Harry Truman in Washington, DC, on November 1 immediately diverted the media's attention away from the drama of the beet fields. Letters about migratory hardship in the Upper Midwest continued to arrive on the island, but after November 1 were rarely printed by the Puerto Rican newspapers—even by the opposition daily El Imparcial. The hysterical equation of Puerto Rican Nationalists with communism and the subsequent arrests of proindependence and other radical Puerto Rican activists silenced allies of Puerto Rican sugar beet workers, both in Michigan and on the island. With the discrediting of all things Puerto Rican and widespread support among Michigan sugar beet farmers, Fred Crawford won his reelection bid. The media and political networks that helped fuel the threat posed by wronged men hoeing in the Michigan beet fields and their wives' bregando on the island largely ground to a halt, leaving thousands of Puerto Rican families in apparently silenced despair, with no sympathetic public venues or organizational allies.

PERSISTENT
BREGAS

Bregar does not offer a leap into the realm of freedom, neither a pure
martyrdom nor a redemption. Rather, it is a system of decisions and indecisions,
a back and forth which has permitted many to construct agency in a
[hostile] world. • Arcadio Díaz Quiñones, *El arte de bregar*

The mounting political crisis of the sugar beet fields may have dissipated
surprisingly quickly, as the men dispersed and a potent fusion of anticommunism and denunciation of Puerto Rican independence activism swept
both the island and the United States, ending media attention to the midwestern farmers' exploitation of Puerto Ricans. However, the tensions surrounding the Michigan experience persisted, extinguished in public, but
not easily resolved for the state or the migrants and their families. The male
sugar beet migrants found that their most enduring allies were not the politicians, journalists, church leaders, and union officials who had spoken publicly on their behalf during the summer and fall of 1950. Rather, the most

effective solidarity flowed from those erased from the public record—the Tejanos who led them into networks of travel and employment in the United States and the women on the island who insisted on locating their dispersed family members and recovering their back wages. Despite the press's abandonment of their cause and their consequent disappearance from public view, the Puerto Rican sugar beet migrants and their women relatives continued to demand that the PPD government somehow make amends. These disaffected men and women remained problematic constituents. After forcing the official admission of horrible exploitation in Michigan and creating the political imperative to pass Law No. 1 in Puerto Rico, the women and male workers' persistent pressure for the recovery of back wages pushed the Puerto Rican state into a brega with them yet again, even as the acute political scandal that had formed around them died down. In the immediate aftermath of the Nationalist rebellion, the PPD attempted to contain the anger and disappointment of the workers and their families and recapture their loyalty by developing routinized methods for filing back pay claims. The state officials' strategies and the results of their advocacy on the workers' behalf remained constrained, however, by their own colonial positions and lack of political will.

By late October 1950, after months of little to no remuneration from Michigan and only meager amounts of material aid from the government, women in Puerto Rico began to demand the back pay owed their husbands and sons in letters and visits to PPD offices. One mother, for example, whose son had worked on two Michigan farms for no pay, and then labored alongside a Tejano family all the way to El Paso, Texas, ordered PPD officials to contact the "mineworkers' union" in Texas, to explore the possibility of locating a permanent job for her son there. She also insisted that the Puerto Rican government was responsible for producing the pay that her son was owed from his months in Michigan. The wife of another Michigan migrant, after successfully winning her husband's back wages from "The Company in Michigan," took up the cases of various neighbors who had also suffered in the sugar beet fields. Many other wives and mothers of Michigan migrants did the same. They also pressed Department of Migration Services officials to locate their loved ones who had disappeared into the search for work in the United States, peppering the Puerto Rican government offices in San Juan, New York City, and Chicago with inquiries about the migrant men's whereabouts.[1]

After leaving Michigan, the male agricultural workers also joined their women relatives in continuing to demand recognition of the minimum remaining shreds of their paternal dignity—if the Puerto Rican government had not been able to protect them in Michigan, they reasoned, it could at least help them recover the wages owed them from the months they had spent suffering there. Hundreds of men wrote letters to Puerto Rico's Department of Labor, demanding that the government intervene with Michigan farmers, as it had so many times with Puerto Rican employers, to ensure that the terms of their contracts were respected and that they received appropriate remuneration for the time they had worked. Many, like Lucas Díaz Rodríguez, wrote from the United States. Armed with a reference from the Migration Services office in Chicago, Díaz Rodríguez had landed work in a greenhouse in Milwaukee, Wisconsin. He had not forgotten, however, that the Michigan farmers had never settled up financially with him; he insisted that they make good on their contractual obligations. "I expect to be treated as I treat others," he proclaimed. Workers wrote from a wide variety of rural and urban locations throughout the United States. Letters came from states as far-flung as Florida, Texas, Wisconsin, California, Ohio, Illinois, Indiana, Minnesota, New Jersey, Pennsylvania, and, of course, New York.[2] Those who had returned to the island also wrote their government and visited its local offices. To a man, the disillusioned workers insisted on being paid for 160 hours for every four weeks of labor, as promised in the renegotiated contract of midsummer. Those who had completed their contracts, laboring well into November in the frozen sugar beet fields, also expected their $1 per acre bonus.

The Michigan migrants and their family members sent so many letters and appeared so many times between late October and early November 1950 at Puerto Rican government offices both on the island and in the United States that top employees of the Puerto Rican Department of Labor and the PPD's Migration Services Division began to inquire with Michigan Field Crops and its member farmers about wages—even for those who had not stayed through the end of the contract. Personnel of the PPD coordinated these efforts between Puerto Rico, New York, and Chicago offices, even hiring new employees for the purpose. The director of the New York office called on Alan Perl, the PPD government's legal counsel in the United States, to negotiate from time to time with particularly recalcitrant growers. Worried about the potential fallout in the looming constitutional referendum, PPD officials in New York and Chicago scrambled to place those fleeing Michigan in industrial jobs as well as to find them clothes and shelter—anything to discourage their return to the island or their turning to the local Spanish-language newspapers for support, several of which in New York

City were sympathetic to the proindependence cause. Finally, the Michigan migrants also insisted that their government advocate for the wages owed them from post-Michigan agricultural employers in rural New York, New Jersey, and Pennsylvania; the PPD bureaucrats ultimately responded to these calls as well.[3]

The director of Migration Services quickly devised a form to be filled out by back pay petitioners in an attempt to transform the flood of demands into a manageable current. No PPD official wanted to relive the "chaos of complaints" that had plagued them throughout the summer of 1950. Decreed necessary in order to have an active file, this signed document authorized the Puerto Rican Commissioner of Labor to "represent [the Michigan workers] in the matter of claims of insufficient wages and noncompliance with the . . . contract" as well as to examine and evaluate all work records and to receive and transmit all back wages recovered. A few additional short spaces were provided to include information about the migrants' personal information, contract number, places and crops worked, and the dates of their labor in Michigan.[4]

These forms and the subsequent chain of written communication between government officials and Michigan growers requesting their records of individual migrants, the calculation of pay owed to the men, and the issuance of checks in their name to be sent to the state's central office for distribution to the workers document the PPD's attempt to capture the uncontrolled disappointment and anger about the Michigan debacle still ricocheting through working-class Puerto Rican networks on the island and in the United States. The act of filling out these forms and the government's "advocacy" on their behalf redirected the migrants' and families' energies toward petitioning the state for a very specific goal—recovery of back pay—rather than reaching out to a broader public in protest of a comprehensively exploitative situation. Thus, in the thousands of files saved in scores of boxes labeled "Querellas de Obreros Migrantes, 1950–52," which fill a significant section of the Archivo General's Fondo del Departamento del Trabajo, lie the remains of a massive, yet diffuse and publicly silenced struggle over the containment of the Michigan crisis. Here, we witness both the migrants' persistence in pressing their claims on the state and the PPD trying to defuse the potential danger of the migrants' disillusionment, even hoping at times to turn it back into a political loyalty reminiscent of that which had undergirded the men's excited clamor to board the Michigan-bound planes.

The tension of this historical moment is embodied in the physical documents themselves. The claim forms did not allow the expression of emotions or the recounting of the lengthy stories of suffering, solidarity, strategizing, and displacement that filled the pages of the workers' and their relatives' letters during the summer of 1950. Rather, the intentionally minimalist information gathering of the government's terse documents stripped away all the complexity of meaning, feeling, and agency that coursed through the stories from and about Michigan. Indeed, it was not uncommon for workers to attach their own unsolicited handwritten testimonies to the formal claims for back pay. They insisted on creating a record not only of basic statistics but also of the monstrous experiences of exploitation, disappointment, and betrayal that overflowed the bureaucratic responses to workers' queries. Miguel Cruz Rivera even refused to fill out the officially endorsed form, stating that "he had no need to fill out that piece of paper." His suffering did not fit within the strictures of government interest; he wanted an acknowledgment of his own narrative of the sugar beet field struggles as well as immediate material results. Cruz Rivera's angry rejection of the government form sharply belied the PPD official's smug note that after telling Cruz Rivera that he was responsible for airfare and food costs and thus would not receive any money for his work in Michigan, Cruz Rivera "accepted without question" the stunning news ("este se quedó conforme").[5]

The written forms and bureaucratic actions that accompanied them sought to reduce the men and women who completed them to powerless supplicants, dependent on the state for any success in pressing their claims. Party officials consistently tried to position themselves as the sole mediators between Michigan Field Crops and the workers; in their responses to claims, meticulously copied and saved along with other relevant documents, bureaucrats reiterated to both workers and growers that all requests for pay had to be channeled through them and that they were the only legitimate agents for transmission of moneys recovered back to the workers.

Many Michigan migrants who remained in the United States did not inform the government consistently of their whereabouts, displaying an unnerving fluidity of residence and employment. Officials of the PPD's Migration Services Division both on the island and in the United States developed a complex surveillance network for locating these workers. They solicited information from families, friends, church clergy, past employers, hospitals where the workers were rumored to have received medical treatment, and local political officials in both Puerto Rican small towns and in the Midwest. Migration Services investigators visited family, friends, and previous residences to locate the men. The PPD's advocacy of recovery of back pay emerged as an additional state strategy to track down the elusive migrants, provide them and their families with some sort of recompense for their months in Michigan, and to continue to discourage them from returning to the island.[6] Indeed, the documents collected in the Department of Labor's section of Puerto Rico's Archivo General do not only record the Puerto Rican state's ultimate concession of the migrants' right to recovery of wages owed to them and its attempts to channel the discontent from Michigan into petitions to a paternalist bureaucracy. The documents also record how the Michigan migrants' persistent pressure helped shape state agencies themselves, pushing government officials and politicians to invent forms, devise legislation and regulations, allocate resources, establish staff positions, initiate investigations, exponentially expand the purview of state inquiry and interventions, and establish networks for the management of large flows of information, human movement, and monetary transfers.

Once growers began to send checks to the Puerto Rican Department of Labor to be forwarded to the workers, the PPD filled the island's radio waves with reports of its allegedly successful advocacy to recover wages earned in Michigan. This may have served the state's interests to a certain extent, by propagating a vision of the PPD government as deeply committed to the welfare of its citizens, willing to confront U.S. agribusiness and wrest wages owed to Puerto Rican workers from the maws of sugar profiteers. This official story resonated well with the narrative spun by the PPD about its beneficent actions on the island. However, such triumphalist tales created increased pressure for wage recovery as more and more Michigan migrants and their relatives responded to the news by demanding a piece of this alleged abundance for themselves.[7]

Ultimately, thousands of Michigan migrants and their families did receive some funds from these cycling currents of pressure from workers and wives to state agencies to growers and back again. However, the letters exchanged in this multitude of cases also expose the colonial power imbalances that permeated U.S.–Puerto Rican relations. Not only did the PPD claims process restrict agricultural workers to requesting advocacy from the Puerto Rican state and its agencies, Puerto Rican officials were sorely limited in their own strategies for recovering wages. Since the U.S. government steadfastly refused to include agricultural laborers in the protections established for citizen workers, the Puerto Rican government's only legal recourse was to petition the growers directly for the back pay claimed. Party officials could not count on any backup from their state counterparts in the United States.[8] When the farmers or agribusiness enterprises refused to respond to PPD inquiries or drastically reduced the amounts of migrants' claims, PPD officials generally accepted the growers' records and logic as final, informing the workers and their relatives in terse form letters that unless they could produce additional evidence that disproved the growers' records, their cases would be closed.[9] Checks sent out to workers through the PPD Department of Labor generally ranged from $2.50 to $16.00; the average back pay check obtained was $6.56, usually for two or more months of work. Not infrequently, growers produced checks such as the 86 cents sent to Rafael Lizardi for his more than five months of labor in Michigan; his time there had included a proud "commitment to the cause of the sugar beet harvest" all the way through late November 1950.[10] Some Michigan growers even continued to claim that the Puerto Rican workers actually owed them money for food and round-trip airfare, although many of the migrants remained abroad, searching for work in the United States.[11]

Despite these frequently discouraging results, the workers and their families persisted in their efforts to receive what they considered just calculations of the wages owed to them. They insisted on payment by the hour rather than by the acre. They pointed to their contracts, which had promised a minimum of 160 hours of work over each period of four weeks. Those who had stayed to finish the renewed contract negotiated by Luis Muñoz Marín in August 1950 resolutely maintained their right to an additional bonus of $1 per acre harvested. Many of the Michigan migrants refused to accept the growers' "final words." They and their wives and mothers convinced the mayors of their Puerto Rican hometowns, local representatives to the Puerto Rican legislature, or employees of other PPD agencies to write letters on their behalf to the Puerto Rican Department of Labor. In the United States, the men also turned to local social workers, state Department of Labor officials, Red Cross chapters, or the Chicago or New York City PPD offices. Meanwhile, their female relatives pressed local officials throughout the island to listen to their husbands' stories.[12] Sometimes these efforts bore some fruit, as when Emilio Cruz Rodríguez and his wife managed to convince Clarence Senior, the director of the New York office of PPD Migration Services, to press a Michigan employer further, ultimately producing an additional $8 in back wages, almost eight months after the filing of their original claim. Most Michigan migrants ended up frustrated, however, like Rafael Lizardi, who demanded his documents back and stormed out of the San Juan PPD office to hire a private attorney when he received his final statement check for 86 cents. After several days of consulting with lawyers, though, all of whom wanted to charge him a sizeable sum even before initiating proceedings against Michigan Field Crops, Lizardi had no recourse but to return to the PPD Department of Labor in San Juan to file a new claim. For all of his political loyalty, hard work in Michigan, and his persistence in the claims process, Lizardi was rewarded the second time with a new finding from the U.S. agricultural corporation—now, they alleged, Lizardi owed the growers $27.80![13] Thus, despite the Michigan migrants' success in pushing PPD officials into an international intervention of unprecedented scale on their behalf, they ultimately could not win this colonial battle for justice and dignity, waged as it was over long geographical distances, without effective, powerful allies, and lacking political rights in the United States, despite the workers' formal citizenship there.

A year after the passage of Law No. 1, the Puerto Rican Department of Labor filed a satisfied report, stating proudly that the legislation was no longer needed. Of the money allocated for aid to beet workers and their families, $37,000 remained unspent. The report's authors congratulated the Departments of Labor and Public Welfare for maintaining such strict control over the program's budget.[14] The painful experiences of Puerto Ricans in rural Michigan briefly reappeared in the press in 1954, when an attorney named Armando Miranda forced a hearing in the Puerto Rican Senate's Labor Commission. There, Miranda accused the Puerto Rican Department of Labor of having failed to protect the sugar beet migrants and having defrauded them of hundreds of thousands of dollars in back wages. Clearly, the wounds of Michigan had not completely healed, at least for the workers whom Miranda claimed to represent. Fernando Sierra Berdecía, who had authored the government report of August 1950 conceding the exploitation suffered by Puerto Ricans in Michigan, took the stand to refute Miranda's charges. Armed with mountains of statistics, documentation of the PPD's "valiant" efforts to recover back wages for thousands of workers, and an accusation of his own—that Miranda had made his living for many years as an informal labor recruiter of Puerto Ricans to work in Florida agriculture— Sierra Berdecía won the sympathy of the Puerto Rican press and seems to have stifled any further investigation of the PPD's actions (or lack thereof) on behalf of the Michigan migrants.[15] No sustained public outcry congealed around the newspaper reports.

Meanwhile, the majority of the sugar beet workers and their families appear to have remained dislocated, separated from each other, and under- or unemployed. The state's refusal of the sugar beet migrants' right to return and its channeling of complaints into a lengthy, individualized petition process were ultimately as—or more—effective methods of excluding emerging dissidents as the crackdowns against nationalists and leftists carried out between 1950 and 1953. This was the softer disciplinary hand of the state in dealing with troublesome groups. Spread throughout the United States, or back on the island, ashamed of their failure to be *padres cumplidos*, the sugar beet workers could spin no heroic narrative of collective resistance or utopian visions for the future. Consequently, they could not sustain a powerful collective memory of their suffering. Luis Muñoz Marín, on the other hand, managed to sustain his paternal authority, thanks to the power of economic exile, a ferocious excoriation of all threats to state power, and the diversion of diffuse political dissatisfaction into individual claims for back wages— but only after a great deal of hard work and strategizing by him and other government officials.

This gaping hole is reflected in broader popular memory as well. In 2002, I visited the house where Maximino and Regalada Cordero lived when they became inadvertent performers in the Muñocista paternalist drama of August 1950. A tiny sliver of the *barriada* Jurutungo still remained, a few winding, barely paved narrow alleyways, lined with cramped wooden houses on stilts, sandwiched almost invisibly between two upscale suburban neighborhoods of Hato Rey. An elderly neighbor told me that Maximino Cordero, then a widower, had moved away several years before. The neighbor still vividly remembered the day when Luis Muñoz Marín and Doña Inés Mendoza had come to the block. She could not recall, however, the purpose of their visit or the fact that thousands of Puerto Ricans, including her neighbor of more than fifty years, had migrated to the Michigan countryside and protested their experience there. Muñoz Marín's populist charisma had successfully outlasted the political crisis of the sugar beet fields that had worried him so deeply.

Fatherhood and Domesticity:
The Sinews of Meaning in Populism, Migration, and Colonialism

The narrative I have spun in this book seems excruciatingly tragic at times. However, excavating the migrants' and families' buried protests from the Midwestern sugar beet fields and Puerto Rico's countryside and cities underscores the active, dynamic nature of la *brega de Michigan* and opens a new interpretation of the island's populist period. The political explosion in response to the exploitation Puerto Rican agricultural migrants encountered in Michigan provides a window into the contentious processes of shaping political culture, physical landscapes, and the state that emerged between 1935 and 1950 on the island. Indeed, the Michigan-related protests and the alliances they constructed were part of a broad Puerto Rican political effervescence in the postwar years that required concerted efforts and a wide variety of strategies by the PPD to contain. Ernesto Laclau argues that part of populist movements' energy comes from their filling of "empty" concepts such as "freedom," "bread," and "citizen" with powerful meanings.[16] For Puerto Ricans, persistent, fervent discussions of domesticity, empowered masculinity, economically secure motherhood, and responsible fatherhood did a great deal of this work, helping to forge social consensus out of a cacophony of political heterogeneity. Laclau also recognizes the profound emotions that undergird populist movements. The PPD faithful were moved by the deep affective bonds of mutual responsibility between fathers and sons that supposedly stretched from U.S. politicians to Luis Muñoz Marín to working-class Puerto Rican men to their own familial dependents. The Michigan migrants' rage at the betrayal of these bonds, combined with their heightened political and economic expectations, drove them to the sharp protests that caught the attention of a wide range of political actors in the summer of 1950, both on the island and in the United States.[17]

Other historians have illuminated the power of populist leaders' paternalism.[18] This book has explored the fatherly charisma of Luis Muñoz Marín, but also the importance of family-based masculinity to working-class participants in populist politics. Their understandings of themselves as fathers and mothers and as creators of domesticity were essential elements in the enduring populist project of the PPD. Fathers, whether humble citizens or powerful politicians, should be held responsible for their paternal responsibilities to their families, they believed.

Indeed, the power of the ideal of the family man and his benevolently patriarchal reign over an idealized domesticity, I have argued, was key to the development of the PPD's colonial populism. Like his Argentinian contemporary Juan Perón, Muñoz Marín proposed "the home as social uplift," changing "the very terrain of politics by connecting utopian ideals of national progress to yearnings for greater security, comfort, and plenty at the household level."[19] Postwar domesticity dreams and their related desires for modern consumption became integral parts of the promises of prosperity offered by the PPD in its march toward industrialization and urbanization, all ostensibly made possible in Puerto Rico by a strengthened relationship with the United States and its many sources of development funds.

The postwar domesticity discourses, begun as an attempt at island uplift and invoked internationally by Puerto Rican officials in order to manage the 1930s crisis of the island's relationship with its colonial metropolis, also spun out of the state's control. Masking their own long-standing tensions over the garnering and distribution of family economic resources, laboring Puerto Rican women and men united in 1950 to wield the domesticity rhetoric against their government's betrayal of its paternalist promises. The solidarity forged in this moment of urgent political and economic need largely obscured the particularity of women's experiences. Women relatives of the Michigan migrants identified outside forces as the sole source of their suffering and emphasized a probably fictitious total dependence on male incomes. Back in the Upper Midwest, the domesticity discourse's power to make the migrants palatable to a hostile North American public ended up for a brief historical moment legitimizing Puerto Rican workers' protests against their government's and the Michigan growers' violated promises.

Working-class dreams of domesticity could also motivate thousands of men to board potentially dangerous airplanes bound to the sugar beet fields of Michigan in the name of an ultramodern migration, one that would ostensibly allow them to foster abundance, build homes, and cement their own legitimacy as paternal providers even as they absented themselves from the very domestic spaces they hoped to rule. Indeed, migration, the Michigan story reminds us, centrally shaped Puerto Rico's populist era. Historians have long noted that PPD officials hoped to rid the island of those they deemed excess population in order to more effectively develop Puerto Rico's economy. In this book, I have argued that the PPD's strategies for doing so depended upon trying to produce particular perceptions and practices of plebeian Puerto Rican femininity and masculinity. This preoccupation with gendered representations also marked PPD officials' methods of responding to anti–Puerto Rican backlash in New York City, their attempts to attract U.S. capital to the island, and their efforts to market Puerto Rican laborers in other parts of the United States. Laboring Puerto Ricans' motivations for migration were also profoundly gendered; the airlift to Michigan provides a compelling case study of this phenomenon.

Finally, Puerto Rican migrants themselves also shaped the trajectory of populist politics. Again, historians have shown us that the huge New York City diaspora community—its labor and civic organizations, often radical politics, and alliances with New York leftist political figures such as Vito Marcantonio—was of deep concern to Luis Muñoz Marín and other PPD leaders throughout the long years of the party's reign.[20] The 1950 migrants to rural Michigan left their mark on Puerto Rico's populism as well, however. These male workers and their women relatives created an international political crisis that PPD officials feared would derail plans for consolidating a reinvigorated colonial relationship with the United States. The migrants' and families' pressure for the wages owed from agricultural migrant labor helped create or accelerated bureaucratic practices of advocacy, resource distribution, and citizen surveillance on the island and abroad. Thus, the actions of Michigan migrants, together with their wives and mothers, constituted part of the larger process of Puerto Rican welfare state formation during the postwar period.

Labor migration has long been one of the methods with which Puerto Ricans have negotiated their position as colonial subjects. This book illuminates some of the strategies that the PPD used to reconfigure popular understandings of U.S. colonialism and how migrant experiences might challenge them. By the 1930s, U.S. rule had come to represent repression and economic exploitation for many Puerto Ricans. During the 1940s and '50s, however, Muñoz Marín and his advisors sought to recast the United States as a generous father willing to dispense resources to his loyal, productive sons in the Caribbean and Latin America. Puerto Rico, they insisted, was the most upstanding and reliable of these worthy children-coming-to-adulthood, led by its own father, Muñoz Marín, whose skill at international paternal collaboration knew no equal. The flow of funds obtained through this newly familial pact would create jobs, build homes, and bring abundant consumer goods to the island, ushering in a liberating age of progress, development, and modernity. Puerto Rican men, especially, were to become respected citizen-fathers of both Puerto Rico and the United States in the process. The airlift to Michigan was part and parcel of this allegedly reciprocal developmentalist project built upon a foundation of fraternal fatherhood. Puerto Rican and U.S. men would join together as they simultaneously battled to save the sugar beet harvest and lift Puerto Rican families out of poverty—Luis Muñoz Marín and Fred Crawford, Michigan growers and Puerto Rican workers all helping each other through great adversity.

But the protests that emanated from Michigan's countryside exposed the duplicity of these promises. Modern sugar beet production meant a return to near slavery, not a dignified partnership of virile collaborators. Colonialism was alive and well in the heartland of the United States. As massive construction of houses, factories, and infrastructure of all kinds transformed Puerto Rico's physical and economic landscape, thousands of men shouted from rural Michigan, "These Americans are savages!" "What of my children's rice and beans?" "We are left without a father here."

The flood of letters from and about the sugar beet fields as well as the Puerto Ricans' refusal to work there under such exploitative conditions shows us how laboring Puerto Rican men and women contested their disillusioning experiences. In the process, they forced those in power to respond, even if rarely in ways they had hoped. Certainly, the Puerto Rican state did not intervene effectively in a lasting way on behalf of agricultural migrants to Michigan in 1950. Island politicians and other officials were limited by their acceptance of the imperative to serve colonial interests as well as by the Puerto Rican state and citizenry's impotence within colonial political structures. Despite their perseverance, Puerto Rican agricultural migrants and their families continually found themselves caught in a net of poverty and constrained choices. However, Muñoz Marín and the PPD's balancing of the demands from colonial metropolis and Puerto Rican working people required substantial attention to grassroots pressure and the cultivation of a variety of methods to manage the crisis it caused.[21] Thus, the Michigan sugar beet saga illuminates the strategies and technologies of power within colonial structures, developed through a persistent, multileveled *brega* often fueled from below.

The Racial Implications of Domesticity Discourses

The Puerto Rican letters from Michigan are intriguingly surreptitious about race. Indeed, as in much of the era's public political discussions in Puerto Rico, gendered identities and yearnings took discursive center stage in these sources. The discourses of fraternal fatherhood and respectable domesticity dreams seem to have eclipsed direct references to race during the Michigan crisis. Ileana Rodríguez argues that in an earlier period, between 1860 and 1930, Puerto Ricans frequently chose to strategically silence public race talk in order to build particular political alliances or assert their political legitimacy, often substituting the language of labor for that of racial groupings.[22] Certainly, during the mid-twentieth century, Muñoz Marín and other PPD activists attempted to downplay racial differences among Puerto Ricans in an attempt to build national unity. The workers in Michigan seem to have followed suit, making not one mention of racial tensions among themselves, despite the wide range of phenotypes and skin colors apparent in photos of men boarding airplanes to the midwestern countryside in the summer of 1950. This silence on internal racial conflicts may, as I have suggested in the case of the persistent gender solidarity expressed by men and women during the Michigan crisis, reflect a political strategy rather than the actual experiences of Puerto Ricans in the sugar beet fields. More surprising is the absence of any references to racial slurs by North Americans in the letters of protest.

We cannot know if those who denounced the bitter experience of "slavery in the land of freedom" considered themselves or were seen by others as of African descent. Certainly, this comment was made frequently enough and echoed so compellingly through press and other popular accounts during the Michigan controversy that it appears to have resonated with a wide spectrum of the Puerto Rican public. By 1950, use of the term "slavery" invoked the worst form of colonial and labor exploitation as well as the denigration of blackness—an experience available to all Puerto Ricans, regardless of their racial identities. Indeed, the protests of sugar beet field slavery exposed an aspect of modernity that PPD triumphalist rhetoric denied; the United States could still indiscriminately exploit those who sought its benefits.

A careful examination of the sources from the period warns us away from a simple conclusion that gender neatly silenced race in postwar Puerto Rican politics. Muñoz Marín's invocations to his followers to become free men probably could not be completely disentangled from their racial resonances—at least for those Puerto Ricans who experienced contemporary racial prejudice and whose families had passed down stories of slavery's oppression. They could also appeal to those who did not identify as black. The powerful language of slavery and freedom, therefore, whether wielded by politicians or laboring protesters, could both incorporate and stretch beyond the historical experience of racialized chattel bondage for Puerto Ricans. It was expansively inclusive. On the other hand, the visual images propagated by the PPD and the privately owned press clearly insisted on the whitening power of the ideal, modern forms of family and domesticity. The security and autonomy embodied in a stable home of one's own, the respectability to be achieved through the separation of private and public spheres, and the hope of enshrining male authority over homebound dependents through men's hard work and decent wages all promised to distance Puerto Ricans from their vulnerable, poverty-stricken—and, for many of them, blackened—pasts. These images, however seductive their intentions, also articulated a profoundly racist vision of modern domesticity—one that invariably excluded blackness. Thus, many of the visual images associated with modernity and respectability that circulated in Puerto Rico during the postwar period vibrated in tension with the carefully deracialized, powerfully inclusive language of liberation that echoed through the speeches and writings of the PPD, particularly of Luis Muñoz Marín, and the denunciations of slavery-like oppression articulated by the Michigan migrants. Populism did not speak with a single voice; perhaps in these very tensions lay part of its emotional power.

Because we still need much research on both popular and elite Puerto Rican postwar understandings of race on the island, we cannot know yet whether those claiming Afro–Puerto Rican identities felt excluded, even alienated, by the whitened images of modern domesticity, families, and workers that circulated so widely in Puerto Rico during this period, or whether in the relatively fluid multiracial heterogeneity of plebeian Puerto Rican society, these discourses beckoned as a positive possibility open to all. More definitive answers to such questions await further research into Puerto Rico's social and cultural history in this era. We must be careful to heed Paul Kramer's insistence that historians examine the workings of race in the specificity of each particular colonial context, with an eye to the actions of the colonized.[23]

Likewise, we cannot yet definitively conclude how or whether long-term Michigan residents who considered themselves white saw either Puerto Ricans or Mexican Americans as racially distinct from themselves or from each other. Certainly, the ease with which most rural Michiganians dismissed the exploitation of migrant workers strongly suggests deep racism against both groups; the local communities who prospered from migrant workers' unacknowledged labor certainly constructed the field laborers as foreigners who were inherently other than themselves. The domesticity discourse that won Puerto Ricans a wide range of urban allies in Michigan may have momentarily deracialized them (or racialized them in a different way) in relation to their Mexican American counterparts—perhaps a particularly important strategy for PPD officials to have developed, given the Puerto Ricans' own phenotypical heterogeneity. Once again, then, as on the island, a gendered respectability may have distanced Puerto Ricans from blackness, or allowed their sympathizers to imagine them in this way. Certainly, the derogatory references to Mexican Americans made by the Puerto Ricans' allies (other than Father Clement Kern in Detroit, who steadfastly stood in solidarity with both groups) often used images of disease, dirt, and questionable morality or family forms that had powerful, if implicit, racial resonances.[24] The precise racial meanings of this differentiation between Puerto Ricans and Mexican Americans, however, awaits further research into the history of the racial dynamics, identities, and relationships of 1950s Michigan—one that would include the assimilation of northern Europeans into landowning whiteness, the changing ways in which different migrant groups may have been racialized in relation to each other and to local growers, and the impact of large-scale African American migration to Michigan's cities between the two world wars.

The comparison of Mexican American and Puerto Rican experiences in rural Michigan during 1950 does powerfully demonstrate that even with a formal citizenship status that eliminates the threat of deportation, physically mobile, ostracized, economically vulnerable people such as migrant agricultural workers can experience a certain degree of "statelessness."[25] All the gestures of political solidarity toward Puerto Ricans did not seem to have altered the growers' abusive treatment of them in the fields and barracks of Michigan's rural counties. Like the migrant Mexican Americans who offered them solidarity, the Puerto Ricans ultimately could not count on forceful protective measures from any government entity, whether local, federal, or colonial.[26] Their plight in Michigan's countryside cautions us that winning justice for migrants, especially in agricultural labor, will require much more than gaining legal citizenship status. Simultaneously, the events of 1950 remind us that even among groups such as Puerto Rican and Mexican American migrant field laborers who performed the same labor and shared the same living conditions, politicized hierarchies can emerge; gendered and/or racialized discourses can legitimize the partial inclusion of particular groups, as they simultaneously exclude others. In Michigan, where the urban-rural divide was particularly acute, Puerto Ricans could be made into deserving citizens by their collaboration with liberal urban allies who largely ignored or denigrated migrant Mexican Americans. This local urban Michiganian response to Puerto Ricans differed dramatically from that produced in New York City, where Puerto Ricans were excoriated as a dangerous invading mass. Such localized levels of analysis allow us to see citizenship not only as a formal political status, but also as a set of gendered and racialized social practices that can be "filled and emptied of contents," creating different types of "debased citizens," conferring certain benefits (such as freedom from deportation fears) while continuing to deny others (such as a decent minimum wage, enforceable standards of health and safety in the workplace, and unemployment and work-related injury compensations).[27]

The Never-Ending *Brega*

The arc of *bregar* opened to us by the Michigan migrants' letters and back pay claims is broad and complicated. The letters' authors slipped frequently from defiant refusals to work, angry orders fired at officials, and personalized political threats to desperate requests for aid. Like the mass demonstrations and other civic and labor activism on the island during the PPD period, the migrants' direct challenges to power often fused with worried supplications for state intervention, rarely constituting solely one strategy or the other. They encourage us to avoid dividing political strategies into rigidly binary categories such as resistance or collaboration. In reconstructing history, we must remember this lesson; our task is not to spin purely romantic or tragic tales. History, gathered up out of the vast, complex "sea of human activities," is much richer than this.[28] It is the stuff of life, with all its daily hopes, pain, and acts of survival—not the flat archetypes of fairy tales with their easy categorizations of good and evil, enduring triumph and utter defeat.

Historical agency does not necessarily translate into definitive political or material success, even when leaving powerful, if unacknowledged, traces. If history's pulsing spirit defies the binary opposites of romance and tragedy, no history telling can ever be complete. All examinations of the past, no matter how richly explored, always leave tangled threads that cannot be fully traced. The story I have told in this book remains incomplete, unable to include those areas not yet deeply explored by historians—the history of mid-twentieth-century Puerto Rican race relations and identities, the social history of rural working-class Puerto Rican families during the 1940s and '50s, the historical experience of women who worked in the factories created during the early years of Operation Bootstrap, laboring Puerto Ricans' interaction with and participation in the island's growing welfare state between 1930 and 1960, and the development of large-scale Puerto Rican agricultural migration to the East Coast of the United States between the 1950s and the 1980s, to name just a few.

Concomitantly, the history of the Michigan sugar beet migrants does not simply end with devastating tragedy for the workers and their families, as it denies the triumphalist narratives about the 1940s and '50s spun by Muñocista enthusiasts and complicates leftist accounts of inexorable PPD hegemony and midcentury Puerto Rican political quiescence beyond the purview of nationalist movements. The many threads of the Michigan crisis continued to spin through history; they did not end in silenced desperation alone. Despite their disappointment in the responses of the Muñocista paternalist state to their demands and the PPD's successful defusing of the political crisis they had created, the Puerto Rican sugar beet migrants forcefully asserted their historical agency. Passive victims they were not. Muñoz Marín was unable to convince most of his compatriots to continue to serve Fred Crawford and the Michigan growers through the fall of 1950. The larger PPD push for massive Puerto Rican migration to the rural Midwest also failed. No Puerto Ricans returned to the beet fields in subsequent years, despite concerted attempts by Michigan Field Crops and Fred Crawford to lure them back.[29] In

1955, the Puerto Rican government announced itself "willing and anxious to serve agricultural mid-America as far west as the Rockies," but in 1960 PPD officials found themselves still unsuccessfully searching for ways to convince Puerto Rican workers to accept temporary rural migrant jobs there.[30]

Hipólito Reyes Sánchez may have said it best when he wrote to the Department of Labor in 1951 to proudly inform its leaders that he had made it to New York City, where friends and relatives had helped him find a permanent job. He would call on the Puerto Rican government no longer, since he could now, he said, "stand up and care for myself and my loved ones." His letter reminds us that those who thrived after the anguished sugar beet struggles of 1950 disappeared from the archival collections focused on the Michigan crisis; their numbers might be larger than we can measure, since their historical traces would only appear in other archives—those of diasporic community building or continued physical movement. Reyes Sánchez hoped to one day forget his experience in Michigan. He reminded his readers, "It's true that there we worked like slaves or worse than slaves." Offering political advice to his unsuccessfully paternalist political leaders, Reyes Sánchez reflected, "More than anything, I think that I will never again work in agriculture. You shouldn't plan any more migrations to put people through what I suffered in those frigid fields."[31]

Ultimately, the Michigan migrants' refusal to accept the exploitative conditions of the rural Midwest set undeniable limits on the plans of the powerful. If the workers' dreams of migratory prosperity remained unrealized, so too did elite dreams of a steady stream of Puerto Ricans moving from the island to the midwestern countryside. Instead, over the years, thousands more Puerto Ricans migrated to join family, friends, and neighbors who had left the sugar beet fields to find work in the industrial centers of New York, Detroit, Milwaukee, Chicago, Gary, Indiana, and Cleveland, Youngstown, and Lorain, Ohio, hoping, in echoes of PPD developmentalist rhetoric, to flourish by abandoning the land in favor of factory jobs. There they built communities in which they made histories of a different sort, resourcefully beginning again, under new circumstances and constraints, to *bregar*.[32]

NOTES

Introduction

Epigraph: AHA Presidential Address, *American Historical Review* 118:1 (February 2013): 19.

1 Esteban Casas Martínez to Honorable Sierra Berdecía, July 12, 1951, File Puerto Ricans in New York and Other States 1951, Box 2276, Tarea 96-20, Fondo de la Oficina del Gobernador (FOG), Archivo General de Puerto Rico (AGPR). All translations from Spanish are my own unless otherwise indicated.

2 Studies of Latin American masculinity generally and Puerto Rican manhood in particular have not yet closely examined labor migration. A notable exception is Garfield, "Tapping Masculinity," 275–308; and Cohen, *Braceros*. For more recent work on Puerto Rican masculinity, see Ramírez, *What It Means to Be a Man*; Ramírez, "Masculinity and Power in Puerto Rico"; García-Toro, Ramírez, and Castillo, *Los hombres no lloran*; Negrón-Muntaner, *Boricua Pop*; Jiménez, *Las prácticas de la carne*.

3 With almost three decades of feminist scholarship on Puerto Rican migration, we have a rich sense of Puerto Rican women's experience of migration to U.S. urban centers. Historians of Puerto Rican migration, however, have not yet embarked upon a study of how understandings of masculinity may have shaped the worldviews and choices of migrants—much less in the all-male world of agricultural migrants, who have also been largely ignored by studies of Puerto Rican movement to and from the United States.

   Virginia E. Sánchez-Korrol provided one of the first discussions of Puerto Rican women migrants to the United States in chapter 4 of *From Colonia to Community*. For some more recent work, see Rúa, *Grounded Identities*; Ruiz and Chavez, *Memories and Migrations*; Pérez, *The Near Northwest Side Story*; Ramos-Zayas, *National Performances*; Delgado, "Rufa Concepción Fernández," 171–180; Toro-Morn, "Boricuas in Chicago."

4 For a call to examine the intimacy of colonial and national politics, see Stoler, "Tense and Tender Ties." In her response to Stoler's article, Mary Renda pointed out that such political intimacy could manifest itself in interactions between men and in working-class expressions writ large—not only in the realm of cross-class heterosexual sex and family formation. Renda, "'Sentiments of a Private Nature.'"

5 Puerto Rico was certainly not unique in this respect, nor was the mid-twentieth century. Sarah Chambers provides an illuminating look into early nineteenth-century Chilean politics of paternity and paternalism in "The Paternal Obligation to Provide."

6 The popular cartoon *Diplo*, which ran in Puerto Rican newspapers through the 1940s and '50s, and the music of Rafael Cortijo and Ismael Rivera are only a few examples of such popular culture phenomena. For a foray into the former venue, see Jiménez Muñoz, "¡Xiomara mi hermana!" Popular music and dance of the 1940s and '50s have received the most scholarly attention of all these racially inflected cultural expressions. See most especially the prolific work of Angel G. Quintero Rivera. A few of his most relevant works are *Cuerpo y cultura* and *Salsa, sabor, y control*. Important, also, are Flores, *La venganza de Cortijo y otros ensayos* and "'¡Ecua Jei!'"; Berrios-Miranda and Dudley, "El Gran Combo, Cortijo, and the Musical Geography of Cangrejos/Santurce." We eagerly await scholarly analysis of other postwar racially inflected cultural venues.

7 An analogous absorption of race by gendered political discussions occurred in the 1890s in the southern Puerto Rican city of Ponce, when an antiprostitution panic helped create a political consensus between elite white liberals and mulatto artisans. See Findlay, *Imposing Decency*, 76–109. Ileana Rodríguez-Silva discusses Puerto Ricans' alternate voicing and avoiding of racial issues in nineteenth- and early twentieth-century political conflicts in *Silencing Race*.

8 Catherine Hall calls for the investigation of "discourses of affect and the livedness of emotional life" experienced by people living through processes of historical change. Hall, "Commentary," 452–468. César Seveso provides a compelling analysis of the emotions experienced by both Peronists and anti-Peronists after the Argentinian coup of 1955 and how they affected subsequent political action and meanings. Seveso, "Political Emotions and the Origins of the Peronist Resistance." See also Karen Kampwirth's discussion of the "passion of populism" in the introduction to her edited volume *Gender and Populism in Latin America*, 1–2.

9 Whalen, "Colonialism, Citizenship, and the Making of a Puerto Rican Diaspora." For early twentieth-century Puerto Rican migration to New York City, see, among others, Thomas, *Puerto Rican Citizen*; Sánchez-Korrol, *From Colonia to Community*; Ayala and Bernabé, *Puerto Rico in the American Century*.

10 See, for example, De Genova and Ramos-Zayas, *Latino Crossings*; Dávila, *Barrio Dreams*; Ruiz and Chávez, *Memories and Migrations*; Fernández, *Brown in the Windy City*.

11 Forthcoming research projects by Ismael García-Colón and Patricia Silver promise rich historical studies of Puerto Rican migrant farm laborers on the U.S. East Coast. They join the company of Duany, *Blurred Borders*, 81–105. Some of Silver's initial findings have been published in "'Culture Is More Than Bingo and Salsa'"; some of García-Colón's in "Claiming Equality." Several of the

articles in Whalen and Vásquez-Hernández's anthology *The Puerto Rican Diaspora* show how some significant Puerto Rican urban U.S. communities formed originally from migrations to surrounding rural areas. See Rivera, "La colonia de Lorain, Ohio"; Glasser, "From Rich Port to Bridgeport." See also Whalen, *From Puerto Rico to Philadelphia*. Cindy Hahamovitch briefly discusses Puerto Ricans' labor in East Coast agricultural camps during World War II in *The Fruits of Their Labor*, 186, 196, 200.

12 The "Mexican" migration to the broader Midwest was actually made up of a wide range of workers, including U.S. citizens of Mexican descent who migrated from the U.S. Southwest during northern planting and harvest seasons, Mexicans recruited through private, informal networks, and Mexicans brought to the United States through the state-supported *bracero* program, which was cosponsored by Mexico and the United States. Valdés, *Al Norte*.

13 Other historical contexts do not seem to have repeated this pattern of solidarity. De Genova, *Working the Boundaries*; Ramos-Zayas, *National Performances*; De Genova and Ramos-Zayas, "Latino Racial Formations in the United States"; Ramos-Zayas, "Delinquent Citizenship, National Performances." Lilia Fernández sees Mexican and Puerto Rican experiences in Chicago as much more parallel than do De Genova and Ramos-Zayas; she finds that the two groups carved out a broad Latino racial, social, and political space between the dominant groups of white European ethnics and black African Americans. Fernández, *Brown in the Windy City*.

   For a much earlier anthropological analysis of Mexicans and Puerto Ricans in Chicago, see Elena Padilla's master's thesis at the University of Chicago, "Puerto Rican Immigrants in New York and Chicago," originally completed in 1947, and its republished version in Rúa, *Latino Urban Ethnography and the Work of Elena Padilla*. De Genova provides an insightful commentary on Padilla's 1947 hopeful prognosis for Puerto Ricans' possible assimilation into Mexicanness in Chicago in "'White' Puerto Rican Migrants, the Mexican Colony, 'Americanization,' and Latino History."

14 As Kathleen Canning points out, struggles over citizenship rights of previously marginalized groups such as women or workers of either sex could "convene new communities, both national and civic" and create "'a new language of democratic participation.'" Canning, *Gender History in Practice*, 218, 216.

15 Carol Gluck urges scholars to analyze "the appeal of the modern to the peoples around the world who co-produced it," dubbing it "aspirational modernity." Gluck, "The End of Elsewhere," 377.

16 In this sense, those who ended up dominating Puerto Rican populism differed dramatically from their counterparts in the rest of Latin America, who not only used nationalist rhetoric but often instituted nationalist economic policies, such as import substitution and the expropriation of land, oil fields, mines, and other "national patrimonies" from U.S. control.

17 Citizens of colonized territories, Frederick Cooper notes, can often make "claims for resources, rights, or access . . . on the basis of *belonging*." Cooper, *Colonialism in Question*, 30, 29. Indeed, Puerto Ricans, if not North Americans, "took imperial space seriously," insisting on the equality of their U.S. citizenship. Thomas, *Puerto Rican Citizen*.

18 Scholars of many different empires have begun to call for careful local-level studies of imperialism. See, for example, Kramer, "Race, Empire, and Transnational History," 200–201; Stoler, *Haunted by Empire*; Ballantyne and Burton, *Bodies in Contact*, 4.

19 Paul A. Kramer calls the United States' method of imperial rule "empire by invitation"; he points out that we need to recognize both that the United States has long functioned as an imperial power and that it also has become skilled at employing "explicitly non-coercive modes of imperial power." Kramer, "Power and Connection," 1381. Alfred W. McCoy, Francisco Scarano, and Courtney Johnson, "On the Tropic of Cancer," 31, agree, noting that the U.S. empire has frequently built upon "an undeniable idealism" that "often fused development, altruism, and democratic ideals."

20 The study of populism in Latin America, especially its emergence throughout the region between the two World Wars, has produced a vast literature, too extensive to cite here. Few if any of these works, however, have studied Latin American migrants' engagement with their home country's populism and its promises, as this study does. For a foundational revisionist approach, see James, *Resistance and Integration*. Subsequent studies have expanded on James's insights to study populist regimes in Mexico and Brazil, among other countries. For a few of the newest historically informed works on Latin American populism, see Kiddle and Muñoz, eds., *Populism in Twentieth-Century Mexico*; Karush and Chamosa, *The New Cultural History of Peronism*; Elena, *Dignifying Argentina*.

Recent feminist scholarship on populist and revolutionary projects in Latin America has enriched the study of populism even further. These works stress women's experiences of subordinate incorporation into or exclusion from state reform projects and how plebeian men's empowerment through labor unions and political parties was often premised upon this female subordination, containment, and outright exclusion. Discourses exalting motherhood in service to the nation fused with exhortations to support working-class men in their aspirations for higher wages. Puerto Rico fits many of these general patterns. For a sampling of the extensive literature on populists' and radical democrats' insistence on similar reforms of gender relations in other parts of Latin America, see Weinstein, "Unskilled Worker, Skilled Housewife"; Klubock, *Contested Communities*; Tinsman, *Partners in Conflict*; Rosemblatt, *Gendered Compromises*; James, *Doña María's Story*; Olcott, *Revolutionary Women in Postrevolutionary Mexico*; Kampwirth, *Gender and Populism in Latin America*. For an interesting exception to the pattern of mobilizing women as mothers rather than as workers, see González-Rivera, *Before the Revolution*.

21 Jocelyn Olcott elaborates a similar analysis of Mexican populism, arguing that popular demands overflowed and expanded the limits of resource redistribution planned by populist leaders. Thus, she shows, populism constitutes an opening for pressure from below as well as a pathway for elite co-optation of popular desires. Olcott, "The Politics of Opportunity."

22 Díaz Quiñones, *El arte de bregar*.

23 Díaz Quiñones, *El arte de bregar*, 22–23, 27.

24 Díaz Quiñones, *El arte de bregar*, 84. For analyses of Muñoz Marín's politics that begin to develop analogous interpretations, see Villaronga, *Toward a Discourse of Consent*; and Álvarez Curbelo, "La conflictividad en el discurso político de Luis Muñoz Marín."

25 Frederick Cooper interprets African decolonization movements similarly: "One needs to appreciate the sense of possibility of these years and to understand what ensued not as an imminent logic of colonial history but as a dynamic process with a tragic end." Cooper, *Colonialism in Question*, 26.

26 Kramer, "Power and Connection," 1365, 1380–1381. See also Kozol and Hofmeyr, "AHR Conversation."

27 Kramer, "Power and Connection," 1383; Renda, "'Sentiments of a Private Nature,'" 885–886.

28 For the archive as sepulchre, predicated on death and burial, but open to the possibility of new life through archival access and users' interpretations, see Mbembe, "The Power of the Archive and Its Limits." For the archive as a space where the "dance of imagination" can occur, see Harris, "A Shaft of Darkness."

29 Burton, "Introduction." Michel-Rolph Trouillot analyzes four key moments when "silence enters the process of historical production": the creation of sources, the creation of archives, the creation of narratives, and the making of "history in the final instance." Trouillot, *Silencing the Past*, 26–30. For a brilliant analysis of the formation of Spanish colonial archives and the role of Andean notaries in the creation of the documents that inhabit them, see Burns, *Into the Archive*.

30 In this, my experience differs profoundly from that of Carolyn Steedman, who writes eloquently of the "loneliness" of the historian, imagining meanings of the past in the archive's solitude. Steedman, *Dust*. My first years of archival research were anything but solitary in Puerto Rico. They were, rather, deeply communal, and their success rested almost entirely on the good will and interest of various levels of archival staff—from the retrievers of documents to formally trained archivists—and other archive users. This research eventually became *Imposing Decency*. Antoinette Burton explores the power-saturated social relations of the archive in "Archive Stories."

31 Valdés, *Al Norte*, 118–134. Genevieve Casey's biography of Father Clement Kern, Catholic priest and advocate for farm worker justice in Detroit, also devotes sections to the priest's collaboration with the Puerto Rican beet workers. Casey, *Father Clem Kern*.

32 The quote is from Mbembe, "The Power of the Archive and Its Limits," 21; Hayes, Silvester, and Hartmann, "'Picturing the Past' in Namibia"; Foucault, *Archaeology of Knowledge and Discourse on Language*; Dirks, "Annals of the Archive"; Milligan, "'What Is An Archive?'"; Fritzche, "The Archive and the Case of the German Nation"; Derrida, *Archive Fever*.

33 Dirks, "Annals of the Archive"; Stoler, *Along the Archival Grain*; Flores Collazo, "Dioramas de la identidad"; Richards, *The Imperial Archive*.

34 Jean Allman writes evocatively of the "accidental" nature of postcolonial archives in Africa, as well as the transnational "shadow collections" that have been produced by weak national states' incapacity or disinterest in creating national archives. Allman, "Phantoms of the Archive." See also Hayes, Silvester, and Hartmann, "Picturing the Past"; and Rafael, *White Love and Other Events in Filipino History*.

35 María Dolores Luque's essay "El Desarrollo de los Archivos Históricos de Puerto Rico" provides a striking example of how the establishment, mainte-nance, and operation of official archives are often deeply bound up with nation formation—both in practice and in metaphor. Luque argues that an archive to gather documents from and for the entire island developed in tandem with an effective Puerto Rican national identity and Puerto Ricans' struggle for self-governance. Under U.S. rule in the early twentieth century, Luque points out, the Puerto Rican legislature created the position of an official historian, but the island's archive languished in a pitiful state, with documents stacked in a moldy, flooded basement. In 1926 a fire destroyed most of the documents; the surviving materials had to be moved to the University of Puerto Rico. Only in 1955, after the consolidation of PPD power in the 1940s, and the approval of the ELA and its new constitution in 1952, was the AGPR established and provided with a solid building and permanent staff who could collect and guard docu-mentation of Puerto Rico's past. Luque describes the AGPR of the early 1990s as an embodiment of Puerto Rico's still unresolved "national question"—poorly funded, but aspiring courageously to preserve Puerto Rico's patrimony and allow its citizens to investigate the questions "Who are we? Where are we headed?" "Archivistic activity in Puerto Rico during the last few decades," Luque asserts, "demonstrates a profound preoccupation with the conservation of documentary sources which has developed along with a maturing historical consciousness and a deeply rooted sense of identity." Thus, the AGPR represents, for Luque (who herself is the director of an archive based at the University of Puerto Rico's history department—the Centro de Investigaciones Históricas), the never-triumphant but ever-persistent search for Puerto Rican nationhood.

36 Dávila, *Sponsored Identities*.

37 Achille Mbembe argues that selection for deposit in the archive transforms documents from mere pieces of data to "a status of proof." Mbembe, "The Power of the Archive and Its Limits," 21. This resonates with Michel-Rolph Trouillot's discussion of the "archival moment" of historical creation. Trouillot, *Silencing the Past*.

38 Stoler, *Along the Archival Grain*, 8. In the boxes marked "obreros de Michigan" in the AGPR, then, we can discern two different archival moments, the originating one of knowledge, investigation, and attempted containment, and a subsequent, extended one, after the documents generated by the political crisis of 1950 were deposited en masse at the AGPR, years after the threats they had expressed had waned, to lie dormant, waiting for the wandering eyes of unsuspecting historians and inquisitive citizens to discover them.

39 Acosta, *La Mordaza*; Seijo Bruno, *La Insurrección Nacionalista en Puerto Rico*; Ferrao, *Pedro Albizu Campos y el nacionalismo puertorriqueño*; Ferrao, "Nacionalismo, hispanismo y élite intelectual en el Puerto Rico de los años treinta."

40 For critiques of the nationalist underpinnings of Puerto Rican studies and history, see Negrón-Muntaner and Grosfoguel, *Puerto Rican Jam*; and Pabón, *Nación postmortem*. Such nation-state-rooted blinders are not unique to Puerto Rico. See Saler and Podruchny, "Glass Curtains and Storied Landscapes."

41 Cooper, *Colonialism in Question*, 29.

42 Arcadio Díaz-Quiñones pointed out that Puerto Rico's diaspora was one of the primary points of "broken memory," the historical amnesia that has allowed Puerto Ricans to maintain a narrative of their painless rise to industrial prosperity out of the ashes of the Great Depression. See *La memoria rota* and especially *El arte de bregar*. Until the last decade, most historians of the island have ignored the Puerto Rican diaspora as a legitimate part of Puerto Rican history. I offer as an example my own book, *Imposing Decency*, in which I fail to consider the importance of travel and extra-island experiences in the lives of many Puerto Rican labor organizers, feminists, and liberal autonomists during the nineteenth and early twentieth centuries. For a few examples of Puerto Rican historians who made similar assumptions, see these pioneering works, among many others: Picó, *Vivir en Caimito*; García and Quintero Rivera, *Desafío y solidaridad*; Pantojas-García, *Development Strategies as Ideology*.

43 At times, the differences in vision and experience among artists from the island and from the diaspora have emerged as direct conflict as well as politically convenient amnesia. See Mohr, "Puerto Rican Writers in the United States." For some examples of classic and more recent diaspora-focused scholarship, see Iglesias, ed., *Memoirs of Bernardo Vega*; Nieves Falcón, *Los emigrantes puertorriqueños*; History Task Force, Centro de Estudios Puertorriqueños, *Labor Migration under Capitalism*; Maldonado-Denis, *The Emigration Dialectic*; Sánchez-Korrol, *From Colonia to Community*; Haslip-Viera and Baver, *Latinos in New York*; Rivera, *New York*

Ricans from the Hip-Hop Zone. See also the Cuadernos series on migration to New York produced in 1974 by the History Task Force and the Migration Workshop of the Center for Puerto Rican Studies at CUNY, Hunter College. These workshops and their subsequent publications were foundational to early scholarly discussions in New York on the Puerto Rican diaspora. I came upon the original 1974 proceedings and papers in the Colección Puertorriqueña of the Universidad de Puerto Rico, Río Piedras. Another important collaboration sponsored by the Center for Puerto Rican Studies was the famous "National Culture and Migration" by Campos and Flores.

44 Oberdeck, "Archives of the Unbuilt Environment," 253. Overmyer-Velázquez makes a similar critique of historians of Mexican and Chicano/a histories in "Histories and Historiographies of Greater Mexico."

45 Jorge Duany and Juan Flores, in their respective fields of anthropology and cultural studies, pioneered the analysis of fused diaspora and island experiences, long before the current explosion of historians' interest in transnational migration and identity formation. Their most recent work comes closest to the type of history I am proposing here, one that traces people's physical movement and its political, social, and cultural effects. Flores, *The Diaspora Strikes Back* and *From Bomba to Hip-Hop*; Duany, *Puerto Rican Nation on the Move* and *Blurred Borders*.

Recent scholarship has begun to integrate diasporic and island historical experiences more fully, seeing them as a unified, although diffuse, field of study. *CENTRO: The Journal of the Center for Puerto Rican Studies* has been crucial in this endeavor over the last decade, as it was in founding the field of Puerto Rican studies in the United States during the 1970s. For some other examples, see Ayala and Bernabé, *Puerto Rico in the American Century*; Torre, Rodríguez Vecchini, and Burgos, *Commuter Nation*; Negrón-Muntaner and Grosfoguel, *Puerto Rican Jam*, especially the essays in section 3; Pérez, *Near Northwest Side Story*; Grosfoguel, *Colonial Subjects*.

46 Ballantyne and Burton, "Introduction," in *Moving Subjects*, 3. See also Lazo, "Migrant Archives"; Bayly et al., "AHR Conversation"; Martinez-San Miguel, *Caribe Two Ways*; and Putnam, *Radical Moves*.

47 Fritzche, "The Archive and the Case of the German Nation," 200, 204.

48 While doing research on the beet field crisis, I did interviews about the controversy on five different local radio talk shows in Puerto Rican communities that sent large numbers of men to Michigan in 1950: San Lorenzo, Cayey, Yauco, Isabela, and San Juan, during which I solicited responses from listeners. Although callers asked probing questions about the event, no one contacted me in response to my pleas for oral history informants. I also wrote letters to the editor about my project and published advertisements in English- and Spanish-language newspapers in Milwaukee, Chicago, Detroit, Cleveland, and Lorain, Ohio, again to no avail. However, when I publicized my research through the

same methods in two small-town Michigan newspapers in counties from which sizable numbers of Puerto Ricans had penned protests in 1950, I received eight responses from elderly Anglo Michigan residents within a week.

49 Stoler, *Along the Archival Grain*, 138, 107.

50 Tinsman, *Partners in Conflict*; Rosas, "Flexible Families"; James, *Doña María's Story*.

51 See Emma Amador's forthcoming dissertation and her paper "Transnational Case Work."

52 Stoler, *Along the Archival Grain*, 33.

53 Fritzche, "The Archive and the Case of the German Nation," 204.

54 Harris, "A Shaft of Darkness," 71.

1 • Family and Fatherhood

1 Puerto Rico's experience with populism echoes that of many others throughout Latin America—from the most famous populist regimes in countries like Argentina (Juan and Eva Perón), Mexico (Lázaro Cárdenas), and Brazil (Getúlio Vargas) to the lesser-known populist leaders-turned-dictators of Central America and the Caribbean like Haiti's François Duvalier, Nicaragua's Anastasio Somoza, the Dominican Republic's Rafael Trujillo, and Cuba's Fulgencio Batista. Cites for important recent works on the South American and Mexican populist regimes are in the introduction, note 20. For key works on Caribbean and Central American populist dictators, see Derby, *The Dictator's Seduction*; Turits, *Foundations of Despotism*; Trouillot, *Haiti*; Gould, *To Lead as Equals*.

2 Scarano, *Sugar and Slavery in Puerto Rico*; Ramos Mattei, *Azúcar y esclavitud*; Ramos Mattei, *La sociedad del azúcar en Puerto Rico*; Scarano, *Puerto Rico*, 426–450.

3 Ramos Mattei, *La hacienda azucarera*; Bergad, *Coffee and the Growth of Agrarian Capitalism in Nineteenth-Century Puerto Rico*; Picó, *Amargo Café*; García and Quintero Rivera, *Desafío y solidaridad*; Quintero Rivera, *Patricios y plebeyos*.

4 Rosario Ferré's short story "Maldito amor" fictionally explores the racial anxiety and historical racial ambiguity of Puerto Rican elites. Ferré, *Maldito amor y otros cuentos*. For historical discussions, see Scarano, "The Jíbaro Masquerade and the Subaltern Politics of Creole Identity Formation in Puerto Rico"; Findlay, *Imposing Decency*; Hoffnung-Garskof, "To Abolish the Law of Castes"; Loveman, "The U.S. Census and the Contested Rules of Racial Classification in Early Twentieth-Century Puerto Rico"; Loveman and Muñiz, "How Puerto Rico Became White"; Rodríguez-Silva, *Silencing Race*; Figueroa, *Sugar, Slavery, and Freedom in Nineteenth-Century Puerto Rico*; Mintz, "Cañamelar"; and Wolf, "San José," 178–181.

For a discussion of how contemporary racial identifications among Puerto Ricans can shift quite deeply, depending on context and perspective, see Findlay, "Slipping and Sliding." Isar Godreau provides an insightful analysis of contemporary Puerto Ricans' complex, shifting verbal racial politics in "Slippery Semantics."

5 Findlay, "Love in the Tropics."

6 Bergad, *Coffee and the Growth of Agrarian Capitalism in Nineteenth-Century Puerto Rico*; Picó, *Libertad y servidumbre en el Puerto Rico del siglo XIX*; Quintero Rivera, *Patricios y plebeyos*.

7 Findlay, "Love in the Tropics," 142–149; Ober, *Puerto Rico and Its Resources*, 162–170; Dinwiddie, *Puerto Rico*, 162–166. Gary Y. Okihiro finds that Puerto Ricans' racialization by U.S. observers at the turn of the twentieth century was not so obvious as their obsessive racial mapping of Filipino phenotypical, geographical, cultural, and religious diversity. Okihiro argues that North Americans' racialization of Puerto Ricans during the early years of the military occupation was primarily implicit and accomplished through the feminization of Puerto Rican men and persistent assertions of their laziness, "tropical backwardness," and allegedly constant sexual activity. According to Okihiro, plebeian Puerto Ricans' racial identities, although undeniably inferior to Anglo North Americans', were subsumed by U.S. officials and reformers into a gendered understanding of incompetence, sexual dissolution, and docility. Okihiro, "Colonial Vision, Racial Visibility." I would agree in large part. However, it is clear that U.S. commentators and officials were quite unnerved by the uncontainable interracial interactions among plebeian Puerto Ricans they observed at the beginning of the twentieth century. By the late 1940s, though, this study will show, explicit discussions of racial identity in Puerto Rico had dropped almost entirely from public political discussions, displaced by an intensification of exhortations toward modernity, represented by a "properly" patriarchal domesticity. By 1950, then, gender had effectively subsumed race as never before in Puerto Rican political venues.

8 Picó, 1898, 73–79; García and Quintero Rivera, *Desafío y solidaridad*; Quintero Rivera, *Patricios y plebeyos*, 99–116; Negrón Portillo, *El Autonomismo puertorriqueño*.

9 Findlay, "Love in the Tropics," 142–149; García and Quintero Rivera, *Desafío y solidaridad*; Silva Gotay, *Protestantismo y política en Puerto Rico*; Coleson, "The Puerto Ricanization of Protestantism in Puerto Rico"; Valdés, *Organized Agriculture and the Labor Movement before the UFW*, 25–59; Sanabria, "Samuel Gompers and the American Federation of Labor in Puerto Rico."

10 Valdés, *Organized Agriculture and the Labor Movment before the UFW*, chapters 1–2; García and Quintero Rivera, *Desafío y solidaridad*; Quintero Rivera, *Conflictos de clase y política en Puerto Rico*; Silvestrini, *Los trabajadores Puertorriqueños y el Partido Socialista*; Scarano, *Puerto Rico*, 654–659.

11 The quotes are from Don Rubén del Pilar, personal communication, September 2, 1991. For other memories of the visceral hunger and poverty suffered in rural areas of Puerto Rico during the 1920s and '30s, see Acevedo González, *¡Que tiempos aquellos!*, 70–120.

12 For discussions of the intensifying protests during the 1930s, see Dietz, *Economic History of Puerto Rico*; García and Quintero Rivera, *Desafío y solidaridad*; Taller de Formación Política, *Huelga en la caña*; Taller de Formación Política, *No estamos pidiendo el cielo*; and Villaronga, *Toward a Discourse of Consent*. Ayala and Bernabé provide an excellent overview of this tension-ridden period in *Puerto Rico in the American Century*, 95–116. See also Valdés, *Organized Agriculture and the Labor Movement before the UFW*, 22–106.

For discussions of women needleworkers' experiences and organizing activities, see Boris, "Needlewomen under the New Deal in Puerto Rico," 39–49; González García, *Una puntada en el tiempo*; and González García, "La industria de la aguja en Puerto Rico y sus orígenes en los Estados Unidos," 59–80; Baerga-Santini, "Las jerarquías sociales y las expresiones de Resistencia"; Muñiz-Mas, "Gender, Work, and Institutional Change in the Early Stage of Industrialization"; and Gallart, "Las mujeres en la discursiva de Luis Muñoz Marín."

13 Scarano, *Puerto Rico*, 692–698; Ferrao, *Pedro Albizu Campos y el nacionalismo puertorriqueño*; Taller de Formación Política, *¡Huelga en la caña!*

14 Despite their impermanence, Manuel Rodríguez argues that these New Deal efforts constituted an important shift in the way the United States attempted to govern Puerto Rico—through the "biopolitics" of ensuring a certain basic standard of living for the population rather than through an overtly exploitative colonialism. Rodríguez, *A New Deal for the Tropics*. For differing interpretations of the 1930s in Puerto Rico, see Pantojas-García, "Puerto Rican Populism Revisited"; González, "La lucha de clases y la política en el Puerto Rico de la década del '40"; Santiago-Valles, *Subject People and Colonial Discourses*; Villaronga, *Toward a Discourse of Consent*.

15 For women social workers' history, see Burgos, *Pioneras de la profesión de trabajo social en Puerto Rico*; and Amador, "Transnational Case Work"; as well as Amador's forthcoming PhD dissertation. For the movements in Puerto Rico in favor of birth control, see Briggs, *Reproducing Empire*, 90–98; and Ramírez de Arellano and Seipp, *Colonialism, Catholicism, and Contraception*.

16 Valdés, *Organized Agriculture and the Labor Movement before the UFW*, 74–83; Ayala and Bernabé, *Puerto Rico in the American Century*, 138–146.

17 The PPD's strategy on this score followed a pattern very common among populist regimes around the world. See Panizza, "Introduction," in *Populism and the Mirror of Democracy*, 1–31.

18 Muñoz Marín, "¡Qué grande es el Partido Popular Democrático!," in *Palabras* (1980), 347–365.

19 This is a common feature of the "passion of populist moments." Panizza, "Introduction," in *Populism and the Mirror of Democracy*, 10–25.

20 James, *Resistance and Integration*, 22.

21 Rodríguez Juliá, *Las tribulaciones de Jonás*, 53.

22 Daniel James discusses how the early Peronist movement in Argentina utilized similar strategies of rehabilitating denigratory descriptions of working-class people. James, *Resistance and Integration*, 31–34.

23 Córdova, "In His Image and Likeness." Córdova argues that the silhouetted jíbaro emblem created an effectively racially and class-neutral (albeit clearly male) image which, like a religious icon, encouraged multiple understandings of the PPD message and thus broadened its appeal. For a compelling, quite different analysis of the changing imagery of rural jíbaros and of Muñoz Marín himself, see González López, "Imágenes."

Muñoz Marín and the PPD certainly were not the first to invoke the jíbaro as part of an attempt to reshape Puerto Rican politics and assert a quasi-national identity. For its earlier uses as both the incorporation of popular interests and as insult, see Scarano, "The Jíbaro Masquerade and the Subaltern Politics of Creole Identity Formation"; Findlay, *Imposing Decency*, 28–52; and Guerra, *Popular Expression and National Identity in Puerto Rico.*

24 James, *Resistance and Integration*, 21, 22.

25 Muñoz Marín, "El proyecto de los mercados PRACO," in *Palabras*, vol. 4, 338. See also "Para hacer la Ley de Tierras aún major," *El Batey*, March 14, 1942.

26 Muñoz Marín, "Decisión del Corte Supremo," in *Palabras* (1980), 289–324.

27 "Lo que se compra con 10 pesos," *El Mundo*, April 14, 1947.

28 Other Latin American populists have presented themselves as priests or spiritual leaders. See Kampwirth, "Introduction," in *Gender and Populism in Latin America*, 13; and Fernandes, "Gender, Popular Participation, and the State in Chávez's Venezuela," 211.

29 Muñoz Marín, "Que grande" and "En la víspera de las elecciones," radio speech, 1940, 366–381, both in *Palabras* (1980).

30 "Esto no es bueno, pero es verdad," *El Batey*, March 14, 1942.

31 Muñoz Marín, "En la víspera de las elecciones." Throughout the early 1940s, Muñoz Marín's radio and mass meeting speeches as well as many articles in *El Batey* directly addressed both men and women in this manner.

32 "Muñoz Marín y los desempleados," *El Batey*, March 15, 1939. For a few more examples, see "Lean esto en todos los barrios—ejemplo del barrio Hoyo Mulas de Carolina," *El Batey*, September 1, 1948, 7; "Filosofía del Partido Popular Democrático," *El Batey*, October 28, 1950; "Muñoz Marín en los campos," *El Batey*, August 15, 1951, 1.

33 "Tributo de Muñoz Marín a las mujeres," *El Batey*, September 1, 1948, 1; "Munoz Marin ante el pueblo," *El Batey*, September 1, 1948. See also "Lean esto las mujeres de nuestros campos," *El Batey*, April 1939; Muñoz Marín, "A las mujeres de Puerto Rico," in *Palabras*, vol. 4, 606–619.

34 For early twentieth-century anarchist and socialist approaches to "the woman question," see Azize Vargas, *La mujer en la lucha*; Baerga-Santini, "Las jerarquías

sociales y las expresiones de resistencia"; Findlay, *Imposing Decency*, 159–166; Valle Ferrer, *Luisa Capetillo*; Ramos, *Amor y anarquía*, 11–58.

35 Muñoz Marín, "Las mujeres dieron el ejemplo en la inscripción," in *Palabras*, vol. 3, 498–501. In these rhetorical flourishes, Muñoz Marín resuscitated the political essays of late nineteenth-century liberals such as Salvador Brau, who saw women's moral and social reform of men as the only hope for creating a productive, moral peasantry. Findlay, *Imposing Decency*, 53–61.

36 "Tributo a las mujeres," *El Batey*, September 1, 1948, 1.

37 See Barceló Miller, "'Un gobierno de hombres,'" 47.

38 "Grupo de Maria Luisa Guerra apela ante Muñoz la decisión de Solá en cuanto a nominación en Río Piedras," *El Imparcial*, August 12, 1948, 3; "Confían en que será cambiado," *El Imparcial*, August 12, 1948; Gallart, "Las mujeres en la discursiva de Luis Muñoz Marín"; Gallart, "Political Empowerment of Puerto Rican Women."

39 Barceló Miller, "'Un gobierno de hombres.'" In this sense, the PPD's dominant vision of women was more limited than that of the early working-class Puerto Rican radicals, who readily acknowledged women's status as wage workers and who did not consistently reduce them to mothers or wives. Many early twentieth-century male radicals, however, were not immune to patriarchal dreams. They did still call for the creation of an idealized society where men would care for women, who in turn would happily accept their enclosure within a utopian domesticity. Findlay, *Imposing Decency*, 156–158; Baerga-Santini, "Las jerarquías sociales y las espresiones de resistencia." For similar historical patterns in Chile and Brazil, see Tinsman, *Partners in Conflict*; and Wolfe, "From Working Mothers to Housewives," 91–109.

40 The most obvious examples of such images are the ubiquitous PPD party symbol of the pava and the advertisements for the Operation Bootstrap industrialization plan that dotted island newspapers throughout the late 1940s.

41 Villaronga, *Toward a Discourse of Consent*, 50–51; Muñoz Marín, "La injusticia sobre los choferes," in *Palabras* (1980), 279–282.

42 Díaz Quiñones, *El arte de bregar*, 65.

43 Muñoz Marín, "Decisión del corte supremo de los Estados Unidos de América sobre la Ley de las 500 cuerdas," in *Palabras* (1980), 289–324. See also "El rancho contra el pueblo," *El Batey*, June 15, 1942; "Su voto es su arma," *El Batey*, April 1939.

44 Jiménez, *Las prácticas de la carne*, 65–67.

45 Muñoz Marín, "Decisión del corte supremo," 317; Muñoz Marín, "Qué grande es el Partido," 362; Muñoz Marín, "Cómo se propulsó la Ley de las 500 cuerdas," in *Palabras* (1980), 283–288.

46 Early twentieth-century labor organizers in Puerto Rico also used similar racially redolent rhetorical strategies in their denunciations of "wage slavery." Findlay, *Imposing Decency*, 141–144. During the late nineteenth century,

Afro–Puerto Rican artisans who constituted the radical wing of the Puerto Rican Liberal Party frequently asserted their manhood as a central strategy in efforts to challenge racial prejudice. Hoffnung-Garskof, "To Abolish the Law of Castes."

47 Turits, *Foundations of Despotism*; Derby, *The Dictator's Seduction*; Fernandes, "Gender, Popular Participation, and the State in Chávez's Venezuela"; and Sosa-Bucholz, "Changing Images of Male and Female in Ecuador."

48 Many Puerto Ricans also interpreted Muñoz Marín's political stature as an inheritance from his father, Luis Muñoz Rivera, a prominent liberal who by the 1930s had been canonized as one of Puerto Rico's founding fathers. Working people wrote letters to Muñoz Marín linking their experiences of seeing him speak to those of his father's public speeches and journalism. See, for example, José Miranda to Luis Muñoz Marín, October 28, 1947, Folder 3, Subseries 13: EEUU, Nueva York, Series 8, Section IV, Fundación Luis Muñoz Marín (hereinafter FLMM); Aurelio Vásquez to Luis Muñoz Marín, Folder 16, Subseries 13: EEUU, Nueva York, Series 8, Section IV, FLMM.

49 Villaronga, *Toward a Discourse of Consent*, 208.

50 González López, "Imágenes," 391–396; Barceló Miller, "'Un gobierno de hombres'"; "Muñoz Marín ante el pueblo," *El Batey*, September 1, 1948. Intensely personalized paternalism has been a long-standing historical pattern in Latin America, particularly cultivated by populist leaders. See Kampwirth, "Introduction," in *Gender and Populism in Latin America*, 12–13. For Porfirio Díaz's role as surrogate father of his loyal children-subjects in late nineteenth-century Mexico, see McNamara, *Sons of the Sierra*. Richard Turits explores how rural Dominicans remembered Trujillo as a "stern but solicitous father, concerned with both maintaining rural values and ushering in progress." Turits, *Foundations of Despotism*, 206–231. Lauren Derby agrees that Trujillo's paternalism was built on his image as a "disciplinary" rather than a tender, caring father. Derby, *The Dictator's Seduction*, 23–24. Muñoz Marín's paternalism was a gentler style; he positioned himself as a redemptive father leading a newly formed national family built on love and respect, rather than fear.

51 Rodríguez Juliá, *Las tribulaciones de Jonás*, 101.

52 See, for example, the letters collected in FLMM, Section IV, Series 8 (Ultramar), Subseries 13, EEUU, Nueva York. For a discussion of highland peasants' personalized loyalty to Muñoz Marín, see Wolf, "San José," 213. For further examples and discussion of the intense personalism of Muñoz Marín's populist appeal, see Rodríguez Juliá, *Las tribulaciones de Jonás*; Díaz Quiñones, *El arte de bregar*. For a few photos of passionate crowds gathering to see Muñoz Marín during his political heyday, see "Muñoz Marín ante el pueblo," *El Batey*, September 1, 1948, 5; *El Batey*, October 20, 1952, 7–10.

53 See, for example, "Lo que es la ley de Constitución y Convenio," *El Batey*, October 28, 1950, 1–2; "Esto no es bueno pero es verdad," *El Batey*, March 14, 1942.

54 Muñoz Marín, "En la víspera de las elecciones," in *Palabras* (1980), 377–378.

55 Box 1, Gen. 2, postcard collection, Centro Archives, Hunter College, New York.

56 See, for example, Muñoz Marín, "Contra la resolución Crawford," in *Palabras*, vol. 3, 343–344; Muñoz Marín, "Democracy Would Be a Hoax," in *Palabras*, vol. 3, 321–323; Muñoz Marín, "La venta de la telefónica," in *Palabras*, vol. 3, 553–554; Ayala and Bernabé, *Puerto Rico in the American Century*, 142. For fiery language in the early years of the PPD that denounced the exploitation visited on Puerto Rican working people by rapacious sugar corporations, see Muñoz Marín, "¿Sabía Usted?," *El Batey*, March 15, 1939; Muñoz Marín, "Decisión del Corte Supremo," in *Palabras* (1980), 295–296, 306–307. By 1950, Muñoz Marín had abandoned such excoriation of elites and absentee sugar barons; instead, even the sugar industry, tamed by government reforms, was now sometimes presented as an important ally in the march to progress. "Una Edición especial dedicada a la industria de Puerto Rico," advertisement for *Puerto Rico Ilustrado* in *El Mundo*, November 26, 1949, 12.

57 See, for example, "La guerra se pelea para que continue la obra de justicia," *El Batey*, March 14, 1942; "Obra de justicia continuara en medio de la guerra," *El Batey*, March 15, 1940. Manuel Rodríguez discusses the high regard in which many working-class Puerto Ricans held Franklin D. and Eleanor Roosevelt, even while critical of U.S. colonial rule itself. Rodríguez, *A New Deal for the Tropics*, 108–111.

58 Muñoz Marín, *Historia del Partido Popular Democrático*, 73, 86.

59 "El Gobernador Rexford G. Tugwell lucha por la Justicia del Pueblo," *El Batey*, March 14, 1942; Muñoz Marín, "La libertad y los derechos del hombre," in *Palabras*, vol. 4, 260–264; Muñoz Marín, "El porvenir de Puerto Rico y del hemisferio Americano es el porvenir de la democracy," in *Palabras* (1980), 333–343. Muñoz Marín, "Homenaje al soldado típico de Puerto Rico, Pedro Ocasio," in *Palabras*, vol. 4, 34–36; Muñoz Marín, "A los soldados en Panamá," in *Palabras*, vol. 4, 32–33. See Álvarez Curbelo, "Las lecciones de la guerra."

60 Ayala and Bernabé, *Puerto Rico in the American Century*, discuss this chilling turn away from political pluralism, 136–178, and its economic ramifications, 179–200. They also trenchantly note that the Muñocista government was the only mid-twentieth-century populist regime in Latin America not to increase its polity's national economic autonomy during this period, 151.

61 Wolf, "San José," 247.

62 Wolf, "San José," 246–247. See also "Srta. Gómez insta a campesinas a ingresar en Clubs de hogar," *El Mundo*, May 2, 1950, 28.

63 Muñoz Marín, "La libertad y los derechos del hombre," in *Palabras*, vol. 4, 260–264; Muñoz Marín, *Historia del Partido Popular Democrático*, 112; Muñoz Marín, "The Overall Picture of Realities in Puerto Rico Is as Follows," in *Palabras*, vol. 4, 311–315; Gutierrez Franqui, "Status politico solo compete a los Estados Unidos y Puerto Rico," *El Imparcial*, July 5, 1947; "Las explicaciones sencillas de

Muñoz Marín," El Batey, September 1, 1948, 8; "Filosofía del Partido Popular Democrático," El Batey, October 28, 1950.

64 Villaronga, *Toward a Discourse of Consent*, 67. See also Ayala and Bernabé, *Puerto Rico in the American Century*, 95–116, 136–161.

65 For a few examples of labor actions during the 1950s, see "Termina huelga," El Imparcial, March 10, 1954; "Diez heridos en motín," El Imparcial, March 22, 1954; "Decretan huelga en muelles isla," El Imparcial, May 26, 1954; "Limitarán derecho declarar huelga," El Imparcial, June 13, 1954; "Última hora termina huelga," El Imparcial, June 17, 1954; "Trabajadores UTM dudan de la buena fe de liderato de la ILA," El Imparcial, June 27, 1954.

66 For just a few examples, see, in El Imparcial: "Huelga en Central Aguirre," February 22, 1947, 6; "Otra huelga de taxis en San Juan," February 27, 1947, 2; "Huelgas paran producción de cemento: Miles quedan sin trabajo," August 16, 1949, 3; "Gestiona de líderes obreros arreglen huelga en puerto de Jobos," April 18, 1947, 4. For a few in El Mundo, see "Hieren a empleados de la fabrica de envases," March 26, 1947; "Tres centrales en paro de producción por una huelga de azucareros," May 12, 1947, 1; "Una fábrica fue atacada a tiros y con pedradas," December 16, 1947, 14; "Obreros van a la huelga hoy en la industria del azucar: Sigue impasse en los salaries," March 7, 1949, 1.

67 See, among many others, "Unión de obreros de 'Los Muchachos' han perdido la fe en JRT," El Imparcial, February 13, 1947; "Obreros del PEG en huelga; dicen no se les paga," El Imparcial, August 10, 1948; and "Protesta obrera en Mayagüez," El Imparcial, August 11, 1948, 1; "Van a la huelga 300 empleados de central Roig," El Mundo, November 8, 1947, 2; Arana Soto, "Imputan discriminacion racial a contratantes de obreros para EEUU," El Imparcial, January 20, 1948; "Está pendiente aún resolución sobre huelga de consumidores," El Mundo, April 14, 1947.

68 "Muñoz mediará crisis de APA y trabajadores," February 26, 1949, 1; "Representante patronal pide reformas en Junta Insular Salario Mínimo," El Imparcial, February 22, 1947; "Sigue el caso de injunction contra los obreros," El Mundo, March 20, 1947, 1.

69 Among others, see Carlos Guzmán, "Unión de Yauco distribuye seguro social a beneficiarios de 23 obreros fenecidos," El Imparcial, January 2, 1947; "El Express ofrece aumentar salaries a trabajadores," El Imparcial, January 29, 1949, 11; Ernesto Cuebas, "Beneficia acerca de 4000 obreros opinión del juez David Chávez," El Imparcial, November 18, 1948; "Asamblea legislative aprueba proyectos sobre seguro para obreros industria azucarera," El Imparcial, December 22, 1948, 2; "Nuevos pagos para obreros de la caña," El Mundo, May 19, 1948, 1; "Celebran ley de seguro a favor obreros azucar," El Mundo, May 19, 1948, 4.

70 In her study of the Dominican Republic during this period, Lauren Derby points out that these sorts of official acts could resonate powerfully with popular practices of patronage between the wealthy and the poor; such gifts

"conceal a relationship of obligation, one that becomes domination when gifts are highly assymetrical. . . . The power it [the gift] carries is the power to compel reciprocity." Derby, *The Dictator's Seduction*, 10–11. See also Muñoz Marín, "Distribución, en fincas de Beneficio Proporcional de la Autoridad de Tierras en Arecibo," in *Palabras*, vol. 3, 616–618; "Gobernador firma leyes sobre desempleo obrero: El seguro queda reducido," *El Mundo*, January 7, 1966; "Choferes van exponer caso a Muñoz Marín," *El Mundo*, March 3, 1949; Muñoz Marín, "El mandato a la Asamblea Legislativa por el pueblo de Puerto Rico," in *Palabras*, vol. 4, 506–524; "Obreros cobran jornales adecuados," *El Imparcial*, November 15, 1948.

71 For just a few cases, see "Conciliadores no logran poner de acuerdo el AAA y el sindicato azucarero," *El Imparcial*, January 11, 1948, 11; "Investigan si agencia de empleos burla la ley," *El Imparcial*, July 11, 1949; Luis O. Burgos, "Denuncian insalubridad caseríos Central Roig," *El Imparcial*, July 14, 1949.

72 "Lcdo. Nestor A. Rodríguez Escudero," *El Imparcial*, September 12, 1948; Antonio Arana Soto, "Imputan discriminacion racial a contratantes de obreros para EEUU," *El Imparcial*, January 20, 1948; "Está pendiente aún resolución sobre huelga de consumidores," *El Mundo*, April 14, 1947; "Entidades obreras en simpatía con asamblea de consumidores," *El Mundo*, April 16, 1947; Ricardo Villamil, "Incidentes ayer en paro de Colegio de Mayagüez," *El Mundo*, April 2, 1947; "Voz del Pueblo," *El Imparcial*, April 1948, Rec. 26; Felix Cohen, "Inquilinos de caserío alegan ser difamados por periódico de ASH," *El Imparcial*, February 11, 1948.

73 In *El Mundo*, see the following: "La manifestación de veteranos frente al Capitolio Insular ayer," April 3, 1947; "HV urge de Gobernador rápida acción en asuntos de viviendas," August 15, 1948; Carlos Nieves Rivera, "Grupo de veteranos gestiona que le reformen su caserío," October 23, 1949, 10; "Hay plan para vender fincas a veteranos," April 24, 1947; "Legión gestiona un caserío para Cayey," December 23, 1947, 30; "Perez insta cumplir carta a veteranos," June 5, 1947, 19; "160 casa para veteranos levantarán Floral Park," March 26, 1947, 14; "Acuerdo para la enseñanza de veteranos," July 11, 1947, 1. "Reclaman prioridad," *El Imparcial*, May 7, 1948, 23; "Doscientos veteranos de Guayama protestan por no haber recibido hace 3 meses pagos por desempleo," August 13, 1948, 6.

74 For a similar process in Peronist Argentina, see Elena, *Dignifying Argentina*, 206–220.

75 "Populares de Cayey se juramentan contra las imposiciones de Muñoz," *El Imparcial*, August 2, 1948. See also "Torrech no acepta petición de Muñoz," *El Imparcial*, August 9, 1948, 2.

76 "Grupo de María Luisa Guerra apela ante Muñoz la deciaión de Solá en cuanto a nominación de Río Piedras," *El Imparcial*, August 12, 1948, 3; "Confían en que

será cambiado," El Imparcial, August 12, 1948. For other controversies of this kind, see "Lío Popular," El Imparcial, August 12, 1948; Gallart, "Political Empowerment of Puerto Rican Women"; and Gallart, "Las mujeres en la discursiva de Luis Muñoz Marín."

77 James, Resistance and Integration, 40. For some worried commentary on labor combativeness and the necessity for calm to attract U.S. investment, see William J. Dorvillier, "De Washington a Puerto Rico," El Mundo, September 11, 1947.

78 Muñoz Marín, "Hay que denunciar a los partidos políticos disfrazados," in Palabras, vol. 4, 250–257; "Muñoz Marín hace gestiones para controlar un periódico," El Imparcial, March 6, 1948, 2; "'El Universal' pasa a poder de Muñoz Marín el lunes," El Imparcial, April 4, 1948; "Acusa Ramón Barreto Pérez a ciertos funcionarios del gobierno de abuser la buena fe de obreros boricuas," El Imparcial, June 27, 1948, 17; "Muñoz invita al pueblo que los compre y que los lea, pero que no crea en 'El Mundo' ni 'El Imparcial,'" El Imparcial, August 1, 1948, 2; "Alcalde de Aguada y otros líderes populares hacen ingreso en el PIP," El Imparcial, August 9, 1948, 2; "Long pide exención de contribuciones," El Imparcial, August 23, 1948, 2; "Condenan a una agencia de empleos a devolver más de $1,000 a obreros," El Imparcial, April 1, 1949, 6.

79 Ayala and Bernabé, Puerto Rico in the American Century, 162–167.

80 Gallart, "Political Empowerment of Puerto Rican Women"; Gallart, "Las mujeres en la discursiva de Luis Muñoz Marín"; Ayala and Bernabé, Puerto Rico in the American Century, 156–162. See, for example, "Luis Muñoz Marín ante el pueblo," El Batey, September 1, 1948, 5; "Lean esto en todos los barrios—el ejemplo del barrio Hoyo Mulas de Carolina," El Batey, September 1, 1948.

81 "Don Luis Siéntese!," El Mundo, January 2, 1949, 37–38. The original is a two-page spread, with the cane workers hoeing across the bottom of both pages. The rest of the first page is filled with a poem paying homage to Muñoz Marín "guiding his people to freedom." This representation of docile working men accepting the leadership and enlightenment offered by progressively minded elites resonates deeply with the discourse of the late nineteenth-century Liberal Autonomist Party—one of whose founding members was Muñoz Marín's father, Luis Muñoz Rivera. Findlay, Imposing Decency, chapters 2 and 3. See also Miguel López, "La mision educadora del Agente Agrícola en la Isla," El Mundo, August 8, 1947.

82 For just a few examples, see Armando Torres Vega, "Pan, Tierra, y Libertad," El Imparcial, February 22, 1948, 11; "Alcalde Villarubia agradece extensión luz a zonas rurales," El Imparcial, March 8, B; A. González Orona, "Muñoz Marín, instrumento del imperialism," El Imparcial, October 3, 1948, 15; "Agencias del gobierno se openen a que obrero reconstruye su casa, que practicamente se le está cayendo," El Imparcial, October 10, 1948, 2; "Alerta a los obreros," El Imparcial, October 18, 1948, 19; "Cuesta $6,000,000 el traslado de familias de zona 'El Fanguito,'" El Imparcial, June 1, 1949, 5, 26.

1 Eduardo Elena discusses an analogous phenomenon in Peronist Argentina. Elena, *Dignifying Argentina*, 67–70, 119–136. See also Milanesio, *Workers Go Shopping in Argentina*.

2 Strasser and Tinsman, "It's a Man's World?" The authors note that such political projects were promoted "with astonishing breadth" in many different nation-building contexts throughout the world over the course of the nineteenth and twentieth centuries.

3 For early critical analyses of the PPD zest for modernity, see the essays in Rivera Medina and Ramírez, *Del cañaveral a la fábrica*. Contrast Rafael Cabrera's interpretation of PPD modernity as a successfully hegemonic, coherent political project with later analyses of the anxieties that lay at the core of Luis Muñoz Marín's and the PPD's drive toward modernization. Cabrera Collazo, "La 'criollización' del desarrollismo y la inclusión de lo puertorriqueño en tres discursos inaugurales de Luis Muñoz Marín," 233–239; Luque de Sánchez, "'La buena vida o la vida buena'"; Alegría Ortega, "La gobernación de Luis Muñoz Marín."

4 Ley de Tierras, Artículos 74, 76.

5 Muñoz Marín, "Cómo se propulsó la Ley de las 500 Cuerdas," in *Palabras* (1980), 283–288; Muñoz Marín, "Decisión del Corte Supremo," in *Palabras* (1980), 289–324; Muñoz Marín, "Distribución en fincas de Beneficio Proporcional de la Autoridad de Tierras en Arecibo," in *Palabras*, vol. 3, 616–628; "Títulos y propiedad en las parcelas," *El Batey*, October 20, 1952, 2.

6 Tinsman, *Partners in Conflict*, 21–24, 34–37, discusses similar concerns for inquilino families in Chile prior to the land reforms of the 1960s.

7 See Acevedo González, *¡Que tiempos aquellos!*, for vivid descriptions of agregado living conditions during the 1920s and '30s. James Dietz discusses the broad outlines of the *parcela* distributions in *Economic History of Puerto Rico*, 200–201.

8 Rubén Nazario Velasco brilliantly analyzes the economic, social, and cultural implications of the PPD's assertion that the majority of Puerto Rican land was unproductive. Nazario Velasco, "Pan, casa, libertad."

9 Ley de Tierras, Artículos 74, 76; "Consideran enmendar el Título Qunto de la Ley de Tierras," *El Mundo*, December 28, 1947, 1. See also Ayala and Bernabé, *Puerto Rico in the American Century*, 184–186; Nazario Velasco, "Pan, casa, libertad"; and Dietz, "La reinvención del subdesarrollo," 194–201.

10 Unfortunately, García Colón's interesting ethnohistorical analysis of *parcela* communities in Cidra does not explore these gendered family dynamics in detail. Hopefully, future researchers will take them up. García-Colón, *Land Reform in Puerto Rico*; García-Colón, "Buscando Ambiente"; and García-Colón, "Playing and Eating Democracy"; "Las comunidades rurales," *El Imparcial*, November 19,

1949; García Carrera, "Explican las funciones de programas sociales de autoridad de tierras," El Mundo, November 27, 1949, 21.

11 Mintz, Three Ancient Colonies, 171–174. For an analogous process with suggestive possibilities for interpreting Puerto Rico's history of rural industrialization, see Tinsman, "Household Patrones."

12 Weinstein, "Developing Inequality." See also Cohen, Braceros, 32–33.

13 Ayala and Bernabé note that Muñoz Marín refused "geographical determinism," insisting that all people, no matter in which part of the world they lived, had the right and the capacity to live materially dignified lives. Ayala and Bernabé, Puerto Rico in the American Century.

14 Nazario Velasco, "Pan, casa, libertad," 153. Velasco even argues that "the reign of the parcela helped to legitimize the suburb," by separating the land completely from its agricultural, productive capacity. He points out sardonically that the first family targeted for expropriation under the Ley de Tierras in Puerto Rico eventually made a fortune by converting their cane fields into a huge urbanización, San Patricio, 160. Silvia Álvarez-Curbelo argues that this desire to abandon agriculture in favor of the modernity of industrial production can be discerned much earlier in Muñoz Marín's speeches. Álvarez-Curbelo, "La conflictividad en el discurso político de Luis Muñoz Marín," 20–37.

James L. Dietz points out that populist regimes throughout Latin America made this turn away from agriculture toward an allegedly modernizing industrialization. Thus, Puerto Rico was not exceptional in this regard. Dietz, "La reinvención del subdesarrollo," 181. The neighboring Dominican Republic implemented a strikingly different path to modernity during this historical period, however. The populist dictator Rafael Trujillo's government effectively created a sedentary, agriculturalist peasantry in much of the Dominican countryside by redistributing large amounts of land for long-term residence and agricultural production between 1932 and 1960; male heads of these newly constituted peasant households were praised as the "men of work" who would provide food for their nation and ensure its transition to modern prosperity. Turits, Foundations of Despotism.

15 Manos a la Obra, El Imparcial, September 8, 1948; see also Manos a la Obra, El Mundo, May 28, 1947; and Nazario Velasco, "Pan, casa, libertad."

16 "Hecho para la industria privada," El Imparcial, February 17, 1947, advertisement for the Red Cape Leather Factory.

17 See, for example, Muñoz Marín, "El mandato a la Asamblea Legislativa por el pueblo de Puerto Rico," in Palabras, vol. 3, 506–524; Muñoz Marín, "Hay que dar la batalla por la producción," in Palabras, vol. 4, 281–286; Muñoz Mariñ, "Es necesario aumentar la producción en la zona cafetalera," in Palabras, vol. 4, 265–267; Muñoz Marín, "El problema poblacional de Puerto Rico," in Palabras, vol. 4, 287–289.

18 Paulo Drinot discusses a similar attempt in Peru to whiten the nation through industrialization and the creation of a factory-based proletariat, imagined as virile, white, and male. Drinot, *The Allure of Labor*. Barbara Weinstein shows how the populist regime of Getúlio Vargas in Brazil equated "citizen workers" with male, skilled industrial laborers, discursively erasing both rural and women workers. Weinstein, "Making Workers Masculine."

19 Paulo Drinot points out that for Peruvian elites, industrialization became a cultural project as much as an economic one, integral to their aspirations for modernizing their nation. Drinot, *The Allure of Labor*.

20 Manos a la Obra, *El Imparcial*, June 16 and 18, 1948. For a few more examples, see Manos a la Obra, *El Imparcial*, February 18, 1948; Toro Calder, "Relato de una familia boricua que se impone a dificultades," *El Mundo*, July 31, 1949, 21; and Manos a la Obra, *El Mundo*, May 28, 1947; Manos a la Obra, *El Imparcial*, February 11, 1948, October 6, 1948, and June 23, 1948, 5; "Hay agua pura para un millón de habitantes," *El Mundo*, June 11, 1947.

Gabriel Villaronga explores the PPD's "imaginative flights" focused on the allegedly extraordinary development potential of manufacture in "Un 'pequeño Pittsburgh' borincano." He discusses how the visual imagery produced by the PPD in newspaper and magazine photos, plans, and pamphlets tried to pull the Puerto Rican public into the industrialization project and "make them feel modern . . . seducing the spectator, stimulating their imagination, and instilling in them a vision of modernity." Villaronga, "Un 'pequeño Pittsburgh' borincano," 190.

21 Valdés, *Organized Agriculture and the Labor Movement before the UFW*, 95–99; Felix Cohen, "Coloniaje es el verdadero problema puertorriqueno y no sobrepoblacion," *El Imparcial*, February 11, 1948, 4; "Los arrabales," *El Imparcial*, April 16, 1949. Rafael Cabrera discusses the renowned cartoonist Filardi's persistent criticism of the PPD's developmentalist project in *Los dibujos del progreso*.

22 For just a few examples, see "Asignan $600,000 a acueductos rurales," *El Imparcial*, May 14, 1949, 3; "Sierra destaca la importancia de la represa Caonillas," *El Imparcial*, January 5, 1949; "Hay agua pura para un millón de habitantes," *El Mundo*, June 11, 1947; "Planificación aprueba proyectos para distintas obras en la isla," *El Imparcial*, September 3, 1948; "Se pedira extension de la zona urbana Mayagüez," *El Mundo*, April 10, 1947, 14.

23 For a few examples, see R. Rivera Santiago, "Siete edificios en construcción que valen $4,230,000," *El Mundo*, March 30, 1947; "Estudio de planes sobre el uso de terrenos urbanos," *El Mundo*, November 2, 1947, 17; Cabrera Collazo, "La 'criollización' del desarrollismo y la inclusión de lo puertorriqueño en tres discursos inaugurales de Luis Muñoz Marín."

24 Sepúlveda Rivera, "Viejos cañaverales, casas nuevas"; and Zapata, "El contratista y la constitución: Leonard Darlington Long y la conspiración contra

la Constitución del Estado Libre Asociado (1951–1952)," analyze the political economy of these suburban developments.

25 Cited in Barceló Miller, "'Un gobierno de hombres.'"

26 Rurico E. Rivera, "Inician plan sorprendente de viviendas," *El Mundo*, December 11, 1949, 11; James F. Cunningham, "Piñero cree es factible plan hogar," *El Mundo*, January 30, 1949, 16; Rurico Rivera, "Diseñan los hogares modelos de construcción a bajo costo," *El Mundo*, January 23, 1949, 6; "Junta Hogares estudia casas prefabricadas," *El Mundo*, November 20, 1947, 7; "Muñoz favorece construir casas más baratas que las de Puerto Nuevo: Plan para edificar 30,000," *El Imparcial*, February 2, 1949; "Piñero anuncia la contrucción de otras tres mil viviendas de bajo costo bajo actual programa," *El Imparcial*, November 11, 1948.

27 Everlasting Development Corporation, advertisement, "Nueva sección de Puerto Nuevo," *El Imparcial*, June 9, 1949.

28 For a now-classic work on Puerto Rican shantytown residents and the communities and families they built, see Safa, *The Urban Poor of Puerto Rico*.

29 For just a few examples, see "Puerto Rico: Senate Committee Finds It an Unsolvable Problem," *Life*, March 8, 1943, 28; "Puerto Rico Moves Ahead," *New York Times*, August 4, 1946, 92; O. G. Villard, "The Coming Crisis in Puerto Rico," *Christian Century*, May 10, 1944, 525–526; O. G. Villard, "The Truth about Puerto Rico," *Christian Century*, October 13, 1944, 1165–1167; Villaronga, "Un 'pequeño Pittsburgh' borincano," 191–193. La Perla, one of the only midcentury *arrabales* to survive in its original location, later became the setting for Oscar Lewis's influential (and much-criticized) work on the "culture of poverty" in Puerto Rico, *La Vida*.

30 Rodríguez, "Suppressing the Slum!"; Tyrell, "Colonizing the New Deal"; Dinsey-Flores, "Disciplining Ponce's Poor entre el Caserío y el Pueblo"; Puerto Rico Housing Authority, *Housing Progress in Puerto Rico*; Carrero, *Housing in Puerto Rico*.

An analogous process unfolded in the United States during this period. For some examples of its manifestations in the areas of Michigan where Puerto Ricans headed in the 1950 airlift, see "Shanty-Town Doom Is Sealed," *Bay City Times*, July 2, section 2, 1; "Two Bedroom Bungalow Pleases This Couple," *Saginaw News*, August 6, 1950, 28.

31 Rurico E. Rivera, "Comienza la limpieza de El Fanguito," *El Mundo*, March 22, 1949, 1; "Trasladan casas desde la zona de El Fanguito a San José," *El Mundo*, April 27, 1949, 2; "Hogares modernos para reemplazar casuchas de La Perla," *El Mundo*, October 26, 1947, 14; "Aboga por eliminación arrabal y mejoramiento de la nutrición," *El Mundo*, July 5, 1947, 1, 10; "Problema del arrabal," *El Mundo*, June 23, 1945, 6; "Tres proyectos sobre hogares aprobados por Senado Insular," *El Mundo*, April 15, 1947; "Revelación trágica," *El Imparcial*, November 30, 1948; "San Juan tendrá 15 millones para zonas arrabal si pasa ley," *El Imparcial*, July 4, 1949. By 1962 the entire *arrabal* where Helen Safa had done fieldwork in 1959 had been razed

and all of its residents relocated. A few managed to purchase homes in the working-class urbanizaciones being built, but most ended up in public housing projects. Safa, *The Urban Poor of Puerto Rico*.

32 "Hacia un Ponce mejor," El Mundo, July 25, 1949, 7. See also "Plano y dibujo de vivienda a bajo costo propuesta para Puerto Rico," June 6, 1952, http://biblio tecadigital.uprrp.edu/cdm/singleitem/collection/ELM4068/id/1442/rec/1, and "Diseño del Caserío Ponce de León, Ponce," December 17, 1948, http://biblio tecadigital.uprrp.edu/cdm/singleitem/collection/ELM4068/id/1430/rec/27. Both in Colección de Fotos del Periódico El Mundo, Biblioteca Digital Puertorriqueña website.

33 "Sin albergue," El Imparcial, May 20, 1949, 1.

34 Guillermo González to Senator Millard E. Tydings, September 23, 1943, and Harold L. Ickes, Secretary of the Interior, to Senator Millard E. Tydings, November 10, 1943, both in U.S. National Archives and Records Administration, Records of the Committee on Territories and Insular Affairs, U.S. Senate, Record Group 46; "Ofrecen marcha sobre San Juan de cincuenta a cien mil trabajadores," El Imparcial, June 28, 1949; "Calles o pantanos?," El Imparcial, July 24, 1947; "Sin albergue" and "Gobierno destruye casa en Cataño," El Imparcial, May 20, 1949; "Destruyen urbanización clandestina," El Imparcial, June 16, 1949, 22; "Alambiqueros de El Fanguito levantan barricadas a la policía e investigadores," El Mundo, July 4, 1949, 2. See also Back, Slums, Projects and People.

35 "Ofrecen marcha sobre San Juan de cincuenta a cien mil trabajadores," El Imparcial, June 28, 1949.

36 Safa, *The Urban Poor of Puerto Rico*, 9–11; Ramírez, El arrabal y la política.

37 See, for example, Manuela Jovet de Salicrup, "La simplificación de las labores domésticas en hogares rurales," El Mundo, April 20, 1947. For a description of the pre-*parcela* household practices, implements, and physical spaces, see Acevedo González, ¡Que tiempos aquellos!, 15–28.

38 See "Con esfuerzo e imaginación puede embellecer el hogar," El Mundo, May 12, 1949, 21; Roberts and Stefani, *Patterns of Living in Puerto Rican Families*, cited in Flores Ramos, Mujer, familia, y prostitución, 158–166; "Darán prestamos para casas de agricultores," El Imparcial, September 13, 1949.

39 Francisco Toro Calder, "Relato de una familia Boricua que se impone a dificultades," El Mundo, July 31, 1947, 21; Treasury of Puerto Rico, "Patrono de la Industria Azucarera: El seguro de empleo le da la oportunidad de aliviar la miseria de sus trabajadores durante el 'Tiempo Muerto,'" advertisement, cited from El Imparcial, February 8, 1949; Servicio de Extensión, "Rincón de la familia," El Mundo, January 2, 1949, 28; "La AHA y su obra en Puerto Rico," El Mundo, April 20, 1947.

40 David Roediger makes an analogous argument for European immigrants to the United States during the mid-twentieth century. For them, owning a home became a marker of potential whiteness, even as it served as a space for

preserving the immigrants' national culture, food, and languages. Roediger, *Working toward Whiteness*. Yolanda Martínez-San Miguel points out that the photographs of Jack Delano, the celebrated documentarian of Puerto Rican daily life during the PPD years, published in the best-selling *Puerto Rico Mío*, unevenly reproduced the PPD's whitening vision of modernity. Martínez-San Miguel, *Caribe Two Ways*, 68–69.

41 The promotion of racial democratization through whitening marked nation-building efforts throughout Latin America. It took many forms, however, from Brazilian and Mexican elites' lauding of racial miscegenation, which they expected would eventually absorb troubling African or indigenous elements in national populations, to Argentina's silencing denial of its citizens of African descent. Racial identities in most Latin American contexts have not been limited solely to biological makeup or phenotype. They also have included educational level, economic status and resources, social and familial networks, and all sorts of cultural elements such as religious beliefs, clothing, hair, and musical style choices, languages spoken, and body movements exhibited. For just a few examples of the vast historical literature analyzing racially inflected nation-building projects in Latin America, see Andrews, *The Afro-Argentines of Buenos Aires*; Wade, *Blackness and Race Mixture*; Twine, *Racism in a Racial Democracy*; Gould, *To Die in This Way*; de la Cadena, *Indigenous Mestizos*; Ferrer, *Insurgent Cuba*; de la Fuente, *A Nation for All*; Appelbaum, MacPherson, and Rosemblatt, *Race and Nation in Latin America*; Sue, *Land of the Cosmic Race*; Telles and Flores, "Not Just Color," 449.

42 For just a few examples of the mass media marketing of domesticity to Puerto Ricans, see "Esta fue una gran residencia," *El Mundo*, November 22, 1947, 12; "Cemento Ponce: Un cemento superior," *El Imparcial*, October 28, 1948; "El nuevo edificio de cafeteras de Puerto Rico," *El Imparcial*, January 23, 1949, 19; "Compare nuestras 100 casas," *El Mundo*, April 15, 1947; "Muebleria La Luz," *El Imparcial*, June 29, 1949; "Philco: Sensacional! Suntuosa!," *El Imparcial*, July 4, 1949, 23; "Un mundo en su Kelvinator," *El Imparcial*, August 22, 1949, 9; "La cocina moderna es un sitio agradable," *El Imparcial*, October 10, 1948; "Llegaron enfriadores eléctricos de agua (de botella)," *El Mundo*, May 28, 1947, 4; "Llegó la nueva nevera Frigidaire Deluxe," *El Imparcial*, August 5, 1948, 30; "Un viejo problema resuelto por un sistema nuevo," *El Mundo*, December 16, 1941, 12; "Sus enseres domésticos G-E valen hoy más de lo que le costaron," *El Mundo*, January 22, 1945, 9. Flores Ramos, *Mujer, familia, y prostitución*, 225–230.

43 Kristin Hoganson argues that domestic consumption can be "a marker of national standing" and of "civilizational attainment." Hoganson, "Buying into Empire," 256. Eduardo Elena shows how Argentinian populist publications attempted to mold Argentinians' consumption desires and practices, channeling their aesthetic sensibilities and modes of conduct into an imitation of elite practices. Elena, "Peronism in 'Good Taste.'" See also his monograph *Dignifying Argentina*, and Milanesio, *Workers Go Shopping in Argentina*. Louis Pérez shows

that access to U.S. goods, culture, and personal styles was integral to Cubans' twentieth-century sense of national identity and their own sense of modernity vis-à-vis the rest of Latin America. Pérez, *On Becoming Cuba*.

44 For men's insistence on the right to extramarital sexual relationships, see Findlay, *Imposing Decency*; Flores Ramos, *Mujer, familia, y prostitución*; Flores Ramos, *Eugenesia, higiene pública y alcanfor para las pasiones*; Cubano Iguina, *Rituals of Violence in Nineteenth-Century Puerto Rico*; Ramirez, *What It Means to Be a Man*.

45 "Aquí si hay," El Mundo, May 12, 1947 (emphasis added). For a few more examples, see "Si la casa es su problema . . . nosotros le ofrecemos la solución," *El Mundo*, March 1, 1947; "La casa que hay en su futuro," *El Mundo*, March 19, 1947, 11; "Urbanización Santa Cruz donde su SALUD Y TRANQUILIDAD son sus mayores dividendos," *El Imparcial*, August 3, 1948.

46 "Nuestras Felicitaciones al Reparto Baldrich," El Mundo, May 6, 1947, 20.

47 "Varios vecinos de Puerto Nuevo elogian el proyecto," El Mundo, February 27, 1949, 5.

48 Findlay, *Imposing Decency*, 153–159. For the 1950s, see the collection of interviews with working-class men in "¿Cree Usted conveniente que la mujer casada trabaje fuera del hogar?," *El Imparcial*, April 4, 1954, 32.

49 Wolf, "San José," 194–235; Acevedo González, *¡Que tiempos aquellos!*, 217–232.

50 Wolf, "San José," 258–259.

51 Quotes from Mintz, "Cañamelar," 379. See also Findlay, *Imposing Decency*, 18–52; Briggs, *Reproducing Empire*, 96; Safa, *The Urban Poor of Puerto Rico*, 20–40; Acevedo González, *¡Que tiempos aquellos!*, 107–120.

52 Roberts and Stefani, *Patterns of Living in Puerto Rican Families*, 275; Safa, *The Urban Poor of Puerto Rico*, 20–60; Mintz, *Worker in the Cane*, 44–50; Findlay, *Imposing Decency*, 110–134.

53 Flores Ramos, *Mujer, familia y prostitución*; Rivera González, "Género y proceso democrático"; Colón Pizarro, "Poetic Pragmatism"; Gallart, "Political Empowerment of Puerto Rican Women"; Marsh Kennerley, *Negociaciones culturales*; Ostman, Colle, and Franco, *Advocating Women's Rights in Literature and Film*.

54 María de Fátima Barceló Miller shows how elite Puerto Rican women elaborated their own earlier discourses of domesticity in an attempt to empower women of their class. Barceló Miller, "Domesticidad, desafío y subversión." See also Findlay, *Imposing Decency*, 62–76.

55 Tom Klubock notes that in early twentieth-century Chile, U.S. copper mining corporations advanced a similar argument to their employees. "Citizenship thus denoted the legal rights enjoyed by men under the nation-state and their social and sexual rights as heads of homes." Klubock, *Contested Communities*, 72. See also Weinstein, "Making Workers Masculine"; Tinsman, *Partners in Conflict*; and Rosemblatt, *Gendered Compromises*.

 As in the United States, this vision of bourgeois domesticity fused with a ferocious anticommunism during the 1950s; their interlacing became an important point of consensus for both the PPD and its opposition. For example, both El Mundo and El Imparcial regularly featured "Charlas de bebés," women's advice sections, fashion articles, a column by Dorothy Dix instructing the public on how to form proper nuclear families, and the daily serial story El médico de las locas. These all wove in and out of sensationalistic reporting on communist advances and threats around the world.

56 "Se pega fuego por estar sin trabajo; vecinos lo salvan," El Imparcial, August 25, 1948. See also Ramírez, What It Means to Be a Man; and Ramírez, "Masculinity and Power in Puerto Rico." For nineteenth- and early twentieth-century struggles of this type, see Findlay, Imposing Decency, 110–134.

57 See, for example, Muñoz Marín, "Distribución en fincas de Beneficio Proporcional de la Autoridad de Tierras en Arecibo," in Palabras, vol. 3, 627–628; Ramón Fernández Marina, "La función del padre en el hogar," and Edmée Doble, "Hogares sin padre," both in Twelfth Annual Conference of the Instituto del Hogar, Río Piedras, University of Puerto Rico, August 23, 1964.

58 Certainly, the exercise of virility was central to earlier quasi-populist, cross-class Puerto Rican political projects. However, the concern of early nineteenth-century male liberals (including Muñoz Marín's father, Luis Muñoz Rivera) with masculine redemption focused much more heavily on relationships between men and less on creating heterosexual domesticity. See Cubano Iguina, Rituals of Violence in Nineteenth-Century Puerto Rico; and Findlay, Imposing Decency, 77–88. See Pablo Piccato's discussion of conflicts over male honor in Mexico's public sphere in The Tyranny of Opinion.

59 Ayala and Bernabé, Puerto Rico in the American Century, 191; Safa, The Myth of the Male Breadwinner; Colón Warren et al., Estirando el peso; Acevedo, "Políticas de industrialización y cambios en el empleo femenino en Puerto Rico"; Acevedo, "Género trabajo asalariado y desarrollo industrial en Puerto Rico"; Sánchez, "Posibles efectos de la industrialización rápida sobre la familia puertorriqueña," 96–107; Gregory, "El desarrollo de la fuerza obrera industrial en Puerto Rico"; Fernández Méndez, "Algunos cambios culturales, económicos y sociales que afectan la familia en Puerto Rico."

60 Mintz, Three Ancient Colonies, 171–174; Safa, The Urban Poor of Puerto Rico; and Safa, Myth of the Male Breadwinner.

61 Several such incidents were reported each week throughout the late 1940s and early 1950s. For just a few examples of such reports, see "Da 'por amor' tres puñaladas a una casada," El Mundo, June 13, 1950, 14; "Regresa para matar amante de su esposa," El Mundo, June 15, 1950, 23; "Veterano mata amante por andar 'chereando,'" El Imparcial, June 26, 1950, 2; "Mata su concubina a puñaladas y se fuga," El Imparcial, July 4, 1950, 7; "Acuchilla esposa le amenazó con dejarlo," El Imparcial, July 17, 1950, 5.

62 Córdova Suárez, "Setting Them Straight," 33. One newspaper columnist moaned, "Soon our country will be filled with nothing but divorcees. We have

to stop this immorality!" "Carta pública y privada," El Imparcial, June 14, 1950, 10, 39. Unions also called for measures to stop the rising rate of divorces. "Asamblea CGT Autentica pide plena soberania para la isla," El Mundo, September 30, 1949, 11. For a few more examples of the kinds of articles that filled the back pages of island newspapers, see "Pide divorcio a los 4 días de casada," El Imparcial, August 9, 1950, 2; "Decretan 22 divorcios en corte de San Juan," El Imparcial, July 26, 1950, 30; Flores Ramos, Mujer, familia y prostitución, 196–208.

Divorce was not new on the island; it had been instituted in Puerto Rico just a few years after the United States' invasion of the island. In the early 1900s, Puerto Rican women responded quickly to the new legal option, turning to the courts to free themselves from abusive or financially inconsistent husbands. Findlay, "Love in the Tropics"; and Findlay, Imposing Decency, 110–134. However, the postwar years saw a marked increase in the incidence of divorce.

63 "Mayoría padres acusados puede sostener hijos," El Imparcial, June 18, 1950, 19; "Nos importa la niñez?," El Imparcial, June 18, 1950, 19; "Protección a la niñez," El Imparcial, August 15, 1950, 15; "Condenan 9 padres a sostener hijos," El Imparcial, September 13, 1950, 11.

3 • Removing "Excess Population"

1 Muñoz Marín, "Decisión del Corte Supremo de los Estados Unidos de América sobre la Ley de las 500 Cuerdas," in Palabras (1980), 43.

2 Rodríguez Juliá, Las tribulaciones de Jonás.

3 Deborah Cohen argues that a similar dynamic operated in the bracero program, which brought single Mexican men as temporary agricultural laborers to the United States after World War II. Cohen, Braceros, 67–86, 173–198. See also Valdés, Organized Agriculture and the Labor Movement before the UFW, 96–103.

4 Briggs, Reproducing Empire, 74–83, 90–98; Ramírez de Arellano and Seipp, Colonialism, Catholicism, and Contraception; Lugo Ortiz, "Sterilization, Birth Control, and Population Control."

5 See Paul Blanshard, "Puerto Rico's Tomorrow," New York Times, January 1, 1950, 108; Perloff, Puerto Rico's Economic Future.

6 The fevered discourses linking overpopulation and birth control in Puerto Rico anticipated by several decades the explosion of such discussions in the rest of Latin America. For the latter, see Pieper Mooney, The Politics of Motherhood.

7 "Comentario semanal de hechos y noticias," Manos a la Obra, El Imparcial, November 10, 1948. For a few more examples of this discourse, which saturated political discussions in the postwar era, see in El Mundo, "Recomiendan la emigración a Venezuela," October 2, 1947, 1; "Plan abarcador para resolver caso población," November 1, 1947, 1; "Economista discute migración," January 2, 1949, 43–44. In El Imparcial, see "Dos universidades hacen estudio sobre problema poblacional Puerto Rico," February 4, 1948, 2; Manos a la Obra, November

24, 1948. See also Muñoz Marín, "Es necesario aumentar la producción en la zona cafetalera," in *Palabras*, vol. 4, 265–267; and Muñoz Marín, "Puerto Rico tiene un desafío ante el destino," in *Palabras*, vol. 4, 523–526; José L. Janer, "La superpoblación en Puerto Rico," paper delivered on April 14, 1949, at a public forum on the island's economy, sponsored by the Faculty of Social Sciences of the University of Puerto Rico. Colección Puertorriqueña, Universidad de Puerto Rico, Río Piedras; Cofresí, *Realidad Poblacional de Puerto Rico*.

8 Luis Sánchez Coppa, "Pérez favorece un ajuste antes de mecanizar la agricultura," *El Mundo*, September 28, 1947, 1.

9 Marta Suárez, personal communication, October 2002. For the postwar explosion in air travel from Puerto Rico, see the "Anuncios clasificados" section in *El Imparcial* during the late 1940s. Every day, the classified section was filled with advertisements for airline flights to and from New York, but also to cities as far afield as Philadelphia, Chicago, Saint Louis, Salt Lake City, and New Orleans. See also in *El Imparcial*, "San Juan a 6 horas de Nueva York; a 4 de Miami," October 18, 1948, 5; "'El Borinquen' presta servicios ruta Miami," October 21, 1948, 5.

10 For reactions to earlier mass immigrations from Europe to New York City, see Roediger, *Working toward Whiteness*; Jacobson, *Barbarian Virtues*; Jacobson, *Whiteness of a Different Color*.

11 *New York Daily News*, October 12, 1947, 100–101. See also, among many others, "Officials Worried about Influx of Puerto Rican Migrants," *New York Times*, August 2, 1947, 1; "Why Puerto Ricans Flock to the U.S.," *New York Times*, June 1, 1947, E5; "Aid Planned Here for Puerto Ricans," *New York Times*, January 12, 1947, 25; "Migrants: The Puerto Ricans," *Newsweek*, March 24, 1947, 7–8; "Puerto Rican Drift to Mainland Gains," *New York Times*, July 31, 1947, 18.

12 Keller, "Migrants Find Even More Misery in City," *New York World-Telegram*, October 20, 1947, 1. For another striking example of this language, see "The World They Never Made," *Time*, June 12, 1950, 24.

13 Allan Keller, "Crime Festers in Bulging Tenements," *New York World-Telegram*, October 23, 1947, 1–2; Allan Keller, "Enormous Birth-Rate Outraces Death in Teeming, Starving Puerto Rico," *New York World-Telegram*, October 24, 1947, 18; "Puerto Rico's Overcrowding Grows Worse," *New York World-Telegram*, September 1, 1949, 7; "Puerto Rico Moves a Step Ahead," *New York Times*, August 4, 1946, 92; "Ask Million People Leave Puerto Rico," *New York Times*, March 29, 1946, 13.

14 Keller, "Crime Festers in Bulging Tenements."

15 "Aid Planned Here for Puerto Ricans"; "Puerto Rican Migrants Jam New York," *Life*, August 25, 1947; Keller, "Migrants Find Even More Misery in City," 1–2.

16 "City's Disease Rate Raised by Migrant Tide," *New York World-Telegram*, October 21, 1950, 1–2; Albert J. Gordon, "Solution Is Sought to Migrant Influx," *New York Times*, August 4, 1947, 19; "Puerto Rico Moves a Step Ahead," 92.

17 Keller, "Crime Festers in Bulging Tenements"; "Racial Tension Up in East Bronx Area," *New York Times*, April 24, 1947, 30; "Crime Increasing in 'Little Spain,'" *New York Times*, August 3, 1947, 12.

18 "Puerto Ricans Bring Schooling Problem," *New York Times*, November 6, 1947, 32; "Better Care Urged for Puerto Ricans," *New York Times*, November 12, 1947, 29; "Special Classes to Help Puerto Ricans," *New York World-Telegram*, November 12, 1947, 3; "Puerto Rican Influx Brings Schools a Puzzle," *New York World-Telegram*, November 5, 1947, 3.

19 "Tide of Migrants Pushing Relief Load through the Roof," *New York World-Telegram*, October 22, 1946, 2; "Influx of Puerto Ricans Drives Up Relief Costs," *New York Times*, May 25, 1947, 3; "Solution Is Sought to Migrant Influx," *New York Times*, August 4, 1947, 19; Keller, "Migrants Find Even More Misery in City," 2; "Puerto Rican Migrants Jam New York," 27; "Ask Million People Leave Puerto Rico," 13.

20 "Sharkey Urges Two Year Residence as Relief Brake," *New York World-Telegram*, November 6, 1947, 3; "Two-Year Residence Is Sought as Qualification for Relief," *New York Times*, November 7, 1947, 14; "Nonresidents and Relief," *New York Times*, November 22, 1947, 10.

21 "Crime Festers," *New York World-Telegram*, October 23, 1947, 2; "Says Welfare Dept. Winked at Immorality," *New York World-Telegram*, November 12, 1947, 1; "Official Winks at Immorality on Dole Probed," *New York World-Telegram*, November 19, 1947, 1.

22 "The World They Never Made," 25. See also "Ask Million People Leave Puerto Rico"; Whalen, "Labor Migrants or Submissive Wives."

23 Meyer, *Vito Marcantonio, Radical Politician*; "Marcantonio Plot Charged by Mayor," *New York Times*, November 7, 1949, 5; "Defends Puerto Ricans," *New York Times*, September 23, 1947, 18; "Marcantonio and Davis Lose: Stinging Blow to Commies," *New York World-Telegram*, November 11, 1949, 4.

24 "Welfare, Reds, and Puerto Ricans," *New York World-Telegram*, October 22, 1947, 34; "Now Clean Out Commies in Relief," *New York World-Telegram*, November 15, 1947, 10; "80$ a Week Worker Got Relief Aid Too," *New York World-Telegram*, November 24, 1947, 1; "Red-Led UPW Gives Top Welfare Jobs as Union Reward," *New York World-Telegram*, October 17, 1947, 11; "Says Welfare Dept. Winked at Immorality," *New York World-Telegram*, November 12, 1947, 18; "Better Care Urged for Puerto Ricans," *New York Times*, November 12, 1947, 29.

25 Mary Nieves Perez, "Conditions in Puerto Rico," *New York Times*, February 16, 1948, 2; Pilar Pacheco, Letter to the Editor, *New York Times*, October 29, 1947, 30; "500 Pickets Blast Newspaper Series of Puerto Ricans," *New York World-Telegram*, October 31, 1947; "Plans to Resettle Migrants Criticized," *New York Times*, November 18, 1947, 43; "Puerto Rican Gains in Harlem Praised," *New York Times*, December 18, 1947, 20. For a few examples of the numerous letters sent to Muñoz Marín protesting the virulent press attacks against Puerto Ricans, see in

Fundacion Luis Munoz Marin (FLMM), Section IV, Series 8, Subseries 13: EEUU, Cartapacio 3, Petra González to Luis Muñoz Marín (hereafter LMM), October 15 and November 4, 1947; José Miranda to LMM, October 28, 1947; Nicolás Martínez Storer to LMM, October 24, 1947; Oliva Cruz to LMM, October 13, 1947.

26 Jesús Piñero, "Piñero afirma hay que llevar emigración a zonas agrícolas," El Mundo, October 6, 1947, 1; Petro América de Pagán, "Programa de Trabajo Migratorio de Puerto Rico a los Estados Unidos," Colección Puertorriqueña, Universidad de Puerto Rico, 6–8; "Speech of Mrs. Petro América de Pagán de Colón, Director Puerto Rico Employment Service, before the Illinois Federation of Women's Clubs," Chicago, May 10, 1955, Folder 16, Box 2830, Ephemeral Publications, Community Organizations and Cultural Affairs 1948–1995, Office of the Government of Puerto Rico in the United States (OGPRUS), Centro Archives, Hunter College, New York.

27 Mills, Senior, and Goldsen, The Puerto Rican Journey; Thomas, Puerto Rican Citizen, 133–161; Meléndez Vélez, "The Puerto Rican Journey Revisited"; Pérez, The Near Northwest Side Story, 45–50; López, "Investigating the Investigators"; "Folleto ilustra el propósito de migración de los boricuas," El Mundo, February 21, 1949, 5; Benjamin Santana, "Oportunidad en el Norte para obreros," El Mundo, April 8, 1948, 1, 16; "Sierra afirma hará cambios en emigración," El Mundo, November 11, 1947, 1; "Perito entrena al personal de Migración," El Mundo, May 12, 1948, 7; "Comisionado industrial NY interesa obreros boricuas; Sierra Berdecía aplaude plan," El Imparcial, February 6, 1948, C; Box 2743, Administration, Monthly Reports, OGPRUS, Centro Archives.

28 The PPD government signed a contract in January 1948 with Hamilton Wright Organization, a New York–based publicity firm, in order to remake the image of the island and its people. Villaronga, "Un 'pequeño Pittsburgh' borincano." See also Maldonado, Teodoro Moscoso and Puerto Rico's Operation Bootstrap, 103–118. For just a few examples of the media coverage produced, see in New York Times: "Work Is Limited for Puerto Ricans, but 90% Are Self-Supporting and They Meet Standards of Wages and Hours," October 6, 1949, 38; "'Migrants' Misery Charged to Bias," April 24, 1949, 38; Charles Grutzner, "City Puerto Ricans Found Ill-Housed: Crowded Conditions, Race Bias Seen as Reasons for the Social Problem," October 4, 1949, 30; "Corsi Offers Plan for Puerto Ricans," April 20, 1950, 25; "City Seeks Aid for Puerto Ricans," April 21, 1950, 25.

29 See the following articles, all in the New York Times: "New Homes for 7,000 Families in Puerto Rico," November 21, 1948, R7; "Puerto Rico Ready to Speed Industry," January 3, 1949, 68; "Puerto Rico Plans First Oil Refinery," December 11, 1949, 74; "Puerto Rico Adds 50 Industries," January 3, 1950, 87; "Textile Plant for Puerto Rico," March 1, 1950, 49; "Boom in Housing Gives 10,000 Jobs for Puerto Ricans," March 28, 1948, R1; "Puerto Rico Looks Up," April 4, 1948, E8; "Ponce de Leon's Isle," October 23, 1950, XX6; "Puerto Rico Opens a $6,000,000 Hotel," December 10, 1949, 29.

30 "A New Puerto Rico Shows Off," *Life*, January 2, 1949, 19–25.

31 Lloyd Staffer, "Puerto Rico Fights Back," *Reader's Digest*, January 1949, 127–130; Grutzner, "City Puerto Ricans Found Ill-Housed"; "Puerto Rican Study," *Newsweek*, July 19, 1948, 78–79.

32 Warren Weaver, "Puerto Ricans Aid Up-State Farmers," *New York Times*, June 16, 1949, 3; "Jersey Welcomes Migrant Workers," *New York Times*, September 6, 1950; "U.S., P.R. Map a Labor Pact," *New York Times*, February 6, 1949, 7; "Alien Farm Labor Is Barred in State," *New York Times*, April 5, 1950, 32; "Alien Farm Labor Protested," *New York Times*, April 4, 1950, 1; "Upstate Farmers Aided," *New York Times*, April 20, 1950, 25; "Puerto Ricans Flown Here to Help in Crop Harvest," *New York Times*, August 13, 1950, 79.

33 "American Imperialism," *New York Times*, July 5, 1950, 18. For a few more examples from the *New York Times*, see "Puerto Rico Plan Called a Success," October 2, 1949; "Puerto Rico Visit Set for Four Point Study," November 26, 1949, 30; "U.N. Group Studies Puerto Rico," May 15, 1950. See also Paul Harrison, "Crawford plantea a subcomite que deterioro en economia de Isla podria derrotar a Munoz," *El Mundo*, June 4, 1948, 1, 18; Muñoz Marín, "La libertad y los derechos del hombre," in *Palabras*, vol. 4, 260–264; and Muñoz Marín, "The Overall Picture of Realities in Puerto Rico Is as Follows," in *Palabras*, vol. 4, 311–315; Ayala and Bernabé, *Puerto Rico in the American Century*, 154–161; Goldstein, "The Attributes of Sovereignty," 319.

34 Grandin, *Empire's Workshop*, 31. This role deepened after the Cuban revolution of 1959; David Sheinin argues that "in the race for Caribbean modernization, Puerto Rico became Cuba's antagonist." Sheinin, "The Caribbean and the Cold War," 495.

35 See, for example, "Puerto Rico Seeks to Curb Migration," *New York Times*, February 23, 1947, 20; "The World They Never Made." For the responses of Puerto Ricans and their allies to the hostile newspaper coverage, see Thomas, *Puerto Rican Citizen*, 148–150.

36 FLMM, Section IV, Series 9 (Asuntos), Subseries 195, "Minutes: Emigration Advisory Committee," September 11, 1947.

37 Petro América de Pagán, "Programa de Trabajo Migratorio de Puerto Rico a los Estados Unidos," 5–6.

38 "No permiten emigración que no se ajuste a lo recomendado por Geigel," *El Imparcial*, February 5, 1947, 4. See also Mario Delgado telegram from Walla Walla, Washington, June 30, 1949; Fernando Sierra Berdecía (FSB) to Gustavo Agrait, September 27, 1949, both in Box 2276, Puerto Ricans in New York and Other States, Tarea 96-20, Fondo de la Oficina del Gobernador (FOG), Archivo General de Puerto Rico (AGPR). Additionally, see Antonio Collazo to LMM, September 20, 1949 and FSB to Collazo, October 7, 1949; "Investigación practicada en relación con diversas actividades de la Agencia de Empleos Friedman, sus agents, empleados y demás relaciones en Puerto Rico y Estados Unidos,"

October 20, 1949, both in File 742: Emigración (second), Box 2275, Tarea 96-10, FOG, AGPR; Statement of Mr. Joseph Monserrat, Chief of the Migration Division, Puerto Rican Department of Labor before the U.S. House of Representatives Select Subcommittee on Labor," May 9, 1961, Folder Pine-Pratta, Box 978, Farm Labor Program, OGPRUS, Centro Archives.

Gunther Peck explores the nefarious strategies of earlier informal labor recruiters among Italian, Greek, and Mexican immigrants to the United States and Canada during the Progressive Era in "Reinventing Free Labor." Peck notes that these labor recruiters presented themselves as the champions of free labor and workers' right to choose their employers, while denying or downplaying contractors' fees, debt peonage to company stores, and requirements to work wherever recruiters left them. The labor recruiters in Puerto Rico seem to have developed similar strategies and recruiting rhetoric, although they were not employed directly by large corporations, nor were they of the same national origin as the workers they recruited.

39 Rúa and Torres, "At the Crossroads of Urban Ethnography and Puerto Rican Latinidad" in Rúa, Latino Urban Ethnography and the Work of Elena Padilla; and Ramos-Zayas, "Gendering 'Latino Public Intellectuals.'" This exciting volume provides a welcome analysis of the importance of Padilla's "anthropolitics." For an earlier examination of Padilla's role in the creation of The People of Puerto Rico, see Lauria-Perricelli, "A Study in Historical and Critical Anthropology"; Steward, The People of Puerto Rico.

40 For a biography of Muna Lee and an evaluation of her literary work, see Cohen, A Pan-American Life, including the volume's moving foreword by Aurora Levins Morales. For an analysis of Doña Inés's public performances of maternity and respectable wifeliness and their importance to PPD politics, see Flores Ramos, Mujer, familia, y prostitución, 173–196.

41 Rúa, "Footnotes of Social Justice: Elena Padilla and Chicago Puerto Rican Communities"; Pérez, The Near Northwest Side Story; Toro-Morn, "Género, trabajo y migración"; and Toro-Morn, "Yo era muy arriesgada."

42 See the following articles in El Imparcial: "Blas Oliveras contesta un artículo sobre emigración obreros boricuas al norte," March 23, 1947; "Geigel Polanco relata quejas de los obreros boricuas en Chicago," January 24, 1947, 6; Frank Torres, "Vicisitudes del coloniaje: Una emigración desastrosa," May 18, 1947, 10; and "Senado aprueba proyecto Geigel reglementando emigraciones de obreros," April 14, 1947, 6. Josephine Ripley, "Investigan importación de domésticas boricuas," El Mundo, May 20, 1947. Some of the correspondence between Elena Padilla and the renowned New York–based leftist organizer and intellectual Jesús Colón concerning this case is preserved in Folder 5, Box 3, Jesús Colón Papers, Centro Archives.

43 See in El Imparcial: "S.G. Friedman alega fue víctima de acto inescrupoloso por parte de firma que no empleó Boricuas," September 12, 1948; "Estudian can-

celación licencia concedida a agencias de empleo," June 17, 1949; "Investigan si agencia de empleos burla la ley," July 11, 1949, 4; "Justicia y trabajo investigan el caso agencia de empleos," July 15, 1949, 23.

44 "Desean más obreros boricuas en EEUU; Trabajo para 10,000," El Imparcial, October 22, 1948; "Introducirán en Puerto Rico el sistema usado en Nueva York para activar labor de emplear obreros," El Imparcial, September 20, 1948; Petro América de Pagán, "Programa de Trabajo Migratorio de PR," 12–13.

45 A columnist for the daily newspaper El Imparcial reported that the Puerto Rican government's attempts to regulate wages and labor conditions gave the impression that Puerto Rican workers "have to be cared for like newborn babies from the moment they leave the island and during their whole stay at work sites." "Obreros boricuas en EEUU narran trágicas condiciones de trabajo," September 15, 1948, 7. Many negotiations for large-scale agricultural employment contracts broke down because growers refused to provide low-cost airfare for Puerto Rican workers. "De 5 a 7 mil trabajadores a Nueva Jersey," El Imparcial, April 5, 1947.

46 "Llegó Cecyl Morales; dirigirá la oficina sobre la emigración," El Mundo, November 27, 1947, 4; "Sanciones, Comisionado," El Imparcial, September 3, 1948; "Sorprenden contrabando de trabajadores; Sierra mismo investiga caso," El Imparcial, August 7, 1949; "Estudian cancelación licencia concedida a agencias de empleo," El Imparcial, June 17, 1949; Rivera, "Friedman dice que un acuerdo impide migración de boricuas," El Mundo, June 21, 1948, 7, 18; "Sierra asegura que se cumple acuerdo con servicio empleos," El Mundo, June 23, 1948, 5; "Detienen contrabando de obreros hacia E.U.," El Imparcial, May 1, 1950, 3, 47.

Philadelphia seems to have been an important center of the sort of private agricultural labor recruitment that the Puerto Rican government sought to supplant. See Whalen, From Puerto Rico to Philadelphia, for a discussion of Samuel Friedman's operations and their ancillary effects in the establishment of a Puerto Rican community in that city.

47 See in El Mundo: "Planean 7 centros adicionales para adiestrar las domésticas," November 19, 1947; "Se celebró en Caguas la inauguración del instituto para adiestrar trabajadores para el hogar," October 25, 1947, 14; "En pos de trabajo en la ciudad de Nueva York," February 22, 1948, 10; "Dieron paseo a las domésticas de Puerto Rico," February 28, 1948; "Domésticas boricuas son bien recibidas en Scarsdale, NY," March 1, 1948, 6; "Times publicó artículo sobre las domésticas," April 1, 1948, 32; "Crearán centros para entrenar mujeres en trabajo del hogar," August 28, 1948; "Inauguran primer centro rural para trabajadoras del hogar," March 6, 1949, 7. Whalen reports that Puerto Rican government officials also hoped that women migrants would marry and remain in the United States, thus hastening the process of migrant assimilation that would ultimately ease the island's alleged population problem, From Puerto Rico to Philadelphia, 58–60.

Barbara Weinstein explores an analogous initiative by the populist government of Getúlio Vargas in her chapter in French and James, The Gendered Worlds of

Latin American Women Workers. The Brazilian women, however, were not destined for migration.

48 See in *El Imparcial*: "Ofrecen oportunidad a 100 muchachas para trabajar en los E.U.," February 21, 1948; "Nuevo curso para entrenar jóvenes como domésticas," October 11, 1948, 10; "Llegan en febrero a N.Y. primeras domésticas ha adiestrado gobierno P.R.," January 31, 1948. Petro América de Pagán, a high-ranking Department of Labor official, admitted that Puerto Rican women migrants consistently "abandoned" the sparse government-sponsored domestic employment in the United States to find factory jobs there. "Programa de Trabajadores Migratorios de Puerto Rico a los Estados Unidos," Colección Puertorriqueña, Universidad de Puerto Rico, Rió Piedras, 7. "Denuncian explotación de sirvientas boricuas," *El Mundo*, April 11, 1948, 4.

Carmen Teresa Whalen reports similar patterns in Philadelphia during the same period. Whalen, *From Puerto Rico to Philadelphia*, 62. A few rather small-scale attempts to employ Puerto Rican men in unionized factories in the Midwest seem to have been much more successful, especially in Lorain, Ohio, and Gary, Indiana. Negotiating membership in local unions seems to have been key to these efforts. Ironically, several of them were initiated by private recruitment agencies. See Rivera, "La colonia de Lorain, Ohio"; "Sierra acepta agencia Freeman lleve obreros para una firma Ohio," *El Imparcial*, January 8, 1948, B; "Obreros felices en Ohio," *El Imparcial*, January 4, 1949, 17. Luis Sánchez Cappa, "Más empresas emplearían a los boricuas," *El Mundo*, June 19, 1948, 1, 20; "Boricuas se ganan efecto en Lorain," *El Mundo*, July 4, 1948, 1.

49 FSB to Alan Perl, Miguel Cabranes, and Estella Draper, June 1, 1949, Folder 35, Box 915, Farm Labor, OGPRUS, Centro Archives.

50 FSB to Perl, Cabranes, and Draper, June 1, 1949; "Sierra Berdecía opuesto a emigración obreros boricuas al sur de E.U.," *El Imparcial*, January 16, 1948, B.

51 FSB to Manuel Cabranes, May 12, 1948, Folder 34, Box 915, Farm Labor, OGPRUS, Centro Archives; Manuel Cabranes to FSB, March 25, 1949; Manuel Cabranes to FSB, May 10, 1949; Alan Perl to FSB, June 23, 1949, all in Folder 35, Box 915, Farm Labor, OGPRUS, Centro Archives; Charles Grutzner, "Alien Farm Labor Protested Amid Political, Racial Rifts," *New York Times*, April 4, 1950, 1, 33.

52 See in *El Imparcial*: "Sale nueva expedición de obreros," June 1, 1949, 2; "Contratarán a 1500 para trabajar en EEUU," July 21, 1949, 5; "Cuentan experiencia, salud, conducta, para trabajos en EEUU," July 22, 1949, 5. "Han emigrado 2,867 obreros al continente," *El Mundo*, June 24, 1949, 4; "Estimularán uso obreros boricuas E.U.," *El Mundo*, February 12, 1949, 1; "Darán paridad al trabajador de Puerto Rico," March 4, 1949, 1; Antonio Arana Soto, "Sierra suspende contratación de obreros a Estados Unidos," *El Imparcial*, August 31, 1948.

53 FSB to Manuel Cabranes, May 12, 1948, Folder 34, Box 915, Farm Labor, OGPRUS, Centro Archives; Juan Martínez Chapel, "Caucus de la mayoría aprobó medida de emigración obrera," *El Mundo*, April 2, 1947; "300 obreros de la Isla ambulan

por Nueva Jersey," El Mundo, April 21, 1948, 1, 14; Whalen, From Puerto Rico to Philadelphia.

54 "Devolverán a la isla a obreros disgustados en fincas de New Jersey," El Imparcial, May 31, 1948, 11; "300 obreros de la isla ambulan por Nueva Jersey," El Mundo, April 21, 1948, 1, 14; Petro América Pagán de Colón to Sra. María Soliván, viuda de Bonilla, December 14, 1950, File—Michigan-A, B, C, Box 2275, Tarea 96-20, FOG, AGPR.

55 "CGT pide discutir el contrato suscrito por obreros que emigrant," El Imparcial, January 24, 1947, 6; "Saez se dirige al secretario de agricultura," El Mundo, August 17, 1948, 4; Antonio Arana Soto, "Imputan discriminación racial a contratantes obreros para EEUU," January 20, 1948, 11; "Asamblea CGT Auténtica pide plena soberanía para la isla," El Mundo, September 30, 1949, 11.

56 See, for example, "Como viven los obreros boricuas en Nueva Jersey," El Mundo, July 17, 1947; "Se denuncia maltrato a boricuas en una finca de Glassboro, New Jersey," El Imparcial, March 21, 1947, 6; "Devolverán a la isla a obreros disgustados en fincas de Nueva Jersey," El Imparcial, May 31, 1948, 11.

57 "Iniciaron envío de obreros a Nueva Jersey," El Mundo, April 2, 1948, 1, 14; "Formalizan contrato para llevar 2,000 boricuas a trabajar en Nueva Jersey," El Imparcial, April 2, 1948.

58 "Expedicionarios boricuas se quejan," El Imparcial, August 22, 1948. See also Manuel Cabranes to FSB, May 14, 1948, Folder 34, Box 915, Farm Labor, OGPRUS, Centro Archives; "Obrero Boricua en Nueva Jersey se queja del trato recibido; dice que norteamericanos ganan más jornal," El Imparcial, June 22, 1948; "Obreros boricuas en EEUU narran trágicas condiciones de trabajo," El Imparcial, September 15, 1948, 7. El Mundo, whose editorial positions seem to have converged with the PPD hierarchy by this point, published nothing on the protests against government-sponsored contracts, instead reiterating Sierra Berdecía's complaints about workers with no agricultural experience.

59 Manuel Cabranes to FSB, May 14, 1948, Folder 34, Box 915, Farm Labor, OGPRUS, Centro Archives; "Obreros boricuas en EEUU narran trágicas condiciones de trabajo."

60 "No emigre para trabajar como agricultor el que no lo sea," El Mundo, May 29, 1948, 10. For a few more examples, see "Devolveran a la isla a obreros disgustados en fincas de Nueva Jersey," El Imparcial, May 31, 1948; "Sierra sugiere a los agricultores de Nueva Jersey importer obreros boricuas de industria azucarera," El Imparcial, June 25, 1948; "Denuncian mal trato a obreros boricuas," El Imparcial, August 11, 1948.

61 "250 obreros firman para trabajar en Nueva Jersey," El Imparcial, August 6, 1948. Interestingly enough, the progovernment newspaper El Mundo mentioned nothing about this incident. It did, however, triumphantly cover the men's original, proud departure for Washington State a few months earlier. "Envian trabajadores puertorriqueños al continente," El Mundo, June 1, 1949, 7.

62 "Friedman organiza a obreros boricuas," El Imparcial, September 14, 1949; Sánchez Cappa, "Crea revuelo la migración a New Jersey," El Mundo, August 19, 1948, 1; "Los obreros puertorriqueños forman entidad en New Jersey," El Mundo, September 1, 1949, 5, 28. This meeting is also mentioned in Whalen, From Puerto Rico to Philadelphia, 78. For Friedman's presentation of himself as a more effective and committed advocate for Puerto Rican workers than the PPD Department of Labor, see his letters and "Confidential Memorandum" to LMM from August 11 and 12, 1949, File 743—Emigración, Box 2275, Tarea 96-20, FOG, AGPR.

63 "Muñoz solicita Tobin realice investigación," El Mundo, August 16, 1948, 1, 14; "Goodwin realice la pesquisa sobre boricuas en Nueva Jersey," El Mundo, August 17, 1949, 1, 12; B. Santiago Sosa, "Contratos a obreros boricuas garantizan alza en los jornales," El Mundo, September 3, 1929, 1, 22; B. Santiago Sosa, "Hay más casos de jornal menor a obreros isla," El Mundo, August 28, 1948, 1, 24. The end of the New Jersey growing season may have helped defuse the controversy in Philadelphia.

For continued individual denunciations of oppressive working conditions in New Jersey agriculture and the "selling" of Puerto Rican migrant workers by the island's Department of Labor, addressed to Luis Muñoz Marín personally and couched in the language of sons seeking paternal protection, see Francisco Segarra to LMM, September 8, 1949, "Solicitud de ayuda," July 20, 1949; and "Emigrante 125" to LMM, August 8, 1949, all in Box 2279, File 743.4, Tarea 96-20, FOG, AGPR. For a typical government brush-off of such petitions, see FSB to Francisco Segarra, September 22, 1949, in File 743.4, Box 2279, Tarea 96-20, FOG, AGPR.

64 Alan Perl to FSB, January 19, 1950; and Alan Perl to FSB, February 2, 1950, both in Folder 35, Box 915, Farm Labor, OGPRUS, Centro Archives.

65 "Salvan cosecha de remolacha en MI," El Mundo, June 19, 1950, 1; "Un periódico de Detroit comenta emigración aerea de boricuas," El Mundo, June 23, 1950, 4.

66 Petro América de Pagán de Colón, "Programa de trabajadores migratorios de Puerto Rico a los Estados Unidos," Colección Puertorriqueña, Universidad de Puerto Rico, Río Piedras; Fernando Sierra Berdecía, "State Commissioner of Labor of Puerto Rico, Fernando Sierra Berdecía, before the Sub-committee of the Committee on Agriculture on the Availability in Puerto Rico of Manpower for Agricultural Work in the Mainland," March 26, 1951, 2, 5–6, Folder 35, Box 915, Farm Labor, OGPRUS, Centro Archives.

67 Sierra Berdecía, "Before the Sub-committee," 2.

4 • Arriving in Michigan

1 "Diez aviones llevarán diariamente obreros a Michigan," and "Companías acceden a petición formulada por el gobernador," El Mundo, June 13, 1950; "Ayer en palacio," El Mundo, June 17, 1950, 7; "Transportación en masa," El Mundo,

June 21, 1950, 6; "Airlines' Sugar Beet Shuttle Hauls 5,000 without a Spill," *Detroit Free Press*, June 20, 1950, 13; Leonard Jackson, "Puerto Rican Farm Workers Embittered by Deplorable Plight," *Bay City Times*, August 6, 1950.

2 "El viaje de Sierra Berdecía," *El Mundo*, July 24, 1950, 6. See also "Enviarán hoy trabajadores a Michigan," *El Mundo*, May 31, 1950, 1; "Obreros en Michigan," *El Mundo*, June 16, 1950, 6.

3 "Salen 186 obreros a 'buscar ambiente' en Michigan," *El Mundo*, June 2, 1950, 1, 10; "El accidente destaca," *El Mundo*, June 9, 1950, 3. The caption for the photo in fig. 4.1 reads in part: "Receiving their last instructions, warnings, and advice before abandoning the island for several months to go to help continental agriculture maintain its high production, a group of Puerto Rican agricultural workers appear in this photo, gathered together in one of the offices of the Bureau of Employment and Migration. In their hands are the work contracts which they have just signed before leaving for Michigan, to work in the plantations of beets, cucumbers, green beans, and other vegetables."

4 The Puerto Ricans' hopes for masculine attainment and affirmation in their migration to Michigan mirrored those of Mexican braceros traveling to the United States as agricultural laborers during the same time period. Cohen, *Braceros*, 69–86.

5 The promised wage of $0.60 per hour would have constituted a tripling or even quadrupling of the migrants' incomes in Puerto Rico; when able to find work, they earned anywhere between $1.00 and $2.80 per day to plant and harvest cane, coffee, or food crops. The men applying to migrate to Michigan routinely listed unemployment or insufficient pay as their primary reasons for wanting to leave the island. See the initial applications collected in Boxes 190–199, Serie Querellas de Obreros Migrantes, Tarea 61-55, Fondo Negociado de Trabajo, Archivo General de Puerto Rico (AGPR).

6 My discussion of the midwestern sugar beet industry's history relies heavily on Mapes, *Sweet Tyranny*. For a more localized study of sugar beet production in the Red River Valley region of Minnesota and North Dakota, see Norris, *North for the Harvest*. For a highly idealized version of a Michigan sugar company's history, see Mahar, *Sweet Energy*.

While these authors focus on the midwestern sugar beet industry, Dionicio Nodín Valdés traces the history of migrant workers of Latin American descent in the rural Upper Midwest in *Al Norte*. Juan R. García discusses the experience of Mexican beet workers between the two world wars in *Mexicans in the Midwest*, 25–104. See also Jesse Hoffnung Garskof's brief but illuminating overview, "Michigan"; and Valdés's wide-ranging *Barrios Norteños*. Zaragosa Vargas touches briefly on the experience of Mexican American and Mexican sugar beet workers in Colorado in *Labor Rights Are Civil Rights*, 27–34.

7 The granting of limited rights for sugar beet workers under the 1937 Jones-Costigan Act and the 1937 Sugar Beet Act, passed while Henry Wallace was sec-

retary of agriculture, did not stop the massive deportation of Mexican workers during the anti-immigrant tirades that exploded during the Great Depression. Mapes, *Sweet Tyranny*, 216–228. See Valdés, *Al Norte*, for a detailed account of the shifting currents of migrant workers who labored in midwestern agriculture through the twentieth century.

8 Anastacio Díaz, interview with Eileen J. Findlay, July 13, 2009. After a few weeks of this suffering, Mr. Díaz left the beet fields and managed to find work fixing trailers in a nearby town. He later was able to obtain a full-time union job in an auto factory in Saginaw and eventually married a Mexican American woman from Texas whose parents also had emigrated to central Michigan. The back-breaking brutality of sugar beet cultivation surfaces in many other recollections of the era. For some examples, see Manuel and Elisa Ochoa, interview with James F. Findlay, August 23, 2009; Donald Turner, interview with James F. Findlay, August 22, 2009, in possession of the author; Testimony of Father Clement Kern, President's Commission on Migratory Labor, Saginaw County Court House, September 11 and 12, 1950, 430. The written transcript of the hearings is located at Harry S. Truman Library, Record Group 220. My heartfelt thanks go to Jesse Hoffnung-Garskof, who came upon these documents and, unsolicited, photocopied them for me.

9 This pattern seems to have been less marked in other types of local crop production. See, for example, the 1949 strike of six hundred southwestern Michigan grape growers (not the migrant workers who picked the grapes) against the Welch juice company. "Grape Pickers Back at Work," *Bay City Times*, September 17, 1949, 3.

10 Testimony of Dr. Frederick Leeder, "Stenographic Report of Proceedings Held at Saginaw, Michigan," President's Commission, 504.

11 See, for example, the *Alma Record*, the *Gratiot County Herald*, the *Isabella County Daily Times-News*, the *Sanilac Jeffersonian*, the *Saginaw News*, and the *Bay City Times* between 1947 and 1952.

12 Documentation of arrests is in Jail Record Books, 1947–1952, Isabella County Sheriff's Department and Jail, Mount Pleasant, Michigan. For the newspaper coverage of the "unruly" Puerto Rican migrants, see "Beet Workers Put on $32 Weekend Binge," June 19, 1950; and "Beet Worker Stabs Companion," July 17, 1950, 1, both in the *Isabella County Daily Times-News*.

13 Doner, *Cloud of Arrows*. See also Turner, *A True Account of My Life's Experiences*. Thanks to Donald Turner for making his father's self-published memoir available to me.

14 Charlotte Hoenig, comments to Eileen J. Findlay, July 15, 2009, Bay City, MI. See also Donald Turner and Harold Neimer, interview with James F. Findlay, August 22, 2009, Croswell, MI; Ralph and Linda Berry, interview with Eileen J. Findlay, July 14, 2009, in possession of the author.

15 Mapes, *Sweet Tyranny*, 91.

16　Mapes, *Sweet Tyranny*, 143–165, 215–239. Perhaps not surprisingly, a novel about the Michigan sugar beet towns published in 1950 described hardworking German smallholders as representing an idealized, whitened past, when nonexploitative relationships between sugar companies and migrant workers allegedly reigned. The author counterposed this supposedly harmonious past (which Mapes's research exposes as a farce) with the horror of Mexican American migrant poverty and degradation. "They [the Germans] represent the kind of migrant labor we dealt with in the old days. There was co-operation, mutual regard, and understanding." Doner, *Cloud of Arrows*, 99. For similar idealized memories of European migrant beet workers, see also Donald Turner and Harold Neimer, interview with James F. Findlay in Croswell, MI, August 22, 2009, in possession of the author.

17　Ngai, *Impossible Subjects*, 50–90, 127–166, quote on 133. This sort of racialized slippage is evident as well in several histories of the sugar beet industry in the northern Midwest; these authors fail to distinguish consistently between Mexican and Mexican American field-workers. See Mapes, *Sweet Tyranny*; Norris, *North for the Harvest*; and Mahar, *Sweet Energy*.

18　Such broad-brush denial of citizenship and respectable racial status to people of Mexican descent produced other sets of conflicts among Tejanos themselves between 1930 and the late 1950s. The Tejanos who migrated to Michigan during the northern growing seasons were rejected as both white and as citizens by more economically prosperous Mexican Americans as well as by Anglos in South Texas. Thus, they were considered neither legitimate citizens nor reliably white in either Texas or Michigan. Foley, "Partly Colored or Other White"; and Foley, *Quest for Equality*. For other conflicts between settled Mexican American community members and recent Mexican immigrants, see García, "Intraethnic Conflict and the *Bracero* Program during World War II."

19　Testimony of Harry Markle, "Stenographic Report of Proceedings Held at Saginaw, Michigan," President's Commission on Migratory Labor, Saginaw County Court House, September 11 and 12, 1950, 18–25; Testimony of Dr. R. L. Loftin, President's Commission, 395–396; Valdés, *Al Norte*, 93–107.

20　Testimonies of Harry Markle, 24, and Joseph Loughney, 48–50, both in President's Commission, 1950; "Sugar Beet Harvest to Start Next Week," *Bay City Times*, September 18, 1949, 11. Valdés describes the corporatization of agriculture in the Great Lakes region in *Al Norte*, 89–117.

21　Testimony of Dr. Edgar G. Johnston, President's Commission, 518–519. For an alternative vision, which also bemoans the loss of farmer paternalism but blames migrant workers for their alleged disinterest in quality work, see the testimony of Max Henderson, representative of Michigan Field Crops, the growers' organization that recruited the Puerto Ricans to Michigan in 1950, President's Commission, 156. A similar historical shift is evident in the memoir of a Michigan cucumber farmer, although he talks of paternalistic intimacy with Mexican workers in the early 1940s. Turner, *A True Account of My Life's Experiences*, 101–115.

22 Mapes, *Sweet Tyranny*, 70–73.

23 See President's Commission, September 1950, especially the testimony of Don Hamilton, 395–397.

24 Ngai, *Impossible Subjects*, 129–138; Hahamovitch, *No Man's Land*, 12–49, 96–134. For a few other examples of Mexican and Mexican American migrant worker histories, most of which focus on the U.S. Southwest and West, see Zamora, *Claiming Rights and Righting Wrongs in Texas*; Stephen, *Transborder Lives*; and Gómez-Quiñones, *Mexican-American Labor*. Rodolfo F. Acuña's sweeping *Corridors of Migration* provides an epic historical account of centuries of Mexican immigration and labor organizing. Ana Elizabeth Rosas analyzes the exploitative gender dynamics of bracero migration to California in "Flexible Families." Deborah Cohen takes a much less pessimistic approach to bracero historical experiences in *Braceros*. For other discussions of the bracero program, see Loza, "Braceros on the Boundaries"; García, *A World of Its Own*; Pitti, *The Devil in Silicon Valley*.

25 Valdés, *Al Norte*, 97–99.

26 Testimony of Russell Evarts, 303, 314–315; Harry Kobel, 59–71; Marvin H. Keil, 229–230; and A. W. Siebenand, 126, all in President's Commission, 1950.

27 See Valdés, *Al Norte*, 51–58, for a description of the changing travel strategies of Tejanos through the 1930s and the political economies of their home communities that pushed them into migration to the Midwest.

28 Valdés, *Al Norte*, 25–27; Sierra Berdecía, "Report for the Governor of Puerto Rico, Hon. Luis Muñoz Marín. Living and Working Conditions of Puerto Rican Workers under Contract in Michigan," August 16, 1950, File 743, Box 2273, Tarea 96-20, Fondo Oficina del Gobierno (FOG), AGPR, 6–8. The following in President's Commission: Testimony of Harry Markle, 22–26, 31–34, 44–46, 50; Testimony of A. B. Love, 73; Testimony of José Chávez, 461–467; Testimony of Cándido Delgado, 469–475; Testimony of Harold Gough, 317–319. John Espinoza, interview with Eileen Findlay, July 24, 2009; Elisa and Manuel Ochoa, interview with James F. Findlay, August 23, 2009; Denison, *America's Son*.

   Marc Simon Rodríguez provides an illuminating analysis of Tejanos' analogous diaspora into the agricultural zones of Wisconsin; he argues that the longstanding seasonal migrations to Wisconsin ended up deeply shaping Chicano political organizing in South Texas. Rodríguez, *The Tejano Diaspora*.

29 The following in President's Commission, September 11–12, 1950: Testimonies of Henry McCusker, 337; Dr. R. L. Loftin, 396–401; Dr. Frederick Leeder, 494–508; Dr. Edgar G. Johnston, 508–522; Ellis Washburn, 576–578; and Philippe Gonzalez, 479–491.

30 Mapes, *Sweet Tyranny*, 222–238; Norris, *North for the Harvest*, 65–81; Valdés, *Al Norte*, 73–86; "Migration to Study Migrants," *Saginaw News*, June 1, 1950, 25.

The 1950 publication of Mary Frances Doner's novel, *Cloud of Arrows*, criticizing the exploitation of migrant workers in Michigan's sugar beet fields is part of the burgeoning interest in migrant agricultural laborers that preceded the Puerto Ricans' arrival in Michigan. See also testimonies in President's Commission, September 1950: Mrs. C. R. Mueller, 352–356; Dr. R. L. Loftin, 395–419; Henry McCusker, 336–351; Dr. Frederick S. Leeder, 492–507; Ellis Washburn, 575–600; as well as "Hunger Strikes Farm Labor Camps," *Life*, March 27, 1950, 38–39.

31 Quotes from the testimony of Reverend R. Norman Hughes, President's Commision, 1950, 535–536. For a few examples from the *Isabella County Daily Times-News*, see "Flaming Cross in the Florida Pines," June 14, 1950; and "Age Is No Barrier," August 16, 1950. Dionicio Nodín Valdés also found that rural European American residents in this part of Michigan routinely assumed that all Mexicans were infected with syphilis, *Al Norte*, 107–109.

32 Mrs. S. L. Durham, "Lansing 1946"; "Report of the Home Mission Council Workers," August 31, 1948; "Summer Report for Marshall Migrant Work," August 31, 1950; "Summer Report for Migrant Work, June 22–Aug., 1951," all in Box 1, Michigan Migrant Ministry Reports, Bentley Historical Library, University of Michigan, Ann Arbor, MI. President's Commission, 1950, testimonies of Mrs. F. D. Hepburn, 258–265; Mrs. S. L. Durham, 286–298; and Ellis Washburn, 575–600. "Saginaw Church Women Entertain Trio Here to Aid Migrant Workers," *Saginaw News*, June 27, 1950, 13; "Migrants Here Are Entertained," *Saginaw News*, July 14, 1950, 2; "Migrant Committee Formed This Week," *Sanilac County Jeffersonian*, June 29, 1950, 1.

33 See Kern's palpable rage at the inhumane conditions suffered by migrant workers in his handwritten manuscript, "Work in the Beet Fields," Affidavits: 1945–46, Box 1, Clement Kern Papers, Walter P. Reuther Library, Wayne State University, Detroit, MI. Also see his testimony before the President's Commission on Migratory Labor, September 12, 1950, 418–422; and Casey, *Father Clem Kern*, 118–158.

34 See, for example, "Other Side of the Coin," *Saginaw Catholic Weekly*, July 23, 1950; "Strong Unions Urged for Migrant Labor," *Saginaw Catholic Weekly*, July 23, 1950, 1; "Obituaries," *Saginaw News*, February 7, 1950, 9; "St. Patrick's Aids Migrant Laborers," *Sanilac County Jeffersonian*, July 13, 1950, 1.

35 Elisa Ochoa, interview with James F. Findlay, August 23, 2009; Sierra Berdecía, "Report to the Governor, 6–8; García, *Mexicans in the Midwest*, 25–104; Valdés, *Al Norte*, 61–128; Herman G. Zimmerman, "The Role of Hand Labor in Monitor Sugar Company History," unpublished manuscript, January 1981, Bay County Historical Society, Bay City, MI; Testimony of José Chávez, 461–467, and Testimony of Cándido Delgado, 469–475, both in President's Commission, 1950; Mapes, *Sweet Tyranny*, 160–161; Norris, *North for the Harvest*, 65.

36 Valdés, *Al Norte*, 118–128.

37 "37 Survivors of Plane Crash Saved," *Detroit Free Press*, June 7, 1950, 15; "A New Migrant Problem," *Detroit Free Press*, June 19, 1950, 1, 9; "Airlines' Sugar Beet Shuttle Hauls 5,000 without a Spill," *Detroit Free Press*, June 20, 1950, 13.

38 "Boricuas salvan la cosecha Michigan," *El Mundo*, June 21, 1950, 1; "Unas palabras de Crawford," *El Mundo*, June 25, 1950, 6; "Dicen obreros de Puerto Rico son los mejores," June 23, 1950, 1; "Salvan la cosecha de remolacha en MI," *El Mundo*, June 19, 1950, 1; "Air Lift of Puerto Ricans Averts Wide Beet Crop Loss in MI," *New York Times*, June 18, 1950, 1; "'Operation Farmlift' Credited with Saving State's Sugar Beet Crop," *Bay City Times*, June 19, 1950, 15; "Huge Stake in 'Farmlift,'" *Saginaw News*, June 14, 1950, 10; "A New Migrant Problem," *Detroit Free Press*, June 19, 1950, 1, 9.

39 "Crawford pide se investigue porqué no acepta la Marina el ingreso de portorriqueños," *El Mundo*, May 29, 1947, 1; "Crawford Gets Committee Post," *Bay City Times*, September 23, 1949, 2; Testimony of Fred Crawford, President's Commission, 1950, 5–15. The following all in the *Saginaw News*: "Crawford Will Offer CCC Probe Resolution," and "Crawford Advises Enforcement Body," June 6, 1950, 3; "U.S. Has Strayed from True Ideal, Crawford Says," July 5, 1950, 17; "Crawford Intends to Testify at Migrant Labor Hearing," September 2, 1950, 2; "Why I Should Be Nominated," October 10, 1950, 8.

Indeed, it might be argued that as Muñoz Marín's political commitments moved away from his early more radical political positions and toward capitalist colonial modernization, Fred Crawford replaced New York representative Vito Marcantonio as Muñoz Marín's most prominent Washington ally. For Muñoz Marín's complicated, shifting relationship with Marcantonio, see Meléndez, "Vito Marcantonio, Puerto Rican Migration, and the 1949 Mayoral Election in New York City," 198–234.

40 "Crawford's Maryland Farm Seen Hot Issue in 8th District Race," *Bay City Times*, July 4, 1950, 5; "Curry Lambasts Crawford Record in Campaign Talk," *Saginaw News*, August 30, 1950, 3; "Leppien Sees 18,000 Votes in Primary," *Saginaw News*, September 8, 1950, 21; "Fred Crawford elogia mensaje de gobernador," *El Mundo*, March 9, 1950, 1; "Se necesitan con urgencia en Michigan," *El Mundo*, June 10, 1950, 1; "En torno a la fortaleza," *El Mundo*, June 10, 1950, 6; "Obreros boricuas ayudan salvar carrera a Crawford," *El Mundo*, July 10, 1950, 6; "Crawford analiza intervención en la contratación de obreros," *El Mundo*, August 10, 1950, 18.

41 "Huge Stake in 'Farmlift,'" *Saginaw News*, June 14, 1950, 10.

42 Testimony of Fred Crawford, President's Commission, 1950, 9, 11. For analogous rhetoric, see also testimony of Max Henderson, President's Commission, 1950, 153–154.

43 $N = 556$. All applications are drawn from the boxes labeled "Querellas de Obreros de Michigan," Tarea 61-55, Departamento de Trabajo, AGPR. For discussions of plebeian and proletarian Puerto Ricans' long-standing tradition of consensual union, within which heterosexual couples often considered themselves

husbands and wives, see Findlay, *Imposing Decency*; Mintz, "Cañamelar"; and Safa, *The Urban Poor of Puerto Rico*.

44 Luis Muñoz Marín (hereafter LMM) to Honorable Fred Crawford, June 21, 1950, and LMM to A. Fernós Isern, June 21, 1950, both in File 743, Box 2273, Tarea 96-20, FOG, AGPR. For chronologies of the contract signing and airlift, see Valdés, *Al Norte*, 120–130; Asencio Camacho, *Itinerario de muerte*; Asencio Camacho, "Of Unscheduled Deaths and Other (Un)Happy Endings"; Asencio Camacho, "Migrants Who Never Arrived"; as well as Sierra Berdecía, "Report to the Governor," 1–2.

45 Luis Asencio Camacho narrates the harrowing experience of the airplane crash in the Atlantic Ocean from the perspective of two survivors from Mayagüez whom he interviewed many years later. Asencio Camacho, *Itinerario de muerte*; Asencio Camacho, "Of Unscheduled Deaths and Other (Un)Happy Endings." See also the following press reports, among many others: "Tragedia avión azota hogares en Mayagüez," *El Imparcial*, June 9, 1950, 5; "Que desgracia," *El Imparcial*, June 10, 1950, 3; "Ramos Antonini dice: Gobierno no aconseja emigración de obreros," *El Imparcial*, June 13, 1950, 3; "Relata terror y muerte a bordo de avión caído," *El Imparcial*, June 13, 1950, 3; "Salvan 37 del avión," *El Mundo*, June 7, 1950, 1; "Supervivientes dan dramático relato a fotógrafo Casenave," *El Mundo*, June 9, 1950, 1; "Llegan a Charleston los supervivientes del desastre aereo," *El Mundo*, June 9, 1950, 7.

46 "Salvan 37 del avión," *El Mundo*, June 7, 1950, 1; "Supervivientes dan dramático relato a fotógrafo Casenave," *El Mundo*, June 9, 1950, 1; "Llegan a Charleston los supervivientes del desastre aereo," *El Mundo*, June 9, 1950, 7.

"Puerto Ricans Excel as Help in Beet Fields: Planes Fly in Eager, Law-Abiding Workers," *Detroit Free Press*, June 19, 1950, 1, 9; "Airlines Sugar Beet Shuttle Hauls 5,000 without a Spill," *Detroit Free Press*, June 20, 1950, 3.

47 For a few examples of *El Imparcial*'s unrelenting criticisms of the PPD's handling of the flights, see "La causa del desastre," June 9, 1950; "Culpa AT de las muertes: Empleado revela el avión salió sin inspección," June 10, 1950, 3; "Otro testigo corrobora no inspeccionaron avión," June 11, 1950; "Una carta acusadora," June 11, 1950, 19.

48 "Tragedia avión azota hogares en Mayagüez," *El Imparcial*, June 9, 1950, 5; "Qué desgracia," *El Imparcial*, June 10, 1950, 3; "Niños se horroriza ante lo incierto de su vida," *El Imparcial*, June 18, 1950, 4.

49 See in *El Mundo*, "Esperan transportación aera a EEUU otros 558 obreros," June 9, 1950, 22; "No se arrepienten: Salieron en últimas horas 248," June 8, 1950, 3; "Llevan más trabajadores al continente," June 7, 1950, 1, 12; "Hacen nueve vuelos al día con obreros," June 12, 1950, 1; "Sierra elogia valor de obreros boricuas despúes del desastre," June 14, 1950, 10.

50 "'Operation Farmlift' Bigtime Aviation Job," *Saginaw News*, June 13, 1950, 17; "Puerto Ricans Flown Here to Work in Fields," *Bay City Times*, June 2, 1950, 1, 2; "Crawford Influence in Puerto Rico Paid Off for State Beet Farmers," *Saginaw*

News, June 18, 1950, 1; "Farmlift Operations Slated for Completion Today," *Bay City Times*, June 18, 1950; "Two Airlines Plan Gigantic 'Airlift,'" *Saginaw News*, June 10, 1950, 1; "Airport Value Emphasized by 'Operation Farmlift,'" *Saginaw News*, June 17, 1950, 4.

51 "Beet Labor Arrives Here Following Airplane Crash," *Gratiot County Herald*, June 15, 1950, 12; "Congressman Crawford Wins Praise of Beet Industry," *Isabella County Daily Times-News*, June 14, 1950; and "Island Supplies Beet Workers," *Isabella County Daily Times-News*, June 15, 1950.

52 The following in *Bay City Times*: "Flying in Puerto Rican Workers Is Costing $500,000," June 13, 1950, 5; "Farmlift Task Is Nearing End," June 16, 1950, 6; and "Farm Workers End Mass Airlift Today," June 18, 1950, part A, 12. The quote is from the last article. See also "5,300 by Weekend Is Farmers' Goal," *Saginaw News*, June 15, 1950; and "'Farmlift' Ends, Crop Job Begins," *Saginaw News*, June 19, 1950, 13.

53 For some examples, see "Operation Sugar Cane: Plans Underway to Fly Puerto Ricans Home in the Fall," *Bay City Times*, June 20, 1950, 4; and "Yanqui 'Know-How,' 1950-Style," *Bay City Times*, June 18, 1950, part A, 13; "Farmlift Clippers at Tri-City Airport," *Saginaw News*, June 13, 1950, 17.

54 "Farmlift Task Is Nearing End," *Bay City Times*, June 16, 1950, 4.

55 Airplanes were an almost magical symbol of postwar modernity in 1950, embodying both peril and triumphant power. While automobiles had become quite commonplace (even migrant agricultural workers owned them), most rural Michigan residents had never boarded a plane. Tragic plane crashes constituted front-page news in Michigan newpapers several times each week. Concomitantly, however, airplanes figured prominently in press accounts of U.S. successes on the battlefield in Korea, creating compelling, heroic images of pilots and their flying machines. For some examples of crash reporting, see the following, all in the *Saginaw News* on page 1: "B-36's Making Long Flight over Ocean," June 23, 1950; "58 on Airliner Feared Dead in Lake," June 24, 1950, "Bits of Plane, People Found, Apparently Blown to Pieces," June 26, 1950; "Armed Forces Charter Major Pacific Airline," July 9, 1950. For stories marveling at wartime airpower, see in the *Saginaw News*: "British Sky Giant Faces Atlantic Test," June 28, 1950, 8; "Delivery Accepted," June 28, 1950, 1; "News in Pictures," July 22, 1950, 8; "U.S. Sends Planes, Ships to Fight Korean Reds," June 27, 1950; and "Morale Transformed by Bombers' Arrival," June 29, 1950, 1. For a discussion of the modernizing impulse associated with airplanes in Africa, see Allman, "Phantoms of the Archive."

56 Donald Turner, interview with Eileen J. Findlay, August 7, 2009; Manuel Ochoa, interview with James F. Findlay, August 23, 2009; Linda Berry, personal communication, July 6, 2009; "More Puerto Ricans," *Saginaw News*, June 7, 1950, 25; and "Puerto Rican Survivor Here, Still Shaky from Air Tragedy," *Saginaw News*, June 10, 1950, 5.

57 For a few examples, see Francisco Rosa "and many others here in Michigan" to
    Tonín Romero, June 27, 1950, Box 195, Serie Querellas de Obreros Migrantes,
    Tarea 61-55, Fondo Negociado de Trabajo, AGPR; Ruperto Muñoz and thirteen
    others to LMM, July 21, 1950, File 743—Michigan-M-N-O, Box 2275, Tarea 96-20,
    FOG, AGPR; Celso González to Carmen González Crespo, September 10, 1950,
    File 743—Michigan-G-H-I; and Celso González Crespo to LMM, September 5,
    1950, File 743—Michigan-G-H-I.

58 See, for example, Ramón Miranda Crespo and others to LMM, July 17, 1950,
    File 743—Michigan-M-N-O, Box 2275, Tarea 96-20, FOG, AGPR; Ramón
    Moreno, August 21, 1950, File 743—Michigan-M-N-O; Domingo LaPorte,
    September 3, 1950, File 743—J-K-L, Box 2275, Tarea 96-20, FOG, AGPR; Ramón
    Guzmán, July 15, 1950, File 743—G-H-I; Pedro Rodríguez, July 20, 1950, File
    743—R, Box 2277.

59 "Cruz roja se hace cargo de boricuas en Michigan," El Imparcial, August 10, 1950,
    4. The two worker protest letters in El Mundo appeared on July 26, 1950, 22, and
    August 26, 1950, 6. See also in El Mundo "El desastre aereo," June 18, 1950, 6;
    "Felicitación," June 10, 1950, 6; "Preguntas a la A.T.," June 17, 1950, 6. El Diario de
    Puerto Rico, which Luis Muñoz Marín had recently purchased, debated El Impar-
    cial's charges that Muñoz Marín was more interested in serving Fred Crawford's
    interests than aiding his own constituents. See in El Diario de Puerto Rico: "La
    cosecha remolachera de MI," and "$117,000 para los obreros boricuas en E.U.,"
    August 21, 1950; "Obreros boricuas en E.U. recibirán .65 la hora," August 24,
    1950; and "Además un dólar por cada acre que trabajen," August 24, 1950.

60 Manuel Cabranes, "Report on Visit to Michigan and Brant, New York," June
    28, 1950, and Eulalio Torres, "Asunto: Visita a Michigan," June 26, 1950, both in
    File 743—1950, Box 2273, Tarea 96-20, FOG, AGPR. See also Alan Perl's report
    on July 17, 1950, File 743—1950, Box 2273, Tarea 96-20, FOG, AGPR. This initial
    response from the Puerto Rican government followed prior practices in the
    prewar period. Whalen, "Colonialism, Citizenship, and the Making of a Puerto
    Rican Diaspora."

61 "Dicen obreros de Puerto Rico son los mejores," El Mundo, June 23, 1950, 1. El
    Mundo also seems to have received letters of protest, beginning in late June,
    but refused to print them, instead warning its readers against "fraudulent
    complaints" and admonishing families of beet workers against sending the
    migrants any cash. "Sierra previene a los obreros contra timos," June 30, 1950,
    5; "Una alerta a los obreros," July 2, 1950, 6.

62 Amos Rivera to Pedro Rivera, August 29, 1950, File 743—R, Box 2277, Tarea 96-
    20, FOG, AGPR. For a few examples of the flood of letters published by El Impar-
    cial, see "Boricuas se quejan de maltrato en MI," June 27, 1950, 5; "Obreros dicen
    en Michigan los tratan como a perros," June 29, 1950, 6; "Miseria en Michigan,"
    September 16, 1950, 17; "Obrero enfermo denuncia atropellos en Michigan,"
    September 9, 1950, 10.

63 Valdés, *Organized Agriculture and the Labor Movement before the UFW*, 60–79; Dietz, *Economic History of Puerto Rico*, 165–166.

    For women's needlework in the 1930s, see Boris, "Needlewomen under the New Deal in Puerto Rico," 33–55; González García, *Una puntada en el tiempo*; Baerga-Santini, "Las jerarquías sociales y las espresiones de resistencia." For the home needlework industry in the 1950s, see Dietz, *Economic History of Puerto Rico*, 225–226.

64 Eric Wolf also tells of the razing of the company store on the coffee plantation in the municipality he studied in central Puerto Rico, "San José," 193, 231; Mintz, "Cañamelar," 324–329, 350–351.

65 Elías Correa and others to LMM, July 27, 1950, File—Michigan-A-B-C, Box 2275, Tarea 96-20, FOG, AGPR; Maximino Cordero to LMM, September 4, 1950, File 743—Emigración, Box 2275, Tarea 96-20, FOG, AGPR.

66 Affidavit of Pablo Tirado, July 3, 1950, Affidavits—Sugar Beets, Box 1, Clement Kern Papers, Walter Reuther Library, Wayne State University, Detroit, MI.

67 Pedro Miranda to LMM, August 1950, File 743—Michigan-M-N-O, Box 2275, Tarea 96-20, FOG, AGPR.

68 Celso González to Carmen González Crespo, September 10, 1950, File 743—G-H-I, Box 2275, Tarea 96-20, FOG, AGPR; Saturnino Lazu Toledo and fifteen others to LMM, July 17, 1950, File 743—J-K-L; Luis de la Cruz Rodríguez, July 31, 1950, File 743—D-E-F; Testimony of Santos Cintrón, President's Commission, 1950, 444–447.

69 I thank Bob Grove for first raising the possibility of workers' rage at enforced sexual abstinence. The quote is from Mintz, "Cañamelar," 379. Men's anxiety over women's possible sexual roaming and the violent lengths to which they were expected to go to prevent such activities surfaced continually in Puerto Rican popular culture and newspapers of the period. See the movie advertisement: "IS THIS YOUR NEIGHBOR'S WIFE?—She might be . . . WITHOUT HONOR!," *El Mundo*, June 16, 1950, 22. "Da 'por amor' tres puñaladas a una casada," *El Mundo*, June 13, 1950, 14; "Regresa para matar amante de su esposa," *El Mundo*, June 15, 1950, 23. For broader historical overviews of these questions, see Findlay, *Imposing Decency*, 18–52, 110–134; Guerra, *Popular Expression and National Identity in Puerto Rico*; Mintz, "Cañamelar," 258–259, 376–380; Wolf, "San José," 257–258; Safa, *The Urban Poor of Puerto Rico*, 20–60.

    It is entirely possible that in Michigan some men developed homoerotic relationships with each other. No hint of this surfaced in the sources available to me, however.

70 "Describen horrores," *El Imparcial*, July 9, 1950, 34, archived in Recortes de periódico, File 743—1950, Box 2273, Tarea 96-20, FOG, AGPR; Saturnino Lazú Toledo and fifteen others to LMM, July 17, 1950, File 743—Michigan-J-K-L, Box 2275, Tarea 96-20, FOG, AGPR; Rafael Arroyo to LMM, August 3, 1950, File 743—Michigan-A-B-C, Box 2275, Tarea 96-20, FOG, AGPR.

71 Tito Oriol Colón to LMM, November 21, 1950, File—Michigan-M-N-O, Tarea 96-20, FOG, AGPR. See also Pedro Miranda, August, 1950, File—Michigan-M-N-O; Luis Reyes, Novembe 13, 1950, File—Michigan-R, Box 2277.

72 Ceferino Echevarría and six others to LMM, August 31, 1950, File 743—S-T, Box 2277, Tarea 96-20, FOG, AGPR.

73 Ceferino Echevarria and six others to LMM, August 31, 1950, File 743—S-T, Box 2277, Tarea 96-20, FOG, AGPR; Antonio López Santiago to LMM, October 9, 1950, File 743—Michigan-J-K-L, Box 2275, Tarea 96-20, FOG, AGPR; Álvaro González and others to LMM, August 3, 1950, File 743—Michigan-G-H-I, Box 2275, Tarea 96-20, FOG, AGPR; Luis de la Cruz Rodríguez to LMM, July 31, 1950, File 743—Michigan-D-E-F, Tarea 96-20, FOG, AGPR; "No somos más populares," El Imparcial, July 19, 1950, 15; "Obreros dicen en Michigan los tratan como a perros," El Imparcial, June 29, 1950, 6.

74 Salomé Hernández Gracias to LMM, September 7, 1950, File 743—Michigan-G-H-I, Box 2275, Tarea 96-20, FOG, AGPR; Virginia Nieves to LMM, September 27, 1950, File 743—Michigan-M-N-O, Box 2275, Tarea 96-20, FOG, AGPR; Viviano Rodríguez to LMM, September 9, 1950, File 743—R, Box 2277, Tarea 96-20, FOG, AGPR; Miguel A. Casul to LMM, September 2, 1950, File 743—Michigan-A-B-C, Box 2275, Tarea 96-20, FOG, AGPR.

75 Fidel Robledo to LMM, September 13, 1950, File 743—Michigan-R, Box 2277, Tarea 96-20, FOG, AGPR; Manuel Andino Gaetan to LMM, August 25, 1950, File 743—Michigan-A-B-C, Box 2275. For the importance of withstanding adversity in the constitution of plebeian masculinity elsewhere in Latin America, see Stern, The Secret History of Gender, 151–188; and Gutmann, The Meanings of Macho.

76 Julia Arzuaga to LMM, July 28, 1950, File 743—Michigan-A-B-C, Box 2275, Tarea 96-20, FOG, AGPR; Juan Rivera and others to LMM, August 26, 1950, File 743—Michigan-R, Box 2277, Tarea 96-20, FOG, AGPR. In El Imparcial see "Quieren Fugarse," July 15, 1950; "Sigue el maltrato," July 16, 1950; "Boricuas en Michigan," July 16, 1950.

77 Anne Shea analyzes how family descriptions in contemporary U.S. farmworker testimonies reject agricultural laborers' reduction to mere commodities. Shea, "'Don't Let Them Make You Feel You Did a Crime.'"

78 Juan Rivera and others to LMM, August 26, 1950, File—Michigan-R, Box 2277, Tarea 96-20, FOG, AGPR; Miguel A. Casul to LMM, September 2, 1950, File 743—Michigan-A-B-C, Box 2275, Tarea 96-20, FOG, AGPR; Porfirio Irizarry to LMM, September 1950, File 743—Michigan-G-H-I, Box 2275, Tarea 96-20, FOG, AGPR.

79 Exequiel Amaroles to LMM, October 3, 1950, File 743—Michigan-M-N-O, Box 2275, Tarea 96-20, FOG, AGPR; Gilberto Vásquez and others to LMM, September 1, 1950, File 743—V-Z, Box 2277, Tarea 96-20, FOG, AGPR; Juan M. Rosado and others to LMM, September 1950; File 743—R, Box 2277, Tarea 96-20, FOG, AGPR; Luís Reyes to LMM, November 13, 1950, File 743—Michigan-R, Box 2277, Tarea 96-20, FOG, AGPR.

80 See Anselmo Colón Balaguer to LMM, September 29, 1950, File 743—Michigan-A-B-C, Box 2275, Tarea 96-20, FOG, AGPR; Carmen Seda Miranda to LMM, September 10, 1950, File 743—Michigan-M-N-O, Box 2275, Tarea 96-20, FOG, AGPR; Ramón Rodríguez to LMM, September 8, 1950, File 743—R, Box 2277, Tarea 96-20, FOG, AGPR. Many letters from impoverished Puerto Ricans to Muñoz Marín during the 1940s requested his intervention on their behalf in an almost prayerful way, as if saying the rosary. Very few letters from the beet fields had this religious tone. Also, although many 1940s letter writers referred to their PPD activism and used a familiar, even intimate language when address-ing the governor, speaking to him as if he were a member of their family, they lacked the sharp egalitarianism that marks many letters from the beet fields.

81 N = 279 for the archival letters; n = 150 for *Imparcial* letters.

82 Miguel A. Casul to LMM, September 2, 1950, File 743—Michigan-A-B-C, Box 2275, Tarea 96-20, FOG, AGPR.

83 Marcial Montalvo to LMM, October 3, 1950, File 743—Michigan-M-N-O, Box 2275, Tarea 96-20, FOG, AGPR. See also Alejandro Padró to LMM, July 24, 1950, File 743—Michigan-P-Q, Box 2275, Tarea 96-20, FOG, AGPR; Antonio López Santiago to LMM, October 9, 1950, File 743—Michigan-J-K-L, Box 2275, Tarea 96-20, FOG, AGPR.

84 Maximino Cordero to LMM, September 4, 1950, File 743—Michigan-A-B-C, Box 2275, Tarea 96-20, FOG, AGPR; Luis de la Cruz Rodríguez, July 31, 1950, File 743—Michigan-D-E-F; "Más atropellos," El Imparcial, July 27, 1950, 17. See also, for example, Juan B. Pérez to LMM, October 5, 1950, File 743—Michigan-P-Q, Box 2275, Tarea 96-20, FOG, AGPR; Rejustino de Jesús to LMM, July 10, 1950, File 743—Michigan-D-E-F, Box 2275, Tarea 96-20, FOG, AGPR; Elías Correa and others to LMM, July 27, 1950, File 743—Michigan-A-B-C, Box 2275, Tarea 96-20, FOG, AGPR; Bienvenido Rodríguez and others to LMM, September 13, 1950, File 743—Michigan-R, Box 2277, Tarea 96-20, FOG, AGPR.

85 "Lo engañaron," El Imparcial, July 3, 1950; "Le agradaría a Ud.?," El Imparcial, July 10, 1950; "Quiere vivir de nosotros," El Imparcial, July 13, 1950, FOL XII. See also, from El Imparcial: "No les pagan," July 7, 1950; "Quejas de Michigan," July 7, 1950; "Condiciones pésimas," July 4, 1950; "Están hastiados," July 1, 1950; "Pide cuentas a comisionado," July 18, 1950.

86 Teófilo Caro to LMM, September 28, 1950, File 743—Michigan-A-B-C, Box 2275, Tarea 96-20, FOG, AGPR. This author's address to Muñoz Marín echoes quite explicitly the ritualized opening words of a satirical weekly political column in El Imparcial, "Cartas Públicas . . . y privadas." For several more examples, see Matías Cabán and others to LMM, October 2, 1950, File 743—Michigan-A-B-C, Box 2275, Tarea 96-20, FOG, AGPR; Victor Burgos to LMM, September 28, 1950, File 743—Michigan-A-B-C, Box 2275, Tarea 96-20, FOG, AGPR; "No somos más populares," El Imparcial, July 19, 1950; "Situación en Michigan," El Imparcial,

August 15, 1950, 15; Pedro Rivera Betances to LMM, September 2, 1950, File 743—R, Box 2277, Tarea 96-20, FOG, AGPR.

87 Rafael Arroyo to LMM, August 3, 1950, File 743—Michigan-A-B-C, Box 2275, Tarea 96-20, FOG, AGPR. See also "No somos más populares," El Imparcial, July 19, 1950, 15; "Rectifican a Nido," and "No es cierto," El Imparcial, July 27, 1950, 17.

88 Inocencio Ortiz to LMM, September 30, 1950; File 743—Michigan-M-N-O, Box 2275, Tarea 96-20, FOG, AGPR.

89 Rejustino de Jesús to LMM, July 10, 1950, File 743—Michigan-D-E-F, Box 2275, Tarea 96-20, FOG, AGPR. See also Ruperto Muñoz and thirteen others to LMM, July 21, 1950, File 743—Michigan-M-N-O, Box 2275, Tarea 96-20, FOG, AGPR; Jenaro López Vega to LMM, September 23, 1950, File 743—Michigan-J-K-L, Box 2275, Tarea 96-20, FOG, AGPR; Celso González to LMM, September 5, 1950, File 743—Michigan-G-H-I, Box 2275, Tarea 96-20, FOG, AGPR.

5 • The *Brega* Expands

1 The Tejano field men who served as intermediaries between migrant workers and the farmers figured prominently in narratives about abusive conditions in the Michigan countryside. While sidestepping their own responsibility for the degrading conditions imposed upon migrant workers, growers frequently blamed crew leaders for stealing Tejano wages, making unenforceable employment agreements, and "loading people like cattle" into their trucks to make the long journey from Texas. See, for example, in President's Commission on Migratory Labor, Saginaw County Court House, September 11 and 12, 1950, written transcript in Harry S. Truman Library, Record Group 220: the testimonies of A. B. Love, 94–95; Albert Hildebrandt, 280–284; Don Hamilton, 394–395; and Max Henderson, 184–187. Manuel Ochoa was one of the lucky ones. After migrating from Texas to Michigan for many years as a field laborer, he managed to parlay his experience as a military policeman in the U.S. armed forces during World War II into a position as a labor recruiter and field man for Michigan Sugar Company in Croswell, MI. Manuel Ochoa, interview with James F. Findlay, August 23, 2009.

2 Álvaro González and others to Luis Muñoz Marín (LMM), August 3, 1950, File 743—Michigan-G-H-I, Box 2275, Tarea 96-20, Fondo de la Oficina del Gobernador (FOG), Archivo General de Puerto Rico (AGPR). See also Ernesto Valdés and others to LMM, August 31, 1950, File 743—V-Z, Box 2277, Tarea 96-20, FOG, AGPR; Marcial Montalvo to LMM, October 3, 1950, File 743—Michigan-M-N-O, Box 2275, Tarea 96-20, FOG, AGPR; Valdés, Al Norte, 127–128.

3 "More Migrant Workers Arrive," Saginaw News, June 23, 1950, 17.

4 Testimony of Mrs. S. S. Durham, President's Commission, 288, 292–295.

5 "Puerto Ricans Thank People of Michigan," Detroit Free Press, July 30, 1950, 2.

6 Félix Pérez and others to LMM, June 24, 1950, Rec. 22, File 743—Michigan-G-H-I, Box 2275, Tarea 96-20, FOG, AGPR.

7 For another example of such political maneuvering, see Eulalio García, December 2, 1950, File 743—Michigan-G-H-I, Box 2275, Tarea 96-20, FOG, AGPR. Lorrin Thomas provides an insightful analysis of other such attempts by Puerto Ricans—and their persistent marginalization—in New York City during this period. Thomas, *Puerto Rican Citizen*.

8 Father Kern, along with his assistants Fathers Elizalde and Talavera, priests from Mexico, was an important figure in the working-class Corktown neighborhood of Detroit, where he organized agricultural, industrial, and even sex workers to defend their rights, helped recent arrivals to the city find employment and housing, and supported residents organizing to fight against freeways being built through the neighborhood. A close friend of Walter Reuther and cofounder of a network of Detroit worker schools in the 1930s, in later years, Kern became a fervent ally of César Chávez's farmworkers' labor union, held regular 2 a.m. masses for labor reporters and other night workers, helped found a social service network for Spanish-speaking prisoners, and walked picket lines in favor of striking Detroit prostitutes demanding a fair wage for their sex work. The community Montessori school, free medical and legal clinics, and a network of alcohol and substance abuse programs that Kern and his pastoral team helped to establish continued to thrive in Detroit's Corktown neighborhood long after Kern's death. Casey, *Father Clem Kern*; "Remembrances for the Tenth Anniversary of Msgr. Clement Kern's Death and Passing to the Good Shepherd" and "The Faithful of Most Holy Trinity Church Remember the Twelfth Anniversary of Msgr. Clement Kern's Death and Passing with This Second Edition of Testimonies of How He Inspires Us Still," unpublished booklets produced by the Trinity Church congregation, in possession of the author. See also Kern's obituary, "Msgr. Clement Kern," *New York Times*, August 16, 1983, D-22.

   Historian Dionicio Nodín Valdés, who grew up in Detroit's Latino community, credits Kern's efforts with creating enduring relations of solidarity between the Puerto Ricans who settled in Detroit after the sugar beet field fiasco and the city's residents of Mexican descent. Dionicio Nodín Valdés, personal communication, June 20, 2006.

9 Statement of Pedro Colón, June 25, 1950, Box 1, Clement Kern Papers, Walter Reuther Library, Wayne State University, Detroit, MI, emphasis added. For some examples of Mexican American protests during this same period, see untitled statement, June 25, 1950, 1950 Affidavits—Sugar Beets.

10 By the end of the summer of 1950, the Puerto Rican government representatives stationed in Michigan routinely sent dissatisfied beet workers to Kern for job placement in the city. Kern also received many letters from Puerto Ricans and their families thanking him for his help. Unprocessed Letters I, Box 1; Box Rec'vd 5–12–86, both in Clement Kern Papers.

11 Although he did not direct a congregation himself, instead serving as executive secretary of the Bay County Council of Churches, Reverend Hughes was an active presence in the Bay City liberal Protestant scene, preaching on Easter Sunday at the First Presbyterian Church, hosting a local radio show, organizing youth delegations to regional peace conferences, welcoming displaced persons from western Europe, and winning a national award for his affordable housing advocacy. Minutes of session, October 4, 1949, March 13, 1950, First Presbyterian Church, Bay City, MI; "Rev. R. Norman Hughes Is Presbyterian Speaker," *Bay City Times*, September 24, 1949, 2; and "Church News," *Bay City Times*, July 1, 1950, 2; Elsie S. Parker, "Citizen Action," *National Municipal Review*, February 1952, 114.

12 "Job Deserters Protest: Beet Field Fraud Charged by Workers," *Detroit Times*, July 16, 1950; "Migrants Seek to Organize," *Michigan Teacher*, October 1950, 4; "47 Puerto Rican Workers Are Flown Back to Island Homes," *Bay City Times*, July 20, 1950; "Migrant Worker Pacts Checked," *Bay City Times*, July 22, 1950, 4; "Excerpts from Frank Edwards' Radio Broadcast 7/12/50 Mutual Broadcasting System," in Folder: Newspapers, Box 1, Clement Kern Papers; "State Beet Growers, Puerto Rican Workers Settle Pay Payment Dispute," *Bay City Times*, July 17, 1950, 4; testimony of Rev. R. Norman Hughes, President's Commission, 1950, 527–531.

Mexican bracero workers also protested farm labor conditions to their consul in Detroit during the 1940s. They were not able to garner the same public support as Puerto Ricans among Michigan constituencies, however, nor do they appear to have provoked any meaningful response from their government. For some examples, see in Affidavits Sugar Beet Workers, Box 1, Clement Kern Papers: "Diario de un bracero: Apuntes de: Fernando Alquicira E.," July 11, 1945, 1945–46 ; "Caso en Millinton," June 18, 1945, 1945–46; Francisco Espinosa Q. and Uvaldo García R. to Marcelino Mendoza, July 8, 1945, 1945–46; "La Recluta en México," n.d. 1950.

13 Carmen González Crespo to LMM, September 18, 1950, File 743—Michigan-G-H-I, Box 2275, Tarea 96-20, FOG, AGPR.

14 Virginia Nieves to LMM, September 27, 1950, File 743—Michigan-M-N-O, Box 2275, Tarea 96-20, FOG, AGPR.

15 Felícita López, October 11, 1950, File 743—V-Z, Box 2277, Tarea 96-20, FOG, AGPR. See also Ana Mercedes Saez Aponte to LMM, July 10, 1950, File 743—Michigan-D-E-F, Box 2275, Tarea 96-20, FOG, AGPR.

16 "Relata miseria familia de obrero en Michigan," *El Imparcial*, July 26, 1950, 5; "Esposa obrero Michigan pide ayuda a Muñoz," *El Imparcial*, August 30, 1950, 26; "Desalojan esposa de obrero," July 21, 1950, 5; Arturo Cruz Estrada to Depto. de Trabajo, May 18, 1951, Box 190, Querellas de los obreros de Michigan, Tarea 61-55, Fondo Negociado de Trabajo, AGPR; Ana Mercedes Saez Aponte to LMM, July 19, 1950, File 743—Michigan-D-E-F, Box 2275, Tarea 96-20, FOG, AGPR; Elenia Albaladejo to LMM, October 30, 1950, File 743—Michigan-P-Q, Box 2275, Tarea 96-20, FOG, AGPR; Carmen González Crespo to LMM, September 18,

1950, File 743—Michigan-G-H-I, Box 2275, Tarea 96-20, FOG, AGPR; LMM to
Ana Esther Pagán, October 26, 1950, File 743—Michigan-D-E-F, Box 2275, Tarea
96-20, FOG, AGPR; Fidencia Feliciano to LMM, October 16, 1950, File 743—
Michigan-D-E-F, Box 2275, Tarea 96-20, FOG, AGPR; Juana González to LMM,
January 29, 1951, File 743—Michigan-G-H-I, Box 2275, Tarea 96-20, FOG, AGPR;
LMM to Rosa E. González, September 19, 1950, File 743—Michigan-G-H-I, Box
2275, Tarea 96-20, FOG, AGPR.

17 *P'allá afuera* is a distinctively Puerto Rican saying that literally translates as
"out there, outside," but which refers to the places beyond the island to which
Puerto Ricans have migrated—in particular, the United States.

18 Elías Correa, July 27, 1950, File 743—Michigan-A-B-C, Box 2275, Tarea 96-20,
FOG, AGPR; Arturo Cruz Estrada to Depto. de Trabajo, May 18, 1951, Box
190, Querellas de los obreros de Michigan, Tarea 61-55, Fondo Negociado de
Trabajo, AGPR; LMM to Sra. Gregoria Candelaria, July 19, 1950, File 743—
Michigan-A-B-C, Box 2275, Tarea 96-20, FOG, AGPR; Severina Aguayo to
LMM, September 6, 1950, File 743—Michigan-A-B-C, Box 2275, Tarea 96-20,
FOG, AGPR; Rosa S. Martínez de Pedroza to LMM, August 8, 1950, File 743—
Michigan-P-Q, Box 2275, Tarea 96-20, FOG, AGPR.

19 Stern, *The Secret History of Gender*, 142.

20 Findlay, *Imposing Decency*, 110–134; Roberts and Stefani, *Patterns of Living in
Puerto Rican Families*, 275; Safa, *The Urban Poor of Puerto Rico*, 20–60; Mintz,
Worker in the Cane, 44–50.

21 See Hutchison, *Labors Appropriate to Their Sex*; Tinsman, *Partners in Conflict*;
Klubock, *Contested Communities*; and Rosemblatt, *Gendered Compromises*, for
contests over masculine rights and responsibilities in twentieth-century
Chile, especially during times of mass mobilization of the working classes. For
Mexico, see Vaughan, "Modernizing Patriarchy"; Olcott, *Revolutionary Women in
Postrevolutionary Mexico*. For Brazil, see Weinstein, "Making Workers Masculine";
and Wolfe, "'Father of the Poor' or 'Mother of the Rich'?"

22 Roberts and Stefani, *Patterns of Living in Puerto Rican Families*; Mintz, "Cañamelar," 362–367; Safa, *The Urban Poor of Puerto Rico*, 20–35.

23 For some examples, see Carmen Seda Miranda to LMM, September 10, 1950,
File 743—Michigan-M-N-O, Box 2275, Tarea 96-20, FOG, AGPR; Virginia
Nieves to LMM, September 27, 1950, File 743—Michigan-M-N-O, Box 2275,
Tarea 96-20, FOG, AGPR. Álvaro Cristos al Comisionado de Trabajo, August
31, 1950, Box 190, Querellas de Obreros de Michigan, Tarea 61-55, Depto.
de Trabajo, AGPR; Pedro Rivera Betances to LMM, September 2, 1950, File
743—Emigración, Box 2275, Tarea 96–20, FOG, AGPR; "Esposa obrero Michigan pide ayuda a Muñoz," *El Imparcial*, August 30, 26; "Desalojan esposa de
obrero," *El Imparcial*, July 21, 1950, 5. For rising prices of lard, ham, bacon, rice,
beans, and bacalao, see "Suben precios de artículos básicos," *El Imparcial*, July

20, 1950, 5; "Surge escasez de manteca en isla," El Imparcial, July 24, 1950, 2; "Vecinos indignados por aumento precio," El Imparcial, July 31, 1950, 10.

24 Fernando Sierra Berdecía, "Informe para el gobernador de Puerto Rico, Hon. Luis Muñoz Marín. Condiciones de vida y trabajo de los obreros puertorriqueños llevados a Michigan bajo contrato," File Migración—MI, Box #244: Correspondencia sobre Migrante a MI, Tarea 61-55, Fondo del Departamento del Trabajo, AGPR, 19. References to suffering families in Puerto Rico and the men's concern for them pepper this report.

25 Ayala and Bernabé, Puerto Rico in the American Century, 162–167. During the summer of 1950, the pages of all the island newspapers were filled with debates over the constitution and its implications for the island's future.

26 Kramer, "Race, Empire, and Transnational History," 201. The politics of recognition was "formally inclusionary, inviting its subjects to participate actively in colonial state-building to the extent that hegemonic authorities recognized their capacities for discipline, political rationality, and self-government. . . . It delivered the highly useful illusion of impermanence . . . [and marked] moments when recognition of the capacities of the colonized would (in theory) translate into counterimperial transfers of sovereignty."

27 Ayala and Bernabé, Puerto Rico in the American Century, 168–173.

28 Manuel Cabranes to Gustavo Agrait, October 2, 1950, "Personal-Confidential," File Puerto Ricans in New York and Other States, Box 2276, Tarea 96-20, FOG, AGPR.

29 Kramer, "Race, Empire, and Transnational History," 201.

30 Just a few months later, Méndez Mejía would find himself expelled from the Confederación General de Trabajadores (CGT) by the new CIO-allied union leadership. He and his fellow union organizer in Guánica, Carlos Báez, would go on to form a new sugar workers' union, the Organización Obrera Insular, which affiliated with the much more progressive International Longshoremen's Association. Valdés, Organized Agriculture and the Labor Movement before the UFW, 85.

31 See in El Mundo, July 22, 1950, 4; September 3, 1950, 2; "El viaje de S.B.," July 24, 1950, 6; "F. Sierra Berdecia partió ayer junto a Howard Davidson," July 25, 1950, 2; "Indigna a Sierra la situación de los boricuas en Michigan," August 19, 1950, 1; "Sierra comprueba son ciertas quejas de obreros en Michigan," August 18, 1950, 1. Even after the union reports, El Mundo continued to provide a platform for Michigan grower commentary as long as possible, while refusing to print worker letters. "Remolachero dice visita Sierra no se debe a malos entendidos," July 26, 1850, 1. The assistant director of the Puerto Rican government's Department of Labor's New York division also told the U.S. press in late July that the men's contracts were satisfactory "except for the methods of cooking." Five dollars per week, she insisted, was sufficient to feed each worker. But "when the men come in from the fields after a hard day's work, no one wants to cook a

good meal. The result is that many are not eating properly." "Pin Puerto Rican Dissent on Food," *Detroit Times*, July 25, 1950.

32 "Hearing Near Conclusion," *Saginaw News*, September 12, 1950; "Other Side of the Coin," *Saginaw Catholic Weekly*, July 23, 1950; "Strong Unions Urged for Migrant Labor," *Saginaw Catholic Weekly*, July 23, 1950, 1.

33 For Puerto Ricans in New Jersey, Ohio, and on the island expressing their solidarity with the Michigan migrants, see in *El Imparcial*, "Pide ayuda," August 3, 1950, 21; "Boricuas atropellados," September 2, 1950, 17; Bombón, "Carta pública . . . y privada," August 3, 1950, 19; "Los obreros de MI," July 16, 1950, 19; "El caso de Michigan," July 23, 1950, 17; "El caso de Michigan," July 29, 1950, 19. For Puerto Rican professionals in Detroit, see Ramón Martínez to LMM, July 19, 1950, File 743—1950, Box 2273, Tarea 96-20, FOG, AGPR. For sympathetic U.S. journalists, see the articles by Leonard Jackson in the *Bay City Times*: "Puerto Rican Field Workers Embittered by Deplorable Plight," August 6, 1950; "Puerto Rican Toils Seven Weeks for 20 Cents," August 7, 1950; and "Puerto Ricans Vow Not to Return," August 8, 1950; "Times Reporter Jackson Wins National Award," *Bay City Times*, March 8, 1951, 1. For a few of the *New York Times* articles, see "Migrant Labor Inquiry," July 25, 1950; "Puerto Rico to Pay for Migrants' Aid," August 21, 1950; "Puerto Rico Seeks Workers' Return," August 20, 1950; and "His Wages 'Minus,' Migrant Relates," September 13, 1950.

Muñoz Marín's staff saved newspaper clippings on the Puerto Rican protests from the cities of Ann Arbor, Traverse City, Bay City, Saginaw, Marshall, Cadillac, Hillsdale, Flint, Ypsilanti, Pontiac, Lansing, and Detroit. For these as well as *New York Times* and European newspaper clippings, see File Recortes de periódico, Box 243, Correspondencia sobre migrantes a Michigan, Tarea 61-55, Fondo del Departamento del Trabajo, AGPR. See also Sierra Berdecía, "Informe para el gobernador," 2–4; Valdés, *Al Norte*, 127–130.

34 For a few examples of the reprinted Kern quote, see "Migrant Laborers Describe Hardships," *Detroit Free Press*, September 13, 1950; "Priest Would Organize Farm Migrants: Announces Intentions after Detailing Working Conditions Here," *Saginaw News*, September 13, 1950. For other examples of the sympathetic family discourse, see "Labor Force Problems Aired: Migrant Body Ends Session," *Saginaw Catholic Weekly*, September 17, 1950; "Puerto Ricans Harvest a Crop of Bitterness in the State," *Detroit News*, August 26, 1950; "Strong Unions Urged for Migrant Labor," *Saginaw Catholic Weekly*, July 23, 1950, 1; "Following the Crops," *Bulletin of National Consumers League*, fall 1950, 1; "10 Weeks' Work? Pay the Boss $9.69," *Sun Herald*, October 12, 1950; "American Atrocities," *Gothic*, December 1950, 17, 48; William Dorvillier, "Desde Washington," *El Mundo*, September 20, 1950; "Time Study Needed: Beet Workers Sleep on Ground in Michigan as Families Sell Furniture to Eat in Puerto Rico," *Wage Earner*, August 26, 1950.

The *Bay City Times* was especially sympathetic to the Puerto Ricans throughout the uproar and invoked the desecration of family sanctity frequently in its discussion of the allegations of abuse and contract violation. In addition to Leonard Jackson's August 1950 series of articles, see in *Bay City Times*: "Puerto Rican Government Gets Report on Migrant Workers," August 14, 1950, 9; "Field Crops, Inc. Offers Better Pay, Living Conditions to Puerto Ricans," August 15, 1950, 4; "Puerto Rico to Aid Workers," August 21, 1950, 1; "Puerto Ricans Get New Pact," August 22, 1950, 4.

35 For example, see "Other Side of the Coin," *Saginaw Catholic Weekly*, July 12, 1950, 1; "Strong Unions Urged for Migrant Labor," *Saginaw Catholic Weekly*, July 23, 1950, 1; "Labor Force Problems Aired: Migrant Body Ends Session," *Saginaw Catholic Weekly*, September 17, 1950; "Migrant Laborers Describe Hardships," *Detroit Free Press*, September 13, 1950; "Priest Would Organize Farm Migrants: Announces Intentions after Detailing Working Conditions Here," *Saginaw News*, September 13, 1950; "Puerto Ricans Harvest a Crop of Bitterness in the State," *Detroit News*, August 26, 1950; "Excerpts from Frank Edwards' Broadcast 7/12/50 Mutual Broadcasting System," Newspapers, Box 1, Clement Kern Papers; Gordon Blake, "American Atrocities," *Gothic*, December 1950, 17, 48. The *Detroit Free Press* covered no farm worker issues in the late 1940s. Only the Puerto Rican "explosion" caught their attention.

36 Sierra Berdecía, "Informe para el gobernador," 10, 13, 27; *Bay City Times*, August 6, 1950; Alan Perl to Fernando Sierra Berdecía, "Field Trip—Michigan," July 17, 1950, File 743, Box 2273, Tarea 96-20, FOG, AGPR; Eulalio Torres, "Asunto: Visita a Michigan," June 26, 1950, File 743, Box 2273, Tarea 96-20, FOG, AGPR; John Merrifield, "Puerto Ricans Fly to State Despite Airplane Tragedy," *Detroit News*, June 8, 1950, 14.

37 Sierra Berdecía, "Informe para el gobernador," 14–25.

38 Sierra Berdecía, "Informe para el gobernador," 4, 7–8, 13–14, 24; Max Henderson to Fernando Sierra Berdecía, August 2, 1950, File 743—1950, Box 2273, Tarea 96-20, FOG, AGPR; Eulalio Torres, "Asunto: Visita a Michigan," June 26, 1950, File 743—1950, Box 2273, Tarea 96-20, FOG, AGPR.

Dionicio Nodín Valdés tantalizingly mentions that by the 1940s, Tejanos migrating to the Upper Midwest still organized their production through family labor, but that their strategies were more diverse than was reported by Sierra Berdecía after his visit in July 1950. Valdés asserts that by the late 1940s, mothers and younger children stayed out of the fields more frequently to concentrate on the all-consuming domestic labor. He even argues that some Tejano family units stretched geographically in ways not dissimilar to the Puerto Rican experience, with the women and young children staying in South Texas and the field labor family units comprising fathers, sons, and other male relatives and friends, all of whom shared field and domestic labor in the camps. Pay, however, continued to be calculated by amount cultivated rather than by the hour, and wages withheld until the end of the season. Valdés, *Al Norte*, 61–62. Valdés's discussion of these points is quite general. Thus, without doing close local studies of the exact areas where Puerto Ricans and Tejanos worked in 1950, we cannot know if the contrast drawn by contemporary observers between the two types of labor was more purely discursive than experiential.

39 Bud Lanker, "Employers Praise Puerto Rican Labor," *Detroit Free Press*, July 15, 1950; "Puerto Rican Colony Grows in Saginaw Valley," *Detroit Times*, June 14, 1950; "A New Migrant Problem," *Detroit Free Press*, June 8, 1950, 6. Valdés cites permanent rural residents of Michigan discussing "Mexicans' filthy ways." Valdés, *Al Norte*, 108–109. Interestingly, Gina Pérez mentions that during the 1950s, "peaceful" Puerto Ricans migrating to Chicago were contrasted to the Mexicans, who "liked to fight." Pérez, *The Near Northwest Side Story*, 75.

40 Gordon Blake, "American Atrocities," *Gothic*, December 1950, 17, 48. See also Leonard Jackson's award-winning denunciation of Puerto Ricans' conditions in the *Bay City Times*, in which he completely ignores the fact that Tejanos, Mexicans, and other groups endured analogous circumstances for many years prior to the arrival of the Puerto Ricans.

41 Republican State Representative David Young insisted of Tejano workers, "'We can't bring up the standard of living of the rest of the world. . . . These people were brought up this way. . . . You can't change human nature.'" "MFC Accused of Violating Contract with Workers," *Bay City Times*, September 1, 1950, 1.

42 "Puerto Ricans Excel as Help in Beet Fields," *Detroit Free Press*, June 19, 1950, 1, 9. We should remember that such language created an implicit contrast as well with the alleged family forms and behaviors of Puerto Ricans who were migrating to New York City during this period. Eugenio Rivera reports a similar pattern of discursive construction of early Puerto Rican male migrants to the steel factories of Lorain, Ohio, as handsome, industrious workers. Once the Puerto Ricans began to bring entire families and their numbers increased beyond the steel mills' capacity to employ them, however, Lorain newspapers began to complain of the town's "Puerto Rican problem." Rivera, "La colonia de Lorain, Ohio," 159–165. For an analogous historical progression in media portrayals of Puerto Ricans in Chicago, see Pérez, *The Near Northwest Side Story*.

43 For connections between U.S. and Puerto Rican unions, see García and Quintero Rivera, *Desafío y solidaridad*; Sanabria, "Samuel Gompers and the American Federation of Labor in Puerto Rico," 140–162; Valdés, *Organized Agriculture and the Labor Movement before the UFW*, 25–106. For the CIO organizing drive in Puerto Rico during 1950, see "Outside Factors to Add Fuel to Beet Workers' Troubles," *Saginaw News*, September 2, 1950. Dionicio Nodín Valdés concludes that ultimately the increasingly anticommunist CIO destroyed the most vibrant organizing currents within the Puerto Rican CGT.

For just some of the labor organizing activity in Michigan, see in *Bay City Times*: "Plumbers Here Ask Wage Hike," May 12, 1950, 4; "Blanket Wage Hike," August 15, 1950; "Labor Unrest May Curtail Defense Plans," August 18, 1950, 1;

"Railroad Dispute Still Deadlocked," August 20, 1950, 1; "Strikes Plague Detroit Workers," August 24, 1950, 2; and "The Strike Plague," August 27, 1950, 6.

For postwar Consumers' League work in Michigan, see the testimony of Mrs. C. R. Mueller, President's Commission, 1950, 352–356. For a broader history of the Consumers' League, see Storrs, *Civilizing Capitalism*.

44 See, for example, the work of the Reverend Norman J. Hughes, of Bay City, who worked to establish low-rent housing projects, promoted the care of displaced person refugees from war-torn Western Europe, and accompanied Detroit and Flint labor leaders to interview Puerto Ricans in labor camps near Saginaw, MI. "Statement of Reverend R. Norman Hughes," President's Commission; Parker, "Citizen Action," 112–114; Minutes of Session, First Presbyterian Church of Bay City, MI, 1949–1951.

For Michigan Protestant missions in Puerto Rico, see "Habrá asamblea presbiteriana en Michigan," El Mundo, May 9, 1947, 25; and in *Bay City Times*: "Bay Cityan Tells of Her Work at Puerto Rican Missionary Project," July 8, 1950, 2; "Presbyterian Mission Aids Puerto Ricans in Agriculture," July 16, 1950, 2; "Mission's Recreational Facilities Compete with Gambling, Liquor," July 22, 1950, 2; "Medical Program Important at Guacio," August 5, 1950, 2; "Social Workers Aid Needy—Cooperatives Prove Big Help in Puerto Rico," July 29, 1950, 2, 4.

45 "Mexican Festival Aspirants Named," *Saginaw News*, June 28, 1950, 21.

46 Flores Ramos, *Mujer, familia, y prostitución*, 131–191. Lorrin Thomas also sensitively explores Puerto Ricans' demands for equal treatment as citizens of the United States while living in New York City. Thomas, *Puerto Rican Citizen*.

47 Valdés, *Al Norte*, 131. Mexican American State Representative John Espinoza, who arrived in Croswell, Michigan, with his migrant laboring family as a youngster from rural Texas, confirms Valdés's analysis on these scores. He remembers his parents' excitement at the possibility of sending their children to the same schools as white children in Michigan. John Espinoza, personal communication, July 24, 2009. Rodolfo Acuña discusses the long history of Mexican and Mexican American agricultural organizing efforts in his sweeping work *Corridors of Migration*.

Not until the 1960s and '70s, with the swelling of the Chicano and farmworker rights movements, would Mexican Americans mount analogous protests against the beet field exploitation, and garner more positive public attention in Michigan. Valdés, *Al Norte*, 165–199. Valdés also notes that liberal reformers during the Progressive Era and the immediate post–World War II years periodically turned their attention to migrant laborers in Michigan. However, their efforts, he argues, were profoundly paternalistic, and generally focused on cultural assimilation rather than on changing the workers' material conditions. Valdés, *Al Norte*, 109–111. Mapes interprets Progressive Era reformers' interventions more positively; Mapes, *Sweet Tyranny*, 142–165.

48 "Some Migrants Going to East," *Saginaw News*, July 26, 1950, 3; and "Beet Workers Get Eastern Jobs," *Saginaw News*, August 2, 1950, 1; "Beet Workers Move
to East," *Bay City Times*, August 2, 1950; and in File 743, Box 2273, Tarea 96-20,
FOG, AGPR: Max Henderson to Fernando Sierra Berdecía, August 4, 1950;
Sierra Berdecía, "Report to the Governor," 28–30 (English translation); and
Manuel Cabranes to Fernando Sierra Berdecía, August 16, 1950; Valdés, *Al Norte*,
127–130; testimonies of Martín González, 458–459, and Santos Cintrón, 452–
454, President's Commission, 1950.

49 The quote is from "Declaración del Comisionado del Trabajo, Señor Fernando
Sierra Berdecía," August 21, 1950, File 743, Box 2273, Tarea 96-20, FOG, AGPR.
See also Fernando Sierra Berdecía to Max Henderson, August 8, 1950, File 743,
Box 2273, Tarea 96-20, FOG, AGPR; in *El Diario de Puerto Rico*: "Próximo año
habrá mejores contraltos obreros PR en EU," August 9, 1950; "MI contratará
15,000 boricuas: Sierra opine esta cifra excesiva," August 16, 1950; "Sierra opine
obreros fueron engañados," August 17, 1950; and "Michigan no puede acoger
15,000 obreros," August 18, 1950; "Puerto Ricans Rushing Home? It's All Con-
fused," *Saginaw News*, August 22, 1950, 25.

50 Luis Muñoz Marín a los obreros en Michigan, August 25, 1950, File 743—MI,
Box 2273, Tarea 96-20, FOG, AGPR; "Puerto Ricans Get New Pact," *Bay City
Times*, August 22, 1950, 4; testimony of Max Henderson, President's Commis-
sion, 1950, 163.

51 "Reglamento promulgado por el comisionado del trabajo para instrumentar la
Ley Num.1 de 23 de agosto de 1950, titulada Ley para declarer que existe un estado de emergencia en relacion con la conservación de las normas mínimas de
vida de trabajadores puertorriqueños llevados al estado de Michigan entre el 31
de mayo y el 18 de junio de 1950; proveer ayuda economica dichos trabajadores
y asignar la suma de $117,400 para llevar a cabo los fines de esta ley," File 743—
MI, Box 2273, Tarea 96-20, FOG, AGPR.

52 Severina Aguayo to LMM, September 6, 1950, File 743—Michigan-A-B-C, Box
2275, Tarea 96-20, FOG, AGPR; Virginia Nieves to LMM, September 27, 1950,
File 743—Michigan-M-N-O, Box 2275, Tarea 96-20, FOG, AGPR; Carmen Seda
Miranda, September 19, 1950, File 743—Michigan-M-N-O, Box 2275, Tarea
96-20, FOG, AGPR; Jenaro López Vega to LMM, September 23, 1950, File 743—
Michigan-J-K-L, Box 2275, Tarea 96-20, FOG, AGPR; Pedro Rivera Betances to
LMM, September 2, 1950, File 743—Emigración (Segundo), Box 2275, Tarea
96-20, FOG, AGPR.

53 "PR to Aid Workers," *Bay City Times*, August 21, 1950, 1, 4; LMM telegram to
Fred Crawford, August 21, 1950, File 743, Box 2273, Tarea 96-20, FOG, AGPR;
"Crawford's Maryland Farm Seen Hot Issue in Eighth District Race," *Bay City
Times*, July 4, 1950, 5; "Rep. Crawford Denies Intent to Sue Now," *Saginaw News*,
July 18, 1950, 2; "Crawford to Defend Importation of Puerto Rican Farm Work-
ers," *Bay City Times*, September 2, 1950, 5.

54 See in *El Mundo*: "Agricultura federal investiga salarias en fincas remolachas," August 24, 1950, 11; "En el momento de prueba," August 21, 1950, 6; "Frente al maltrato," August 19, 1950, 6; "Acusa a Sierra hacer política caso obrero," August 21, 1950, 1; "Alegan existe trama contra Fred Crawford," August 31, 1950, 1; "Crawford alega investigación le perjudica," September 1, 1950, 1; "Muñoz pide boricuas cooperen a terminar labor en Michigan," August 29, 1950, 1, 14; Luis Muñoz Marín telegram to Fred Crawford, August 21, 1950, File 743, Box 2273, Tarea 96-20, FOG, AGPR.

55 "Muñoz pide boricuas cooperen a terminar labor en Michigan," *El Mundo*, August 29, 1950, 1.

56 Emilio González to LMM, October 2, 1950, File 743—Michigan-G-H-I, Box 2275, Tarea 96-20, FOG, AGPR; Eulalio Torres to Manuel Cabranes, "Resumen de operaciones en Michigan," October 2, 1950, File 743—Emigration, Box 2276, Tarea 96-20, FOG, AGPR. See also "U.S. 'Gobbles Up' Vast Army of Puerto Rican Migrant Workers," *Bay City Times*, November 11, 1950, 4; "Puerto Ricans' Work Nearly Done, but Will They Return to Island?," *Saginaw News*, November 9, 1950, 2.

57 Solicitud de Maximino Cordero, Querellas de Obreros de Michigan 1950, Box 191—II, Tarea 61-55, Fondo del Departamento del Trabajo, AGPR.

58 Maximino Cordero to LMM, August 10, 1950, File 743—Emigración, Box 2275, Tarea 96-20, FOG, AGPR.

59 Maximino Cordero to LMM, September 4, 1950, File 743—Michigan-A-B-C, Box 2275, Tarea 96-20, FOG, AGPR.

60 Gustavo Agrait to María, n.d., File 743—Michigan-A-B-C, Box 2275, Tarea 96-20, FOG, AGPR; "Muñoz Marín oye episodios sobre obreros en Michigan," *El Imparcial*, September 9, 1950, 4.

61 LMM to Maximino Cordero, September 9, 1950, File 743—Michigan-A-B-C, Box 2275, Tarea 96-20, FOG, AGPR.

62 The leaders of the CGT sugar workers union, in collaboration with the CIO, continued to demand that Muñoz Marín publish Sierra Berdecía's report on the Michigan conditions. "Lideres CGT-CIO propulsan pedir a Muñoz publique informe Sierra," *El Diario de Puerto Rico*, September 12, 1950.

63 Viviano Rodríguez to LMM, September 9, 1950, File 743—7, Box 2277, Tarea 96-20, FOG, AGPR. For just a few others, see also Angel Reyes and others to LMM, September 30, 1950, File 743—Michigan-J-K-L, Box 2275, Tarea 96-20, FOG, AGPR; Fidel Robledo to LMM, September 13, 1950, File 743—R, Box 2277, FOG, AGPR; Erasmo Torado to LMM, August 29, 1950, File 743—S-T, Box 2277, Tarea 96-20, FOG, AGPR; Joaquín Torres to LMM, September 8, 1950, File 743—S-T, Box 2277, Tarea 96-20, FOG, AGPR.

64 Luis de la Cruz Rodríguez to LMM, July 31, 1950, File 743—Michigan-D-E-F, Box 2275, Tarea 96-20, FOG, AGPR.

65 Antonio López Santiago to LMM, October 9, 1950, File 743—Michigan-J-K-L, Box 2275, Tarea 96-20, FOG, AGPR. For more examples, see Inocencio

Ortiz to LMM, September 30, 1950, File 743—Michigan-M-N-O, Box 2275, Tarea 96-20, FOG, AGPR; Marcial Montalvo to LMM, October 3, 1950, File 743—Michigan-M-N-O, Box 2275, Tarea 96-20, FOG, AGPR.

66 Porfirio Irizarry to LMM, October 15, 1950, File 743—Michigan-G-H-I, Box 2275, Tarea 96-20, FOG, AGPR. See also Emilio González to LMM, October 2, 1950, File 743—Michigan-G-H-I, Box 2275, Tarea 96-20, FOG, AGPR.

67 For more on the various strategies of men leaving Michigan, see Maximino Cordero to LMM, September 4, 1950, File 743—Michigan-A-B-C, Box 2275, Tarea 96-20, FOG, AGPR; Luis Rivera Santos to LMM, August 27, 1950, File 743—MI, Box 2273, Tarea 96-20, FOG, AGPR; Ramón Miranda Crespo to LMM, July 17, 1950, File 743—Michigan-M-N-O, Box 2275, Tarea 96-20, FOG, AGPR; Gabriel Vásquez to LMM, September 11, 1950; File 743—V-Z, Box 2277, Tarea 96-20, FOG, AGPR; Eulalio García to LMM, December 3, 1950, File 743—Michigan-G-H-I, Box 2275, Tarea 96-20, FOG, AGPR. Sugar beet workers protested their lack of income in the Chicago office of the Puerto Rican Dept. of Migration. Anthony Vega to Petro América de Pagán, January 8, 1951, File Puerto Ricans in New York and Other States, Box 2276, Tarea 96-20, FOG, AGPR. "Obreros se niegan a renovar contrato en fincas Michigan," El Imparcial, October 22, 1950, 2.

68 Diego Candelario and Rumardo Rodríguez to LMM, October 4, 1950, File 743—Michigan-A-B-C, Box 2275, Tarea 96-20, FOG, AGPR; Angel L. Chabuissant and others to LMM, September 8, 1950, File 743—Michigan-A-B-C, Box 2275, Tarea 96-20, FOG, AGPR; Victor Vargas and others to LMM, August 1950, File V-Z, Box 2277, Tarea 96-20, FOG, AGPR; Eulalio García to LMM, December 3, 1950, File 743—Michigan-G-H-I, Box 2275, Tarea 96-20, FOG, AGPR.

69 William López to Andrés Montañez, March 12, 1951, File 743—Michigan-M-N-O, Box 2275, Tarea 96-20, FOG, AGPR; Elenia Albaladejo de Pintor to LMM, File 743—Michigan-P-Q, Box 2275, Tarea 96-20, FOG, AGPR; Emeterio Lazu to LMM, December 25, 1950, File 743—Michigan-J-K-L, Box 2275, Tarea 96-20, FOG, AGPR; Carmen Campbell to LMM, December 11, 1950, File 743—Michigan-J-K-L, Box 2275, Tarea 96-20, FOG, AGPR; "Obreros quieren volver a Puerto Rico," El Imparcial, October 8, 1950, 17; Manuel Cabranes to Petro América Pagán, February 9, 1951, File of José Rivera Cosme, Serie Querellas de Obreros Migrantes, Box 199, Tarea 61-55, Fondo Negociado de Trabajo, AGPR; February 13, 1951, File of Pablo Figueroa Robles, Serie Querellas de Obreros Migrantes, Box 206, Tarea 61-55, Fondo Negociado de Trabajo, AGPR.

70 Manuel Cabranes to Fernando Sierra Berdecía, September 27, 1950, File 743—Emigration, Box 2276, Tarea 96-20, FOG, AGPR.

71 This included workers who had transferred to New Jersey and New York to do agricultural labor, under the auspices of the Puerto Rican Department of Labor. Sixto González to LMM, September 15, 1950, File—Michigan-G-H-I, Box 2275, FOG, AGPR; Vicente Ramos González and others to LMM, October 18, 1950, File—Michigan-G-H-I, Box 2275, FOG, AGPR. For a few examples of the flood

of requests, see Juan Paxots to LMM, September 1950, File 743—Michigan-P-Q, Box 2275, Tarea 96-20, FOG, AGPR; Pedro Rodríguez and nine others to LMM, July 20, 1950, File—R, Box 2277, Tarea 96-20, FOG, AGPR; Victor Vargas and others to LMM, August 1950, File V-Z, Box 2277, Tarea 96-20, FOG, AGPR; Victor Torres to LMM, September 25, 1950, File S-T, Box 2277, FOG, AGPR.

72 "Explica Cabranes," El Diario de Nueva York, October 6, 1950; Sierra Berdecía to LMM, September 27, 1950, File 743—Emigration, Box 2276, Tarea 96-20, FOG, AGPR. "Sierra afirma se ayuda a obreros en Michigan," El Imparcial, October 3, 1950, 4.

73 Félix Vásquez to Gabriel Vásquez, September 11, 1950, File V-Z, Box 2277, Tarea 96-20, FOG, AGPR. For just a few others, see Napoleón Rodríguez Pacheco to Sra. Celestina Zalduondo de Goodsaid, August 31, 1950, and "Petición de ayuda al gobierno por el trabajador Gaspar Febres," September 27, 1950, both in Box 206, Serie Querellas de Obreros Migrantes, Tarea 61-55, Fondo del Departamento del Trabajo, AGPR.

74 Manuel Andino Gaitan to LMM, August 25, 1950, File 743—Michigan-A-B-C, Box 2275, FOG, AGPR.

75 Rosa S. Martínez de Pedroza to LMM, August 21, 1950, File 743—Michigan-P-Q, Box 2275, FOG, AGPR.

76 LMM telegram to Fred Crawford, August 21, 1950, File 743, Box 2273, Tarea 96-20, FOG, AGPR; Manuel Cabranes to Gustavo Agrait, August 17, 1950, File 743.5 (B), Box 2280, Tarea 96-20, FOG, AGPR; Fernando Sierra Berdecía, "Condiciones de vida y trabajo de los obreros puertorriqueños llevados a Michigan bajo contrato," August 16, 1950, File Migración—MI Correspondencia, Box Correspondencia sobre Migrantes a MI #244, Tarea 61-55, Fondo del Departamento del Trabajo, AGPR.

77 Ramón González Rodríguez to LMM, October 15, 1950, File—Michigan-G-H-I, Box 2275, Tarea 96-20, FOG, AGPR; Ceferino Alicea Negrón to LMM, August 26, 1950, File—Michigan-A-B-C, Box 2275, FOG, AGPR; Andrés Cortés and others to LMM, September 13, 1950, File—Michigan-A-B-C, Box 2275, FOG, AGPR; Pedro Rivera Meléndez to LMM, November 21, 1950, File—Michigan-R, Box 2277, Tarea 96-20, FOG, AGPR; Adelita M. de Iguina to LMM, November 6, 1950, File 743—S-T, Box 2277, Tarea 96-20, FOG, AGPR. See in El Imparcial: "Victima de Michigan se queja no lo atienden," September 27, 1950, 26; "Pide que se le atienda," October 21, 1950, 17; "Quién es él que paga?," November 4, 1950; "Más Justicia," November 8, 1950, 15; "Otra vez?," December 9, 1950, 25; "Obreros de Michigan alegan se les engaña," January 7, 1951.

Conclusion

1 Rosa Robles de Figueroa to F. Sierra Berdecía, January 26, 1951, File of Pablo Figueroa Robles, Box 206, Serie Querellas de Obreros Migrantes, Tarea 61-55, Fondo del Departamento del Trabajo, AGPR; Francisco Rivera Méndez

to Petro América Pagán, June 16, 1951, Box 199, Serie Querellas de Obreros Migrantes, Tarea 61-55, Fondo del Departamento del Trabajo, Archivo General de Puerto Rico (AGPR). For just a few more examples, see Matilde Rosado Quiñones to Petro América Pagán, November 24, 1950, Box 199, Serie Querellas de Obreros Migrantes, Tarea 61-55, Fondo del Departamento del Trabajo, AGPR; Anthony Vega report, March 31, 1951, File of Juan José Cruz Román, Box 190, Serie Querellas de Obreros Migrantes, Tarea 61-55, Fondo del Departamento del Trabajo, AGPR; Petro América Pagán to Hilda Molina, November 5, 1950, Box 199, Serie Querellas de Obreros Migrantes, Tarea 61-55, Fondo del Departamento del Trabajo, AGPR; File of Andrés Crespo, Box 190, Serie Querellas de Obreros Migrantes, Tarea 61-55, Fondo del Departamento del Trabajo, AGPR.

2 Lucas Díaz Rodríguez, April 17, 1951, File 743—Michigan-D-E-F, Box 2275, Tarea 96-20, Fondo de la Oficina del Gobernador (FOG), AGPR. For just a few examples of migrants' demands for back pay from the United States, see Antonio Román to Dept. de Trabajo, January 15, 1951, Box 199, Serie Querellas de Obreros Migrantes, Fondo del Departamento del Trabajo, AGPR; Manuel Cabranes to Michigan Field Crops, February 23, 1951, Box 190, Serie Querellas de Obreros Migrantes, Fondo del Departamento del Trabajo, AGPR; Andrés Crespo to F. Sierra Berdecía, December 18, 1950, and May 18, 1951, Box 190, Serie Querellas de Obreros Migrantes, Fondo del Departamento del Trabajo, AGPR.

3 For a few examples, see files in Querellas de Obreros Migrantes, Tarea 61-55, Fondo del Departamento del Trabajo, AGPR: Julio López, Box 209, Francisco Mendoza Rivera, Box 195, Oscar Menéndez Arce, Box 192, Gustavo Menéndez Arroyo, Box 192.

4 For such Migration Division officials' commentary about early worker complaints from Michigan, see Estella Draper to Eliseo Meléndez, July 11, 1950, Box 206, Serie Querellas de Obreros Migrantes, Fondo del Departamento del Trabajo, AGPR.

5 File of Miguel Cruz Rivera, Box 190, Querellas de Obreros Migrantes, Tarea 61-55, Fondo del Departamento del Trabajo, AGPR. For a few other particularly poignant cases, see in Querellas de Obreros Migrantes, Tarea 61-55, Fondo del Departamento del Trabajo, AGPR: Pedro José Malavé, November 6, 1950, Box 199; File of Rafael Lizardi, Box 209; and Urbano Rivera to Fernando Sierra Berdecía, January 9, 1951, Box 199.

6 See, for example, in Box 206, Querellas de Obreros Migrantes, Tarea 61-55, Fondo del Departamento del Trabajo, AGPR: A. San Antonio Mimoso to Petro América Pagán, June 27, 1952; File of Luis Manuel de la Cruz, Eugenio Pérez to Petro América Pagán, March 20, 1951; and Rafael Olivencia Valladares to Petro América Pagán. Also Ezequiel Marrero, alcalde, to Petro América Pagán, June 22, 1951, Box 199.

7 Numerous claim letters cite such radio reports and the authors' irritation at not having received their own back pay. For a few examples, see in Querellas de Obreros Migrantes, Tarea 61-55, Fondo del Departamento del Trabajo, AGPR: the files of Eduviges López, Box 209; Urbano Rivera to Fernando Sierra Berdecía, January 9, 1951, Box 199; A. San Antonio Mimoso, Box 206; and Miguel Cruz Rivera, Box 190.

8 Cynthia Hahamovitch provides a devastating comparative global analysis of these issues. She notes the radically different results of the U.S. guest worker programs, where the federal government consistently stayed out of guest-worker regulation, leaving labor recruitment and maintenance of living and working conditions to private employers and thus abandoning imported guest workers to consistently deplorable exploitation, and western European guest worker programs, where nation-states recruited migrant laborers who then worked alongside citizens and were eligible for union membership and other state protections. Hahamovitch, *No Man's Land*.

9 For example, see in Serie Querellas de Obreros Migrantes, Tarea 61-55, Fondo del Departamento del Trabajo, AGPR: File of Rafael Lizardi, Box 209; File of Miguel Flores Ruiz, Box 206; and File of Emilio Cruz Rodríguez, Box 190.

10 N = 233 (a random sample from the more than 2,500 files in Boxes 190–195, Serie Querellas de Obreros Migrantes, 1950–1952, Tarea 61-55, Fondo del Departamento del Trabajo, AGPR). File of Rafael Lizardi, Box 209. The lowest payment I encountered was for 40 cents. For a few other such cases, see in Serie Querellas de Obreros Migrantes, Tarea 61-55, Fondo del Departamento del Trabajo, AGPR: File of Bernabé Maldonado Vásquez, Box 193; File of Martín Moyes Reyes, Box 195; and File of Manuel Martínez Ramos, Box 193.

11 See Eulalio Torres to Petro América Pagán, July 13, 1951, and File of Rafael Lizardi, Box 209, Serie Querellas de Obreros Migrantes, Tarea 61-55, Fondo del Departamento del Trabajo, AGPR.

12 For a few examples, see in Serie Querellas de Obreros Migrantes, Tarea 61-55, Fondo del Departamento del Trabajo, AGPR: files of Gaspar Febres Figueroa, Box 206; Antonio López Santiago, Box 209; José Rivera Corredor, Box 199; Telesforo Rivera, Box 199; Eduviges López, Box 209; Victor López Díaz, Box 209; and Santiago Emmanuelli, Box 206.

13 File of Emilio Cruz Rodríguez, Box 190, and File of Rafael Lizardi, Box 209, Serie Querellas de Obreros Migrantes, Tarea 61-55, Fondo del Departamento del Trabajo, AGPR.

14 "Informe del Comisionado del Trabajo," July 24, 1951, File 743, Box 2274, Tarea 96-20, FOG, AGPR.

15 Rurico E. Rivera, "Sierra niega negligencia en migración: Refuta alegación en caso Michigan," *El Mundo*, April 13, 1954; Antonio Ramos Llompart, "Sierra refuta a Lic. Miranda," *El Imparcial*, April 14, 1954.

16 Laclau, *On Populist Reason*. See also Laclau, "Populism."

17 For the passion undergirding populism, see also Kampwirth, "Introduction," in *Gender and Populism in Latin America*, 1–2, 18; Fernandes, "Gender, Popular Participation, and the State in Chávez's Venezuela," 212. For other definitions of populism, see from the same volume Wolfe, "From Working Mothers to Housewives," 93; Olcott, "The Politics of Opportunity," 27–31; and Kampwirth, "Introduction," 2; as well as Panizza, "Introduction," in *Populism and the Mirror of Democracy*, 1–31.

18 See introduction, note 20.

19 Elena, *Dignifying Argentina*, 253.

20 For just a few examples, see Ayala and Bernabé, *Puerto Rico in the American Century*; Meléndez, "Vito Marcantonio, Puerto Rican Migration, and the 1949 Mayoral Election in New York City"; Lapp, "Managing Migration."

21 See Whalen, "Colonialism, Citizenship, and the Making of the Puerto Rican Diaspora," for the Puerto Rican government's complete disinterest in complaints from migrants between 1915 and 1935.

22 Rodríguez-Silva, *Silencing Race*.

23 Kramer, *The Blood of Government*, 434–435.

24 Ann Laura Stoler reminds us that "intimate matters and narratives about them figured in defining the racial coordinates and social discriminations of empire. . . . [Such discussions] point to strategies of exclusion on the basis of social credentials, sensibility, and cultural knowledge." Stoler, "Tense and Tender Ties," 832.

25 For discussions of the threat of deportation in shaping the experiences of guest workers, see Hahamovitch, *No Man's Land*; Ngai, *Impossible Subjects*; and Pitti, *The Devil in Silicon Valley*. For a sobering meditation on the workings of statelessness, see Kerber, "The Stateless as the Citizen's Other." Deborah Cohen reflects on the liminality of transnational subjects, which often poses a perceived threat to the fixed, bounded nation-state, in *Braceros*.

26 Indeed, it may well be no coincidence that both Puerto Ricans' and Tejanos' home territories had been conquered during the nineteenth century by the United States. The subsequent experiences of imperial rule, one resulting in perpetual colonial status, the other in eventual statehood—due mainly to Anglos' consolidation of political and economic hegemony in Texas—accumulated for both of these migrant groups in different versions of colonial citizenship. Puerto Ricans came to be considered, in Pedro Cabán's words, "unassimilable wards"—"U.S. citizens who could not become Americans." Cabán, "The Puerto Rican Colonial Matrix." For further elaboration of questions of Puerto Ricans' changing legal citizenship status, see Venator-Santiago, "Extending Citizenship to Puerto Rico"; Baldoz and Ayala, "The Bordering of America"; and Meléndez, "Citizenship and the Alien Exclusion in the Insular Cases."

27 Canning and Rose discuss the practices of citizenship in the introduction to *Gender, Citizenships and Subjectivities*. Claudio Lomnitz ruminates on the workings

of what he calls debased citizenship in "Modes of Citizenship in Mexico," 324. See also Glenn, *Unequal Freedom*. Neil Foley in *Quest for Equality* and Marc Simon Rodríguez in *The Tejano Diaspora* examine Tejanos' struggle for recognition as full citizens. See also the tantalizing article by Jennifer McCormick and César J. Ayala, which shows how different local contexts of racially stigmatizing Puerto Rican citizenship could create a radically inclusive political consciousness for a Puerto Rican–naturalized Mexican family emerging out of encounters between different Latin American migrant agricultural workers in California. Ayala and McCormick, "Felícita 'La Prieta' Méndez (1916–1998) and the End of Latino School Segregation in California," 12–32.

28 Kramer, "Power and Connection," 1381.

29 "Siervos a Michigan," *El Diario de Nueva York*, March 26, 1952; Fernando Sierra Berdecía, Memo to Luis Muñoz Marín, "Meeting with Max Henderson on the possibility of employing Puerto Rican workers for the sugar beet industry in Michigan—PERSONAL AND CONFIDENTIAL," April 16, 1952, File 743, Box 2275, Tarea 96-20, FOG, AGPR.

30 "Operation Breadbasket," pamphlet, 1955, File 743—Emigración, Box 2275, Tarea 96-20, FOG, AGPR; see in Box 2407, Administrative Monthly Reports, Office of the Government of Puerto Rico in the United States (OGPRUS), Centro Archives, Center for Puerto Rican Studies, Hunter College, New York: Carlos Gómez, "Weekly Report," September 2 and 9, 1960; and Katz and Friedman Law Firm to Anthony Vega, June 6, 1957.

31 Hipólito Reyes Sánchez to Petro América Pagán, April 28, 1951, Box 199, Serie Querellas de Obreros Migrantes, Tarea 61-55, Fondo del Departamento del Trabajo, AGPR.

32 A report on the Puerto Rican community in Milwaukee traced its genesis to men leaving Michigan sugar beet work who found a foothold in the Milwaukee steel foundries: State of Wisconsin, Industrial Commission, State Employment Service, "In-Migration of Puerto Rican Workers," September 3, 1952, File 743—Emigration, Box 2276, Tarea 96-20, FOG, AGPR. See also Paul M. McMahon, "It's a New Life in Strange City, but Puerto Ricans Happy Here," *Milwaukee Journal*, November 13, 1955, Part II, 2; Valdés, *Al Norte*, 132; Carlos Gómez, "Weekly Report," September 2 and 9, 1960, Box 2407, Administrative Monthly Reports, OGPRUS, Centro Archives; and Katz and Friedman Law Firm to Anthony Vega, June 6, 1957, Box 2407, Administrative Monthly Reports, OGPRUS, Centro Archives; Dionicio Nodín Valdés, personal communication, June 20, 2006.

BIBLIOGRAPHY

Primary Sources

Oral History Interviews

Anastacio Díaz, July 14, 2009
John Espinosa, July 24, 2009
Elisa Ochoa, August 23, 2009
Manuel Ochoa, August 23, 2009
Donald Turner, August 7 and 22, 2009

Newspapers and Periodicals

MICHIGAN
Alma Morning Sun
Bay City Times
Catholic Weekly
Detroit Free Press
Detroit Times
Gratiot County Herald
Isabella County Republican
Isabella County Times-News
Michigan Teacher
Night Hawk
Saginaw News
Saint Louis Leader-Press
Sanilac Jeffersonian
Sun Herald
Tri-County Banner
Wage Earner

PUERTO RICO
El Batey
El Diario de Puerto Rico
El Imparcial
El Mundo
Puerto Rico Ilustrado

NEW YORK CITY
Daily Mirror
El Diario de Nueva York
New Leader
New York Daily News
New York Times
New York World-Telegram

OTHER U.S. CITIES
Chicago Daily Tribune
Milwaukee Journal
Youngstown Vindicator

UNITED STATES—NATIONAL
American Mercury
Asia and Americas
Atlantic Monthly
Catholic World
Christian Century
Christian Science Monitor
Collier's
Commonweal
Gothic
Life
Nation
New Republic
Newsweek
Reader's Digest
Time

Archives and Libraries

PUERTO RICO

Archivo General de Puerto Rico, Puerta de Tierra (AGPR)

Colección Puertorriqueña, Universidad de Puerto Rico, Río Piedras

Fundación Luis Muñoz Marín, Trujillo Alto (FLMM)

UNITED STATES

Alice and Jack Wirt Public Library, Bay City, MI

Archives of Labor and Union Affairs, Wayne State University, Detroit, MI

Archives of Michigan, Lansing, MI

Bay County Historical Society, Bay City, MI

Bentley Historical Library, University of Michigan, Ann Arbor, MI

Centro Archives, Center for Puerto Rican Studies, Hunter College, City University of New York, New York City, NY

Clarke Historical Library, Central Michigan University, Mount Pleasant, MI

Detroit Public Library, Detroit, MI

First Presbyterian Church of Bay City, MI

Harry S. Truman Presidential Library, Independence, MO

Hoyt Public Library, Saginaw, MI

Library of Congress, Washington, DC

National Archives and Records Administration, Washington, DC

Presbyterian Historical Society, Philadelphia, PA

William H. Aitkin Public Library, Croswell, MI

Secondary Sources

Acevedo, Luz del Alba. "Género trabajo asalariado y desarrollo industrial en Puerto Rico: La división sexual del trabajo en la manufactura." In *Género y trabajo: La industria de la aguja en Puerto Rico y el Caribe hispánico*, edited by María del Carmen Baerga-Santini, 161–212. Río Piedras: Editorial de la Universidad de Puerto Rico, 1993.

———. "Políticas de industrialización y cambios en el empleo femenino en Puerto Rico, 1947–1982." In "Mujeres puertorriqueñas, protagonistas en el Caribe," special issue, *Homines* 4 (1987): 40–69.

Acevedo González, Andino. *¡Que tiempos aquellos!* Río Piedras: Editorial de la Universidad de Puerto Rico, 1989.

Acosta, Ivonne. *La Mordaza: Puerto Rico, 1948–1957*. Río Piedras: Editorial Edil, 1987.

Acosta-Belen, Edna, ed. *The Puerto Rican Woman: Perspectives on Culture, History, and Society*. New York: Praeger, 1986.

Acuña, Rodolfo F. *Corridors of Migration: The Odyssey of Mexican Laborers, 1600–1933*. Tucson: University of Arizona Press, 2007.

Adams, Julia, Elisabeth S. Clemens, and Ann Shola Orloff, eds. *Rethinking Modernity: Politics, History, and Sociology*. Durham, NC: Duke University Press, 2005.

Agosín, Marjorie, ed. *Inhabiting Memory: Essays on Memory and Human Rights in the Americas*. San Antonio, TX: Wings Press, 2011.

Alanís Enciso, Fernando Saúl. "The Repatriation of Mexicans from the United States and Mexican Nationalism, 1929–1940." In *Beyond la Frontera: The History of Mexico-U.S. Migration*, edited by Mark Overmyer-Velázquez, 51–78. New York: Oxford University Press, 2011.

Alegría Ortega, Idsa. "La gobernación de Luis Muñoz Marín: Una mirada a sus resistencias." In *Luis Muñoz Marín: Imágenes de la memoria*, edited by Fernando Picó, 195–217. Trujillo Alto: Fundación Luis Muñoz Marín, 2008.

Alegría Ortega, Idsa, and Palmira N. Ríos González, eds. *Contrapunto de género y raza en Puerto Rico*. Río Piedras: Centro de Investigaciones Sociales, 2005.

Alicea, Marixsa. "'A Chambered Nautilus': The Contradictory Nature of Puerto Rican Women's Role in the Social Construction of a Transnational Community." *Gender and Society* 2 (1997): 597–626.

Allman, Jean. "Phantoms of the Archive: Kwame Nkrumah, a Nazi Pilot Named Hanna, and the Contingencies of Postcolonial History-Writing." *American Historical Review* 118:1 (February 2013): 104–129.

Álvarez-Curbelo, Silvia. "La bandera en la colina: Luis Muñoz Marín en los tiempos de la guerra de Corea." In *Luis Muñoz Marín: Perfiles de su gobernación*, edited by Fernando Picó, 1–19. Trujillo Alto: Fundación Luis Muñoz Marín, 2003.

———. "La conflictividad en el discurso político de Luis Muñoz Marín: 1926–1936." In *Del nacionalismo al populismo: Cultura y política en Puerto Rico*, edited by Silvia Álvarez-Curbelo and María Elena Rodríguez Castro, 13–37. Río Piedras: Ediciones Huracán, 1993.

———. "Las lecciones de la guerra: Luis Muñoz Marín y la segunda guerra mundial, 1943–1946." In *Luis Muñoz Marín: Ensayos del centenario*, edited by Fernando Picó, 30–59. Trujillo Alto: Fundación Luis Muñoz Marín, 1999.

———. *Un país del porvenir: El afán de modernidad en Puerto Rico (siglo XIX)*. San Juan: Ediciones Callejón, 2001.

Álvarez-Curbelo, Silvia, and María Elena Rodríguez Castro, eds. *Del nacionalismo al populismo: Cultura y política en Puerto Rico*. Río Piedras: Ediciones Huracán, 1993.

Amador, Emma. "Transnational Case Work: Social Workers, Migrant Workers, and Puerto Rican Citizenship, 1950–66." Paper presented at the meeting of the Puerto Rican Studies Association, State University of New York, Albany, NY, October 2012.

Andrews, George Reid. *The Afro-Argentines of Buenos Aires*. Madison: University of Wisconsin Press, 1980.

Aparicio, Frances R. *Listening to Salsa: Gender, Latin Popular Music, and Puerto Rican Cultures*. Hanover, NH: University Press of New England, 1998.

Appadurai, Arjun. *Modernity at Large: Cultural Dimensions of Globalization*. Minneapolis: University of Minnesota Press, 1996.

Appelbaum, Nancy, Anne MacPherson, and Karin Alejandra Rosemblatt, eds. *Race and Nation in Latin America*. Chapel Hill: University of North Carolina Press, 2003.

Argenti, Nicolas, and Katharina Schramm, eds. *Remembering Violence: Anthropological Perspectives on Intergenerational Transmission.* New York: Berghahn, 2010.

Arredondo, Gabriela F. *Mexican Chicago: Race, Identity, and Nation, 1916–39.* Urbana: University of Illinois Press, 2008.

Asencio Camacho, Luis. *Itinerario de muerte: Relato de un vuelo sin itinerario fletado con 62 obreros puertorriqueños, con rumbo a los Estados Unidos, que se vio forzado a amarar al norte de las Bahamas la noche del 5 de junio de 1950, dejando a sus pasajeros a la deriva y a la merced de la competencia de un piloto, la presteza de los guardacostas y la ferocidad de los tiburones, antes de su dramático rescate.* Yauco: Imprenta y Editorial Coquí, 2012.

———. "Migrants Who Never Arrived: The Crash of Westair Transport's N1248N in 1950." CENTRO: *Journal of the Center for Puerto Rican Studies* 25:11 (fall 2013): 120–139.

———. "Of Unscheduled Deaths and Other (Un)Happy Endings: The Ditching of Westair's N1248N and Its Sequels." Scribd, 2013. http://www.scribd.com.

Auyero, Javier. *Poor People's Politics: Peronist Survival Networks and the Legacy of Evita.* Durham, NC: Duke University Press, 2000.

Ayala, César J. *American Sugar Kingdom: The Plantation Economy of the Spanish Caribbean, 1898–1934.* Chapel Hill: University of North Carolina Press, 1999.

———. "The American Sugar Kingdom, 1898–1934." In *The Caribbean: A History of the Region and Its Peoples,* edited by Stephan Palmié and Francisco Scarano, 433–444. Chicago: University of Chicago Press, 2011.

Ayala, César J., and Rick Baldoz. "The Bordering of America: Colonialism and Citizenship in the Philippines and Puerto Rico." CENTRO: *Journal of the Center for Puerto Rican Studies* 25:1 (spring 2013): 76–105.

Ayala, César J., and Rafael Bernabé. *Puerto Rico in the American Century: A History since 1898.* Chapel Hill: University of North Carolina Press, 2007.

Ayala, César J., and Jennifer McCormick. "Felícita 'La Prieta' Méndez (1916–1998) and the End of Latino School Segregation in California." CENTRO: *Journal of the Center for Puerto Rican Studies* 19:2 (fall 2007): 12–32.

Azize Vargas, Yamila. *La mujer en la lucha.* Río Piedras: Editorial Cultural, 1985.

———, ed. *La mujer en Puerto Rico: Ensayos de investigación.* Río Piedras: Ediciones Huracán, 1987.

Back, Kurt J. *Slums, Projects, and People: Social Psychological Problems of Relocation in Puerto Rico.* Durham, NC: Duke University Press, 1962.

Baerga-Santini, María del Carmen. "Cuerpo subversivo, norma seductora: Un capítulo de la historia de la heterosexualidad en Puerto Rico." *Op. Cit.* 14 (2002): 49–96.

———. "El género y la construcción social de la marginalidad del trabajo femenino en la industria de la confección de ropa." In *Género y trabajo: La industria de la aguja en Puerto Rico y el Caribe hispánico,* edited by María del Carmen Baerga-Santini, 3–59. Río Piedras: Editorial de la Universidad de Puerto Rico, 1993.

———, ed. *Género y trabajo: La industria de la aguja en Puerto Rico y el Caribe hispánico.* Río Piedras: Editorial de la Universidad de Puerto Rico, 1993.

————. "History and the Contours of Meaning: The Abjection of Luisa Nevárez, First Woman Condemned to the Gallows in Puerto Rico, 1905." *Hispanic American Historical Review* 89:4 (November 2009): 643–674.

————. "La articulación del trabajo asalariado y no asalariado: Hacia un reevaluación de la contruibución femenina a la sociedad puertorriqueña (el caso de la industria de la aguja)." In *La mujer en Puerto Rico: Ensayos de investigación*, edited by Yamila Azize Vargas, 89–112. Río Piedras: Ediciones Huracán, 1987.

————. "Las jerarquías sociales y las espresiones de resistencia: Género, clase y edad en la industria de aguja en Puerto Rico." In *Género y trabajo: La industria de la aguja en Puerto Rico y el Caribe hispánico*, edited by María del Carmen Baerga-Santini, 103–137. Río Piedras: Editorial de la Universidad de Puerto Rico, 1993.

Baldoz, Rick, and César Ayala. "The Bordering of America: Colonialism and Citizenship in the Philippines and Puerto Rico." *CENTRO: Journal of the Center for Puerto Rican Studies* 25:1 (spring 2013): 76–105.

Baldrich, Juan José. "Gender and the Decomposition of the Cigar-Making Craft in Puerto Rico, 1899–1934." In *Puerto Rican Women's History: New Perspectives*, edited by Félix V. Matos-Rodriguez and Linda Delgado, 105–125. Armonk, NY: M. E. Sharpe, 1998.

Ballantyne, Tony, and Antoinette Burton. *Bodies in Contact: Rethinking Colonial Encounters in World History*. Durham, NC: Duke University Press, 2005.

————, eds. *Moving Subjects: Gender, Mobility, and Intimacy in an Age of Global Empire*. Urbana: University of Illinois Press, 2009.

Barceló Miller, María de Fátima. "Domesticidad, desafío y subversión: La discursividad femenina sobre el progreso y el orden social, 1910–1930." *Op. Cit.* 14 (2002): 187–212.

————. "Halfhearted Solidarity: Women Workers and the Women's Suffrage Movement in Puerto Rico during the 1920s." In *Puerto Rican Women's History: New Perspectives*, edited by Félix V. Matos-Rodriguez and Linda Delgado, 126–142. Armonk, NY: M. E. Sharpe, 1998.

————. *La lucha por el sufragio femenino en Puerto Rico, 1896–1935*. Río Piedras: Ediciones Huracán, 1997.

————. "'Un gobierno de hombres': Género y populismo en los discursos de Muñoz, 1940–1950." In *Luis Muñoz Marín: Imágenes de la memoria*, edited by Fernando Picó, 38–61. Trujillo Alto: Fundación Luis Muñoz Marín, 2008.

Barrero, Mario. "Are Latinos a Racialized Minority?" *Sociological Perspectives* 51 (summer 2008): 301–324.

Bayly, C. A., Sven Beckert, Matthew Connelly, Isabel Hofmeyr, Wendy Kozol, and Patricia Seed. "AHR Conversation: On Transnational History." *American Historical Review* 111:5 (December 2006): 1440–1464.

Bederman, Gail. *Manliness and Civilization: A Cultural History of Gender and Race in the United States, 1880–1917*. Chicago: University of Chicago Press, 1995.

Benmayor, Rina, Ana Juarbe, Blanca Vásquez Erazo, and Celia Álvarez. "Stories to Live By: Continuity and Change in Three Generations of Puerto Rican Women." *Oral History Review* 16:2 (fall 1988): 1–48.

Bennett-Kimble, Laura. "Sweet Smell of Success." *Michigan History Magazine* (March–April 2000): 40–45.

Bergad, Laird. *Coffee and the Growth of Agrarian Capitalism in Nineteenth-Century Puerto Rico*. Princeton, NJ: Princeton University Press, 1983.

Berlin, Ira. *The Making of African America: The Four Great Migrations*. New York: Viking, 2010.

Berrios-Miranda, Marisol, and Shannon Dudley. "El Gran Combo, Cortijo, and the Musical Geography of Cangrejos/Santurce." *Caribbean Studies* 36:2 (July 2008): 121–151.

Blum, Ann. *Domestic Economies: Family, Work, and Welfare in Mexico City, 1884–1943*. Lincoln: University of Nebraska Press, 2009.

Bolívar Fresneda, José L. "The Development Bank and the Initial Failure of the Industrial Program in Puerto Rico, 1942–1948." *CENTRO: Journal of the Center for Puerto Rican Studies* 20:2 (fall 2008): 127–147.

Bolland, O. Nigel. "Labor Protests, Rebellions, and the Rise of Nationalism during Depression and War." In *The Caribbean: A History of the Region and Its Peoples*, edited by Stephan Palmié and Francisco Scarano, 459–474. Chicago: University of Chicago Press, 2011.

Bon Tempo, Carl J. *Americans at the Gate: The United States and Refugees during the Cold War*. Princeton, NJ: Princeton University Press, 2008.

Booth, W. James. *Communities of Memory: On Witness, Identity, and Justice*. Ithaca, NY: Cornell University Press, 2006.

Boris, Eileen. *Home to Work: Motherhood and the Politics of Industrial Homework in the United States*. New York: Cambridge University Press, 1994.

———. "Needlewomen under the New Deal in Puerto Rico, 1920–1945." In *Puerto Rican Women and Work: Bridges in Transnational Labor*, edited by Altagracia Ortiz, 33–54. Philadelphia: Temple University Press, 1996.

Briggs, Laura. *Reproducing Empire: Race, Sex, Science, and U.S. Imperialism in Puerto Rico*. Berkeley: University of California Press, 2002.

Briggs, Laura, Gladys McCormick, and J. T. Way. "Transnationalism: A Category of Analysis." *American Quarterly* 60:3 (September 2008): 625–648.

Brown, Kathleen. "What Do Sex and Laundry Have to Do with It? Thinking about Daily Life as a Source of Historical Change." Paper presented at the National Women's History Museum, Washington, DC, March 14, 2012.

Burgos, Nilsa. *Pioneras de la profesión de trabajo social en Puerto Rico*. Hato Rey: Publicaciones Puertorriqueñas, 1997.

Burnett, Christina Duffy, and Burke Marshall, eds. *Foreign in a Domestic Sense: Puerto Rico, American Expansion, and the Constitution*. Durham, NC: Duke University Press, 2001.

————, eds. *Puerto Rico, American Expansionism, and the Constitution*. Durham, NC: Duke University Press, 2001.

Burns, Kathryn. *Into the Archive: Writing and Power in Colonial Peru*. Durham, NC: Duke University Press, 2010.

Burton, Antoinette, ed. *Archive Stories: Facts, Fictions, and the Writing of History*. Durham, NC: Duke University Press, 2005.

————. "Archive Stories: Gender in the Making of Imperial and Colonial Histories." In *Gender and Empire*, edited by Philippa Levine, 281–293. Oxford: Oxford University Press, 2004.

————, ed. *Gender, Sexuality, and Colonial Modernities*. New York: Routledge, 1999.

————. "Introduction." In *Archive Stories: Facts, Fictions, and the Writing of History*, edited by Antoinette Burton, 1–21. Durham, NC: Duke University Press, 2005.

Cabán, Pedro. "The Puerto Rican Colonial Matrix: The Etiology of Citizenship—an Introduction." *CENTRO: Journal of the Center for Puerto Rican Studies* 25:1 (spring 2013): 4–21.

Cabrera Collazo, Rafael L. "La 'criollización' del desarrollismo y la inclusión de lo puertorriqueño en tres discursos inaugurales de Luis Muñoz Marín: 1949, 1953, 1957." In *Luis Muñoz Marín: Ensayos del centenario*, edited by Fernando Picó, 233–249. Trujillo Alto: Fundación Luis Muñoz Marín, 1999.

————. *Los dibujos del progreso: El mundo caricaturesco de Filardi y la crítica el desarrollismo muñocista, 1950–1960*. San Juan: Publicaciones Puertorriqueñas Editores, 2006.

Camacho, Alicia Schmidt. *Migrant Imaginaries: Latino Cultural Politics in the U.S.-Mexico Borderlands*. New York: New York University, 2008.

Campos, Ricardo, and Juan Flores. "National Culture and Migration: Perspectives from the Puerto Rican Working Class." Centro Working Papers. New York: Centro de Estudios Puertorriqueños, 1978.

Canning, Kathleen. *Gender History in Practice: Historical Perspectives on Bodies, Class, and Citizenship*. Ithaca, NY: Cornell University Press, 2006.

Canning, Kathleen, and Sonya O. Rose, eds. *Gender, Citizenships and Subjectivities*. London: Blackwell, 2002.

Carrero, Telesforo. *Housing in Puerto Rico*. Santurce: Junta de Planificación de Puerto Rico, 1950.

Casey, Genevieve M. *Father Clem Kern: Conscience of Detroit*. Detroit: Marygrove College Press, 1989.

Chambers, Sarah. "The Paternal Obligation to Provide: Political Familialism in Early Nineteenth-Century Chile." *American Historical Review* 117:4 (October 2012): 1123–1148.

Chávez, Leo. *The Latino Threat: Constructing Immigrants, Citizens, and the Nation*. Palo Alto: Stanford University Press, 2008.

Cobas, José A., Jorge Duany, and Joe R. Feagin. *How the United States Racializes Latinos: White Hegemony and Its Consequences*. Boulder, CO: Paradigm, 2009.

Cofresí, Emilio. *Realidad Poblacional de Puerto Rico*. San Juan, Puerto Rico: n.p., 1951.

Cohen, Deborah. *Braceros: Migrant Citizens and Transnational Subjects in the Postwar United States and Mexico*. Chapel Hill: University of North Carolina Press, 2011.

Cohen, Jonathon. *A Pan-American Life: Selected Poetry and Prose by Muna Lee*. Madison: University of Wisconsin Press, 2004.

Coleson, Jeanene M. "The Puerto Ricanization of Protestantism in Puerto Rico, 1898–1939." PhD diss., Universidad de Puerto Rico, 2007.

Colistete, Renato P. "Trade Unions and the ICFTU in the Age of Developmentalism in Brazil, 1953–1962." *Hispanic American Historical Review* 92:4 (November 2012): 669–701.

Colón Pizarro, Mariam. "Poetic Pragmatism: The Puerto Rican Division of Community Education (DIVEDCO) and the Politics of Cultural Production, 1949–1968." PhD diss., University of Michigan, 2011.

Colón Warren, Alice. "The Impact of Job Losses on Puerto Rican Women in the Middle Atlantic Region, 1970–1980." In *Puerto Rican Women and Work: Bridges in Transnational Labor*, edited by Altagracia Ortiz, 105–138. Philadelphia: Temple University Press, 1996.

———. "Mujeres, familias y trabajos en Puerto Rico: Discusiones en la investigación social." *Revista de Ciencias Sociales* 12 (2003): 68–101.

Colón Warren, Alice, María Maite Mulero, Luis Santiago, and Nilsa Burgos. *Estirando el peso: Acciones de ajuste y relaciones de género ante el cierre de fábricas en Puerto Rico*. Río Piedras: Centro de Investigaciones Sociales, 2008.

Colón Warren, Alice, and Rhoda Reddock. "Cambios en la situación de las mujeres en el Caribe a través del siglo XX." *Op. Cit.* 14 (2002): 213–246.

Conniff, Michael, ed. *Populism in Latin America*. Tuscaloosa: University of Alabama Press, 1999.

Cooper, Frederick. *Colonialism in Question: Theory, Knowledge, History*. Berkeley: University of California Press, 2005.

Cooper, Frederick, and Ann Laura Stoler. "Between Metropole and Colony: Toward a Research Agenda." In *Tensions of Empire: Colonial Cultures in a Bourgeois World*, edited by Frederick Cooper and Ann Laura Stoler, 1–56. Berkeley: University of California Press, 1997.

———, eds. *Tensions of Empire: Colonial Cultures in a Bourgeois World*. Berkeley: University of California Press, 1997.

Córdova, Nathaniel I. "In His Image and Likeness: The Puerto Rican Jíbaro as Political Icon." *CENTRO: Journal of the Center for Puerto Rican Studies* 17:2 (fall 2005): 170–191.

Córdova Suárez, Isabel. "Setting Them Straight: Social Services, Youth, Sexuality, and Modernization in Postwar (WWII) Puerto Rico." *CENTRO: Journal of the Center for Puerto Rican Studies* 19:1 (spring 2007): 27–49.

Crespo-Kebler, Elizabeth. "¿Y las trabajadoras domésticas, dónde están? Raza, género y trabajo." In *Contrapunto de género y raza en Puerto Rico*, edited by Idsa Alegría

Ortega and Palmira N. Ríos González, 135–154. Río Piedras: Centro de Investigaciones Sociales, 2005.

Cronon, William. "Storytelling." *American Historical Review* 118:1 (February 2013): 1–19.

Cubano Iguina, Astrid. "Con 'arrebato y obcecación': Violencia doméstica y otras violencias contra las mujeres en Puerto Rico, 1870–1890." *Op. Cit.* 14 (2002): 129–146.

———. "Luis Muñoz Marín, la utopía liberal y los consumidores: Apuntes para una genealogía de la cultura política en Puerto Rico." In *Luis Muñoz Marín: Ensayos del centenario*, edited by Fernando Picó, 14–29. Trujillo Alto: Fundación Luis Muñoz Marín, 1999.

———. *Rituals of Violence in Nineteenth-Century Puerto Rico: Individual Conflict, Gender, and the Law*. Gainesville: University Press of Florida, 2006.

Dávila, Arlene M. *Barrio Dreams: Puerto Ricans, Latinos, and the Neo-liberal City*. Berkeley: University of California Press, 2004.

———. *Latino Spin: Public Image and the Whitewashing of Race*. New York: New York University Press, 2008.

———. *Sponsored Identities: Cultural Politics in Puerto Rico*. Philadelphia: Temple University Press, 1997.

Dávila, Arlene M., and Agustín Lao, eds. *Mambo Montage: The Latinization of New York*. New York: Columbia University Press, 2001.

De Genova, Nicholas. "Race, Space, and the Reinvention of Latin America in Mexican Chicago." *Latin American Perspectives* 102:25 (September 1998): 87–116.

———, ed. *Racial Transformations: Latinos and Asians Remaking the United States*. Durham, NC: Duke University Press, 2006.

———. "'White' Puerto Rican Migrants, the Mexican Colony, 'Americanization,' and Latino History." In *Latino Urban Ethnography and the Work of Elena Padilla*, edited by Mérida M. Rúa, 157–177. Urbana: University of Illinois Press, 2010.

———. *Working the Boundaries: Race, Space, and "Illegality" in Mexican Chicago*. Durham, NC: Duke University Press, 2005.

De Genova, Nicholas, and Ana Y. Ramos-Zayas. *Latino Crossings: Mexicans, Puerto Ricans, and the Politics of Race and Citizenship*. New York: Routledge, 2003.

———. "Latino Racial Formations in the United States: An Introduction." *Journal of Latin American Anthropology* 8:2 (June 2003): 2–16.

de la Cadena, Marisol. *Indigenous Mestizos: The Politics of Race and Culture in Cuzco, Peru, 1919–1991*. Durham, NC: Duke University Press, 2000.

de la Fuente, Alejandro. *A Nation for All: Race, Inequality, and Politics in Twentieth Century Cuba*. Chapel Hill: University of North Carolina Press, 2001.

de la Torre, Carlos. *Populist Seduction in Latin America: The Ecuadorian Experience*. Athens: Ohio University Press, 2000.

Delgado, Linda. "Rufa Concepción Fernández: The Role of Gender in the Migration Process." In *Puerto Rican Women's History: New Perspectives*, edited by Félix V. Matos-Rodriguez and Linda Delgado, 171–180. Armonk, NY: M. E. Sharpe, 1998.

Delgado, Richard, and Jean Stefancic, eds. *The Latino/a Condition: A Critical Reader.* New York: New York University Press, 2011.

del Moral, Solsiree. *Negotiating Empire: The Cultural Politics of Schools in Puerto Rico, 1898–1952.* Madison: University of Wisconsin Press, 2013.

Denison, Ray W. *America's Son: The Odyssey of John Espinoza: From the Texas Cotton Fields to Vietnam and the Michigan Legislature.* Port Sanilac, MI: Denison Arts, 2006.

Derby, Lauren. *The Dictator's Seduction: Politics and the Popular Imagination in the Era of Trujillo.* Durham, NC: Duke University Press, 2009.

———. "Imperial Secrets: Vampires and Nationhood in Puerto Rico." *Past and Present* 199, suppl. 3 (2008): 290–312.

Derrida, Jacques. *Archive Fever: A Freudian Impression.* Chicago: University of Chicago Press, 1995.

Diamond, Andrew. *Mean Streets: Chicago Youths and the Everyday Struggle for Empowerment in the Multiracial City, 1908–1969.* Berkeley: University of California Press, 2009.

Díaz Quiñones, Arcadio. *El arte de bregar: Ensayos.* San Juan: Ediciones Callejón, 2000.

———. *La memoria rota.* Río Piedras: Ediciones Huracán, 1993.

———. *Sobre los principios: Los intelectuales caribeños y la tradición.* Bernal, Argentina: Editorial de la Universidad Nacional de Quilmes, 2006.

Dietz, James L. *Economic History of Puerto Rico: Institutional Change and Capitalist Development.* Princeton, NJ: Princeton University Press, 1986.

———. "La reinvención del subdesarrollo: Errores fundamentales del proyecto de industrialización." In *Del nacionalismo al populismo: Cultura y política en Puerto Rico*, edited by Silvia Álvarez-Curbelo and María Elena Rodríguez Castro, 179–205. Río Piedras: Ediciones Huracán, 1993.

———. *Puerto Rico: Negotiating Development and Change.* Boulder, CO: Lynne Rienner, 2003.

Dinsey-Flores, Zaire. "Disciplining Ponce's Poor entre el Caserío y el Pueblo." Paper presented at the meeting of the Puerto Rican Studies Association, Hartford, CT, October 2010.

Dinwiddie, William. *Puerto Rico: Its Conditions and Possibilities.* New York: Harper and Brothers, 1899.

Dirks, Nicholas B. "Annals of the Archive: Ethnographic Notes on the Sources of History." In *From the Margins: Historical Anthropology and Its Futures*, edited by Brian Keith Axel, 47–65. Durham, NC: Duke University Press, 2002.

Doner, Mary Frances. *Cloud of Arrows.* New York: Doubleday, 1950.

Dore, Elizabeth, and Maxine Molyneux, eds. *Hidden Histories of Gender and the State in Latin America.* Durham, NC: Duke University Press, 2000.

Drinot, Paulo. *The Allure of Labor: Workers, Race, and the Making of the Peruvian State.* Durham, NC: Duke University Press, 2011.

———. "Creole Anti-communism: Labor, the Peruvian Communist Party, and APRA, 1930–34." *Hispanic American Historical Review* 92:4 (November 2012): 703–736.

Duany, Jorge. *Blurred Borders: Transnational Migration between the Hispanic Caribbean and the United States*. Chapel Hill: University of North Carolina Press, 2011.

———. *The Puerto Rican Nation on the Move: Identities on the Island and in the United States*. Chapel Hill: University of North Carolina Press, 2002.

Duarte, Adriano Luiz. "Neighborhood Associations, Social Movements, and Populism in Brazil, 1945–1953." *Hispanic American Historical Review* 89:1 (February 2009): 111–139.

Dubois, Christine. "Caribbean Migrations and Diasporas." In *The Caribbean: A History of the Region and Its Peoples*, edited by Stephan Palmié and Francisco Scarano, 583–596. Chicago: University of Chicago Press, 2011.

DuBois, Laurent. *A Colony of Citizens: Revolution and Slave Emancipation, 1787–1804*. Chapel Hill: University of North Carolina Press, 2006.

Duffy Burnett, Christina, and Burke Marshall, eds. *Foreign in a Domestic Sense: Puerto Rico, American Expansion, and the Constitution*. Durham, NC: Duke University Press, 2001.

Dufoix, Stephanie. *Diasporas*. Berkeley: University of California Press, 2008.

Durand, Jorge, ed. *Braceros: Las miradas mexicana y estadounidense*. Mexico: Universidad Autónoma de Zacatecas, 2007.

Elena, Eduardo. *Dignifying Argentina: Peronism, Citizenship, and Mass Consumption*. Pittsburgh: University of Pittsburgh Press, 2011.

———. "Peronism in 'Good Taste': Culture and Consumption in the Magazine *Argentina*." In *The New Cultural History of Peronism: Power and Identity in Mid-Twentieth-Century Argentina*, edited by Matthew Karush and Oscar Chamosa, 209–239. Durham, NC: Duke University Press, 2010.

Erman, Samuel C. "Puerto Rico and the Promise of U.S. Citizenship: Struggles around Status in a New Empire, 1898–1917." PhD diss., University of Michigan, 2010.

Esterrich, Carmelo. "Edenes Insostenibles: El campo de la ciudad en la intentona cultural de los cincuenta." *CENTRO: Journal of the Center for Puerto Rican Studies* 21:1 (spring 2009): 181–199.

———. "La Vida and the New Life: Pedro Juan Soto and José Luis González Take On Oscar Lewis's *La Vida*." Paper presented at the meeting of the Puerto Rican Studies Association, Albany, NY, October 2012.

Ettinger, Patrick. *Imaginary Lines: Border Enforcement and the Origins of Undocumented Immigration: 1882–1930*. Austin: University of Texas Press, 2009.

Feder, Ellen K. *Family Bonds: Genealogies of Race and Gender*. New York: Oxford University Press, 2007.

Ferguson, Susan J., ed. *Race, Gender, Sexuality, and Social Class: Dimensions of Inequality*. Thousand Oaks, CA: Sage, 2013.

Fernandes, Sujatha. "Gender, Popular Participation, and the State in Chávez's Venezuela." In *Gender and Populism in Latin America: Passionate Politics*, edited by Karen Kampwirth, 202–221. University Park: Penn State University Press, 2010.

Fernández, Lilia. *Brown in the Windy City: Mexicans and Puerto Ricans in Post-war Chicago.* Chicago: University of Chicago Press, 2012.

———. "Of Immigrants and Migrants: Mexican and Puerto Rican Labor Migration in Comparative Perspective, 1945–62." *Journal of American Ethnic History* 29:30 (spring 2010): 6–39.

Fernández Méndez, Eugenio. "Algunos cambios culturales, económicos y sociales que afectan la familia en Puerto Rico." *Revista de Ciencias Sociales* 7:2 (1964): 167–172.

Ferrao, Luís Angel. "Nacionalismo, hispanismo y élite intellectual en el Puerto Rico de los años treinta." In *Del nacionalismo al populismo: Cultura y política en Puerto Rico,* edited by Silvia Álvarez-Curbelo and María Elena Rodríguez Castro, 37–60. Río Piedras: Ediciones Huracán, 1993.

———. *Pedro Albizu Campos y el nacionalismo puertorriqueñño.* Río Piedras: Editorial Cultural, 1990.

Ferré, Rosario. *Maldito amor y otros cuentos.* New York: Vintage, 1998.

Ferrer, Ada. *Insurgent Cuba: Race, Nation, and Revolution.* Chapel Hill: University of North Carolina Press, 1999.

Figueroa, Luis. *Sugar, Slavery, and Freedom in Nineteenth-Century Puerto Rico.* Chapel Hill: University of North Carolina Press, 2005.

Figueroa Mercado, Loida. *Arenales.* Mayagüez: Antillian College Press, 1985 [1961].

Findlay, Eileen J. "Artful Narration: Puerto Rican Women Return Migrants' Life Stories." *Journal of Women's History* 22:4 (winter 2010): 162–185.

———. "Courtroom Tales of Sex and Honor: Rapto and Rape in Late Nineteenth-Century Puerto Rico." In *Honor, Status, and Law in Modern Latin America,* edited by Sueann Caulfield, Sarah C. Chambers, and Lara Putnam, 201–223. Durham, NC: Duke University Press, 2005.

———. *Imposing Decency: The Politics of Sexuality and Race in Puerto Rico, 1870–1920.* Durham, NC: Duke University Press, 1999.

———. "La raza y lo respetable: La política de la ciudadania, la moralidad, y las identidades raciales en el Puerto Rico decimónico." *Op. Cit.* 16 (2005): 99–135.

———. "Love in the Tropics: Marriage, Divorce, and the Construction of Benevolent Colonialism in Puerto Rico." In *Close Encounters of Empire: Writing the Cultural History of U.S.-Latin American Relations,* edited by Catherine C. LeGrand and Ricardo D. Salvatore, 139–172. Durham, NC: Duke University Press, 1998.

———. "Portable Roots: Latin New Yorker Community Building and the Meanings of Women's Return Migration in San Juan, Puerto Rico, 1960–2000." *Caribbean Studies* 37:2 (July–December 2009): 3–44.

———. "Slipping and Sliding: The Many Meanings of Race in Life Histories of New York Puerto Rican Return Migrants in San Juan." *CENTRO: Journal of the Center for Puerto Rican Studies* 24:1 (spring 2012): 4–21.

Flores, Juan. *The Diaspora Strikes Back: Caribeño Tales of Learning and Turning.* New York: Routledge, 2009.

————. "'¡Ecua Jei!' Ismael Rivera, el Sonero Mayor." *CENTRO: Journal of the Center for Puerto Rican Studies* 16:2 (fall 2004): 62–77.

————. *From Bomba to Hip-Hop: Puerto Rican Culture and Latino Identity*. New York: Columbia University Press, 2000.

————. *La venganza de Cortijo y otros ensayos*. Río Piedras: Ediciones Huracán, 1997.

Flores, Juan, and Miriam Jiménez Román, eds. *The Afro-Latin@ Reader: History and Culture in the United States*. Durham, NC: Duke University Press, 2010.

Flores Collazo, María Margarita. "Dioramas de la identidad: Los museos como difusores del paradigm estado nación." In *El pasado ya no es lo que era: La historia en tiempos de incertidumbre*, edited by Carlos Pabón, 109–140. San Juan: Ediciones Vértigo, 2005.

Flores Ramos, José Enrique. "El Instituto del Hogar: 'Hogares estables y felices.'" *Op. Cit.* 14 (2002): 247–282.

————. *Eugenesia, higiene pública y alcanfor para las pasiones: La prostitución en San Juan de Puerto Rico, 1876–1919*. Hato Rey: Publicaciones Puertorriqueñas, 2006.

————. *Mujer, familia y prostitución: La construcción del género bajo la hegemonía del PPD, 1940–1968*. San Juan: Oficina de la Procuradora de las Mujeres, 2007.

————. "Virgins, Whores, and Martyrs: Prostitution in the Colony, 1898–1917." In *Puerto Rican Women's History: New Perspectives*, edited by Félix V. Matos-Rodriguez and Linda Delgado, 83–104. Armonk, NY: M. E. Sharpe, 1998.

Foley, Neil. "Partly Colored or Other White: Mexican Americans and Their Problem with the Color Line." In *American Dreaming, Global Realities: Rethinking U.S. Immigration History*, edited by Donna Gabaccia and Vicki Ruiz, 361–378. Urbana: University of Illinois Press, 2006.

————. *Quest for Equality: The Failed Promise of Black-Brown Solidarity*. Cambridge, MA: Harvard University Press, 2010.

Foner, Nancy. *In a New Land: A Comparative View of Immigration*. New York: New York University Press, 2005.

Foucault, Michel. *Archaeology of Knowledge and Discourse on Language*. New York: Pantheon, 1972.

Frazer, Lessie Jo. *Salt in the Sand: Memory, Violence, and the Nation-State in Chile, 1890 to the Present*. Durham, NC: Duke University Press, 2007.

French, John, and Daniel James, eds. *The Gendered Worlds of Latin American Women Workers: From Household and Factory to the Union Hall and Ballot Box*. Durham, NC: Duke University Press, 1997.

French, William E., and Katherine Elaine Bliss, eds. *Gender, Sexuality, and Power in Latin America since Independence*. Lanham, MD: Rowman and Littlefield, 2007.

Fritzche, Peter. "The Archive and the Case of the German Nation." In *Archive Stories: Facts, Fictions, and the Writing of History*, edited by Antoinette Burton, 184–208. Durham, NC: Duke University Press, 2005.

Gabaccia, Donna. "When Migrants Are Men: Italy's Women and Transnationalism as a Working-Class Way of Life." In *American Dreaming, Global Realities: Rethinking U.S.

Immigration History, edited by Donna Gabaccia and Vicki Ruiz, 190–206. Urbana: University of Illinois Press, 2006.

Gabaccia, Donna, and Franca Iacovetta. *Women, Gender, and Transnational Lives: Italian Workers of the World.* Toronto: University of Toronto Press, 2002.

Gabaccia, Donna, and Vicki Ruiz, eds. *American Dreaming, Global Realities: Rethinking U.S. Immigration History.* Urbana: University of Illinois Press, 2006.

Gallart, Mary Frances. "Conversaciones con el pueblo." In *Luis Muñoz Marín: Perfiles de su gobernación*, edited by Fernando Picó, 287–306. Trujillo Alto: Fundación Luis Muñoz Marín, 2003.

———. "Las mujeres en la discursiva de Luis Muñoz Marín: Primeras décadas." In *Luis Muñoz Marín: Ensayos del centenario*, edited by Fernando Picó, 187–207. Trujillo Alto: Fundación Luis Muñoz Marín, 1999.

———. "Political Empowerment of Puerto Rican Women, 1952–1956." In *Puerto Rican Women's History: New Perspectives*, edited by Félix V. Matos-Rodriguez and Linda Delgado, 227–252. Armonk, NY: M. E. Sharpe, 1998.

Gamboa, Erasmo. *Mexican Labor and World War II: Braceros in the Pacific Northwest, 1942–1947.* Austin: University of Texas Press, 1990.

Gaonkar, Dilip Parameshwar, ed. *Alternative Modernities.* Durham, NC: Duke University Press, 2001.

García, Gervasio, and Angel G. Quintero Rivera. *Desafío y solidaridad: Breve historia del movimiento obrero puertorriqueño.* Río Piedras: Ediciones Huracán, 1982.

García, Juan R. *Mexicans in the Midwest: 1900–1982.* Tucson: University of Arizona Press, 1996.

García, Matt. "Ambassadors in Overalls: Mexican Guest Workers and the Future of Labor." *Boom: A Journal of California* 1:4 (winter 2011): 31–44.

———. *A World of Its Own: Race, Labor, and Citrus in the Making of Greater Los Angeles, 1900–1970.* Chapel Hill: University of North Carolina Press, 2002.

García, Matthew. "Intraethnic Conflict and the *Bracero* Program during World War II." In *American Dreaming, Global Realities: Rethinking U.S. Immigration History*, edited by Donna Gabaccia and Vicki Ruiz, 399–410. Urbana: University of Illinois Press, 2006.

García Canclini, Nestor. *Hybrid Cultures: Strategies for Entering and Leaving Modernity.* Minneapolis: University of Minnesota Press, 1995.

García-Colón, Ismael. "Buscando Ambiente: Hegemony and Subaltern Tactics of Survival in Puerto Rico's Land Distribution Program." *Latin American Perspectives* 33:1 (January 2006): 42–65.

———. "Claiming Equality: Puerto Rican Farmworkers in Western New York." *Latino Studies* 6:3 (fall 2008): 269–289.

———. *Land Reform in Puerto Rico: Modernizing the Colonial State, 1941–1969.* Gainesville: University Press of Florida, 2009.

———. "Playing and Eating Democracy: The Case of Puerto Rico's Land Distribution Programs." *CENTRO: Journal of the Center for Puerto Rican Studies* 18:2 (fall 2006): 167–189.

García-Colón, Ismael, and Edwin Meléndez. "Enduring Migration: Puerto Rican Workers on U.S. Farms." *CENTRO: Journal of the Center for Puerto Rican Studies* 25:2 (fall 2013): 96–119.

García Muñíz, Humberto. "The Colonial Persuasion: Puerto Rico and the Dutch and French Antilles." In *The Caribbean: A History of the Region and Its Peoples*, edited by Stephan Palmié and Francisco Scarano, 537–551. Chicago: University of Chicago Press, 2011.

García-Toro, Victor, Rafael I. Ramírez, and Luis Solano Castillo. *Los hombres no lloran: Ensayos sobre las masculinidades.* Río Piedras: Ediciones Huracán, 2007.

Garfield, Seth. "Tapping Masculinity: Labor Recruitment to the Brazilian Amazon." *Hispanic American Historical Review* 86:2 (May 2006): 275–308.

Glasser, Ruth. "From 'Indianola' to 'Ño Colá': The Strange Career of the Afro-Puerto Rican Musician." In *The Afro-Latin@ Reader: History and Culture in the United States*, edited by Juan Flores and Miriam Jiménez Román, 157–175. Durham, NC: Duke University Press, 2010.

———. "From Rich Port to Bridgeport: Puerto Ricans in Connecticut." In *The Puerto Rican Diaspora: Historical Perspectives*, edited by Carmen Theresa Whalen and Victor Vásquez-Hernández, 174–199. Philadelphia: Temple University Press, 2005.

———. *My Music Is My Flag: Puerto Rican Musicians and Their New York Communities, 1917–1940.* Berkeley: University of California Press, 1994.

Glenn, Evelyn Nakano. *Unequal Freedom: How Race and Gender Shaped American Citizenship and Labor.* Cambridge, MA: Harvard University Press, 2002.

Gluck, Carol. "The End of Elsewhere: Writing Modernity Now." *American Historical Review* 116:3 (June 2011): 676–687.

Godreau, Isar P. "Missing the Mix: San Antón and the Racial Dynamics of Nationalism in Puerto Rico." PhD diss., University of California, 1999.

———. "Slippery Semantics: Race Talk and Everyday Uses of Racial Terminology in Puerto Rico." *CENTRO: Journal of the Center for Puerto Rican Studies* 20:2 (fall 2008): 5–33.

Goldin, Liliana R., ed. *Identities on the Move: Transnational Processes in North America and the Caribbean Basin.* Albany, NY: Institute for Mesoamerican Studies, 1999.

Goldstein, Alyosha. "The Attributes of Sovereignty: The Cold War, Colonialism, and Community Education in Puerto Rico." In *Imagining Our Americas: Toward a Transnational Frame*, edited by Sandyha Shukla and Heidi Tinsman, 313–337. Durham, NC: Duke University Press, 2007.

Gómez-Barris, Macarena. *Where Memory Dwells: Culture and State Violence in Chile.* Berkeley: University of California Press, 2009.

Gómez-Quiñones, Juan. *Mexican-American Labor: 1790–1990.* Albuquerque: University of New Mexico Press, 1994.

González, Emilio. "La lucha de clases y la política en el Puerto Rico de la década del '40: El Ascenso del PPD." *Revista de Ciencias Sociales* 22 (March–June 1980): 35–67.

González, Gilbert G., Rual Fernández, Vivian Price, David Smith, and Linda Trinh Vo. *Labor versus Empire: Race, Gender, and Migration.* New York: Routledge, 2004.

González García, Lydia Milagros. "La industria de la aguja de Puerto Rico y sus orígenes en los Estado Unidos." In *Género y trabajo: La industria de la aguja en Puerto Rico y el Caribe hispánico*, edited by María del Carmen Baerga-Santini, 59–82. Río Piedras: Editorial de la Universidad de Puerto Rico, 1993.

———. *Una puntada en el tiempo: La industria de la aguja en Puerto Rico (1900–1929)*. Río Piedras: CEREP, 1990.

González López, Libia M. "Imágenes: Muñoz y el pueblo." In *Luis Muñoz Marín: Imágenes de la memoria*, edited by Fernando Picó, 299–431. Trujillo Alto: Fundación Luis Muñoz Marín, 2008.

———. *Puerto Rico en fotos: La colección menonita, 1940–1950*. San Juan: Fundación Luis Muñoz Marín, 2009.

González Pérez, Cándido. *El programa bracero*. Mexico City: Universidad Autónoma de México, Centro Universitario de Ciencias Sociales y Humanidades, 2010.

González-Rivera, Victoria. *Before the Revolution: Women's Rights and Right-Wing Politics, 1821–1979*. University Park: Penn State University Press, 2011.

———. "Gender, Clientelistic Populism, and Memory: Somocista and Neo-Somocista Women's Narratives in Liberal Nicaragua." In *Gender and Populism in Latin America: Passionate Politics*, edited by Karen Kampwirth, 67–90. University Park: Penn State University Press, 2010.

González-Rivera, Victoria, and Karen Kampwirth, eds. *Radical Women in Latin America: Left and Right*. University Park: Penn State University Press, 2001.

Gordon, Linda. *The Great Arizona Orphan Abduction*. Cambridge, MA: Harvard University Press, 1999.

———. "Internal Colonialism and Gender." In *Haunted by Empire: Geographies of Intimacy in North American History*, edited by Ann Laura Stoler, 427–451. Durham, NC: Duke University Press, 2006.

Gould, Jeffrey L. *To Die in This Way: Nicaraguan Indians and the Myth of Mestizaje, 1880–1965*. Durham, NC: Duke University Press, 1998.

———. *To Lead as Equals: Rural Protest and Political Consciousness in Chinandega, Nicaragua, 1912–1979*. Chapel Hill: University of North Carolina Press, 1990.

Grandin, Greg. *Empire's Workshop: Latin America, the United States, and the Rise of the New Imperialism*. New York: Holt, 2006.

———. "The Instruction of Great Catastrophe: Truth Commissions, National History, and State Formation in Argentina, Chile, and Guatemala." *American Historical Review* 110:2 (February 2005): 46–67.

———. *The Last Colonial Massacre: Latin America in the Cold War*. Chicago: University of Chicago Press, 2004.

Grandin, Greg, and Thomas Klubock, eds. *Truth Commissions: State Terror, History, and Memory*. Brooklyn, NY: Radical History Review, 2007.

Greenbaum, Susan D. *More Than Black: Afro-Cubans in Tampa*. Gainesville: University Press of Florida, 2002.

Greene, Julie. *The Canal Builders: Making America's Empire at the Panama Canal*. New York: Penguin, 2009.

Gregory, Peter. "El desarrollo de la fuerza obrera industrial en Puerto Rico." *Revista de Ciencias Sociales* 2:4 (1958): 447–468.

Grewal, Inderpal, and Caren Kaplan, eds. *Scattered Hegemonies: Postmodernity and Transnational Feminist Practices*. Minneapolis: University of Minnesota Press, 2004.

Grosfoguel, Ramón. *Colonial Subjects: Puerto Ricans in a Global Perspective*. Berkeley: University of California Press, 2003.

Grosfoguel, Ramón, and Héctor Cordero-Guzmán. "International Migration in a Global Context: Recent Approaches to Migration Theory." *Diaspora* 7:3 (1998): 351–368.

Guerra, Lillian. *Popular Expression and National Identity in Puerto Rico: The Struggle for Self, Community, and Nation*. Gainesville: University Press of Florida, 1998.

Gutiérrez, David, ed. *The Columbia History of Latinos in the United States since 1960*. New York: Columbia University Press, 2004.

Gutierrez, Ramón. "What's Love Got to Do with It?" *Journal of American History* 88:3 (December 2001): 866–869.

Gutmann, Matthew, ed. *Changing Men and Masculinities*. Durham, NC: Duke University Press, 2003.

———. *The Meanings of Macho: Being a Man in Mexico City*. Berkeley: University of California Press, 1996.

Guy, Donna. *Women Build the Welfare State: Performing Charity and Creating Rights in Argentina, 1880–1935*. Durham, NC: Duke University Press, 2009.

Guzmán Merced, Rosa. *Las narraciones autobiográficas puertorriqueñas: Invención, confesión, apología, y afectividad*. Hato Rey: Publicaciones Puertorriqueñas, 2000.

Hahamovitch, Cynthia. *The Fruits of Their Labor: Atlantic Coast Farmworkers and the Making of Migrant Poverty, 1875–1945*. Chapel Hill: University of North Carolina Press, 1997.

———. *No Man's Land: Jamaican Guestworkers in America and the Global History of Deportable Labor*. Princeton, NJ: Princeton University Press, 2011.

———. "'The Worst Job in the World': Reform, Revolution, and the Secret Rebellion in Florida's Cane Fields." *Journal of Peasant Studies* 35:4 (2008): 770–800.

Hall, Catherine. "Commentary." In *Haunted by Empire: Geographies of Intimacy in North American History*, edited by Ann Laura Stoler, 452–468. Durham, NC: Duke University Press, 2006.

Hamilton, Carolyn, Verne Harris, Jane Taylor, Michele Pickover, Graeme Reid, and Razia Sheh, eds. *Refiguring the Archive*. Boston: Kluwer, 2002.

Harris, Verne. "A Shaft of Darkness: Derrida in the Archive." In *Refiguring the Archive*, edited by Carolyn Hamilton, Verne Harris, Jane Taylor, Michele Pickover, Graeme Reid, and Razia Sheh, 61–80. Boston: Kluwer, 2002.

Haslip-Viera, Gabriel. "Changed Identities: A Racial Portrait of Two Extended Families, 1909–Present." *CENTRO: Journal of the Center for Puerto Rican Studies* 21:1 (spring 2009): 37–51.

Haslip-Viera, Gabriel, and Sherrie L. Baver, eds. *Latinos in New York: Communities in Transition.* Notre Dame, IN: University of Notre Dame Press, 1996.

Hayes, Patricia, Jeremy Silvester, and Wolfram Hartmann. "'Picturing the Past' in Namibia: The Visual Archive and Its Energies." In *Refiguring the Archive*, edited by Carolyn Hamilton, Verne Harris, Jane Taylor, Michele Pickover, Graeme Reid and Razia Sheh, 103–134. Boston: Kluwer, 2002.

Henley, Ronald L. "Sweet Success . . . the Story of Michigan's Beet Sugar Industry." *Great Lakes Informant Series* 3, no. 4. Michigan Industries, Michigan History Division, Michigan Department of State (1980): 1–6.

Hernández Angueira, Luisa. "El trabajo femenino a domicilio y la industria de la aguja en Puerto Rico, 1914–1940." In *Género y trabajo: La industria de la aguja en Puerto Rico y el Caribe hispánico*, edited by María del Carmen Baerga-Santini, 83–102. Río Piedras: Editorial de la Universidad de Puerto Rico, 1993.

Hirschman, Charles, Philip Kasinitz, and Josh DeWind, eds. *The Handbook of International Migration: The American Experience.* New York: Russell Sage Foundation, 1999.

History Task Force, Centro de Estudios Puertorriqueños. *Labor Migration under Capitalism: The Puerto Rican Experience.* New York: Monthly Review, 1979.

Hoerder, Dirk, and Nora Faires, eds. *Migrants and Migration in Modern North America: Cross-Border Lives, Labor Markets, and Politics.* Durham, NC: Duke University Press, 2011.

Hoffnung-Garskof, Jesse. "Michigan." In *Latino America: A State by State Encyclopedia*, edited by Mark Overmyer-Velásquez, 405–426. Westport, CT: Greenwood, 2008.

———. "The Migrations of Arturo Schomburg: On Being Antillano, Negro, and Puerto Rican in New York, 1891–1938." *Journal of American Ethnic History* 21:1 (fall 2001): 1–49.

———. *A Tale of Two Cities: Santo Domingo and New York after 1950.* Princeton, NJ: Princeton University Press, 2008.

———. "To Abolish the Law of Castes: Merit, Manhood and the Problem of Colour in the Puerto Rican Liberal Movement, 1873–92." *Social History* 36:3 (August 2011): 312–342.

Hoganson, Kristen. "Buying into Empire: American Consumption at the Turn of the Twentieth Century." In *Colonial Crucible: Empire in the Making of the Modern American State*, edited by Alfred W. McCoy and Francisco Scarano, 248–260. Madison: University of Wisconsin Press, 2009.

———. *Consumers' Imperium: The Global Production of American Domesticity, 1865–1920.* Chapel Hill: University of North Carolina Press, 2007.

———. *Fighting for American Manhood: How Gender Politics Provoked the Spanish-American and Philippine-American Wars.* New Haven, CT: Yale University Press, 1998.

Holston, James. *Insurgent Citizenship: Disjunctions of Democracy and Modernity in Brazil.* Princeton, NJ: Princeton University Press, 2008.

Hondagneu-Sotelo, Pierrette. "Families on the Frontier: From Braceros in the Field to Braceras in the Home." In *Latinos: Remaking America*, edited by Marcelo

M. Suárez-Orozco and Mariela Páez, 259–273. Berkeley: University of California Press, 2002.

———, ed. *Gender and U.S. Immigration: Contemporary Trends*. Berkeley: University of California Press, 2003.

Hondagneu-Sotelo, Pierrette, and Ernestine Avila. "'I'm Here but I'm There': The Meanings of Latina Transnational Motherhood." *Gender and Society* 11:5 (October 1997): 548–571.

Hutchison, Elizabeth. *Labors Appropriate to Their Sex: Gender, Labor, and Politics in Urban Chile, 1900–1930*. Durham, NC: Duke University Press, 2001.

Iglesias, César Andreu, ed. *Memoirs of Bernardo Vega: A Contribution to the History of the Puerto Rican Community in New York*. New York: Monthly Review, 1984.

Ignatiev, Noel. *How the Irish Became White*. New York: Routledge, 1995.

Irwin McKee, Robert. *Mexican Masculinities*. Albuquerque: University of New Mexico Press, 2003.

Jacobson, Matthew Frye. *Barbarian Virtues: The United States Encounters Foreign Peoples at Home and Abroad*. New York: Hill and Wang, 2000.

———. *Whiteness of a Different Color: European Immigrants and the Alchemy of Race*. Cambridge, MA: Harvard University Press, 1998.

Jaffe, Rivke, ed. *The Caribbean City*. Kingston, Jamaica: Ian Randle, 2008.

James, Daniel. *Doña María's Story: Life History, Memory, and Political Identity*. Durham, NC: Duke University Press, 2000.

———. *Resistance and Integration: Peronism and the Argentine Working Class, 1946–1976*. Cambridge: Oxford University Press, 1988.

Jiménez, Félix. *Las prácticas de la carne: Construcción y representación de las masculinidades puertorriqueñas*. San Juan: Ediciones Vértigo, 2004.

Jiménez Muñoz, Gladys M. "¡Xiomara mi hermana! Diplo y el travestismo racial en el Puerto rico de los años cincuenta." *Bordes* 2 (1995).

Jiménez Román, Miriam, and Juan Flores, eds. *The Afro-Latin@ Reader: History and Culture in the United States*. Durham, NC: Duke University Press, 2010.

Jiménez Wagenheim, Olga. "From Aguada to Dover: Puerto Ricans Rebuild Their World in Morris County, New Jersey, 1948–2000." In *The Puerto Rican Diaspora: Historical Perspectives*, edited by Carmen Theresa Whalen and Victor Vásquez-Hernández, 106–127. Philadelphia: Temple University Press, 2005.

Joseph, Gilbert M., ed., *Reclaiming the Political in Latin American History: Essays from the North*. Durham, NC: Duke University Press, 2001.

———. "What We Now Know and What We Should Know: Bring Latin America More Meaningfully into Cold War Studies." In *In from the Cold: Latin America's New Encounter with the Cold War*, edited by Gilbert M. Joseph and Daniela Spenser, 3–46. Durham, NC: Duke University Press, 2008.

Joseph, Gilbert M., Catherine C. LeGrand, and Ricardo D. Salvatore, eds. *Close Encounters of Empire: Writing the Cultural History of U.S.-Latin American Relations*. Durham, NC: Duke University Press, 1998.

Joseph, Gilbert M., Anne Rubenstein, and Eric Zolov, eds. *Fragments of a Golden Age: The Politics of Culture in Mexico since 1940*. Durham, NC: Duke University Press, 2001.

Joseph, Gilbert M., and Daniela Spenser, eds. *In from the Cold: Latin America's New Encounter with the Cold War*. Durham, NC: Duke University Press, 2008.

Kampwirth, Karen, ed. *Gender and Populism in Latin America: Passionate Politics*. University Park: Penn State University Press, 2010.

Karush, Matthew, and Oscar Chamosa, eds. *The New Cultural History of Peronism: Power and Identity in Mid-Twentieth-Century Argentina*. Durham, NC: Duke University Press, 2010.

Katzman, Laura, and Beverly W. Brannan. *Re-viewing Documentary: The Photographic Life of Louise Rosskam*. Washington, DC: American University Museum, 2011.

Kaufman, Alejandro. *La pregunta por lo acontecido: Ensayos de anamnesis en el presente argentino*. Avellaneda, Buenos Aires: La Cebra, 2012.

Kerber, Linda K. "The Stateless as the Citizen's Other: A View from the United States." *American Historical Review* (February 2007): 1–33.

Kiddle, Amelia, and María L. O. Muñoz, eds. *Populism in Twentieth-Century Mexico: The Presidencies of Lázaro Cárdenas and Luis Echevarría*. Tucson: University of Arizona Press, 2010.

Klubock, Thomas Miller. *Contested Communities: Class, Gender, and Politics in Chile's El Teniente Copper Mine, 1904–1951*. Durham, NC: Duke University Press, 1998.

———. "Nationalism, Race, and the Politics of Imperialism: Workers and North American Capital in the Chilean Copper Industry." In *Reclaiming the Political in Latin American History: Essays from the North*, edited by Gilbert M. Joseph, 231–267. Durham, NC: Duke University Press, 2001.

Kozol, Wendy, and Isabel Hofmeyr. "AHR Conversation: On Transnational History." *American Historical Review* 111:5 (December 2006): 1450–1451.

Kramer, Paul A. *The Blood of Government: Race, Empire, the United States, and the Philippines*. Chapel Hill: University of North Carolina Press, 2006.

———. "Power and Connection: Imperial Histories of the United States in the World." *American Historical Review* 116:5 (December 2011): 1348–1393.

———. "Race, Empire, and Transnational History." In *Colonial Crucible: Empire in the Making of the Modern American State*, edited by Alfred W. McCoy and Francisco Scarano, 199–209. Madison: University of Wisconsin Press, 2009.

Krishnaswamy, Revathi, and John C. Hawley, eds. *The Postcolonial and the Global*. Minneapolis: University of Minnesota Press, 2008.

Laclau, Ernesto. *On Populist Reason*. London: Verso, 2005.

———. "Populism: What's in a Name?" In *Populism and the Mirror of Democracy*, edited by Francisco Panizza, 32–49. London: Verso, 2005.

Lao, Agustín. "Islands at the Crossroads: Puerto Ricanness Travelling between the Translocal Nation and the Global City." In *Puerto Rican Jam: Rethinking Colonialism and Nationalism*, edited by Frances Negrón-Muntaner and Ramón Grosfoguel, 169–188. Minneapolis: University of Minnesota Press, 1996.

Laó-Montes, Agustín, and Arlene Dávila, eds. *Mambo Montage: The Latinization of New York*. New York: Columbia University Press, 2001.

Lapp, Michael. "Managing Migration: The Migration Division of Puerto Rico and Puerto Ricans in New York City, 1948–1968." PhD diss., Johns Hopkins University, 1990.

Lauria-Perricelli, Antonio. "A Study in Historical and Critical Anthropology: The Making of 'The People of Puerto Rico.'" PhD diss., New School for Social Research, 1989.

Lazo, Rodrigo. "Migrant Archives: New Routes in and out of American Studies." In *States of Emergency: The Object of American Studies*, edited by Russ Castronovo and Susan Gillman, 36–54. Chapel Hill: University of North Carolina Press, 2009.

Levine, Philippa, ed. *Gender and Empire*. Oxford: Oxford University Press, 2004.

Lewis, Oscar. *La Vida: A Puerto Rican Family in the Culture of Poverty—San Juan and New York*. New York: Vintage, 1968.

Lomnitz, Claudio. "Modes of Citizenship in Mexico." In *Alternative Modernities*, edited by Dilip Parameshwar Gaonkar, 299–326. Durham, NC: Duke University Press, 2001.

López, Madeleine E. "Investigating the Investigators: An Analysis of *The Puerto Rican Study*." *CENTRO: Journal of the Center for Puerto Rican Studies* 19:2 (fall 2007): 60–85.

Love, Eric T. L. *Race over Empire: Racism and U.S. Imperialism, 1865–1900*. Chapel Hill: University of North Carolina Press, 2004.

Loveman, Mara. "The U.S. Census and the Contested Rules of Racial Classification in Early Twentieth-Century Puerto Rico." *Caribbean Studies* 35:2 (2007): 79–114.

Loveman, Mara, and Jerónimo O. Muñiz. "How Puerto Rico Became White: Boundary Dynamics and Inter-census Racial Reclassification." *American Sociological Review* 72 (2007): 915–939.

Lowe, Lisa. "Work, Immigration, Gender: New Subjects of Cultural Politics." In *The Politics of Culture in the Shadow of Capital*, edited by Lisa Lowe and David Lloyd, 354–374. Durham, NC: Duke University Press, 1997.

Loza, Mireya. "Braceros on the Boundaries: Activism, Race, Masculinity, and the Legacies of the Bracero Program." PhD diss., Brown University, 2010.

Lugo Ortiz, Lourdes de María. "Sterilization, Birth Control, and Population Control: News Coverage of 'El Mundo,' 'El Imparcial,' and 'Claridad.'" PhD diss., University of Wisconsin–Madison, 1994.

Luibhéid, Eithne, and Robert Buffington. "Gender, Sexuality, and Mexican Migration." In *Beyond la Frontera: The History of Mexico-U.S. Migration*, edited by Mark Overmyer-Velázquez, 204–226. New York: Oxford University Press, 2011.

Luna, Lola. "Populismo, nacionalismo, y maternalismo: Casos peronista y gaitanista." *Boletín Americanista* 50:1 (2000): 189–200.

Luque de Sánchez, María Dolores. "El Desarrollo de los Archivos Históricos de Puerto Rico." Paper presented at "Os Arquivos Insulares," conference sponsored by the Secretaria Regional da Educação e Recursos Humanos, Madeira. Conference proceedings available at http://www.madeira-edu.pt/Portals/31/CEHA/ bdigital/ai1_002.pdf, accessed March 17, 2014.

———. "'La buena vida o la vida buena': Muñoz Marín ante la industrialización y el consumismo en Puerto Rico, 1948–1974." In *Luis Muñoz Marín: Imágenes de la memoria*, edited by Fernando Picó, 219–257. Trujillo Alto: Fundación Luis Muñoz Marín, 2008.

MacPherson, Anne. "Toward Decolonization: Impulses, Presses, and Consequences since the 1930s." In *The Caribbean: A History of the Region and Its Peoples*, edited by Stephan Palmié and Francisco Scarano, 475–490. Chicago: University of Chicago Press, 2011.

Mahar, Thomas. *Sweet Energy: The Story of Monitor Sugar Company.* Bay City, MI: Monitor Sugar, 2000.

Maldonado, A. W. *Luis Muñoz Marín: Puerto Rico's Democratic Revolution.* San Juan: Universidad de Puerto Rico, 2009.

———. *Teodoro Moscoso and Puerto Rico's Operation Bootstrap.* Gainesville: University Press of Florida, 1997.

Maldonado-Denis, Manuel. *The Emigration Dialectic: Puerto Rico and the USA.* New York: International, 1980.

Mallon, Florencia E. "Barbudos, Warriors, and Rotos: The MIR, Masculinity, and Power in the Chilean Agrarian Reform, 1965–1974." In *Changing Men and Masculinities*, edited by Matthew Gutmann, 179–215. Durham, NC: Duke University Press, 2003.

Mapes, Kathleen. *Sweet Tyranny: Migrant Labor, Industrial Agriculture, and Imperial Politics.* Urbana: University of Illinois Press, 2009.

Marsh Kennerley, Catherine. *Negociaciones culturales: Los intelectuales y el proyecto pedagógico del estado muñocista.* Rio Piedras: Ediciones Callejón, 2009.

Martínez-Fernández, Luis. "The Rise of the American Mediterranean." In *The Caribbean: A History of the Region and Its Peoples*, edited by Stephan Palmié and Francisco Scarano, 373–384. Chicago: University of Chicago Press, 2011.

Martínez-San Miguel, Yolanda. *Caribe Two Ways: Cultura de la migración en el Caribe insular hispánico.* Río Piedras: Ediciones Callejón, 2003.

Matos-Rodríguez, Félix V., ed. *A Nation of Women: An Early Feminist Speaks Out.* Houston: Arte Público Press, 2004.

———. "Saving the Parcela: A Short History of Boston's Puerto Rican Community." In *The Puerto Rican Diaspora: Historical Perspectives*, edited by Carmen Theresa Whalen and Victor Vásquez-Hernández, 200–227. Philadelphia: Temple University Press, 2005.

Matos-Rodríguez, Félix V., and Linda Delgado, eds. *Puerto Rican Women's History: New Perspectives.* Armonk, NY: M. E. Sharpe, 1998.

May, Elaine Tyler. *Homeward Bound: American Families in the Cold War Era.* New York: Basic Books, 1988.

Mbembe, Achille. "The Power of the Archive and Its Limits." In *Refiguring the Archive*, edited by Carolyn Hamilton, Verne Harris, Jane Taylor, Michele Pickover, Graeme Reid, and Razia Sheh, 18–26. Boston: Kluwer, 2002.

McCormick, Jennifer, and César J. Ayala. "Felícita 'La Prieta' Méndez (1916–1998) and the End of Latino School Segregation in California." CENTRO: Journal of the Center for Puerto Rican Studies 19:2 (fall 2007): 12–32.

McCoy, Alfred W., and Francisco A. Scarano, eds. Colonial Crucible: Empire in the Making of the American State. Madison: University of Wisconsin Press, 2009.

McCoy, Alfred W., Francisco A. Scarano, and Courtney Johnson. "On the Tropic of Cancer: Transitions and Transformations in the U.S. Imperial State." In Colonial Crucible: Empire in the Making of the Modern American State, edited by Alfred W. McCoy and Francisco Scarano, 3–33. Madison: University of Wisconsin Press, 2009.

McKeown, Adam M. Melancholy Order: Asian Migration and the Globalization of Borders. New York: Columbia University Press, 2008.

McNamara, Patrick. Sons of the Sierra: Juárez, Díaz, and the People of Ixtlán, Oaxaca, 1855–1920. Chapel Hill: University of North Carolina Press, 2007.

McPherson, Alan. "The Irony of Legal Pluralism in U.S. Occupations." American Historical Review 117:4 (October 2012): 1149–1172.

———. "Rioting for Dignity: Masculinity, National Identity, and Anti-U.S. Resistance in Panama." Gender and History 19:2 (August 2007): 219–241.

Meléndez, Edgardo. "Citizenship and the Alien Exclusion in the Insular Cases: Puerto Ricans in the Periphery of American Empire." CENTRO: Journal of the Center for Puerto Rican Studies 25:1 (spring 2013): 106–145.

———. "Vito Marcantonio, Puerto Rican Migration, and the 1949 Mayoral Election in New York City." CENTRO: Journal of the Center for Puerto Rican Studies 22:2 (fall 2010): 198–232.

Meléndez Vélez, Edgardo. "The Puerto Rican Journey Revisited: Politics and the Study of Puerto Rican Migration." CENTRO: Journal of the Center for Puerto Rican Studies 17:2 (fall 2005): 192–221.

Meyer, Gerald. Vito Marcantonio, Radical Politician, 1902–1954. Albany: State University of New York Press, 1989.

Michel, Sonya. "Doing Well by Doing Good: American Women's Long Tradition of Reform." Paper presented at the Woodrow Wilson International Center for Scholars, Washington, DC, May 16, 2012.

Mignolo, Walter. Local Histories / Global Designs: Coloniality, Subaltern Knowledges, and Border Thinking. Princeton, NJ: Princeton University Press, 2000.

Milanesio, Natalia. Workers Go Shopping in Argentina: The Rise of Popular Consumer Culture. Albuquerque, NM: University of New Mexico Press, 2013.

Milanich, Nara B. Children of Fate: Childhood, Class, and the State in Chile, 1850–1930. Durham, NC: Duke University Press, 2009.

Millard, Ann V., and Jorge Chapa. Apple Pie and Enchiladas: Latino Newcomers in the Rural Midwest. Austin: University of Texas Press, 2004.

Milligan, Jennifer S. "'What Is an Archive?' in the History of Modern France." In Archive Stories: Facts, Fictions, and the Writing of History, edited by Antoinette Burton, 159–183. Durham, NC: Duke University Press, 2005.

Mills, C. Wright, Clarence Senior, and Rose Kohn Goldsen. *The Puerto Rican Journey: New York's Newest Migrants.* New York: Russell and Russell, 1950.

Mintz, Sidney. "Cañamelar: The Subculture of a Rural Sugar Plantation Proletariat." In *The People of Puerto Rico: A Study in Social Anthropology,* edited by Julian Steward. Urbana: University of Illinois Press, 1956.

———. *Three Ancient Colonies: Caribbean Themes and Variations.* Cambridge, MA: Harvard University Press, 2010.

———. *Worker in the Cane: A Puerto Rican Life Story.* New York: Norton, 1974.

Mohr, Nicholasa. "Puerto Rican Writers in the United States, Puerto Rican Writers in Puerto Rico: A Separation beyond Language." In *Barrios and Borderlands,* edited by Denis Lynn Daly Heyck, 264–269. New York: Routledge, 1994.

Moon, Yumi. "Immoral Rights: Korean Populist Collaborators and the Japanese Colonization of Korea, 1904–1910." *American Historical Review* 118:1 (February 2013): 20–44.

Morrissey, Marietta. "The Making of a Colonial Welfare State: U.S. Social Insurance and Public Assistance in Puerto Rico." *Latin American Perspectives* 33:1 (January 2006): 23–41.

Muñiz-Mas, Félix O. "Gender, Work, and Institutional Change in the Early Stage of Industrialization: The Case of the Women's Bureau and the Home Needlework Industry in Puerto Rico, 1940–1952." In *Puerto Rican Women's History: New Perspectives,* edited by Félix V. Matos-Rodriguez and Linda Delgado, 181–205. Armonk, NY: M. E. Sharpe, 1998.

Muñoz Marín, Luis. *Historia del Partido Popular Democrático.* San Juan: Editorial El Batey, 1984.

———. *Palabras: Luis Muñoz Marín, 1936–1940.* Trujillo Alto: Fundación Luis Muñoz Marín, 1980.

———. *Palabras de Luis Muñoz Marín,* vol. 3, *1941–1944.* Trujillo Alto: Fundación Luis Muñoz Marín, 2005.

———. *Palabras de Luis Muñoz Marín,* vol. 4, *1945–1948.* Trujillo Alto: Fundación Luis Muñoz Marín, 2005.

Nazario Velasco, Rubén. "Pan, casa, libertad: De la reforma agraria a la especulación inmobilaria." In *Luis Muñoz Marín: Perfiles de su gobernación,* edited by Fernando Picó, 145–164. Trujillo Alto: Fundación Luis Muñoz Marín, 2003.

Negrón-Muntaner, Frances, ed. *Boricua Pop: Puerto Ricans and the Latinization of American Culture.* New York: New York University Press, 2004.

———. *None of the Above: Puerto Ricans in the Global Era.* New York: Palgrave, 2007.

Negrón-Muntaner, Frances, and Ramón Grosfoguel, eds. *Puerto Rican Jam: Rethinking Colonialism and Nationalism.* Minneapolis: University of Minnesota Press, 1996.

Negrón Portillo, Mariano. *El Autonomismo puertorriqueño: Su transformación ideológica (1895–1914).* Río Piedras: Ediciones Huracán, 1981.

———. *Las turbas republicanas, 1900–1904.* Río Piedras: Ediciones Huracán, 1990.

————. "Puerto Rico: Surviving Colonialism and Nationalism." In *Puerto Rican Jam: Rethinking Colonialism and Nationalism*, edited by Frances Negrón-Muntaner and Ramón Grosfoguel, 39–56. Minneapolis: University of Minnesota Press, 1996.

Ngai, Mae M. *Impossible Subjects: Illegal Aliens and the Making of Modern America*. Princeton, NJ: Princeton University Press, 2004.

Nieves Falcón, Luís. *Los emigrantes puertorriqueños*. Río Piedras: Editorial Edil, 1975.

Norris, Jim. *North for the Harvest: Mexican Workers, Growers, and the Sugar Beet Industry*. Saint Paul: Minnesota Historical Society, 2009.

Ober, Frederick. *Puerto Rico and Its Resources*. New York: D. Appleton, 1898.

Oberdeck, Kathryn J. "Archives of the Unbuilt Environment: Documents and Discourses of Imagined Space in Twentieth-Century Kohler, Wisconsin." In *Archive Stories: Facts, Fictions, and the Writing of History*, edited by Antoinette Burton, 251–273. Durham, NC: Duke University Press, 2005.

Oboler, Suzanne, ed. *Latinos and Citizenship: The Dilemma of Belonging*. New York: Palgrave Macmillan, 2006.

Okihiro, Gary Y. "Colonial Vision, Racial Visibility: Racializations in Puerto Rico and the Philippines during the Initial Period of U.S. Colonization." In *Racial Transformations: Latinos and Asians Remaking the United States*, edited by Nicholas De Genova, 23–40. Durham, NC: Duke University Press, 2006.

Olcott, Jocelyn. "The Politics of Opportunity: Mexican Populism under Lázaro Cárdenas and Luis Echevarría." In *Gender and Populism in Latin America: Passionate Politics*, edited by Karen Kampwirth, 25–46. University Park: Penn State University Press, 2010.

————. *Revolutionary Women in Postrevolutionary Mexico*. Durham, NC: Duke University Press, 2005.

Olcott, Jocelyn, Mary Kay Vaughan, and Gabriela Cano, eds. *Sex in Revolution: Gender, Politics, and Power in Modern Mexico*. Durham, NC: Duke University Press, 2006.

Orozco, Cynthia. *No Mexicans, Women, or Dogs Allowed: The Rise of the Mexican-American Civil Rights Movement*. Austin: University of Texas Press, 2009.

Ortiz, Altagracia. "'En la aguja y el pedal eché la hiel': Puerto Rican Women in the Garment Industry of New York City, 1920–1980." In *Puerto Rican Women and Work: Bridges in Transnational Labor*, edited by Altagracia Ortiz, 55–82. Philadelphia: Temple University Press, 1996.

————, ed. *Puerto Rican Women and Work: Bridges in Transnational Labor*. Philadelphia: Temple University Press, 1996.

————. "Puerto Rican Women Workers in the Twentieth Century: A Historical Appraisal of the Literature." In *Puerto Rican Women's History: New Perspectives*, edited by Félix V. Matos-Rodriguez and Linda Delgado, 38–61. Armonk, NY: M. E. Sharpe, 1998.

Ostman, Ronald E., Royal D. Colle, and Vivian Franco. *Advocating Women's Rights in Literature and Film: Gender and the Puerto Rican Family*. Working Paper Series, Cornell

University, Population and Development Program 94.10. Ithaca, NY: Department of Rural Sociology, Cornell University, 1994.

Overmyer-Velásquez, Mark, ed. *Beyond la Frontera: The History of Mexico-U.S. Migration*. New York: Oxford University Press, 2011.

———. "Histories and Historiographies of Greater Mexico." In *Beyond la Frontera: The History of Mexico-U.S. Migration*, xxiv–xxviii. New York: Oxford University Press, 2011.

———, ed. *Latino America: A State by State Encyclopedia*. 2 vols. Westport, CT: Greenwood, 2008.

———. "Transforming Race and Nation: New Trends in Latin(o) American Migration." *Latin American Perspectives* 35:6 (2008): 196–205.

Pabón, Carlos, ed. *El pasado ya no es lo que era: La historia en tiempos de incertidumbre*. San Juan: Ediciones Vértigo, 2005.

———. *Nación postmortem: Ensayos sobre los tiempos de insoportable ambigüedad*. San Juan: Ediciones Callejón, 2002.

Padilla, Elena. "Puerto Rican Immigrants in New York and Chicago: A Study in Comparative Assimilation." MA thesis., University of Chicago, 1947.

Palmié, Stephan, and Francisco Scarano, eds. *The Caribbean: A History of the Region and Its Peoples*. Chicago: University of Chicago Press, 2011.

Panizza, Francisco, ed. *Populism and the Mirror of Democracy*. London: Verso, 2005.

Pantojas-García, Emilio. *Development Strategies as Ideology: Puerto Rico's Export-Led Industrialization Experience*. Boulder, CO: Lynne Rienner, 1990.

———. "Puerto Rican Populism Revisited: The PPD during the 1940s." *Journal of Latin American Studies* 21 (1989): 521–557.

Peck, Gunther. "Reinventing Free Labor: Immigrant Padrones and Contract Laborers in North America, 1885–1925." In *American Dreaming, Global Realities: Rethinking U.S. Immigration History*, edited by Donna Gabaccia and Vicki Ruiz, 263–284. Urbana: University of Illinois Press, 2006.

Pérez, Gina. *The Near Northwest Side Story: Migration, Displacement, and Puerto Rican Families*. Berkeley: University of California Press, 2004.

Pérez, Louis A., Jr. *Cuba in the American Imagination: Metaphor and the Imperial Ethos*. Chapel Hill: University of North Carolina Press, 2008.

———. *On Becoming Cuba: Identity, Nationality, and Culture*. Chapel Hill: University of North Carolina Press, 1999.

Perloff, Harvey S. *Puerto Rico's Economic Future*. Chicago: University of Chicago Press, 1949.

Pessar, Patricia, and Sarah J. Mahler. "Transnational Migration: Bringing Gender In." *International Migration Review* 37:3 (2003): 812–846.

Piccato, Pablo. *The Tyranny of Opinion: Honor in the Construction of the Mexican Public Sphere*. Durham, NC: Duke University Press, 2010.

Picó, Fernando. *Amargo Café (los pequeños y medianos caficultores de Utuado en la segunda mitad del siglo XIX)*. Río Piedras: Ediciones Huracán, 1981.

————. *Cayeyanos: Familias y solidaridades en la historia de Cayey*. Río Piedras: Ediciones Huracán, 2007.

————. *1898: La guerra despúes de la guerra*. Río Piedras: Ediciones Huracán, 1987.

————. *Libertad y servidumbre en el Puerto Rico del siglo XIX*. Río Piedras: Ediciones Huracán, 1983.

————, ed. *Luis Muñoz Marín: Ensayos del centenario*. Trujillo Alto: Fundación Luis Muñoz Marín, 1999.

————, ed. *Luis Muñoz Marín: Imágenes de la memoria*. Trujillo Alto: Fundación Luis Muñoz Marín, 2008.

————, ed. *Luis Muñoz Marín: Perfiles de su gobernación*. Trujillo Alto: Fundación Luis Muñoz Marín, 2003.

————. *Puerto Rico Remembered, Recuerdos de Puerto Rico: Photographs from the Collection of Tom Lehman*. San Diego: Thunder Bay Press, 2010.

————. *Vivir en Caimito*. Río Piedras: Ediciones Huracán, 1988.

Pieper Mooney, Jadwiga. *The Politics of Motherhood: Maternity and Women's Rights in Twentieth-Century Chile*. Pittsburgh: University of Pittsburgh Press, 2009.

Piker, Joshua. "Lying Together: The Imperial Implications of Cross-Cultural Untruths." *American Historical Review* 116:4 (October 2011): 964–968.

Pitti, Stephen J. "Chicano Cold Warriors: César Chávez, Mexican American Politics, and California Farmworkers." In *In from the Cold: Latin America's New Encounter with the Cold War*, edited by Gilbert M. Joseph and Daniela Spenser, 273–307. Durham, NC: Duke University Press, 2008.

————. *The Devil in Silicon Valley: Northern California, Race, and Mexican-Americans*. Princeton, NJ: Princeton University Press, 2003.

Plummer, Brenda Gayle. "Building U.S. Hegemony in the Caribbean." In *The Caribbean: A History of the Region and Its Peoples*, edited by Stephan Palmié and Francisco Scarano, 417–432. Chicago: University of Chicago Press, 2011.

Puerto Rico Housing Authority. *Housing Progress in Puerto Rico, 1938–1948*. San Juan: Puerto Rican Housing Authority, 1948.

Putnam, Lara. *Radical Moves: Caribbean Migrants and the Politics of Race in the Jazz Age*. Chapel Hill: University of North Carolina Press, 2013.

————. "To Study the Fragments/Whole: Microhistory and the Atlantic World." *Journal of Social History* 39:3 (spring 2006): 615–630.

Quintero Rivera, Angel G. *Conflictos de clase y política en Puerto Rico*. Río Piedras: Ediciones Huracán, 1976.

————. *Cuerpo y cultura: Las músicas "mulatas" y la subversión del baile*. Madrid: Iberoamericana, 2009.

————. "La ideología populista y la institucionalización universitaria de las ciencias sociales." In *Del nacionalismo al populismo: Cultura y política en Puerto Rico*, edited by Silvia Álvarez-Curbelo and María Elena Rodríguez Castro, 107–145. Río Piedras: Ediciones Huracán, 1993.

———. *Patricios y plebeyos: Burgueses, hacendados, artesanos y obreros: Las relaciones de clase en el Puerto Rico de cambio de siglo*. Río Piedras: Ediciones Huracán, 1988.

———. *Salsa, sabor, y control: Sociología de una música tropical*. Madrid: Siglo XXI, 1998.

Rafael, Vicente. *White Love and Other Events in Filipino History*. Durham, NC: Duke University Press, 2000.

Ramírez, Catherine S. *The Woman in the Zoot Suit: Gender, Nationalism, and the Cultural Politics of Memory*. Durham, NC: Duke University Press, 2009.

Ramírez, Rafael. *El arrabal y la política*. Río Piedras: Editorial Universitaria, 1977.

———. "Masculinity and Power in Puerto Rico." In *The Culture of Gender and Sexuality in the Caribbean*, edited by Linden Lewis, 234–250. Gainesville: University Press of Florida, 2003.

———. *What It Means to Be a Man: Reflections on Puerto Rican Masculinity*, translated by Rosa E. Casper. New Brunswick, NJ: Rutgers University Press, 1999.

Ramírez, Rafael, Victor García Toro, and Luis Solano Castillo. *Los hombres no lloran: Ensayos sobre las masculinidades*. San Juan: Ediciones Huracán, 2007.

Ramírez de Arellano, Annette B., and Conrad Seipp. *Colonialism, Catholicism, and Contraception: A History of Birth Control in Puerto Rico*. Chapel Hill: University of North Carolina Press, 1983.

Ramos, Julio. *Amor y anarquía: Los escritos de Luisa Capetillo*. Río Piedras: Ediciones Huracán, 1992.

Ramos, María E. *La muerte de un gigante: Historia de la Central Guánica y el poblado de Enseñada*. San Juan: Editorial Plaza Mayor, 1999.

Ramos Mattei, Andrés, ed. *Azúcar y esclavitud*. Río Piedras: Universidad de Puerto Rico, 1982.

———. *La hacienda azucarera: Su crecimiento y crisis en Puerto Rico (Siglo XIX)*. Río Piedras: CEREP, 1986.

———. *La sociedad del azúcar en Puerto Rico: 1870–1920*. Río Piedras: Universidad de Puerto Rico, 1988.

Ramos Rosado, Marie. *La mujer negra en la literatura puertorriqueña*. Río Piedras: Editorial de la Universidad de Puerto Rico, 1989.

Ramos-Zayas, Ana Y. "Delinquent Citizenship, National Performances: Racialization, Surveillance, and the Politics of 'Worthiness' in Puerto Rican Chicago." In *Latinos and Citizenship: The Dilemma of Belonging*, edited by Suzanne Oboler, 275–300. New York: Palgrave Macmillan, 2006.

———. "Gendering 'Latino Public Intellectuals': Personal Narratives in the Ethnography of Elena Padilla." In *Latino Urban Ethnography and the Work of Elena Padilla*, edited by Mérida M. Rúa, 178–205. Urbana: University of Illinois Press, 2010.

———. *National Performances: The Politics of Class, Race, and Space in Puerto Rican Chicago*. Chicago: University of Chicago Press, 2003.

Rapport, Nigel, and Andrew Dawson, eds. *Migrations of Identity: Perceptions of Home in a World of Movement*. London: Berg, 1988.

Renda, Mary. "'Sentiments of a Private Nature': A Comment on Ann Laura Stoler's 'Tense and Tender Ties.'" *Journal of American History* 88:3 (December 2001): 882–887.

Richards, Thomas. *The Imperial Archive: Knowledge and the Fantasy of Empire*. London: Verso, 1993.

Rivera, Edward. *Family Installments: Memories of Growing Up Hispanic*. New York: Penguin, 1982.

Rivera, Eugenio. "La colonia de Lorain, Ohio." In *The Puerto Rican Diaspora: Historical Perspectives*, edited by Carmen Theresa Whalen and Victor Vásquez-Hernández, 151–173. Philadelphia: Temple University Press, 2005.

Rivera, Raquel. *New York Ricans from the Hip-Hop Zone*. New York: Palgrave, 2003.

Rivera González, José Antonio. "Género y proceso democrático: Las películas de DIVEDCO, 1950–1970." PhD diss., Universidad de Puerto Rico, 2003.

Rivera Medina, Eduardo, and Rafael L. Ramírez, eds. *Del cañaveral a la fábrica*. Río Piedras: Huracán-Academia, 1985.

Rivera Ramos, Efren. *The Legal Construction of Identity: The Judicial and Social Legacy of American Colonialism in Puerto Rico*. Washington, DC: American Psychological Association, 2001.

Rivera-Rideau, Petra R. "Cocolos Modernos: Salsa, Reggaetón, and Puerto Rico's Cultural Politics of Blackness." *Latin American and Caribbean Ethnic Studies* 8:1 (March 2013): 1–19.

Roberts, Lydia J., and Rosa Luisa Stefani, eds. *Patterns of Living in Puerto Rican Families*. Río Piedras: University of Puerto Rico, 1949.

Rodríguez, Luz Marie. "Suppressing the Slum! Architecture and Social Change in San Juan's Public Housing." In *San Juan Siempre Nuevo: Arquitectura y Modernización en el Siglo XX*, edited by Enrique Vivoni Falagio. Río Piedras: Archivo de Arquitectura y Construcción Universidad de Puerto Rico, 2000.

Rodríguez, Manuel R. *A New Deal for the Tropics: Puerto Rico during the Depression Era, 1932–1935*. Princeton, NJ: Marcus Weiner, 2011.

Rodríguez, Marc Simon. *The Tejano Diaspora: Mexican Americanism and Ethnic Politics in Texas and Wisconsin*. Chapel Hill: University of North Carolina Press, 2011.

Rodríguez Baruff, Jorge. "La pugna entre dos grandes sistemas: La guerra en ele discurso político de Luis Muñoz Marín hasta Pearl Harbor." In *Luis Muñoz Marín: Ensayos del centenario*, edited by Fernando Picó, 126–152. Trujillo Alto: Fundación Luis Muñoz Marín, 1999.

Rodríguez Castro, María Elena. "Foro de 1940: Las pasiones y los intereses se dan la mano." In *Del nacionalismo al populismo: Cultura y política en Puerto Rico*, edited by Silvia Álvarez-Curbelo and María Elena Rodríguez Castro, 61–105. Río Piedras: Ediciones Huracán, 1993.

Rodríguez Domínguez, Victor M. *Latino Politics in the United States: Race, Ethnicity, Class, and Gender in the Mexican American and Puerto Rican Experience*. Dubuque, IA: Kendall/Hunt, 2005.

————. "The Racialization of Mexican Americans and Puerto Ricans, 1890s–1930s." *CENTRO: Journal of the Center for Puerto Rican Studies* 17:1 (spring 2005): 70–105.

Rodríguez Juliá, Edgardo. *El entierro de Cortijo*. Río Piedras: Ediciones Huracán, 1983.

————. *Las tribulaciones de Jonás*. Río Piedras: Ediciones Huracán, 1981.

————. *Puertorriqueños: Album de la sagrada familia puertorriqueña a partir de 1898*. Madrid: Editorial Playor, 1988.

Rodríguez-Silva, Ileana M. *Silencing Race: Disentangling Blackness, Colonialism, and National Identities in Puerto Rico*. New York: Palgrave Macmillan, 2012.

Roediger, David. *The Wages of Whiteness: Race and the Making of the American Working Class*. London: Verso, 1991.

————. *Working toward Whiteness: How America's Immigrants Became White; the Strange Journey from Ellis Island to the Suburbs*. New York: Basic Books, 2005.

Ros, Ana. *The Post-dictatorship Generation in Argentina, Chile, and Uruguay: Collective Memory and Cultural Production*. New York: Palgrave Macmillan, 2012.

Rosario Natal, Carmelo. "Muñoz y Albizu: El choque en la víspera de la insurrección, 1947–1950." In *Luis Muñoz Marín: Perfiles de su gobernación*, edited by Fernando Picó, 309–341. Trujillo Alto: Fundación Luis Muñoz Marín, 2003.

Rosario Urrutia, Mayra. "'La tentación de la suerte: Criminalización y representaciones del castigo a las boliteras, 1948–1960." *Op. Cit.* 14 (2002): 147–186.

————. "'Mogollas, entendidos y malas mañas': La regeneración del partido político en el discurso muñocista, 1938–1948." In *Luis Muñoz Marín: Ensayos del centenario*, edited by Fernando Picó, 208–232. Trujillo Alto: Fundación Luis Muñoz Marín, 1999.

Rosario Urrutia, Mayra, and María Margarita Flores. "El reclamo de una adolescente al derecho femenino a la educación, 1937–1941: Entrevista a Henrietta Orlandi." *Op. Cit.* 14 (2002): 303–332.

Rosas, Ana Elizabeth. "Breaking the Silence: Mexican Children and Women's Confrontation of *Bracero* Family Separation." *Gender and History* 23:2 (August 2011): 382–400.

————. "Flexible Families: Bracero Families' Lives across Cultures, Communities, and Countries, 1942–1965." PhD diss., University of Southern California, 2006.

Rosemblatt, Karin Alejandra. *Gendered Compromises: Political Cultures and the State in Chile, 1920–1950*. Chapel Hill: University of North Carolina Press, 2000.

Roy-Féquiére, Magali. *Women, Creole Identity, and Intellectual Life in Early Twentieth-Century Puerto Rico*. Philadelphia: Temple University Press, 2004.

Rúa, Mérida M. "Footnotes of Social Justice: Elena Padilla and Chicago Puerto Rican Communities." In *Latino Urban Ethnography and the Work of Elena Padilla*, edited by Mérida M. Rúa, 128–139. Urbana: University of Illinois Press, 2010.

————. *Grounded Identidades: Making New Lives in Chicago's Puerto Rican Neighborhoods*. New York: Oxford University Press, 2012.

————, ed. *Latino Urban Ethnography and the Work of Elena Padilla*. Urbana: University of Illinois Press, 2010.

Ruiz, Vicki L., and John R. Chávez. *Memories and Migrations: Mapping Boricua and Chicana Histories*. Urbana: University of Illinois Press, 2008.

Safa, Helen Icken. "Changing Forms of U.S. Hegemony: The Impact on the Family and Sexuality." *Urban Anthropology and Studies of Cultural Systems and World Economic Development* 32:1 (spring 2003): 7–40.

———. "Las mujeres y la industrialización en el Caribe: Una comparación de Puerto Rico y la República Dominicana." In *Género y trabajo: La industria de la aguja en Puerto Rico y el Caribe hispánico*, edited by María del Carmen Baerga-Santini, 213–262. Río Piedras: Editorial de la Universidad de Puerto Rico, 1993.

———. *The Myth of the Male Breadwinner: Women and Industrialization in the Caribbean*. Boulder, CO: Westview, 1995.

———. *The Urban Poor of Puerto Rico: A Study in Development and Inequality*. New York: Holt, Rinehart, and Winston, 1974.

Saler, Bethel, and Carolyn Podruchny. "Glass Curtains and Storied Landscapes: The Fur Trade, National Boundaries, and Historians." In *Bridging National Borders in North America: Transnational and Comparative Histories*, edited by Benjamin Johnson and Andrew R. Graybill, 275–302. Durham, NC: Duke University Press, 2010.

Sanabria, Carlos. "Samuel Gompers and the American Federation of Labor in Puerto Rico." *CENTRO: Journal of the Center for Puerto Rican Studies* 17:1 (spring 2005): 140–161.

Sánchez, Efraín. "Posibles efectos de la industrialización rápida sobre la familia puertorriqueña." In *Octava Convención de Orientación Social de Puerto Rico*, n.p. San Juan: Imp. Venezuela, 1954.

Sánchez-Korrol, Virginia. *From Colonia to Community: The History of Puerto Ricans in New York City, 1917–1948*. Westport, CT: Greenwood, 1983.

Sanders, James E. *Contentious Republicans: Popular Politics, Race, and Class in Nineteenth-Century Colombia*. Durham, NC: Duke University Press, 2004.

Sanders, Nicole. *Gender and Welfare in Mexico: The Consolidation of a Post-revolutionary State*. University Park: Penn State University Press, 2011.

Sandoval Sánchez, Alberto. "Puerto Rican Identity up in the Air: Air Migration, Its Cultural Representations, and Me 'Cruzando el Charco.'" In *Puerto Rican Jam: Rethinking Colonialism and Nationalism*, edited by Frances Negrón-Muntaner and Ramón Grosfoguel, 189–208. Minneapolis: University of Minnesota Press, 1996.

Santiago Caraballo, Josefa. "Política colonial: El Partido Popular Democrático y los projectos de reformas políticas." In *Luis Muñoz Marín: Imágenes de la memoria*, edited by Fernando Picó, 62–87. Trujillo Alto: Fundación Luis Muñoz Marín, 2008.

Santiago-Valles, Kelvin A. "Colonialidad, trabajo sexualmente racializado y nuevos circuitos migratorios." In *Contrapunto de género y raza en Puerto Rico*, edited by Idsa Alegría Ortega and Palmira N. Ríos González, 187–214. Río Piedras: Centro de Investigaciones Sociales, 2005.

———. *Subject People and Colonial Discourses: Economic Transformation and Social Disorder in Puerto Rico, 1898–1947*. Albany: State University of New York Press, 1994.

Santiago-Valles, Kelvin A., and Gladys M. Jiménez Muñoz. "Social Polarization and Colonized Labor: Puerto Ricans in the United States, 1945–2000." In *The Columbia History of Latinos in the United States since 1960*, edited by David Gutiérrez, 87–145. New York: Columbia University Press, 2004.

Scarano, Francisco A. *Inmigración y clases sociales en el Puerto Rico del siglo XIX*. Río Piedras: Ediciones Huracán, 1981.

———. "The Jíbaro Masquerade and the Subaltern Politics of Creole Identity Formation, 1745–1823." *American Historical Review* 101:5 (December 1996): 1398–1431.

———. *Puerto Rico: Cinco siglos de historia*. San Juan: McGraw-Hill, 1993.

———. *Sugar and Slavery in Puerto Rico: The Plantation Economy of Ponce, 1800–1850*. Madison: University of Wisconsin Press, 1984.

Scarano, Francisco A., and Alfred W. McCoy. *Colonial Crucible: Empire in the Making of the Modern American State*. Madison: University of Wisconsin Press, 2009.

Schiller, Nina Glick. "Transmigrants and Nation-States: Something Old and Something New in the U.S. Immigration Experience." In *The Handbook of International Migration: The American Experience*, edited by Charles Hirschman, Philip Kasinitz, and Josh DeWind, 94–119. New York: Russell Sage Foundation, 1999.

———. "'Who Are These Guys?': A Transnational Reading of the U.S. Immigrant Experience." In *Identities on the Move: Transnational Processes in North America and the Caribbean Basin*, edited by Liliana R. Goldin, 15–45. Albany, NY: Institute for Mesoamerican Studies, 1999.

Schiller, Nina Glick, Linda Basch, and Cristina Szanton Blanc. "From Immigrant to Transmigrant: Theorizing Transnational Migration." *Anthropological Quarterly* 68:1 (2005): 48–63.

———, eds. *Towards a Transnational Perspective on Migration: Race, Class, Ethnicity, and Nationalism Reconsidered*. New York: New York Academy of Sciences, 1992.

Scott, Rebecca. "The Provincial Archive as a Place of Memory: The Role of Former Slaves in the Cuban War of Independence (1895–98)." *History Workshop Journal* 59:1 (2005): 149–166.

Seda Bonilla, Eduardo. *Social Change and Personality in a Puerto Rican Agrarian Reform Community*. Evansville, IL: Northwestern University Press, 1973.

Seijo Bruno, Miñi. *La Insurrección Nacionalista en Puerto Rico, 1950*. Río Piedras: Editorial Edil, 1989.

Sepúlveda Rivera, Aníbal. "Viejos cañaverales, casas nuevas: Muñoz versus el síndrome Long." In *Luis Muñoz Marín: Perfiles de su gobernación*, edited by Fernando Picó, 167–207. Trujillo Alto: Fundación Luis Muñoz Marín, 2003.

Seveso, César. "Political Emotions and the Origins of the Peronist Resistance." In *The New Cultural History of Peronism: Power and Identity in Mid-Twentieth-Century Argentina*, edited by Matthew Karush and Oscar Chamosa, 239–270. Durham, NC: Duke University Press, 2010.

Shea, Anne. "'Don't Let Them Make You Feel You Did a Crime': Immigration Law, Labor Rights, and Farmworker Testimony." *MELUS* 28:1 (spring 2003): 123–144.

Sheinin, David. "The Caribbean and the Cold War: Between Reform and Revolution." In *The Caribbean: A History of the Region and Its Peoples*, edited by Stephan Palmié and Francisco Scarano, 491–504. Chicago: University of Chicago Press, 2011.

Shukla, Sandyha, and Heidi Tinsman, eds. *Imagining Our Americas: Toward a Transnational Frame*. Durham, NC: Duke University Press, 2007.

Silva Gotay, Samuel. *Protestantismo y política en Puerto Rico, 1898–1930: Hacia una historia del protestantismo evangélico en Puerto Rico*. Río Piedras: Editorial de la Universidad de Puerto Rico, 1997.

Silver, Patricia. "'Culture Is More Than Bingo and Salsa': Making Puertorriqueñidad in Central Florida." *CENTRO: Journal of the Center for Puerto Rican Studies* 22:1 (spring 2010): 57–83.

Silvestrini, Blanca. *Los trabajadores Puertorriqueños y el Partido Socialista, 1932–1940*. Río Piedras: Editorial Universitaria, 1979.

———. "Women as Workers: The Experience of Puerto Rican Women in the 1930s." In *The Puerto Rican Woman: Perspectives on Culture, History, and Society*, edited by Edna Acosta-Belen, 59–74. New York: Praeger, 1986.

Snodgrass, Michael. "The Bracero Program, 1942–1962." In *Beyond la Frontera: The History of Mexico-U.S. Migration*, edited by Mark Overmyer-Velázquez, 79–102. New York: Oxford University Press, 2011.

Sosa-Buchholz, Sara. "Changing Images of Male and Female in Ecuador: José María Velaso Iarra and Abdalá Bucaram." In *Gender and Populism in Latin America: Passionate Politics*, edited by Karen Kampwirth, 47–66. University Park: Penn State University Press, 2010.

Soto-Crespo, Ramón E. *Mainland Passage: The Cultural Anomaly of Puerto Rico*. Minneapolis: University of Minnesota Press, 2009.

Spenser, Daniela. "Standing Conventional Cold War History on Its Head." In *In from the Cold: Latin America's New Encounter with the Cold War*, edited by Gilbert M. Joseph and Daniela Spenser, 381–396. Durham, NC: Duke University Press, 2008.

Spickard, Paul. *Almost All Aliens: Immigration, Race, and Colonialism in American History and Identity*. New York: Routledge, 2007.

Spiegel, Gabrielle M. "The Task of the Historian." *American Historical Review* 114:1 (February 2009): 1–15.

Steedman, Carolyn. *Dust: The Archive and Cultural History*. Manchester: Manchester University Press, 2000.

Steel, Frances. "Suva under Steam: Mobile Men and a Colonial Port Capital, 1880s–1910." In *Moving Subjects: Gender, Mobility, and Intimacy in an Age of Global Empire*, edited by Tony Ballantyne and Antoinette Burton, 110–126. Urbana: University of Illinois Press, 2009.

Stephen, Lynn. *Transborder Lives: Indigenous Oaxacans in Mexico, California, and Oregon*. Durham, NC: Duke University Press, 2007.

Stern, Steve J. *Battling for Hearts and Minds: Memory Struggles in Pinochet's Chile, 1973–1988*. Durham, NC: Duke University Press, 2006.

————. *Reckoning with Pinochet: The Memory Question in Democratic Chile, 1989–2006*. Durham, NC: Duke University Press, 2010.

————. *Remembering Pinochet's Chile: On the Eve of London, 1998*. Durham, NC: Duke University Press, 2004.

————. *The Secret History of Gender: Women, Men, and Power in Late Colonial Mexico*. Chapel Hill: University of North Carolina Press, 1995.

Steward, Julian, ed. *The People of Puerto Rico: A Study in Social Anthropology*. Urbana: University of Illinois Press, 1956.

Stoler, Ann Laura. *Along the Archival Grain: Epistemic Anxieties and Colonial Common Sense*. Princeton, NJ: Princeton University Press, 2009.

————, ed. *Haunted by Empire: Geographies of Intimacy in North American History*. Durham, NC: Duke University Press, 2006.

————. "Tense and Tender Ties: The Politics of Comparison in North American and (Post) Colonial Studies." *Journal of American History* 88:3 (December 2001): 829–865.

Stoler, Ann Laura, and Frederick Cooper, eds. *Tensions of Empire: Colonial Cultures in a Bourgeois World*. Berkeley: University of California Press, 1997.

Stoler, Ann Laura, Carole McGranahan, and Peter C. Perdue, eds. *Imperial Formations*. Santa Fe, NM: School for Advanced Research Press, 2007.

Storrs, Landon. *Civilizing Capitalism: The National Consumers' League, Women's Activism, and Labor Standards in the New Deal Era*. Chapel Hill: University of North Carolina Press, 2000.

Strasser, Ulrike, and Heidi Tinsman. "It's a Man's World? World History Meets the History of Masculinity." *Journal of World History* 21:10 (March 2010): 75–96.

Suárez-Orozco, Marcelo M., and Mariela Páez, eds. *Latinos: Remaking America*. Berkeley: University of California Press, 2009.

Sue, Christina A. *Land of the Cosmic Race: Race Mixture, Racism, and Blackness in Mexico*. New York: Oxford University Press, 2013.

Surkis, Judith. "Sex, Sovereignty, and Transnational Intimacies." *American Historical Review* 115:4 (October 2010): 1089–1096.

Taller de Formación Política. *Huelga en la caña: 1933–34*. Río Piedras: Ediciones Huracán, 1982.

————. *No estamos pidiendo el cielo: Huelga porturaria de 1938*. Río Piedras: Ediciones Huracán, 1988.

Taylor, Jane. "Holdings: Refiguring the Archive." In *Refiguring the Archive*, edited by Carolyn Hamilton, Verne Harris, Jane Taylor, Michele Pickover, Graeme Reid, and Razia Sheh, 242–281. Boston: Kluwer, 2002.

Telles, Edward, and René Flores. "Not Just Color: Whiteness, Nation, and Status in Latin America." *Hispanic American Historical Review* 93:3 (August 2013): 413–449.

Thomas, Lorrin. "'How They Ignore Our Rights as American Citizens': Puerto Rican Migrants and the Politics of Citizenship in the New Deal Era." In *Latinos and Citizenship: The Dilemma of Belonging*, edited by Suzanne Oboler, 33–58. New York: Palgrave Macmillan, 2006.

————. *Puerto Rican Citizen: History and Political Identity in Twentieth-Century New York City.* Chicago: University of Chicago Press, 2010.

————. "Resisting the Racial Binary? Puerto Ricans' Encounter with Race in Depression-Era New York City." *CENTRO: Journal of the Center for Puerto Rican Studies* 21:1 (spring 2009): 5–35.

Thomas, Piri. *Down These Mean Streets.* New York: Alfred A. Knopf, 1967.

Tinsman, Heidi. "Good Wives, Bad Girls, and Unfaithful Men: Sexual Negotiation and Labor Struggle in Chile's Agrarian Reform, 1964–73." In *Reclaiming the Political in Latin American History: Essays from the North*, edited by Gilbert M. Joseph, 268–308. Durham, NC: Duke University Press, 2001.

————. "Household *Patrones*: Wife-Beating and Sexual Control in Rural Chile." In *The Gendered Worlds of Latin American Women Workers: From Household and Factory to the Union Hall and Ballot Box*, edited by John French and Daniel James, 264–296. Durham, NC: Duke University Press, 1997.

————. "A Paradigm of Our Own: Joan Scott in Latin American History." *American Historical Review* 113:5 (December 2008): 1357–1374.

————. *Partners in Conflict: The Politics of Gender, Sexuality, and Labor in the Chilean Agrarian Reform, 1950–1973.* Durham, NC: Duke University Press, 2002.

Toro-Morn, Maura I. "Boricuas in Chicago: Gender and Class in the Migration and Settlement of Puerto Ricans." In *The Puerto Rican Diaspora: Historical Perspectives*, edited by Carmen Theresa Whalen and Victor Vásquez-Hernández, 128–150. Philadelphia: Temple University Press, 2005.

————. "Género, trabajo y migración: Las empleadas domésticas Puertorriqueñas en Chicago." *Revista de Ciencias Sociales* 7 (1999): 102–125.

————. "Yo era muy arriesgada: A Historical Overview of the Work Experiences of Puerto Rican Women in Chicago." *CENTRO: Journal of the Center for Puerto Rican Studies* 8:2 (fall 2001): 25–43.

Toro-Morn, Maura I., and Alicea Marixsa, eds. *Migration and Immigration: A Global View.* Westport, CT: Greenwood, 2004.

Torre, Carlos Antonio, Hugo Rodríguez Vecchini, and William Burgos, eds. *Commuter Nation: Perspectives on Puerto Rican Migration.* Río Piedras: University of Puerto Rico, 1994.

Trouillot, Michel-Rolph. *Haiti: State against Nation: The Origins and Legacy of Duvalierism.* New York: Monthly Review, 1990.

————. *Silencing the Past: Power and the Production of History.* Boston: Beacon, 1995.

Turits, Richard Lee. *Foundations of Despotism: Peasants, the Trujillo Regime, and Modernity in Dominican History.* Stanford, CA: Stanford University Press, 2003.

Turner, Herbert. *A True Account of My Life's Experiences.* Herbert Turner, 1991.

Twine, France Winddance. *Racism in a Racial Democracy: The Maintenance of White Supremacy in Brazil.* New Brunswick, NJ: Rutgers University Press, 1998.

Tyrell, Marygrace. "Colonizing the New Deal: Federal Housing in San Juan, Puerto Rico." In *The Caribbean City*, edited by Rivke Jaffe. Kingston, Jamaica: Ian Randle, 2008.

Valdés, Dionicio Nodín. *Al Norte: Agricultural Workers in the Great Lakes Region, 1917–1970.* Austin: University of Texas Press, 1991.

———. *Barrios Norteños: Saint Paul and Midwestern Mexican Communities in the Twentieth Century.* Austin: University of Texas Press, 2000.

———. *Organized Agriculture and the Labor Movement before the UFW: Puerto Rico, Hawaii, California.* Austin: University of Texas Press, 2011.

Valdés, Dionicio Nodín, and Bill Holm. *Mexicans in Minnesota.* Minneapolis: Minnesota Historical Society Press, 2005.

Valle Ferrer, Norma. *Luisa Capetillo: Historia de una mujer proscrita.* Río Piedras: Editorial Cultural, 1990.

Vargas, Zaragosa. *Labor Rights Are Civil Rights: Mexican-American Workers in Twentieth-Century America.* Princeton, NJ: Princeton University Press, 2005.

Vásquez-Hernández, Victor. "From Pan-Latino Enclaves to a Community: Puerto Ricans in Philadelphia, 1910–2000." In *The Puerto Rican Diaspora: Historical Perspectives,* edited by Carmen Theresa Whalen and Victor Vásquez-Hernández, 88–105. Philadelphia: Temple University Press, 2005.

Vaughan, Mary Kay. "Modernizing Patriarchy: State Policies, Rural Households, and Women in Mexico, 1930–1940." In *Hidden Histories of Gender and the State in Latin America,* edited by Elizabeth Dore and Maxine Molyneux, 194–214. Durham, NC: Duke University Press, 2000.

Vaughan, Mary Kay, and Stephen E. Lewis, eds. *The Eagle and the Virgin: Nation and Cultural Revolution in Mexico, 1930–1960.* Durham, NC: Duke University Press, 2006.

Venator-Santiago, Charles R. "Extending Citizenship to Puerto Rico: Three Traditions of Inclusive Exclusion." *CENTRO: Journal of the Center for Puerto Rican Studies* 25:1 (spring 2013): 50–75.

Villaronga, Gabriel. "Constructing Muñocismo: Colonial Politics and the Rise of the PPD, 1934–1940." *CENTRO: Journal of the Center for Puerto Rican Studies* 22:2 (fall 2010): 172–196.

———. *Toward a Discourse of Consent: Mass Mobilization and Colonial Politics in Puerto Rico, 1932–1948.* Westport, CT: Praeger, 2004.

———. "Un 'pequeño Pittsburgh' borincano: La ciudad imaginada del discurso desarrollista de Fomento." *CENTRO: Journal of the Center for Puerto Rican Studies* 19:2 (fall 2007): 182–205.

Vivoni Falagio, Enrique, ed. *San Juan Siempre Nuevo: Arquitectura y Modernización en el Siglo XX.* Río Piedras: Archivo de Arquitectura y Construcción Universidad de Puerto Rico, 2000.

Wade, Peter. *Blackness and Race Mixture: The Dynamics of Racial Mixture in Colombia.* Baltimore, MD: Johns Hopkins University Press, 1993.

Weinstein, Barbara. "Developing Inequality." *American Historical Review* 113:1 (February 2008): 1–18.

———. *For Social Peace in Brazil: Industrialists and the Remaking of the Working Class in São Paulo, Brazil, 1920–1964.* Chapel Hill: University of North Carolina Press, 1996.

———. "History without a Cause? Grand Narratives, World History, and the Post-colonial Dilemma." *International Review of Social History* 50 (2005): 71–93.

———. "Inventing the 'Mulher Paulista': Politics, Rebellion, and the Gendering of Brazilian Regional Identities." *Journal of Women's History* 18:1 (March 2006): 22–49.

———. "Making Workers Masculine: The (Re)Construction of Male Worker Identity in Twentieth-Century Brazil." In *Masculinities in Politics and War: Gendering Modern History,* edited by Stefan Dudink, Karen Hagemann, and John Tosh, 276–294. Manchester: Manchester University Press, 2004.

———. "'They Don't Even Look Like Women Workers': Femininity and Class in Twentieth-Century Latin America." *International Labor and Working-Class History* 69:1 (April 2006): 161–176.

———. "Unskilled Worker, Skilled Housewife: Constructing the Working-Class Woman in Sao Paulo, Brazil." In *The Gendered Worlds of Latin American Women Workers: From Household and Factory to the Union Hall and Ballot Box,* edited by John French and Daniel James, 72–99. Durham, NC: Duke University Press, 1997.

Werner, Michael, and Bénédicte Zimmerman. "Beyond Comparison: *Histoire Croisée* and the Challenge of Reflexivity." *History and Theory* 45:1 (2006): 30–50.

Weyland, Kurt. "Clarifying a Contested Concept: Populism in the Study of Latin American Politics." *Comparative Politics* 34:1 (2001): 1–22.

Whalen, Carmen Teresa. "Colonialism, Citizenship, and the Making of the Puerto Rican Diaspora: An Introduction." In *The Puerto Rican Diaspora: Historical Perspectives,* edited by Carmen Teresa Whalen and Victor Vásquez-Hernández, 1–43. Philadelphia: Temple University Press, 2005.

———. *From Puerto Rico to Philadelphia: Puerto Rican Workers and Postwar Economies.* Philadelphia: Temple University Press, 2001.

———. "Labor Migrants or Submissive Wives: Competing Narratives of Puerto Rican Women in the Post–World War II Era." In *Puerto Rican Women's History: New Perspectives,* edited by Félix V. Matos-Rodriguez and Linda Delgado, 206–227. Armonk, NY: M. E. Sharpe, 1998.

———. "Radical Contexts: Puerto Rican Politics in the 1960s and '70s and the Center for Puerto Rican Studies." *CENTRO: Journal of the Center for Puerto Rican Studies* 21:2 (fall 2009): 221–255.

Whalen, Carmen Teresa, and Victor Vásquez-Hernández, eds. *The Puerto Rican Diaspora: Historical Perspectives.* Philadelphia: Temple University Press, 2005.

White, Luise. *Speaking with Vampires: Rumor and History in Colonial Africa.* Berkeley: University of California Press, 2000.

Wilson, Kathleen. *The Island Race: Englishness, Empire, and Gender in the Eighteenth Century.* New York: Routledge, 2003.

———. "Rethinking the Colonial State: Family, Gender, and Governmentality in Eighteenth-Century British Frontiers." *American Historical Review* 116:5 (December 2011): 1294–1323.

Wolf, Eric. "San José: Subcultures of a 'Traditional' Coffee Municipality." In *The People of Puerto Rico: A Study in Social Anthropology*, edited by Julian Steward. Urbana: University of Illinois Press, 1956.

Wolfe, Joel. "'Father of the Poor' or 'Mother of the Rich'? Getúlio Vargas, Industrial Workers, and Constructions of Class, Gender, and Populism in São Paulo, 1930–1954." *Radical History Review* 58 (winter 1994): 80–111.

———. "From Working Mothers to Housewives: Gender and Brazilian Populism from Getúlio Vargas to Joscelino Kubitschek." In *Gender and Populism in Latin America: Passionate Politics*, edited by Karen Kampwirth, 91–110. University Park: Penn State University Press, 2010.

———. "Populism and Developmentalism." In *A Companion to Latin American History*, edited by Thomas H. Holloway, 347–364. Malden, MA: Blackwell, 2008.

———. *Working Women, Working Men: Sao Paulo and the Rise of Brazil's Industrial Working Class, 1900–1950*. Durham, NC: Duke University Press, 1993.

Zamora, Emilio. *Claiming Rights and Righting Wrongs in Texas: Mexican Workers and Job Politics during World War II*. College Station: Texas A&M University Press, 2009.

Zapata, Carlos. "El contratista y la constitución: Leonard Darlington Long y la conspiración contra la Constitución del Estado Libre Asociado (1951–1952)." In *Luis Muñoz Marín: Perfiles de su gobernación (1948–1964)*, edited by Fernando Picó, 228–275. Toa Alta: Fundación Luis Muñoz Marín, 2003.

Zimmerman, Herman C. "The Role of Hand Labor in Monitor Sugar Company History." Bay County Historical Society, MI, January 1981.